Beating Time & Measuring Music in the Early Modern Era

OXFORD STUDIES IN MUSIC THEORY

Series Editor Richard Cohn

Beating Time & Measuring Music in the Early Modern Era

Roger Mathew Grant

OXFORD
UNIVERSITY PRESS

OXFORD
UNIVERSITY PRESS

Oxford University Press is a department of the University of Oxford.
It furthers the University's objective of excellence in research, scholarship,
and education by publishing worldwide.

Oxford   New York
Auckland   Cape Town   Dar es Salaam   Hong Kong   Karachi
Kuala Lumpur   Madrid   Melbourne   Mexico City   Nairobi
New Delhi   Shanghai   Taipei   Toronto

With offices in
Argentina   Austria   Brazil   Chile   Czech Republic   France   Greece
Guatemala   Hungary   Italy   Japan   Poland   Portugal   Singapore
South Korea   Switzerland   Thailand   Turkey   Ukraine   Vietnam

Oxford is a registered trademark of Oxford University Press
in the UK and certain other countries.

Published in the United States of America by
Oxford University Press
198 Madison Avenue, New York, NY 10016

This volume is published with the generous support of the AMS 75 PAYS
Endowment of the American Musicological Society, funded in part by the
National Endowment for the Humanities and the Andrew W. Mellon Foundation.

Library of Congress Cataloging-in-Publication Data
Grant, Roger Mathew.
Beating time & measuring music in the early modern era/Roger Mathew Grant.
p cm.— (Oxford studies in music theory)
Includes bibliographical references and index.
ISBN 978–0–19–936728–3 (hardback : alk. paper)   1. Musical meter and
rhythm—Hmistory.   I. Title.
ML174.G73 2014
781.2'209—dc23   2014005414

9 8 7 6 5 4 3 2 1
Printed in the United States of America
on acid-free paper

CONTENTS

Part III

ACKNOWLEDGMENTS

For the past ten years people have been helping me to think about meter. I got into this beautiful mess in college, when Mary Arlin suggested I undertake an independent study in theories of rhythm and meter and Rebecca Jemian encouraged me to work through Harald Krebs's *Fantasy Pieces*. I fell in love with the topic of time in music then, and I have Professors Arlin and Jemian to thank. In my first semester of graduate school, during a key seminar with Cristle Collins Judd, I began to explore the historical legacy of meter theory, focusing my paper on the relationship between eighteenth-century theories of meter and conceptualizations of time during the period. I have been writing that seminar paper ever since. With the help of countless supportive friends and teachers, generous institutions, sympathetic archivists, and unhealthy doses of coffee, I have finally reached a point at which this study needs to be shared; shared so that it can be completed by all of you who have thought through other aspects of the material I discuss here and who can—I hope—offer other versions of the story I tell herein.

Many people talk about the writing of their book manuscripts as a difficult and trying process, taking them away from other things to which they would have preferred to attend. I am almost afraid to admit it, but my experience has been just the opposite. Because so many friends and mentors in my queer intellectual family have committed themselves to helping me think through this project (and others), I have had an amazingly enjoyable time writing this book. It has not taken me away from people—instead it has brought me closer to them. For this, I cannot be more grateful.

The writing of this book would not have been possible without the University of Michigan Society of Fellows, the institution that supported me financially and intellectually for two crucial years. Thanks are also due to the University of Michigan Libraries (and Kristen Castellana in particular), the University of Pennsylvania Libraries, the British Library, the Staatsbibliothek zu Berlin, the Newberry Library, the Beinecke Rare Book and Manuscript Library and the Irving S. Gilmore Music Library, Yale University, for their assistance during this time. This project also received generous support in the form of publication subventions from the University of Oregon School of Music, the University of Oregon Humanities Center, and the AMS 75 PAYS Endowment of the American Musicological Society, which is funded in part by the National Endowment for the Humanities and the Andrew W. Mellon Foundation.

While still in graduate school at the University of Pennsylvania I was lucky to have formative conversations with Eugene Narmour and Jairo Moreno; although they may not know it, they have made significant impacts on this project. Emily I. Dolan and Gary Tomlinson read every word of my dissertation, transformed my prose, and challenged me to explain the relevance of my project to the humanities in general. Mark J. Butler has been a foundational support from the very beginning and has continued to shepherd this project through its final stages, providing invaluable insights along the way. Don Lopez, Dena Goodman, Yopie Prins, Louise Stein, Stefano Mengozzi, and many others at Michigan were expert sounding boards as I began to put the project together. I am very fortunate to share the field of eighteenth-century music theory with Martin Küster, who provided astute and friendly assistance with issues related to Kirnberger, Marpurg, the *alla breve*, and countless other topics.

I owe a tremendous debt of gratitude to Rick Cohn and Brian Hyer, who both read the manuscript in its entirety and provided me with extensive feedback; I will never forget their generosity and support. I would also like to thank two anonymous reviewers, who graciously shared ideas with me. Suzanne Ryan, Adam Cohen, and their team at Oxford University Press have been nothing short of magical, and I am extremely fortune to work with them. Toward the completion of the project, Tony Solitro assisted me in the technical details of the manuscript preparation and expertly proofread my musical examples. Broude Brothers, Georg Olms Verlag, and the Staatsbibliothek zu Berlin—Preußischer Kulturbesitz, Musikabteilung mit Mendelssohn-Archiv were all very generous in allowing me to reproduce images from their texts free of cost. Through the entire process of writing and producing this book, my parents, Henry A. Grant and Lorraine T. Grant, my brother, Daniel Grant, and my grandparents, Matthew Triggiani, Jean Triggiani, and Mary Grant, have remained unflaggingly supportive and enthusiastic.

Finally, those who shared the days of writing with me deserve special mention. They have, each in their own way, allowed me to think through their writing projects as a means of better understanding my own. They have kept me working, distracted me, supported me, and made my life possible. Thank you to Darien Lamen, for all of our lunch dates; to Joshua Tweedy, for every routine and good habit; to Clare Croft, for her keen sense of prose related to movement; to Sara McClelland, Sarah Quinn, and Lily Cox-Richard, for their brilliance and for inspiring me; to Scott De Orio, for feigning sleep if I took too long to explain my argument (and thereby forcing me to articulate it) and for all of his boundless energy; to Joseph Salvatore Ackley for all of the Kaffeepausen, work dates, and tours; to David Halperin, for being a profoundly influential role model; to Sergio Rigoletto and Pranjal Mehta, for all of the manhattans and for keeping me moving; to William E. Wieczorek, who made the final stages of this project a joy; to the brilliant and heroic Gavin Steingo, who I am sure has read more of my prose than any other person on earth, I am forever happily indebted. I could not be luckier to have such amazing intellectual interlocutors. To all of you and all of the others: you are my teachers. This book is dedicated to you.

ABBREVIATIONS

AmZ	*Allgemeine musikalishe Zeitung*
AmB	Amalienbibliothek
D-B	Staatsbibliothek zu Berlin—Preußischer Kulturbesitz
D-Bsa	Sing-Akademie zu Berlin, Notenarchiv
GB-Lbl	The British Library

NOTES ON ORTHOGRAPHY AND TRANSLATION

Quotations preserve the spelling and idiosyncracies of the original wherever possible. All translations are my own unless otherwise indicated.

Beating Time & Measuring Music in the Early Modern Era

Introduction

We begin at the conclusion, in a moment of great anxiety. In December of 1826 Beethoven wrote to his publisher Schott:

> The metronome markings [for the *Missa Solemnis*] will be sent to you very soon. Do wait for them. In our century such indications are certainly necessary. Moreover I have received letters from Berlin informing me that the first performance of the [ninth] symphony was received with enthusiastic applause, which I ascribe largely to the metronome markings. We can scarcely have *tempi ordinari* any longer...[1]

Beethoven's extensive connection to and interest in Maelzel's metronome has long been recorded, and his letter of late 1826 is only one of many in which he expresses a deep dissatisfaction with the ability of musical notation to specify tempo.[2] He locates the problem with the end of *tempo ordinario*, or what now typically goes by the name *tempo giusto*: the idea that music's "just" or "ordinary" tempo could be determined from its particular combination of meter, note values, and character. At the time of his writing, the reliability of meters to do this work had fallen into serious question, and Beethoven sought a solution in Maelzel's metronome. The efficacy of the system that had once allowed meter to communicate tempo was coming to an end.

Beethoven's 1826 letter was written in a time of tremendous stylistic innovation in Western music. Composers began to experiment with sudden shifts in the meter of their compositions—what I call "integrated metric shifts"—playing with the structure of measurement without altering the tempo, note values, or character of the music. They also began to conceptualize the measure itself as a

---

1. Ludwig van Beethoven to Bernhard Schotts Söhne, Vienna, ca. December 18, 1826, in *Beethoven's Letters*, ed. and trans. Emily Anderson (New York: St Martin's, 1961), 3:1325. See also Rudolph Kolisch, "Tempo and Character in Beethoven's Music," trans. Arthur Mendel, *The Musical Quarterly* 29, nos. 1–2 (1943): 169–87, 291–312, reissued in *The Musical Quarterly* 77, nos. 1–2 (1993): 90–131, 268–342.
2. The extensive bibliography surrounding tempo and performance practice in Beethoven's music is covered in greater detail in chapter 7. In general, see Clive Brown, "Historical Performance, Metronome Marks and Tempo in Beethoven's Symphonies," *Early Music* 19 (1991): 247–58; and Kolisch, "Tempo and Character in Beethoven's Music."

subdivision of a larger metrical unit, availing themselves of compositional manipulations at the level of what Edward T. Cone called the "hypermeasure."[3] They began to reconceive of the relationship between meter and notation in ways that afforded a wealth of stylistic possibilities for new composition.[4]

In this book, I contend that the early nineteenth-century anxieties over tempo specification and the concomitant changes in compositional possibility were intimately related, and that both were deeply involved in a reconceptualization of both meter and time itself. Over the course of the early modern era, the relationships between time, meter, and motion were fundamentally rearranged, and the theory and experience of meter changed forever. Meter was once tightly linked with motion, as the language of sixteenth- and seventeenth-century music theory makes clear. The beat was thought of as both a physical act—the movement of a hand through space, for instance—and a description of temporal passage. These two meanings persist in our twenty-first century definitions for the beat, though they are now separated: the word beat is now either a verb with physical implications or a noun that indicates an abstract temporal interval. Writers on music did not draw this distinction before the eighteenth century. In the science of the period, or natural philosophy as it was then called, time was understood within the broader rubric of motion or change. The beat was a temporal concept that was made explicable through motion and bound up with notated durations and tempo.

During the eighteenth century, the concept of the beat became separated from its motion and a different nexus of terms, including the terms for the newly ubiquitous notated measure, began to do the work of explaining meter. Theorists devoted more attention to the properties of the space between the barlines. It was during this period that they began to express a new concern about temporal specificity in music, worrying that the notation of meter and rhythm no longer communicated tempo. They responded to this problem with an explosion of didactic detail on the many different meters possible (in some cases they described more than fifty different meter signatures), which had nuanced connections to note values, character, and tempo. The eighteenth century's multiplicity of measures shifted the focus of explanation away from the physical implementation of the beat onto the relationship between timekeeping and notation. This change in meter's theorization came alongside a rethinking of time, in which natural philosophy began to conceptualize time as a quantity entirely independent of earthly motions and physical changes. At the end of the century and into the nineteenth, theorists were able to describe meter as a way of measuring the unending progression of homogenous, "absolute" time, and offered a universal theory of measurement that would account for any of the meters they described. Meter became a mutable way of dividing, newly separated from the elaborate complex that had once joined it with notational practices, character, and tempo. Through this slow process of dissociation at the end of the early modern era, tempo became the

---

3. Edward T. Cone, *Musical Form and Musical Performance* (New York: Norton, 1968), 79.
4. Joel Lester, *The Rhythms of Tonal Music* (Carbondale, IL: Southern Illinois University Press, 1986), 107–12.

calculable dimension of music's temporality, and Maelzel's metronome provided a way of prescribing tempo in universally translatable units. By the early nineteenth century, as Beethoven would tell us, the system of tempo indication that relied on the work of the meter signatures in *tempo giusto* was no longer effective.

Meter might seem to be fairly self-evident: a rudiment, one of the backbones of musical structure, it is said to be a framework against which we hear other things. The narrative traced in this book demonstrates just the opposite. Theorists have long grappled with the nature of meter, struggling to explain music's temporal unfolding and its relationship to time and notation. In their efforts, they make recourse to a huge diversity of concepts on time informed by natural philosophy, aesthetics, and mathematics (to name only a few domains of thought). The crucial differences in the underpinnings of meter theories tell us about different ways of knowing music. Taking these historical understandings seriously entails nothing short of a rethinking of musical experience. It entails challenging the tacit assumptions about the way we engage with the musical material of the past, and taking a close look at the manner in which recent theories of meter construct a particular view of musical organization.

For these reasons, *Beating Time and Measuring Music in the Early Modern Era* inspects important changes in musical style and structure through the lens of historical music theory and its intellectual contexts. In order to paint a clear picture of the change that occurred during the eighteenth century, it takes a long view of meter's history and demonstrates how time and the beat transformed from the age of Zarlino to the invention of the metronome. Ultimately concerned with new analytical insights, this book goes about attaining them by means of a curious path. It devotes a great deal of attention to historical music theory and its place in intellectual history, reconstructing notions of meter very different from our own. These historically distant ideas about meter are uniquely positioned to instruct us on the interconnectedness of music theory with a wider universe of knowledge on time. It is this knowledge that underwrote the musical structures we seek to understand in analysis, and this book attempts not only to explain those structures but also to explain the very structures of knowledge that supported them.

A History of Meter Theory, Or, the Rules of the Rules

In an effort to evince something about the way meter worked in music of the period here inspected, this book focuses a great deal of attention on the history of music theory. More specifically, it attempts to understand what larger systems of organization or rules of formation supported the ideas about time found in the writings on music of this period. It asks, in other words, not about the "rules" of music theory—the compositional prescriptions and dicta of performance practice—but instead about the rules of those rules. It is concerned with the knowledge they reflect more than the information they explicitly offer.

The writings of historical music theory are one significant site for evidence on the way people made sense of temporality, and together with evidence from nonmusical discourses and practices they shed light on the dramatic change in the conceptualization of meter that took place during the eighteenth century. The relationship between theory and analysis with which this study is concerned is therefore rather out of the ordinary, even for studies concerned with the history of music theory. The analysis that results is not the product of an application of historical theories onto contemporaneous music. In fact, the perfunctory nature of most of these historical writings means that they would not lend themselves to such an adaptation in any case—at least not one that would resemble the type of analytical work that has been done with applications of Hugo Riemann's *Tonnetz*, for example, or even early modern theories of the modes.[5] Instead, the analyses found in the pages that follow are the result of imagining musical knowledge and experience differently; they are based on a reconstruction of and dialogue with conceptualizations of time unlike our own, a significant source of which is historical music theory. These theories and the musical repertoire inspected must be understood as two divergent manifestations of a foundational principle of temporality. This book does not relate them to each other directly, but relates them instead through their mutual relationships to the larger networks of knowledge on time.

The eighteenth-century transformation of meter at the turning point of this book is of major consequence to its analyses. This change bears resemblance to other shifts charted in important narratives of the period's intellectual and aesthetic history. Of these, the transformation from what Foucault called the classical episteme to the modern episteme and from what Rancière called the representative regime to the aesthetic regime are the most significant.[6] As will become apparent, both historiographical frameworks have informed the writing of this book, though neither is its model. Whereas a strictly Foucauldian archaeology would have the question of the subject at its center, this study focuses deliberately on the more specific claims to knowledge made about time. Like Rancière's work it is invested in the nature of intelligibility and signification at different historical moments, though an understanding of their political potential is not the purpose of the investigation here.

Precisely because conceptual change is at the heart of this book's narrative, the concepts traced do not share one, uniform name. The phenomenon that the

5. On Riemannian and Neo-Riemannian analysis, see the essays collected in *The Oxford Handbook of Neo-Riemannian Music Theories*, ed. Edward Gollin and Alexander Rehding (Oxford: Oxford University Press, 2011); on the issue of implementing Riemann's theories see Steven Rings, "Riemannian Analytical Values, Paleo- and Neo-," in *The Oxford Handbook of Neo-Riemannian Music Theories*, 487–511. For applications of early modern modal theories, see for instance Bernhard Meier, *The Modes of Classical Vocal Polyphony*, trans. Ellen S. Beebe (New York: Broude Brothers, 1988); and Robert Luoma, *Music, Mode and Words in Orlando di Lasso's Last Works* (New York: Edwin Mellen, 1989); for a critique of this analytical practice see Peter Schubert, "Authentic Analysis," *Journal of Musicology* 12, no. 1 (1994): 3–18.
6. Michel Foucault, *The Order of Things* (New York: Pantheon Books, 1970; repr.,New York: Vintage, 1973); Foucault, *The Archaeology of Knowledge*, trans. A. M. Sheridan Smith (New York: Pantheon Books, 1972); Jacques Rancière, *The Politics of Aesthetics: The Distribution of the Sensible*, trans. and with an introduction by Gabriel Rockhill (London: Continuum, 2004); Rancière, *The Politics of Literature* (Cambridge: Polity, 2011).

twenty-first century calls meter went by many other words and was described with many groups of terms in centuries previous. Roughly translated, these include beat, measure, and even pulse. Related terminology included words that would translate as tempo, time, affect, and movement in the twenty-first century—words that now indicate concepts no longer included under the rubric of meter. The unifying thread, then, is not located in any word (say, *Takt*) but the ideas surrounding the regularly recurring temporal division of music: the experience that we call meter in the twenty-first century, which scholars often explain as a mode of attending at regular temporal intervals.[7] It is important to acknowledge that twenty-first century understandings of this phenomenon have necessarily shaped the results of the historical inquiry, encouraging the incorporation of some sources at the exclusion of others. The twentieth- and twenty-first century distinction between meter and rhythm, for example, has made a significant impact on the investigation: understood here as accounts of a different phenomenon, theories of rhythm—or, discourses on the temporal patterning we currently call rhythm—are not included.

Starting from a presumption of unfamiliarity and conceptual distance, a preliminary goal of this book is to identify historical writings that seem to describe the phenomenon we now call meter and to reconstruct their ways of knowing it. This aspect of the book is closest to Foucault's archaeological method; it bears resemblance to other recent work in music studies and in intellectual history.[8] This part of the methodology interrogates the strategies of explanation in historical music theory and seeks to situate them among other discourses in order to find out what structures of knowledge buttressed them all. Rather than simply identifying the practices of borrowing and citation between these writings, it aims to map the pathways common in their logic. It seeks to uncover their ways of interpreting and understanding temporality and duration, and the tools through which they rendered these categories explicable. It provides an account of the sometimes-unarticulated tactics of knowledge production they employed, and an assessment of how those tactics changed.

Consider the words used in Zarlino's chapter "Della battuta" in *Le istitutioni harmoniche*, a text treated in detail in this book's first two chapters. Zarlino theorizes meter through the action of the beat: a lowering and raising of the hand "regulated in the manner of the human pulse."[9] Between these two motions are moments of repose, Zarlino tells us, "because, according to Aristotle, between

---

7. For a survey of the relevant literature see Justin London, *Hearing in Time* (2004; 2nd ed., Oxford: Oxford University Press, 2012).

8. For example, Lorraine Daston and Peter Galison, *Objectivity* (New York: Zone Books, 2007); Jairo Moreno, *Musical Representations, Subjects, and Objects* (Bloomington: Indiana University Press, 2004); Gary Tomlinson, *Metaphysical Song* (Princeton: Princeton University Press, 1999); and ibid., *Music in Renaissance Magic* (Chicago: University of Chicago Press, 1993). This method is also the topic of the essays collected in Ian Hacking's *Historical Ontology* (Cambridge, MA: Harvard University Press, 2002).

9. "Et s'imaginarono che fusse bene, se cotal segno fusse fatto con la mano; accioche ogn' uno de i cantori lo potesse vedere, et fusse regolato nel suo movimento alla guisa del Polso humano." Zarlino, *Le istitutioni harmoniche* (Venice: Francesco de i Franceschi Senese, 1558), 207.

motions [resting points] are always to be found."[10] Zarlino's text offers an explanation of meter through embodied action and physical theorization. The division of time is made legible in the passage of a hand gesture—real or imagined—recurring in two-part succession. Zarlino's explanation makes reference to discourses on anatomy, motion, and natural philosophy in order to place itself in a system of relationships that would have done the work of explaining the division of time to the readers of the era. The images used and the prescription for this practice need detailed and careful reconstruction in order to elucidate the embedded claims about meter and the greater understanding of time they reveal. Just over two hundred years later, the Berlin theorist Johann Philipp Kirnberger would mobilize an entirely different world of images, ideas, and experiences in his theory of meter.[11] He asked his readers to imagine "a series of equal beats that are repeated one after the next with an equal space of time," and explained that "we, in our mind," divide these equally spaced beats into segments. "Indeed," Kirnberger wrote, "we do this such that we place an accent on the first beat of each segment or we imagine that we hear it stronger than the other beats."[12] Kirnberger's explanation involves an imaginary stretch of undifferentiated durations segmented through an operation of the mind that employs accent as a tool of division. Like the passage from Zarlino, this text contains ideas that cannot be accessed directly; the meanings of its terms are not transparent. It requires a process of reconstruction in order for us to appreciate the work its words accomplished and the world of sense-making in which they partook. The texts of Zarlino and Kirnberger reference ways of thinking about meter that are quite different from each other and from our own. Twenty-first century readers may find Kirnberger's description acceptable if quixotic as a theory of meter, but may find Zarlino's writings to be off the topic entirely (for this readership Zarlino's bodily referents more readily call up images of conducting than meter, a problem taken up in chapter 2). Placed next to each other here, these texts demonstrate the diversity of concepts at play in the historical scope of this study and the amount of interpretive work the sources call for.

Insofar as reading these sources will always engage our own understandings of meter, the process of reconstruction necessitates a dialogue. The very provocation of suggesting that some of these writings theorize the same phenomenon addressed in twenty-first century texts on meter is itself indicative of the transformative power they might have if allowed into serious conversation with recent

---

10. "percioche (secondo la mente di Aristotele) tra questi movimenti...sempre si [quiete] ritrovano." Zarlino, *Le istitutioni harmoniche*, 207.
11. I have chosen to identify Kirnberger as the author of the theory as it is presented in *Die Kunst des reinen Satzes in der Musik* (Berlin: Christian Friedrich Voss, 1771–79). I take up the issue of authorship in chapter 4, footnote 1.
12. "Wenn man eine Folge von gleichen Schlägen, die in gleichem Zeitraum nach einander widerholet werden...so lehrt die Erfahrung, daß wir in unsern Gedanken alsobald eine tacktmäßige Eintheilung dieser Schläge machen, indem wir sie in Glieder ordnen, die eine gleiche Anzahl Schläge in sich fassen, und zwar so, daß wir auf den ersten Schlag eines jeden Gliedes einen Accent legen, oder ihn stärker als die übrigen Schläge zu vernehmen glauben." Kirnberger, *Die Kunst des reinen Satzes in der Musik*, 2:114–15. This passage is discussed in detail in chapter 4.

music theory. These historical texts present us with the opportunity to trouble our theories and casual assumptions about meter. In a way, they are also the recipients of information on the other side of the dialogue, shaped as they are by the projection of our own beliefs and expectations about music theory. The acknowledgement of this hermeneutic circle—characteristic in the recent intellectual histories of Dominick LaCapra and Ian Hacking—is thematized and embraced in this book.[13] It has the potential to create productive tension and reveal important, if unsettling, information about old theory as well as new. Furthermore, the process of dialogue provides an opportunity to build on the exciting proliferation of work on meter from the past fifty years. Like much of that scholarship, this investigation has an analytical goal in mind. Reconstructing the networks of ideas that created historical theories of meter and placing those in an interrogative relationship with our own, we are better able to inquire about the specific compositional designs of the music contemporaneous with them.

In order to develop a broadly relevant account of these knowledge-making practices, this study inspects a chronology of materials that spans more than three centuries. A *longue durée* approach, it supplies synthetic understandings of a great number of different historical objects in order to say something about time and meter over a large portion of history.[14] It sacrifices the ideal of comprehensiveness for a commitment to a broad historical look at a single question.[15] The results of this method afford us the opportunity to dialogue across the historical distance, always bringing our notions of meter in tow. Reflecting back on them, we are given the chance to understand how else they might be, and how meter, in each instance, could be said to work in musical composition, thought, and experience.

Reading in the Dark

Although it is true that the preparation of this book has required a great many late nights at the library, it is not because of the lighting that I have been reading in the

---

13. For a concise summary of what LaCapra calls "dialogic reading," see his *History and Reading: Tocqueville, Foucault, French Studies* (Toronto: University of Toronto Press, 2000), 64–72. Although Hacking does not use the same terms, his method is very much in line with LaCapra's concerns. See Hacking, "Historical Ontology," in *Historical Ontology*, 1–26; see also ibid., "Historical Meta-Epistemology," in *Wahrheit und Geschichte*, ed. Wolfgang Carl and Lorraine Daston (Göttingen: Valdenhoeck und Ruprecht, 1999), 53–77.

14. For this reason, and because of an investment in the material and embodied manifestations of knowledge, this study is sympathetic to the approach of the *Annales* school. For a general introduction see Peter Burke, *The French Historical Revolution: The Annales School, 1929-89* (Cambridge: Polity Press, 1990); and Michel Vovelle, *Ideologies and Mentalities*, trans. Eamon O'Flaherty (Cambridge: Polity Press, 1990).

15. Taking a cue, for instance, from Lucien Febvre's *Le Problème de l'incroyance au XVIᵉ siècle: la religion de Rabelais* (Paris: Albin Michel, 1942); translated as *The Problem of Unbelief in the Sixteenth Century, The Religion of Rabelais*, trans. Beatrice Gottlieb (Cambridge, MA: Harvard University Press, 1982).

dark. The sources for the history of meter theory are not great in number or length. There is a reason that recent scholarship has paid less attention to the history of meter than it has to the history of tonality: there is less to study. Fewer pages in our historical texts are taken up with describing meter, and precious fewer attempt what twenty-first century scholars would customarily call a theory of meter. In coping with these dim circumstances I have come to understand the scarcity of the material as a defining condition of this study. The very frustration of searching for "theories" of meter between 1500 and 1830 is a transformative one—one that asks us to reframe the terms of the investigation. What if the history of music theory were to attend to the knowledge left unarticulated or barely written in its texts? What if we took the reconstruction of the almost-recorded as a goal, shifting the focus away from what theorists tell us outright? As Alberto Manguel observes, "Every library conjures up its own dark ghost; every ordering sets up, in its wake, a shadow library of absences."[16] I have been purposefully reading in the dark.

The narrative created out of these conditions can be read as a counterhistory of music theory. It provides an alternative view of the history of music theory not just because it focuses on meter but also because in order to do so it opens out theoretical texts onto a world of ideas, acts, and material objects. It takes advantage of the sparse conditions of documentation by engaging the lived, tangible manifestations of the period's knowledge networks. It is far too easy to slip into a mode of reading music theory that pays little regard to its material implications. We must bear in mind that theories of meter were the result of a deep interconnection between historical actors, the world they experienced, and their techniques for manipulating and measuring it.[17] These techniques involved timekeeping practices that were means of moving through the world and organizing life's unfolding. As ways of relating to the world changed, so too did techniques for understanding time and construing meter.[18]

This study pairs a deep investment in the intellectual heritage of ideas in music theory with an equal investment in their location within systems of human action, manufactured objects, and nature. Responding to the recent growth of scholarship on materiality and technology in historical studies of science, it investigates the physical implementations of music theory under the rubric of technique: a term that encompasses both human activities and their objectification in the form of things.[19] Among the techniques of musical timekeeping

---

16. Alberto Manguel, *The Library at Night* (New Haven: Yale University Press, 2008), 107.
17. The form of this interconnection is eloquently set out in Karl Marx's *Capital*, trans. Ben Fowkes (New York: Vintage Books, 1977), 1:283–91.
18. Acknowledging that theories of meter are part of social and material process, they can be said to reflect what Raymond Williams called a "structure of experience" or "structure of feeling"; they help us to understand the characteristics and "specific hierarchies" involved in time's unfolding. Williams, "Structures of Feeling," in *Marxism and Literature* (Oxford: Oxford University Press, 1977), 128–35, at 132.
19. In so doing it also responds to the recent turn in literary studies toward material processes and materialist critique, or what Susan Wolfson calls an "activist" new formalism. Wolfson, "Reading for Form," *Modern Language Quarterly* 61, no. 1 (2001): 1–16. See also Marjorie Levinson, "What is New Formalism?" *PMLA* 122, no. 2 (2007): 558–69.

inspected here are the metronome and other early musical chronometers, the printed formats music theory took on, and the motions of the hand and heart associated with beating time in sixteenth- and seventeenth-century treatises. Each of these techniques mediates the world in a distinctive way and has much to tell us about the implementation of knowledge on time.

Focusing on the differences in the material manifestations of meter theories also allows us to rethink the claims we make about musical style and structure. If it is easy to forget historical distance in the reading of music theoretical texts, it is much easier to forget it in the analysis of musical compositions. Our familiarity with musical works and methods for interpreting them brings them far too close, frustrating our efforts to understand them further or understand them otherwise. The elusive objects of our music analysis were once also part of the network connecting knowledge, objects, and ways of experiencing time that this study aims to reconstruct. In order to acknowledge the historical gap between us and the compositions we analyze, this study places recent and historical theories in dialogue at the site of analysis. It stages a confrontation between different modes of understanding, contrasting not only our theories of meter with theirs, but also the foundational assumptions of both. Analysis in this sense should be understood as a process of revealing the various ways of knowing that are available in the context of a composition. It asks us to rethink the self-evidence and givenness of our customary theoretical frameworks for meter, creating an interchange with other modes of understanding and the theories of meter based on them. Sometimes we are too familiar in the analytical encounter, and the light we shed actually occludes more than it reveals. Analysis, too, can be conducted in the dark.

A reconstruction of and dialogue with past ways of knowing time, an account of the physical and material techniques used to understand it, and an analytical engagement with the contemporaneous music: these form the three methodological impulses that have shaped the writing and organization of this book. The text is comprised of eight chapters within three large sections. Each section takes on the three themes of theory, technique, and analysis; the first two sections of the book devote a chapter to each of these while the final section combines the theory and analysis chapters for a single study on integrated metric shifts. The book's three sections are organized chronologically into porously delineated historical periods. The first, comprising the first three chapters, covers the era from the birth of print music theory around 1500 through the end of the seventeenth century. Chapter 1, focused on theory, documents the persistence of a single conception of the beat through this lengthy period of changing notational conventions. Detailed case studies of writings on the beat by Ornithoparchus, Zarlino, Lippius, and Loulié elucidate the centrality of motion to the theories of meter written during these two centuries. The second chapter shifts the focus from theory to technique, fleshing out the motion-driven concept of the beat through a focus on the act of beating itself. It demonstrates how the beat was used as a technical and physical solution for the conceptual problem of temporal continuity in theories of meter. Chapter 3 draws on the insights of the first two in order to tackle a particular analytical problem in the music of the era. Its goal is the revitalization of an unequal account of triple meter, in which the basic duality of the *thesis* and *arsis* time-beating motion prescribes the division of triple meters into two, unequal parts. Representative analyses focus on the music of Schein, Susato, Gervaise, Purcell, and Handel.

The second section of the book chronicles a fundamental shift in the conceptualizations of time and meter. Chapter 4 describes how theorists in the eighteenth century shifted the focus of their explanations from the physical act of the beat to the properties of the measure (in every sense of that term). The scaffold that had once joined together meter, note values, character, and tempo began to fragment, and meter was retheorized. With special attention to the continental reception of Newtonian absolute time and the work of Kirnberger and his circle, the chapter provides an intellectual context in which to understand this transformation. The fifth chapter looks again toward the technical, and connects the ubiquity and growing precision of timepieces—and the time discipline they offered—with a burgeoning eighteenth-century anxiety about tempo communication. This anxiety was tied up with an elaborate taxonomic project. During this period theorists created print responses to the problem of tempo specification, attempting to codify the moribund system of *tempo giusto* and to stipulate the relationships between meters, note values, characters, and tempi. Chapter 6 focuses on the same issue through an analytical perspective on the eighteenth-century *alla breve*. Often recalled in the context of musical topics, the *alla breve* in the eighteenth century had the ability to indicate meter, tempo, style, and potential combinations thereof. This chapter shows how the many possible meanings of the *alla breve* capture a final moment in the history of the relationships that created *tempo giusto*. It includes analyses of works both celebrated and obscure by Handel, Quantz, Carl Heinrich Graun, Mozart, Michael Haydn, and Joseph Haydn.

The third and final section of the book traces the narrative through to its conclusion in the early nineteenth century. Chapter 7, focused on technique, provides an extended study of the celebrated machine Maelzel patented and its reception in the music theory of the era. Writings on the metronome returned again and again to the issue of standardization, anxiously attempting to avoid the disparity that Western Europe's many sorts of measurement systems created. With distant and future destinations in mind, these writings reveal as much concern about the communication of quantifiable standards as they do about tempo. The eighth and concluding chapter of the book situates integrated metric shifts as outgrowths of meter's divorce from character and tempo. Described anew in the language of absolute time, meter was no longer linked to specific durations or stylistic traits but became, instead, a flexible way of measuring. The early nineteenth century saw the use of sudden shifts in meter that were otherwise integrated into the compositional fabric of the music. It should be no surprise, then, that some of the most famous of these integrated metric shifts were composed by a passionate advocate of the metronome and a composer that experimented with hypermeter: Beethoven. With tempo regulation mechanized, meter became a tool with which to organize the ongoing flow of absolute time in continually shifting regularities.

I ask for patience from readers who may expect analysis from the beginning or consistently throughout the book. They will find the analytical chapters—the third, sixth, and eighth—well prepared by the theoretical and historical work in those that precede them. The division of the book's sections into chapters is meant to highlight the distinctive contributions of each method of exploration, providing multiple paths through the same historical material. With an eye toward their deep interconnection, the separate arguments of these chapters afford a space for breathing otherwise unavailable in an account related *ad seriatim*.

As a result of reading and listening in the dark there emerges a very different kind of relationship between historical music theory and music analysis. If compositions and theories are understood to say something about the modes of conceptualization and structures of experience under which they were written, then both types of sources must form an inextricably intertwined story about evolving understandings of meter. Out of the conversation among theoretical, philosophical, musical, and material sources both past and present, we are afforded the opportunity to discover many ways of knowing music. Locating ourselves within that conversation and assuming an active role, we have the chance to reconsider our histories of meter, our theories of meter, and what they have to say to each other.

PART I

CHAPTER One

Beating Time

Themes in Meter Theory, 1500–1700

We usually think of the period demarcated by the sixteenth and seventeenth centuries as a time of great change and upheaval in the history of music. Radical transformations took place with regard to musical style, and the conceptualizations of pitch, mode, and temperament were dramatically reimagined and recast. Theories of meter also underwent great revisions over the course of these two centuries, as changing stylistic and notational conventions warranted revised explanation. At the same time, however, certain themes in the tradition of writing on meter persist throughout the sixteenth and seventeenth centuries, and these continuities supersede the differences. These themes were grounded in larger networks of knowledge on time.

Specifically, sixteenth- and seventeenth-century writers on music conceptualized meter through motion. This conceptualization was linked to an understanding of time as a measurement of motion. Time for these thinkers was a way to count or number motion, as the Aristotelian commentators put it.[1] In this doctrine, motion and change were less abstract than time, and time was only rendered sensible as a description or quantification of enacted motions or changes. Although in some cases the references to Aristotelian thinking were explicit, in most cases these two understandings were connected by a shared epistemological configuration that provided the basis for thinking and knowing

---

1. Aristotle, *Physics* 4.11.219b1; cf. commentaries on the *Physics* such as the *Commentarii Collegii Conimbricensis e Societate Jesu in octo libros Physicorum Aristotelis Stagiritae*, facsimile ed. (1594; Hildesheim: Georg Olms, 1984), 2:81; Eustachius, *Summa philosophiae quadripartita* (Leiden: Franciscum Moyardum, 1647), 2:158; or contemporary commentaries including Ursula Coope, *Time for Aristotle* (Oxford: Clarendon Press, 2005), esp. 47–59. On the historical commentaries, see Dennis Des Chene, *Physiologia: Natural Philosophy in Late Aristotelian and Cartesian Thought* (Ithaca: Cornell University Press, 1996), esp. 21–52. On the use of the term "Aristotelian," see Edward Grant, "Ways to Interpret the Terms 'Aristotelian' and 'Aristotelianism' in Medieval and Renaissance Natural Philosophy," *History of Science* 25, no. 4 (1987): 335–58.

all things temporal in this period.[2] Writings on time in natural philosophy and writings on meter were part of a group of knowledge relationships in early modern Europe. These relationships were created, sanctioned, and controlled in specific institutions and within certain written traditions; this nexus of relationships supported a single conception of the beat through changing notational conventions, as barred music slowly replaced unbarred white mensural notation.

The table in appendix 1 catalogues and describes sixty-seven works of music theory published between the 1496 *Practica musice* of Gaffurius and Pablo Nassarre's 1723 *Escuela música según la práctica moderna*. These documents form a representative sample of the writings in music theory from this era that included explanations of meter. The collection cuts across many divisions—it includes treatises extremely lengthy and learned and others as short as a few pages, printed cheaply, and concerned with only the very rudimentary. These books were published in many different languages in locations across Western Europe. Some were meant for school children, while others were studded with Greek and dressed in the right citations to show that they were intended for a highly literate and erudite audience.

Nevertheless, what emerges out of these sources is a surprising continuity. In their explanations of meter, the overwhelming majority of these treatises employ the language of motion. These explanations begin by defining the basic elements of notation: its signs, shapes, and durations, some of them including an explanation of *modus, tempus*, and *prolatio*. At this point, they introduce the concept of the beat. In these texts, the beat is a lowering and raising of the hand—sometimes the foot, the finger, or the heart—that measures and organizes the notated durations in accordance with the structure of mensuration. This lowering and raising motion was as much an action as it was a physical theorization of temporal measurement. Whether it was performed or served as a figure of imagined demonstration, the motion of the beat rendered temporal division sensible in these theories. Differences, of course, abound between these documents. But the apparent opposition of the viewpoints, the different methods of presentation and varying sources of authority, the variety of musical repertoire to which these sources refer—all of these important differences add to the rich texture of the corpus while simultaneously reinforcing the overarching recourse made to the matrix of relationships connecting meter, motion, and time.

There is a profound contrast between this set of relationships and that which governs recent theories of meter. In twentieth- and twenty-first-century theories, the beat is commonly described as a temporal interval or, in some cases, a durationless timepoint that marks the onset of such a unit. The beat has become a location within the metric grid or one of the elements out of which that grid is built.[3] There was something like that hierarchy involved in the sixteenth and

2. My use of the term "epistemological configuration" is related specifically to Foucault's use of this term. See Michel Foucault, *The Order of Things* (New York: Pantheon Books, 1970; repr., New York: Vintage, 1973), 31 and 365.

3. To cite only three recent influential writings, see for instance Fred Lerdahl and Ray Jackendoff, *A Generative Theory of Tonal Music* (Cambridge, MA: MIT Press, 1983), 18; Carl Schachter, "Rhythm and Linear Analysis: Aspects of Meter," in *The Music Forum* VI, ed. Felix Salzer, Carl

seventeenth century theories also, but it was conceptualized, put into effect, and explained within a very different framework of knowledge. For the musicians and theorists of that era, the hierarchy involved in duration was made sensible through the idea of a beat that was simultaneously a motion and a temporal interval. The words they left us on the beat demonstrate an investment in the explicatory power of motion in the theorization of temporal passage.

The space dedicated to meter in sixteenth- and seventeenth-century treatises is a variable component, but in most cases this space is small. Particularly in comparison to the lengthy and grand explanations of pitch and harmony, the writings on meter do not hold any pride of place. In a certain sense, then, the lack of scholarship on the conceptualizations of meter in this period is congruous with the sources themselves; lacking lengthy prose on which to reflect, scholars have concentrated their effort on the interpretation of notational systems (which were in great flux during this period) rather than on aspects of theory. While a recent growth of scholarship on mensuration and proportion signs has helped to elucidate long-standing problems in the history of notation and questions of performance practice—particularly with regard to tempo—little scholarship exists that addresses the theories of meter and conceptions of the beat that were in place during the sixteenth and seventeenth centuries.[4]

Schachter, and Hedi Segel (New York: Columbia University Press, 1987), as reprinted in Carl Schachter, *Unfoldings*, ed. Joseph N. Straus (Oxford: Oxford University Press, 1999), 80, 81; Harald Krebs, *Fantasy Pieces* (Oxford: Oxford University Press, 1999), 23.

4. Some recent exceptions include Graeme M. Boone, "Marking Mensural Time," *Music Theory Spectrum* 22, no. 1 (2000): 1–43; and Alexander Blachly, "*Mensura versus Tactus*," in *Quellen und Studien zur Musiktheorie des Mittelalters III*, ed. Michael Bernhard (München: Bayerischen Akademie der Wissenshaften, 2001), 425–67. Jane Hatter's article on depictions of the *tactus* in early modern paintings, "*Col tempo*: Musical Time, Aging and Sexuality in 16th-Century Venetian Paintings," *Early Music* 39, no. 1 (2011): 3–14, is also of interest, though Hatter does not discuss meter. In addition to these, the outpouring of scholarship on mensuration and proportion signs is significant, and much of the work of the present chapter would not be possible without it. Outstanding of course is Busse Berger's *Mensuration and Proportion Signs* (Oxford: Clarendon Press, 1993), but other secondary sources are also important, including Ruth I. DeFord, "Tempo Relationships between Duple and Triple Time in the Sixteenth Century," *Early Music History* 14 (1995): 1–51; DeFord, "Zacconi's Theories of Tactus and Mensuration," *Journal of Musicology* 14, no. 2 (1996): 151–82; DeFord, "The Evolution of Rhythmic Style in Italian Secular Music of the Late Sixteenth Century," *Studi musicali* 10, no. 1 (1981): 43–74; and Uwe Wolf, *Notation und Aufführungspraxis: Studien zum Wandel von Notenschrift und Notenbild in italienischen Musikdrucken der Jahre 1571-1630* (Berlin: Merseburger, 1992). Older studies that paved the way are still relevant to this day, though many of their points have been treated more systematically in recent writings. These include George Houle, *Meter in Music, 1600–1800* (Bloomington: Indiana University Press, 1987); Carl Dahlhaus, "Die Tactus- und Proportionenlehre des 15. bis 17. Jahrhunderts," in *Hören, Messen und Rechnen in der frühen Neuzeit*, Geschichte der Musiktheorie 6, ed. Frieder Zaminer (Darmstadt: Wissenschafliche Buchgesellschaft, 1987), 333–61; Dahlhaus, "Zur Geschichte des Taktschlagen im frühen 17. Jahrhundert," in *Studies in Renaissance and Baroque Music in Honor of Arthur Mendel*, ed. Robert L. Marshall (Kassel: Bärenreiter, 1974), 117–23; Dahlhaus, "Zur Rhythmic und Metrik um 1600," in *Studien zur Theorie und Geschichte der musikalischen Rhythmic und Metrik*, ed. Ernst Apfel and Carl Dahlhaus (Munich: Emil Katzbichler, 1974), 1:273–90; J. A. Bank, *Tactus, Tempo and Notation in Mensural Music From the Thirteenth to the Seventeenth Century* (Amsterdam: Annie Bank, Anna Vondelstraat 13, 1972); Wolf Frobenius, "Tactus," in *Handwörterbuch der musikalischen Terminologie*, ed. Hans Heinrich

Although the interpretation of notation might seem at first to outweigh in importance the theories of the beat here inspected, it is precisely the perfunctory and unassuming character of these theories that should draw our attention. Because the information passed down to us is little, it is exactly the unwritten knowledge reflected in these small pieces of writing that we should aim to reconstruct. In this way, the writings on meter from this period represent an almost-written or a barely written history; the paucity of their substance offers us an opportunity to investigate the larger statements about time of which the theories are components. Doing so allows us to view these writings as music theoretical linkages to the institutional networks and intellectual legacies of a complex body of thought on time, change, and motion.

The Theoretical Work of the Beat

An exemplary period account of meter can be found within the pages of Martin Agricola's *Musica figuralis deudsch* of 1532. Agricola's writings on the beat are standard not only in their content and their brevity but also in their placement within the text. At the sixth of twelve chapters, it is easy to flip past these few pages, hidden as they are between elaborate musical examples and complicated prose. But part of the reason that this important chapter is tucked so far into Argricola's treatise is that it is conceptually central to the material that surrounds it. Agricola arrives at the topic of the beat only after explaining the components of the notational system, their relationships to each other, and their associations with the signs of mensuration. The chapter on the beat provides the theoretical apparatus that unites and integrates the system of markings thus far described, allowing for a transition to the subsequent topics, which concern alterations to the normative mensurations in augmentation, diminution, and proportional tempo relationships.

Following on the introductory material, Agricola begins his theoretical exposition with the smallest units of musical organization. He describes all of the note shapes, including the *maxima* (the longest duration), the *longa* (or long), *brevis* (breve), *semibrevis* (semibreve or whole note), *minima* (minim or half note), *semiminima* (semiminim or quarter note), *fusa* (or eighth note), *semifusa* (or sixteenth note), and the rests that correspond to these durations. Agricola's next topic is a description of the system of ligatures in which two or more notes are combined in a single shape, a practice already somewhat outdated in musical notation by the time of his treatise's publication.[5] With these preliminaries in place, he begins a short tutorial on the mensuration system. Agricola's basic

Eggebrecht (Wiesbaden: Franz Steiner, 1972–2005 [1971]), 6:1–11; Antoine Auda, *Théorie et pratique du tactus: Transcription et exécution de la musique antérieure aux environs de 1650* (Brussels: Woluwé St. Lambert, 1965); Putnam Aldrich, *Rhythm in Seventeenth-Century Italian Monody* (London: J. M. Dent, 1966); Kurt Sachs, *Rhythm and Tempo* (New York: Norton, 1953); and Georg Schünemann, *Zur Geschichte des Dirigierens* (Leipzig: Breitkopf & Härtel, 1913).
5. Martin Agricola, *Musica figuralis deudsch*, facsimile ed. (1532; Hildesheim: Georg Olms, 1969), Cr–D3r.

outline of the "three gradients," or *modus, tempus*, and *prolatio*, follows a pattern common for sixteenth-century texts which describes the relationships between the various types of durations: the amount of breves that correspond to a long, the amount of semibreves that correspond to a breve, and so on. Agricola describes a *modus major* ("der grosse"), which specifies the division of the maxima, either in perfect division into three longs or imperfect division into two longs; a *modus minor* ("der kleine") likewise divides longs perfectly or imperfectly into breves; *tempus* divides breves into semibreves in the same way; and *prolatio*, semibreves into minims. Each various type of division is coordinated with its respective mensuration signature, and together they account for the normative system of durational relationships among the note shapes.[6]

The chapter that consolidates these rudiments of notation, located in the center of the book, is on the topic of the beat. Agricola opens with a clear and concise definition: "The beat [*Tact odder Schlag*], as it is usually understood, is a steady and measured motion of the hand of the singer, by means of which—like a gauge—the notes of song are measured in accordance with the [mensuration] signs."[7] The motion Agricola describes has two parts: a lowering and a raising of the hand. While duple meters consist of two even motions, triple meter (the *Proporcien Tact*) begins with a lowering of the hand twice as long as the following raising of the hand.[8]

Here, in this central chapter, the beat puts into action the structure of the relationships described in the preceding chapters. The beat, like a ruler or tool of measurement, renders the integration of durations legible through its real or imagined motions. Its action provides a structured temporality with which to unfold the written note shapes, providing for them the logic of ordered recurrence—it breaks these figures out into a regulated, dynamic temporality. It is no surprise, then, that this is the juncture of the text at which tempo becomes a crucial factor and central point of discussion. In the chapters that follow, Agricola explains how augmentation, diminution, and proportion signs work to alter the normative structure of mensuration. In this sense, the beat as a physical gesture cannot help but be inextricably intertwined with its particular rate of action. It serves as the interface between the basic structure of mensuration and the alterations thereof. Under this mode of thinking, tempo and meter are part of the same organizing concept.

Agricola's explanation of meter through motion—specifically of a hand—and his distinction between duple, even meter and triple, uneven meter were

6. Agricola, "Von den dreien Gradibus," in *Musica figuralis deudsch*, D2v–G3r. This vast simplification is intended to capture the essence of the mensuration system so as to elucidate the function of the beat within that theoretical framework. For a more detailed explanation of the signs of mensuration and their interrelationships in treatises like Agricola's, see Busse Berger, *Mensuration and Proportion Signs*.

7. "Der Tact odder schlag, wie er alhie genomen wird ist eine stete und messige bewegung der hand des sengers, durch welche gleichsam ein richtscheit, nach ausweisung der zeichen, die gleicheit der stymmen und Noten des gesangs recht geleitet und gemessen wird…" Agricola, *Musica figuralis deudsch*, G3v.

8. Agricola, *Musica figuralis deudsch*, G3v–G4v.

especially important and recurrent components of writings on meter between 1500 and 1700. In a certain sense, the beat as Agricola and his contemporaries described it is something easy for us to comprehend. The *tactus*, or *Schlag*, or *battuta*, was a hand gesture not altogether dissimilar from the type of casual beating of time one might perform today, only restricted to the binary motion of down and up. These two basic movements consisted of the "downbeat," or lowering of the hand to the point of termination and moment of repose, and the subsequent "upbeat," or raising of the hand in preparation for the next downbeat.

The way in which the beat seems familiar, though, is also what keeps us from knowing it more intimately. Reading Agricola's words in the twenty-first century, we might mistakenly suppose that they are meant to explain some quaint aspect of ensemble performance; we might think that they are limited to describing some sort of archaic form of what we now call conducting, and it is therefore easy to understand how these pieces of language might be excluded from consideration under the rubric of knowledge on meter. But to presume that these explications had to do only with performance is to misread their importance entirely; it is to miss out on a glimpse of a world in which motion—though perhaps unexpectedly—is the foundation for knowledge on time. Other aspects of these writings make the differences more obvious or even jarring, not the least of which is the unfamiliar rendering of triple meter into two unequal parts. This notion of triple meter as an unequal meter, which is discussed in detail in chapter 3, is much closer to our twenty-first-century understanding of unbalanced meters in fives and sevens than it is to our knowledge and theories of triple meter. Confronting both the subtle and the glaring dissimilarities affords us the opportunity to explore and critique the epistemological configurations through which we come to know meter, and to ask questions about earlier ways of knowing and the institutional frameworks that supported them.

Institutions and Traditions

Agricola's text had the ability to explain meter through the motion of a hand because of its participation in certain institutionalized patterns and received traditions that made its knowledge available. Agricola's is a classic book of *musica practica*, the type of music theory treatise that concerned itself with musical literacy and composition. Indeed, the traditional distinction between speculative music theory, or *musica theorica*, and practical music theory, or *musica practica*, is one that usually has theories of pitch in mind in the first place. Aspiring to quadrivial knowledge, works on pitch of the *theorica* variety participated in the long tradition of canonics, demonstrating the mathematical relations that governed both music and the cosmos. Pitch for those writing in this tradition was, in the words of Daniel Chua, "*ratio*-nality itself."[9] Meter, by contrast, found itself among the elements of the practical tradition, in texts that provided guidance for the interpretation and reading of music and offered theoretical explanation

9. Daniel Chua, "Vincenzo Galilei, Modernity, and the Division of Nature," in *Music Theory and Natural Order*, ed. Suzannah Clark and Alexander Rehding (Cambridge: Cambridge University

where necessary to account for the systems of notation and the rules of composition. In this context meter was a foundational concept to be learned and understood at the beginning of musical instruction. As such, discussions of meter in these books take a tone of presumed knowledge, as though their presence were a formality insuring the comprehensiveness of the teachings. The similarity of the language used in these descriptions and their casual concision suggest that the explanations they offered were already commonly held.

Agricola's treatise in particular was part of a distinct tradition of *musica practica* books on "figural music" (expressed variously as *musica figuralis, musica figurativa, de figures notarum*, and other related names). This strand of writings distinguished itself from texts on plainchant in its treatment of the written "figures" or notational practices of measured polyphony. Some of these texts occupied entire works (which might bear corresponding titles, such as *Musica figuralis deudsch*), while others were contained within *musica practica* texts that placed a section on *musica choralis* (or plainchant) before the *figuralis* section. The moniker indicated a focus on the written units of musical literacy, but most of these texts provided more than the identification of musical symbols. In the space of a few pithy lines of theory or in multiple, lengthy chapters, *figuralis* texts helped their audience to understand the hierarchical organization of the mensural system in a way that was understood to be intimately linked with the period's systems of notation and tempo. The label and its variants appeared consistently throughout the sixteenth century, fading from view early in the seventeenth.[10]

The *figuralis* texts shared with many period books of music theory a set of common strategies for organizing and presenting information. Within the portion of the text devoted to fundamentals these treatises routinely explained the various shapes of the notes and the durations to which they corresponded, the notation of pitch on the staff and the signs of the clefs, mensuration and proportion signs, and the relationship of these signs to the beat. Within the relatively brief sections on meter, the use of terms related to movement (such as *tactus, Schlag*, and *battuta*), and the explanation of meter through motion were part of the shared repertoire of materials.

Although the order of presentation varied somewhat, the topics listed above were staples within the *practica* tradition. As a result, the visual similarity of these texts—published in different languages, in different formats, all across Europe—is remarkable. Chapter headings and basic illustrations correspond in

Press, 1993), 17–29 at 21. Because the *musica theorica* tradition is and was so heavily identified with canonics, it is difficult to say what type of work might qualify as *theorica* writing on meter. The distinction itself rests on the assumed primacy of pitch theory. This is not to say that theorists refused to treat of music's temporal elements in learned tracts. On the contrary, some theorists touched on rhythm in their speculative works and some even produced erudite texts entirely devoted to rhythm and meter (such as Agostino Pisa's two publications of 1611, the *Breve dichiaratione della battuta musica* and *Battuta della musicale*, discussed below).

10. Daniel Friderici's *Musica figuralis*, first printed in 1618, is one of the latest in this tradition that I have inspected.

texts published more than one hundred years apart.[11] These organizing forces shaped the group of knowledge relations that ran through many strands of practical music texts, cutting across geographic and institutional boundaries. In addition, texts that did not align themselves with the strictly practical nevertheless participated in these same organizing principles.[12] The Roman humanist Nicola Vicentino, for example, allotted the requisite space for the *battuta* in the standard rudiments sequence of his *L'antica musica ridotta alla moderna prattica*, though his text is remembered today for its reception of Greek theory.[13] Even Fludd, Mersenne, and Kircher, the authors of lengthy seventeenth-century tomes, found a way to echo the order of the practical texts somewhere within the interiors of their own. Though the physical elements of their publication—the size of the books and the quality of their printing, for example—would suggest that their content differed radically, the framework of their rudiments, in fact, did not. Their books supplied much more extended treatments of the mensural system than did many others, but the foundational understanding of the beat as a motion was still a central component in the organization of their theories, and their theories of the beat were still to be found among the familiar elements explaining modes, scales, and notation, albeit in a rather expansive manner.[14]

Aristotelianisms in Theories of Meter

Like many of his contemporaries, Zarlino included his discussion of the beat in the context of his practical writings. The chapter "Della battuta," to which he devoted two pages, can be found in the third and practical book on counterpoint of *Le istitutioni harmoniche*. But unlike many other discussions of meter, Zarlino's treatment of the beat imported ancient authority in the way that definitions in the

11. Daniel Friderici's *Musica figuralis* (Rostock: J. Fuess, 1618) and Johannes Cochlaeus's *Tetrachordum musices* (Nuremberg: Johann Weyssenburger, 1511) are an exemplary pair.

12. Francisco Salinas's writings on the temporal elements of music are an instructive example. His speculative, humanist treatise, *De musica libri septem*, first explicates distinctive rhythmic patterns through an elaborate system of poetic feet. Following this exposition, Salinas then theorizes the temporal unfolding of the various poetic feet through the two-part logic of thesis and arsis. Salinas, *De musica libri septem* (Salamanca: Mathias Gastius, 1577), bk. V:235–85. On Salinas's theories of rhythm and meter, see Matthew S. Royal, "Tradition and Innovation in Sixteenth-Century Rhythmic Theory: Francisco Salinas's *De Musica Libri Septem*," *Music Theory Spectrum* 34, no. 2 (2012): 26–47.

13. Nicola Vicentino, "Regola di batter la misura con tre ordini con l'essempio," in *L'antica musica ridotta alla moderna prattica*, facsimile ed. (1555; Kassel: Bärenreiter, 1965), 8:76.

14. Fludd accomplishes the treatment of the musical rudiments through the use and explanation of his "Templum musicae," the explanation of which comprised part II of the second tract, book I of *Utriusque cosmi*... For Fludd's writings on meter, see *Utriusque cosmi*... (Oppenheim: Johann Theodor de Bry, 1617), 1:190. Mersenne discusses the rudiments in his books on composition. For his treatment of the beat, see Marin Mersenne, *Harmonie universelle*, facsimile ed. (1636–37; Paris: Centre national de la recherché scientifique, 1963), vol. 2, "Livre cinquiesme de la Composition," prop. XI, 324–25. Various rudiments are found in the Lib. VIII (Musicam Mirificam) of book II of Kircher's *Musurgia universalis*. For Kircher's treatment of the beat, see *Musurgia universalis*, facsimile ed. (1650; Hildesheim: Georg Olms, 1970), 2:52.

realm of pitch had done in unbroken tradition for hundreds of years. Zarlino explains that which some call "beat" (*battuta*), or "sounding time" (*tempo sonoro*), and which Augustine ("the very saintly doctor") calls *plauso*, is a motion consisting of two parts.[15] These two parts, a lowering and a raising of the hand, are called *thesis* and *arsis* and are similar to the systole and diastole of the pulse in medicine described by Paul of Aegina and Galen. Between the two, Zarlino continues, there must be some resting points "because, according to Aristotle, between motions [resting points] are always to be found."[16]

The content of Zarlino's chapter on the beat is consistent with most other texts of sixteenth-century music theory: it includes a description of the hand motion and some detail on its particularities in addition to an explanation of the relationship of the beat to the written signs of musical notation. Zarlino's description also includes the detail about the moments of repose between the motions of the hand, which—as chapter 2 demonstrates—highlights the explanatory importance of the distinctly two-part structure of the motion. By contrast to its contemporaries, Zarlino's description is inflated with authoritative citation. In quick succession, he invokes Augustine, a definition from medicine authorized by none other than Galen, and Aristotle's *Physics*. In addition to their connection to the speculative traditions (in which such learned references were common), Zarlino's citations were a part of an important and enduring relationship between writings on meter and natural philosophy that was at times more visible and at times obscured. Long before the publication of *Le istitutioni harmoniche*, a number of medieval theorists had cited Aristotle's *Physics* alongside their discussions of the beat. Marchetto of Padua, in his *Pomerium* of 1318–24, explained the beat as a motion, in that "every measure is [made] in a certain quantity and time," and "every time is the measure of change (according to the philosopher, *Physics* IV)."[17] The anonymous author of the *Tractatus de musica* of ca. 1471 (Coussemaker's Anonymous 12) may have had Marchetto in mind when invoking the Aristotelian doctrine on time, change, and motion and relating these to the continuous motion of the beat.[18] After Zarlino, too, authors took up the practice of citing or even discussing Aristotle's *Physics* in the context of the

---

15. Zarlino, *Le istitutioni harmoniche* (Venice: Francesco de i Franceschi Senese, 1558), 207.

16. "percioche (secondo la mente di Aristotele) tra questi movimenti…sempre si [quiete] ritrovano." Zarlino, *Le istitutioni harmoniche*, 207.

17. Marchetto of Padua, *Pomerium*, in *Marcheti de Padua Pomerium*, ed. Giuseppe Vecchi, Corpus Scriptorum de Musica 6 (Rome: American Institute of Musicology, 1961), 75, as cited and translated in Blachly, "*Mensura* versus *Tactus*," 438.

18. Blachly, "*Mensura* versus *Tactus*," 438–39. On the relationship between medieval Aristotelianism and theories of meter in general, see Dorit Tanay, *Noting Music, Marking Culture: The Intellectual Context of Rhythmic Notation, 1250-1400*, Musicological Studies and Documents 46 (American Institute of Musicology: Hänssler-Verlag, 1999). Interestingly, Tanay and I are both concerned to contextualize our theorists with respect to the various types of Aristotelianism and Aristotelian conceptions of time that informed them—even though the types of theories and the types of Aristoteliansims we discuss are significantly different and chronologically disparate. Taney was not the first to contextualize medieval theories of rhythm in this way. Most notable is Max Hass's work, in "Studien zur mittelalterlichen Musiklehre: I. Eine Übersicht über die Musiklehre im Kontext der Philosophie der 13. und frühen 14. Jahrhunderts," in *Aktuelle Fragen der musikbezogenen Mittelalterforschung: Texte zu einem Basler Kolloquium des Jahres 1975*, ed. Hans

musical beat, some devoting pages of detailed explanation to this relationship.[19] As late a text as Nassarre's 1723 *Escuela música según la práctica moderna* would still include a reference to Aristotle in this context (see the texts listed in appendix 1).

What are these references to Aristotle doing in theories of the beat? More important than the lines of influence they may reflect is their shared relationship to a general set of beliefs about time and motion, and the institutional control and sanctioning of these beliefs. The appearance of Aristotle citations around writings on meter in texts from the twelfth and eighteenth centuries does not speak to a uniformity in the transmission of music theories but rather to the persistence and relative continuity of the Scholastic tradition over this same period.[20] Within this tradition time was rendered sensible through the enacting of motion and change.

The long tradition of commentaries on and translations of Aristotle's texts was bound up with education in the medieval and early modern eras. Although histories of sixteenth- and seventeenth-century culture (and especially histories of music) have traditionally emphasized the innovations of humanism, Scholasticism remained a dominating and exceptional force during this time. Anyone who attempted to gain book learning or professed any sort of education was schooled in Aristotelian thought. Aristotelian texts on logic, metaphysics, and particularly physics were taught nearly universally across Europe as the foundations for learning. In Italy and Spain this tradition was supported and even controlled through the Catholic Church; teaching the *Physics*, though, was so foundational that it was a requirement even in the most progressive and humanist-influenced environments.[21] The reformed institutions of Germany and the North were no exception: even long after these schools had developed their own texts for the teaching of theology and metaphysics, they remained

Oesch and Wulf Arlt (Winterthur: Amadeus, 1982), 323–456; and Hass, "Die Musiklehre im 13. Jahrhundert von Johannes de Garlandia bis Franco," in *Die mittelalterliche Lehre von der Mehrstimmigkeit*, ed. Frieder Zaminer (Darmstadt: Wissenschaftliche Buchgesellschaft, 1984), 89–159.

19. Such as the passages found in Agostino Pisa's *Breve dichiaratione della battuta musicale*, facsimile ed., ed. Piero Gargiulo, with extracts from *Battuta della musica* (1611; Lucca: Libreria Musicale Italiana Editrice, 1996); and idem., *Battuta della musica* (Rome: Bartolomeo Zanetti, 1611), facsimile ed. in Pisa, *Breve dichiarazione della battuta musicale* [*sic*], ed. Walther Dürr (Bologna: Forni, 1969). I refer to Pisa's texts by their original titles (and not the titles of the facsimile editions). These texts are treated in detail below.

20. See Charles B. Schmitt, *Aristotle and the Renaissance* (Cambridge, MA: Harvard University Press, 1983); and Paul F. Grendler, "Universities of the Renaissance and Reformation," *Renaissance Quarterly* 57, no. 1 (2004): 1–42; on the importance of Aristotelianism in natural philosophy see Des Chene, *Physiologia*, esp. 1–16; and Charles H. Lohr, "The Sixteenth-Century Transformation of the Aristotelian Natural Philosophy," in *Aristotelismus und Renaissance: In memoriam Charles B. Schmitt*, ed. Eckhard Keßler, Charles H. Lohr, and Walter Sparn (Wiesbaden: Otto Harrassowitz, 1988), 89–99.

21. Grendler, *The Roman Inquisition and the Venetian Press, 1540-1605* (Princeton: Princeton University Press, 1977), esp. 286–93; and Grendler, "The Universities of the Renaissance and Reformation." See also Gary Tomlinson, *Monteverdi and the End of the Renaissance* (Berkeley: University of California Press, 1987), 234–60; finally, Carlo Giacon's classic study *La seconda scholastica*, 3 vols. (Milan: Fratelli Bocca, 1950), remains useful to this day.

committed to Aristotelian texts on natural philosophy.[22] This tradition persisted well into the seventeenth century and developed alongside humanist thought.

The most important thing about the Aristotle citations, however, is not their mere existence, or even the longevity of the tradition, but the fact that their presence or absence did not alter the content of the explanations of meter. Early modern commentators on Aristotle produced and remade knowledge on time in a way that reflected a larger set of thoughts on the nature of time as motion. Texts on music sometimes made a relationship to these Aristotelian texts explicit and sometimes did not, but in either case both sets of texts—those on music and those on Aristotle—were connected to the same epistemological network that explained time through motion. The citation of Aristotle, then, was an institutional overlay that had its own dynamic, and which resulted in an uneven distribution of visible evidence (the scattering of explicit citations from the twelfth through eighteenth centuries). The more important continuity is found in the pattern of knowledge relations surrounding time and motion, which was made evident as clearly in theories of meter as it was in commentaries on the *Physics*.

To say that texts of music theory made reference to Aristotle, though, is less than clear. The corpus of writings attributed to Aristotle in the medieval and early modern era constitutes a huge variety of translations, interpretations, and commentaries that circulated widely. Thousands of editions (perhaps over three thousand) of Aristotle's works were published in the age of print before 1600 alone, and well over six thousand commentaries on Aristotle's works are identifiable from the period before 1650.[23] Unfortunately, it is rare for writers on music to credit particular commentaries on Aristotle if they cite the philosopher in the context of meter at all.

An interesting and exceptional window into this world of circulating Aristotelianisms is the work of Agostino Pisa. Pisa, a Roman intellectual and a self-described "doctor of canon and civil law," published two texts on the beat in 1611: the *Breve dichiaratione della battuta musica* and *Battuta della musicale*. These documents are unusual in their exclusive focus on musical meter. In the midst of virulent criticism of his contemporaries' time-beating practices, Pisa created lengthy explanations and prescriptions for the act of beating meter supported with Aristotelian authority. In order to do so, he reproduced entire

---

22. Grendler, "The Universities of the Renaissance and Reformation," 3–4, 20.
23. Luca Bianchi, "Continuity and Change in the Aristotelian Tradition," in *The Cambridge Companion to Renaissance Philosophy*, ed. James Hankins (Cambridge: Cambridge University Press, 2007), 50; Richard Blum, "Der Standardkursus der katholischen Schulphilosophie im 17. Jahrhundert," in *Aristotelismus und Renaissance*, ed. Keßler, 141–48. These commentaries took a variety of forms; particularly popular was the *quaestio*, a formal debate on a specific topic, which could serve as the commentary for a translated text of Aristotle's such as the *Physics*. Through the seventeenth century these types of commentaries were gradually replaced by the *cursus*, which reorganized the debates by topic rather than following the structure of the translated text of Aristotle. See Walter Ong, *Ramus, Method, and the Decay of Dialogue* (Cambridge, MA: Harvard University Press, 1983); Brian Lawn, *The Rise and Decline of the Scholastic 'Quaestio disputata': With Special Emphasis on its Use in the Teaching of Medicine and Science* (Leiden: E.J. Brill, 1993), esp. 129–44; Des Chene, *Physiologia*, 7–8.

26 ∾ Beating Time & Measuring Music in the Early Modern Era

definitions on time and motion taken from Aristotelian commentaries on the *Physics*. These widely circulated definitions can be understood as points of commonality in the effort to describe time on the part of Scholastic commentators and writers on music.

Pisa's physical explanation of the beat, in the fifth chapter of the *Battuta della musica*, includes two Aristotelian definitions of motion. The first is "Motus est actus entis in potentia, prout in potentia": motion or change is the actualization of what is in potential, insofar as it is in potential.[24] This phrase (explained in detail below) is from *Physics* 3.1; Pisa credits the third book of the *Physics* in *testo* 6. The Latin phrase itself, generally recognized as Aristotle's definition of motion, is found in this form in many Aristotelian texts from Pisa's era. It appears in Franciscus Suárez's *Disputationes metaphysicæ* (1597; this text was reprinted throughout the first half of the seventeenth century), but Eustachius's *Summa philosophica quadripartite…*(1609) also comes close, with "quatenus" for "prout."[25] So, too, does the older… *Super octo libros Physicorum Aristotelis quaestiones* (1555) of Domingo de Soto, which has "secundum quod est," instead of "prout."[26] The second definition of motion Pisa cites is "Motus est actus mobilis, prout mobile": motion is the action of what is mobile, insofar as it is mobile, also from *Physics* 3.1.[27] This quotation is nearly paralleled in the *Commentarii Collegii Conimbricensis e Societate Jesu in octo libros Physicorum Aristotelis Stagiritae* (1594, with later editions), a set of commentaries compiled for the Jesuit University of Coimbria.[28] Further on in his text, Pisa employs Aristotelian logic on continual motion to justify the momentary resting points at either end of the time-beating motion. For this purpose he reproduced texts from *Physics* 8.8, using Latin phrases that closely parallel Soto's… *Super octo libros Physicorum Aristotelis quaestiones* and the commentaries on the *Physics* of Thomas Aquinas.[29]

24. Pisa, *Battuta della musica*, 75 (Pisa uses these same definitions in the *Breve dichiarazione della battuta musicale*, p. 9).
25. Franciscus Suárez, *Metaphysicarum disputationum* (Paris: Apud Michaelem Sonnium, 1605), 49.2.2, 2:622. Like Pisa, Suárez credits "3. Physicorum, text. 6." With regard to Eustachius, copies of the 1609 edition (the only one available to Pisa) are scarce, but see Eustachius, *Summa philosophiae quadripartite* (Leiden: Franciscum Moyardum, 1647), 2:161. See also Des Chene, *Physiologia*, 26n11.
26. Domingo de Soto, *Reuerendi patris Dominici Soto Segobiensis theologi Ordinis Praedicatorum Super octo libros Physicorum Aristotelis quaestiones* (Salamanca: Andrea de Portonaris, 1555), 39.
27. Pisa, *Battuta della musica*, 75; idem., *Breve dichiarazione della battuta musicale*, 9.
28. *Commentarii Collegii Conimbricensis e Societate Jesu in octo libros Physicorum Aristotelis Stagiritae*, facsimile ed. (1594; Hildesheim: Georg Olms, 1984), 1:332. Mário S. de Carvalho identifies Father Manuel de Góis as the primary author of the commenteries, though there is reason to believe that much of the writing resulted from collobartions. See de Carvalho, "Time According to the Coimbra Commentaries," in *The Medieval Concept of Time*, ed. Pasquale Porro (Deiden: Brill, 2001), 353–82 at 353–57.
29. Soto,…*Super octo libros Physicorum Aristotelis quaestiones*, 138–39; Aquinas, "De Physico Auditu," in *Doctoris Angelici divi Thomæ Aquinatis Opera Omnia*, ed. Eduard Fretté (Paris: Ludovicum Vivès, 1875), 22:678.

Pisa, like other theorists, made reference to passages on motion in the *Physics* commentaries because of the logical dependence, in Aristotelian natural philosophy, of time on *motus* (a concept impoverished in its English translations, change or motion). On the concept of time specifically, the Aristotelian account is obscure; in the *Physics*, the account of time begins with a series of puzzles in which the nature and very existence of time is questioned.[30]

The logical endpoint to this series of puzzles is that time is something of *motus*, rather than really something in itself. Time is said to be the number of change (this is how the formulation is often relayed in English); it is less basic than change and logically descended from it.[31] Features of time rely for their logical explication on features of change.

Aristotelian natural philosophy focused on logical explanations for the progression from what was only in potential to what actually existed. This progression—change, motion, *motus*—was the "primary *explanandum* in natural philosophy."[32] The conceptual category of *motus* helped to organize logically and explain all natural types in the world.[33] As a part of *motus*, the construction of time was conjoined with that of the progressions and changes that explained all of nature. Aristotelians accounted for the continuity of time through the continuity of *motus*. They understood parts of time as parts of movement, and understood time to continue simply because there was always some type of change taking place.[34]

For writers on music in this era, *motus* was the obvious framework for theorizing meter. Specifically, the subcategory of local motion (change of place) best described the action of measuring made in the physical motion of beating meter. The description of beating in the period's treatises shifted the focus of the text momentarily away from the figures of musical literacy and onto the motion of the hand—which could be visualized and experienced—in order to make clear the concept of temporal division. Beating, then, served as a kind of demonstration, or a physical theorization of a temporal concept.

Pisa's dissection of the time-beating process makes the relationship to the parts of *motus* explicit. Within local motion, he asks us to consider three

30. The account of time is found in *Physics* 4.10–14. The first puzzle concerns the nature of time's existence, since time seems to be composed of all that has not yet occurred and all that has ceased to occur. The second interrogates the part of time that is colloquially said to exist: the now. The now, however, is not a part of time. A part of time would measure the whole, and time cannot simply consist of nows. Furthermore (the third puzzle), it is even difficult to say if the now is a single now, always the same, or different in every instant. The translation to which I will refer for books III and IV is *Aristotle's Physics Books III and IV*, ed., trans., and with commentary by Edward Hussey (Oxford: Clarendon Press, 1983), chaps. 10–14 are found on pp. 41–54. On the series of puzzles that begin the account of time in *Physics* IV, see Coope, *Time for Aristotle*, 17–30.

31. Aristotle *Physics*, 4.11.219b1; *Aristotle's* Physics *Books III and IV*, trans. Hussey, 44; Coope, *Time for Aristotle*, 85–98.

32. Des Chene, *Physiologia*, 22.

33. Des Chene, *Physiologia*, 21.

34. Coope, *Time for Aristotle*, 55–57.

things: the *mobile*, the *motus*, and the termination. The *mobile* is the thing moved, the mobile entity, such as the sphere of the moon (rather than its path). The motion describes the "intelligence" driving the movement ("l'intelligenza assistente motrice")—it is the heart of the *motus*. The termination is double, and denotes the points from which the movement begins and ends, or the spatial positions that demarcate the path of the hand in beating time.[35]

What Pisa describes is the Aristotelian doctrine of *motus, potentia*, and *actus*, of which the Aristotelian definitions of motion were a part.[36] In this doctrine, all change begins with *potentia*, the capacity for change. *Actus* puts into practice a *potentia* that inheres in something. It does so in the form of *motus*. *Motus* is not simply movement, but the form of all change: as the Aristotelians wrote, "*motus* is the *actus* of what is in *potentia*, insofar as it is in *potentia*," or "*motus* is the *actus* of a *mobile*, insofar as it is *mobile*."[37] Pisa found it useful to quote these definitions directly in his text. As he carefully points out, *mobile, motus*, and termination are all found in music. The *mobile*, the thing moved, is the hand, while the terminations are the points at the boundaries of its motion. The *motus*, the guiding "intelligence," is the beat: inseparable from the concept of change and motion, described through the precise construction of Aristotelian time, and applied to the temporal interval we today call by a name (beat) devoid of its physical implications. For Pisa, a long, explicit engagement with the Aristotelian account of *motus* served as the primary tool for theorizing meter. He asked his readers to understand the nature of the beat, its being, its intelligence, as *motus*.

Pisa's documents are distinctive in the way that they borrow language directly from the Aristotelian doctrines, and in the way that they prescribe an odd and specific manner of beating time (Pisa thought that the motion should be completely smooth and continuous, with only the most brief of pauses on either end of the motion).[38] His citations to Aristotle, however, are significant in their reference to the shared knowledge on time and motion that was officially sanctioned and dispersed in the commentaries on the *Physics*. *Motus*, then, was the endorsed period term used to describe the beliefs about change, motion, and time that were more fundamental than the specific doctrines of the Aristotelian commentaries or the writings on music. Regardless of the citations they made or the time-beating techniques they supplied, sixteenth- and

---

35. Pisa, *Battuta della musica*, 75; idem., *Breve dichiarazione della battuta musicale*, 10.

36. Des Chene, *Physiologia*, 21–52.

37. The nitpicky "insofar as..." in the first definition clarifies that *actus* works on something in *potentia*, rather than *potentia* itself which is not a thing. Des Chene, *Physiologia*, 26–30. The definitions cited appear here as Des Chene so usefully renders them in hybrid Latin-English in *Physiologia*, 26–27.

38. Pisa's idiosyncratic take on the time-beating motion was later harshly critiqued in Pier Francesco Valentini's equally Aristotelian doctrine, set forth in the *Trattato della battuta musicale* (Rome: Biblioteca Apostolica Vaticana, Ms. Barb. Lat. 4417, [ca. 1643]). For more on the disagreement between Pisa and Valentini, see Houle, *Meter in Music, 1600–1800*, 5–8; and Roger Mathew Grant, "Four Hundred Years of Meter: Theories, Ideologies, and Technologies of Musical Periodicity since 1611" (PhD diss., University of Pennsylvania, 2010), 68–73.

seventeenth-century texts structured the explanation of meter in similar ways. In these texts the hierarchy of temporal mensuration was controlled and organized through the central technique of beating, which consisted of a lowering and raising of the hand.

The Organizing Principle of Meter Theory: Four Approaches

The conceptual dependence of time on change explains the odd and sometimes unexpected turn to the physical motion of time beating in the musical texts of this era. Amidst information on notation, note shapes, and even mensuration, the explanation of the beat might seem like an out of place prescription for performance in texts that were otherwise concerned with the practices of music writing and music reading. Indeed, one secondary source on these early treatises notes, "with the exception of sporadic references to the necessity of physically beating the *tactus*...most of the elementary primers contain no reference to the activity of performance."[39] But to understand the description of the beat as an activity of performance is to miss its significance as understood through the rubric of temporality included in *motus*.

The beat, as described in this period, was simultaneously an embodiment and demonstration of temporal measurement. Its place in performance notwithstanding, it took on a role in which it provided the logical framework of division for theories of meter. It demonstrated, through a specific form of local motion, the change that occurred in the passage of measured time in music. It explained this temporal change in an act of physical change that would have been understood to encompass both. Though the efficacy of this demonstration is difficult to understand today—in a world in which the time of the beat can be thought of and represented without a relationship to motion—it worked well enough to merit centuries of repetition, outlasting notational systems and style periods. The beat, the very conceptual and organizational center of meter, was always explained through motion: the intelligence of *motus*.

While theories of meter in the sixteenth and seventeenth centuries all relied on a certain demonstration of the beat, they differed substantially in terms of the notational practices that they set out to theorize. During this period, the complex system of unbarred white mensural notation fell out of fashion in much of Western Europe, and notation that included regular barlines became more common. Through a slow and uneven process, theories of meter shifted their focus, explaining fewer complexities of the older mensural system. The fairly extended treatments of the temporal hierarchies in that system—the levels of *modus, tempus,* and *prolatio*—became increasingly scarce in theoretical texts as the sixteenth century progressed. The intimate relationship between the beat and

39. John Butt, *Music Education and the Art of Performance in the German Baroque* (Cambridge: Cambridge University Press, 1994), 55.

tempo also changed during this period. Although the two concepts remained entwined well into the nineteenth century (and, to a certain extent, remain this way in the twenty-first), the system of determining tempo by means of the diachronic and synchronic relationships between meter signatures slowly faded from practice; more music was composed with a single meter signature related to a particular configuration of note values, character, and intended affect.[40] But quite apart from this linear narrative, writings on meter were essentially invariant in their basic content. Though the concept of the beat was employed to differing ends, its important organizational work remained central to the changing theories of these centuries.

In order to demonstrate an abiding continuity in theories of meter that span chronology, geography, and stylistic practice, I examine four representative texts known to have been influential in their day. The different approaches they offer demonstrate how a single understanding of the beat functioned in rather divergent theoretical systems.

Ornithoparchus, Musicae activae micrologus *(1517)*

Published in Leipzig and Cologne between the years of 1517 and 1555, Ornithoparchus's *Musicae activae micrologus* was a widely circulated text on performed (or practical) music. The text enjoyed a revival in the later sixteenth century, when John Dowland published his English translation.[41] More generous than some of its *practica* contemporaries in the depth of its explanation, the *Musicae activae micrologus* provides clarifications in the form of figures and tables in the sections on meter. Perhaps its depth of explanation played a role in the adoption of the work as a textbook at Kraków University in the mid-sixteenth century, and the absorption of some of its material in later texts such as Angelo da Picitono's *Fior angelico di musica* of 1547 (which borrowed entire chapters), and Sebastiani's *Bellum musicale* of 1563.[42]

Opening its pages, we first encounter the book on plainsong, which covers the descriptions of the types of music and the topics of scales, intervals, solmization, musica ficta, and other issues related to pitch. It is only after the conclusion of this book that the book on mensural music begins. As with Agricola's explanation, this short introduction to the mensural system includes an identification of the note shapes from the *maxima* to the *semifusa*, a description of the standard ligatures that join these durations, and a brief account of *modus major, modus minor, tempus,* and *prolatio,* each of which can show perfect division into three or

---

40. The changing relationship of tempo to meter is taken up in detail in the fifth and seventh chapters of this book.
41. Andreas Ornithoparchus, *Musicae activae micrologus* (Leipzig: Valentin Schumann, 1517); 2nd ed. (Leipzig: Valentin Schumann, 1519); facsimile ed. (Hildesheim: Georg Olms, 1970). Translated by John Dowland as *Andreas Ornithoparcus: His Micrologus, or Introduction, Containing the Art of Singing…* (London: Thomas Adams, 1609).
42. *Oxford Music Online,* s.v. "Ornithoparchus, Andreas," by Klaus Wolfgang Niemöller, accessed October 29, 2010, <www.oxfordmusiconline.org>.

imperfect division into two.[43] In order to indicate these various divisions, Ornithoparchus recommends the use of mensuration signs (O, C, ☉ and ☾) in combination with the numbers two and three.[44]

Having outlined the basic system of mensuration, Ornithoparchus employs the use of his first table (reproduced as plate 1.1 below) in order to condense the information thus far presented. This table indicates hierarchies, but only those between adjacent levels of normative division: each numeral in the table indicates the number of durations in the level below that correspond to one of the durations in the level above. It serves, then, as a tool of clarification and an initial reference point for the relationship between *modus, tempus, prolatio*, and the mensuration signs, which sit at the bottom of the table.

It is only after the exposition of this preliminary material that Ornithoparchus introduces the concept of the beat. His definition is familiar: "*Tactus* is a successive motion in song that directs measure in an equal manner; or, it is the *motus*, signaled by the hand of the chief singer, which directs the measure of song in accordance with the [mensuration] signs."[45] The logic of this motion measures song and divides

Plate 1.1 Ornithoparchus's first table, from *Musicae activae micrologus*, facsimile ed. (1519; Hildesheim: Georg Olms, 1970), F3r.

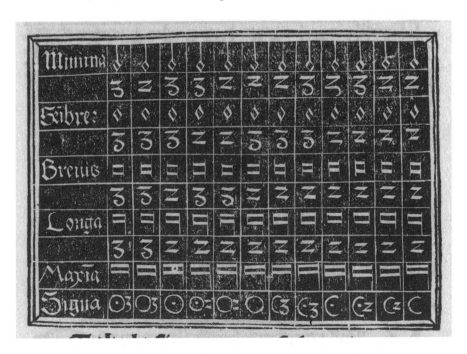

43. Ornithoparchus, *Musicae activae micrologus*, Fv–F2r.
44. On Ornithoparchus's somewhat unorthodox use of the mensuration and proportion signs, see Busse Berger, *Mensuration and Proportion Signs*, esp. 31–32 and 137–39.
45. "Unde Tactus est motio seccessiva in cantu, mensure equalitatem dirigens. Vel est quidam motus, manu precentoris signorum indicio formatus, cantum dirigens mensuraliter."

its durations in the ways allowed for by *modus, tempus,* and *prolatio.* In order to explain the relationship between these concepts, Ornithoparchus produces a second table (reproduced below as plate 1.2).[46] Of this table, which he calls the "table of *Tactuum* resolved," Ornithoparchus writes, "the beat measures the semibreve in all signs."[47] Unlike the first table, this table shows the hierarchy of division between all of the durations related horizontally to the given mensuration sign. Thus in the first row, which shows perfection at each level of *modus, tempus,* and *prolatio* under the sign ⊙3, one *maxima* receives twenty-seven beats, one *longa* receives nine beats, one *brevis* receives three beats, and one *semibrevis* receives the value of the beat. Alternatively the table can be read vertically in order to find out how the different mensuration signs award a number of beats to each note shape. So, for example, the *brevis*—reading from the top of its column—receives three beats under ⊙3, O3, and C3, but two beats under ⊙2, and so forth. The alterations of augmentation and diminution, which are the topics of Ornithoparchus's next chapters, refer back to the normative organization in this table.

At the center of the table, relating all of the durations to the mensuration signs, is the semibreve (or whole note)—the note shape to which the *tactus* is attached. This column, the column of the beat level, is the moment of identity in the table. Here, the beat marshals and organizes the durations into their structured relationships, creating a coherent system. This column provides the unit of measure for the terms in each row, and aligns the shifting relationships of the columns on either side into identity. Understood in this way, the beat in this

Plate 1.2 Ornithoparchus's second table, from *Musicae activae micrologus,* facsimile ed. (1519; Hildesheim: Georg Olms, 1970), F4r.

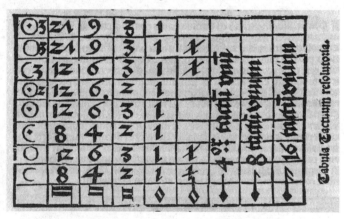

Ornithoparchus, *Musicae activae micrologus,* F3v. Dowland, trans. *Andreas Ornithoparcus: His Micrologus,* 46; in Ornithoparchus and Dowland, *A Compendium of Musical Practice,* 166.

46. This chart resembles, in many ways, a chart in Nicolaus Wollick's *Opus aureum* (Cologne, 1501); rev. ed. (Cologne, 1508), G1v.

47. "Semibrevis in omnibus signis…tactu mensuratur integro." Ornithoparchus, *Musicae activae micrologus,* F4r. Dowland, trans. *Andreas Ornithoparcus: His Micrologus,* 46; in Ornithoparchus and Dowland, *A Compendium of Musical Practice,* 166.

system is a motion that makes the otherwise abstract durational units concrete. It is an act that renders the marks of the table legible. This table, then, concerns not only the manner and hierarchy of mensural division but also the system through which the division is administered. The beat, shown in the column of the semibreve, organizes and explains this system.

Zarlino, Le istitutioni harmoniche *(1558)*

Zarlino's heavily citational definition for the beat, discussed above, is found in the forty-eighth chapter of his book on counterpoint.[48] Turning the pages of *Le istitutioni harmoniche,* one immediately notices how much information Zarlino presents before introducing the topic of the beat. Like Ornithoparchus, he begins his practical book with an identification of the basic elements of musical notation, including the note shapes, the staff, and the clefs. Zarlino's text then departs from the organization of Ornithoparchus's; in this book on counterpoint, the next topic concerns the intervals. Several chapters on simple contrapuntal composition intervene before the discussion of the beat, and still more intervene between the chapter on the beat and the sequence of chapters on *modus, tempus,* and *prolatio.* The reason for this odd arrangement is that Zarlino was able to explain an updated (and much abbreviated) mensuration system within his two-page chapter on the beat. His sequence of chapters on *modus, tempus,* and *prolatio*—some of the final chapters of the book—are written in past tense, and describe a system no longer in use.[49] Changes in notational practices in the forty years since the first publication of Ornithoparchus's *Musicae activae micrologus* had rendered this explanation an exercise in obligation to the older masters.

Zarlino's chapter on the beat, "Della battuta," can be divided into three distinct sections. After establishing the beat as a two-part motion in the first section, Zarlino goes on to discuss the signs of mensuration in the second and the appropriate rhythms for each meter in the third. He clarifies that the beat is fundamentally of two different varieties: equal and unequal (*Equale & Inequale*). The equal beat consists of a lowering and raising of the hand equal in duration, whereas the unequal beat consists of a lowering of the hand twice the length of the following raise. The distinction between equal and unequal dominates the second and third sections of the chapter. Zarlino introduces the mensuration signs in order to indicate those appropriate to the equal beat (these include O, C, ₵, and ₵) and those appropriate to the unequal beat (which include ⊙, ℂ, ₵, and ₵). In addition to these signs, he discusses the sign 3/2, which can also indicate the unequal measure (not only in a proportional relationship to other meters, but also on its own, "when no other competing numerals appear that denote other proportions of the figures").[50]

---

48. Zarlino, *Le istitutioni harmoniche,* 207–9.
49. Zarlino, *Le istitutioni harmoniche,* 268–80.
50. "maßimamente quando non vi concorreno altre cifre numerali, che dinotino alcuna proportione nelle figure." Zarlino, *Le istitutioni harmoniche,* 208.

Zarlino's next and final topic is the relationship between poetic feet and the equal and unequal measures. The equal measure, he suggests, can accommodate the pyrrhic (*v v*), spondee (— —), dactyl (— *v v*), and anapest (*v v* —). The unequal measure suits the iamb (*v* —), trochee (—*v*), and tribrach (*v v v*), as well as the major and minor ionic (— —*v v* and *v v* — — respectively), choriamb (— *v v* —), antispast (*v v* — *v v*), and "many other feet."[51] In this inventory, Zarlino is accounting for some of the rhythmic patterns that each meter can measure. The crucial distinction here is between those rhythms that can be divided into two parts equally and those that must be divided into two parts unequally; it rests on the presumption that each short syllable takes half the time of each long.[52] The tribrach pattern, for instance, might consist of three half notes, while a major ionic might consist of two whole notes followed by two half notes. What results, then, is a way of knowing and experiencing these rhythms under the auspices of the beat's moving division. The structure of the lowering and raising of the hand oriented and explained these otherwise abstracted durations, depicting and demonstrating the experience of their unfolding. Zarlino invites us to envision a performance of rhythm in which the organizing principle is not an imagined grid within which these rhythms are placed, but instead an action that marks and distinguishes a means for their measurement.

For Zarlino, the distinction between an equal and unequal beat segregated the mensuration and proportion signs into distinct categories, and did the same for the combinations of rhythms indicated in poetic feet. This important and lasting distinction between equal and unequal was at root related to the interior division of the beat into two parts: parts that could be equal to each other (in duple meters) or in an unequal—specifically, 2:1—relationship (in triple meters). The two-part motion of the beat translated the many patterns of duration into lucid temporal measures.

Lippius, Synopsis musicæ *(1612)*

Lippius's text is unique among the four inspected here in that the practical and speculative topics it treats are not separated out into different books. This is, in part, due to the extremely condensed nature of the text. Imitated and reproduced in the works of many later writers (including Alsted, Crüger, and Werkmeister) Lippius's influential *Synopsis musicæ* is remembered in the twenty-first century for its description of the *trias harmonica*. But within its small pages it also contains writings on the temporal elements of music.

Perhaps because Lippius does not give over a particular part of the text to the practical musical elements, he places his first treatment of the beat within a portion of the text on the "quantity of sound" (*De Soni Quantitate*). Lippius begins with the assertion "All sound is quantity," and explains that sound has various

---

51. Zarlino, *Le istitutioni harmoniche*, 209.
52. Zarlino, *Le istitutioni harmoniche*, 208–9.

dimensions in which this quantity adheres.[53] These include the dimension of pitch, of course, (*De Soni Numerabili Crassitudine*) as well as volume (*De Soni Latitudine Numerabili*), but the first discussed is the "longitudinal," or durational dimension (*De Soni Longitudine*). As Lippius explains, "all sounds have a length that can be numbered," because "all sounds, [considered] with their *motu*, endure either extendedly or briefly."[54] He continues:

> This temporal flux of sound is numbered in musical science by observing a constant musical *tactus* patterned after the heartbeat. This involves a raising and lowering in definite proportion, mainly duple proportion in geometric proportionality.[55]

The *tactus*, then, is the motion that measures the "flux" (*fluxio*) or *motus* of song and gives it number. Inherently two-part, (as for Zarlino) Lippius's *tactus* is either equal or unequal. Again, this distinction divides poetic feet into those appropriate for each kind of beat, and here Lippius gives only two examples: the spondaic, with its equal parts, suits the equal or duple beat, while the trochaic, with its unequal parts, suits the unequal or triple beat.[56]

Unlike Ornithoparchus or Zarlino, Lippius places the identification of note shapes and other notational basics following, rather than preceding, his explanation of meter. In fact, since he has already identified and described the *tactus*, he can then intertwine his identification of the note names with the "numberable length" that the *tactus* measures.[57] In this text, the relationship between physical demonstration and number is explicit—the first literally makes the second possible. Lippius specifies the number of beats assigned to each note shape with a list that resembles Ornithoparchus's second table in some ways (reproduced below as plate 1.3). These durations can go on *ad infinitum* "with notes of larger or smaller duration." But Lippius decides not to include further note shapes because these "will suffice."[58] The idea that the divisions represented should continue infinitely reflects Lippius's Aristotelian belief in the infinite divisibility of time.

For Lippius, as for Ornithoparchus, the semibreve corresponds to the beat. He therefore assigns it the numeric marker 1/1 in his table, signaling identity. The other note shapes in the vertical list are referred to this central marker and bear a relationship to it: the *brevis* 2/1, the *minima* 1/2, and so forth. Importantly, their values are not referred to each other (as they were in Ornithoparchus's first table).

53. Johannes Lippius, *Synopsis musicæ*, facsimile ed. (1612; Hildesheim: Georg Olms, 2004), B4v.
54. "Omnis Sonus est longus numerabiliter…Quandoquidem omnis Sonus cum suo motu aliquantisper & aut breviter, aut diu durat." Lippius, *Synopsis musicæ*, B5r. For Lippius's writings I have adjusted Benito Rivera's translation. Lippius, *Synopsis of New Music*, trans. Benito Rivera (Colorado Springs: Colorado College Music Press, 1977), 16.
55. "Quò hæc Soni fluxio temporanea numeretur Tactus Musicus ad Cordis motum in scientiâ Musicâ observatur constans depreßione & elevatione juxta Proportiones certas præsertim duplas in Proportionalitate Geometricâ." Lippius, *Synopsis musicæ*, B5r. Lippius, *Synopsis of New Music*, trans. Rivera, 16.
56. Lippius, *Synopsis musicæ*, B5v.
57. Lippius, *Synopsis musicæ*, Dv.
58. "Quamlibet plures majores & minores dari possent Notæ longitudinis potentiâ infinitæ: hæ tamen sufficiunt…" Lippius, *Synopsis musicæ*, D2v. Lippius, *Synopsis of New Music*, trans. Rivera, 27.

Plate 1.3 Lippius's list, assigning the number of beats to each note shape, from *Synopsis musicæ*, facsimile ed. (1612; Hildesheim: Georg Olms, 2004), D2r–D2v.

Maxima		$\frac{8}{1}$
Vel quater, Longa		$\frac{4}{1}$
	D	2
Vel bis, Brevis		$\frac{2}{1}$
		$\frac{1}{1}$
Vel semel, Semibrevis: ◊		$\frac{1}{1}$
Si partem, vel dimidiam & vocatur Minima		$\frac{1}{2}$
Vel quartam, Semiminima.		$\frac{1}{4}$
Vel octavam, Fusa		$\frac{1}{8}$
Vel sedecimam, Semifusa		$\frac{1}{16}$

Lippius's straightforward list makes no room for perfect division—a topic not considered in his volume. This list simply serves to demonstrate how the "notational signs represent the horizontal duration of sound as measurable by the *tactus.*"[59] This vertical list also appears in the texts (listed in appendix 1) that draw heavily from Lippius.

59. "Signum soni longi numerabilis denotat ejus longitudinem durationis mensurabilem Tactu." Lippius, *Synopsis musicæ*, D2r. Lippius, *Synopsis of New Music*, trans. Rivera, 26.

Mensuration and proportion signs, which Lippius only treats briefly, serve either to augment or diminute the values of the note shapes. These signs put the notation into a relationship with the normative division given in Lippius's list. Here again, while the text provides an explanation for the work they do, their effect is understood as a deviation from the pattern established by reference to the central unit attached to the semibreve.[60] This central unit—the beat—does the work of sorting and coordinating the durations both within normative division and in proportion to it. For Lippius, the marking and knowing of music's number of temporal *fluxus* was understood through the basic organization of the beat.

Loulié, Éléments ou principes de musique (1696)

Loulié's text, devoted to the practical principles of music making, essentially covers the same facets of *musica practica* three times over in its three sections: the first devoted to children, the second to "persons more advanced in age," and the final section to "those who are capable of reasoning on the principles of music."[61] As a result, Loulié writes on meter in three locations in the text, at varying stages of detail.

Loulié's text is fundamentally different from the three texts above in its ability to describe a measure (*mesure*) as something distinct from the beat (*temps* or *battement*). Notational changes, including the more frequent use of regular barlines, afforded the possibility to treat the measure as a distinct object.[62] Nevertheless, the identity of the measure for Loulié is constructed entirely through the beat: "The measure," Loulié explains, "is a number of equal beats [*battements*] that serve to regulate the duration of sounds."[63]

A further complication of this distinction is Loulié's use of the terms *battement* and *temps*. Loulié describes *battement* as the earlier authors described the beat: "*Battement* is a small movement of the foot or the hand that one makes down and up."[64] Both terms indicate the beat, and Loulié explains, "*Le Battement* is also called *Temps*." But the two are not exactly identical in meaning in this text. Loulié continues, "*Le Temps* is properly the duration of a *Battement*, up to the start of the next *Battement*."[65] Therefore the measure (*mesure*) is constructed out of the physical act of *battement*, which prescribes durations known as *temps*.

---

60. Lippius, *Synopsis musicæ*, D2v–D3r.
61. "La Premiere pour les Enfans. La Seconde pour les Personnes plus avancez en âge. La Troiseiéme pour ceux qui sont capables de raisonner sur les Principes de la Musique." Étienne Loulié, *Éléments ous principes de musique* (Paris: Christophe Ballard, 1696), unpaginated title page.
62. On the evolution of the notated measure itself, see Claus Bockmaier, *Die instrumentale Gestalt des Taktes* (Tutzing: Hans Schneider, 2001).
63. "La Mesure est un nombre de Battements égaux qui servent à regler la durée des Sons." Loulié, *Éléments*, 30.
64. "*Battement* est un petit mouvement du pied ou de la main, qui se fait de bas en haut." Loulié, *Éléments*, 30. Italics in quotations from Loulié are found in the original.
65. "Le Battement s'appelle encore *Temps*"; "Le *Temps* est proprement la durée d'un Battement jusqu'au commencement d'un autre Battement." Loulié, *Éléments*, 31.

Each measure can be said to have a certain number of *battements* or *temps*. The nexus of these three terms does the work of describing meter.

Loulié's account provides us with an opportunity to observe a system of relationships at the brink of transition. *Mesure* and *temps* are temporal concepts at a level of remove from the motion of the beat. While they both borrow from the beat's physical theorization they are nevertheless conceptualized as different from it; they create the possibility for an abstracted *mesure* hierarchically divided into the *temps* that mark the duration from one beat to the next. Although not fully articulated in Loulié's text, the idea of the measure as an entity independent from the beat is latent in the arrangement of terms he employs.

Loulié takes great care to distinguish and catalogue the different types of measures created through the various signs for meter. All types of meter fall into six basic categories: duple, triple, quadruple, compound duple, compound triple, and compound quadruple. Loulié devotes a section of his text to each of these six categories, listing the signatures for each and the appropriate manners for beating the measure.[66] Triple meter, for instance, can be indicated with the signs 3/1, 3/2, 3/4, 3/8, 3/16, and 3. This meter is understood through three different styles of beating. In the first style, the hand falls twice for each of the first two beats and is raised once for the third beat; in the second style, the lowering of the hand describes the first two beats and is twice as long as the raising of the hand, which describes the third beat; in the third style, the hand simply falls once, taking the time of three beats. These three styles correspond to different tempi, and lend different characters to the different types of triple meters.[67] As his contemporaries De La Voye-Mignot and Masson had put it in their treatises, "the beat is the soul [*l'ame*] of music…its movements supply music with the diversity of its effects."[68]

Still, all of the pages spent on the diversity of meter signatures and the varieties of beating meter did not satisfy Loulié's desire to create a system that would specify tempi.

> Even if one had, in music, enough signs or terms to express all of the different proportions of speed or slowness of the beat, this would not suffice, because it is not enough to mark the way in which the beats of one measure are faster or slower than the beats of another measure. We must mark the speed or slowness of the beats themselves.[69]

66. Loulié, *Éléments*, 32–39.
67. Loulié, *Éléments*, 33–35.
68. "On peut dire que la mesure est veritablement l'ame de la Musique, puis qu'elle luy donne tous ses mouvements, et que par son moyen elle produit ses plus rares effets." De La Voye-Mignot, *Traité de musique*, facsimile ed. (1666; Geneva: Minkoff Reprints, 1972), 11; "La Mesure est l'ame de la Musique, puisqu'elle fait agir avec tant de justesse un grand nombre de Personnes, & que par la variété de ses mouvemens elle peut encore émouvoir tant de differentes passions." Charles Masson, *Nouveua Traité des regles pour la composition de la musique*, facsimile ed. with an introduction by Imogene Horsley (1699; New York: Da Capo, 1967), 6.
69. "Quand bien mesme ou auroit dans la Musique assez de Signes ou de termes pour exprimer toutes les differentes proportions de vitesse ou de lenteur des Battemens de la Mesure, cela ne pourroit pas suffire, car ce n'est pas assez de marquer de combien les Battemens d'une Mesure sont plus vistes ou plus lents que les Battemens d'une autre Mesure, il faut encore marquer de quelle vitesse ou de quelle lenteur sont ces Battemens en eux mesmes." Loulié, *Éléments*, 81–83.

Loulié's frustration responds to a shift in the conceptualization of the interconnection between meter and tempo. As the system of mensuration signs and proportional tempo relationships waned in relevance, composers more frequently employed a single meter signature for an entire musical work that was meant to indicate the correct tempo in tandem with the note values and character of the music. Loulié was one of the first to express explicit dissatisfaction with this system, pointing out its inability to specify durations themselves. In response to this problem, he describes an instrument of his own design called the *chronomètre*. One of the early musical timekeepers, the *chronomètre* specified temporal intervals through spatial measure, marking the lengths of a pendulum that would render specified durations when set in motion.[70] This timekeeper is discussed in greater detail in chapter 5, alongside other early musical chronometers. Although it never became popular for indicating tempo, Loulié's instrument is instructive in that it was a part of a historical moment in which theorists felt that the categories of meter and the specification of tempi required more care than they had customarily received.

* * *

Between Ornithoparchus and Loulié, then, the system of *modus, tempus,* and *prolatio* had lost its place in meter theories, different sorts of measures were appropriate for certain durations, and the time of the measure itself had become something of a concern as manifest in Loulié's *chronomètre*. But beyond the developments in notation, beyond the changes in the emphasis of explanation, beyond the different systems employed in the four texts surveyed here, the beat finds a function common to each. Whatever the hierarchies of notated duration may be, the beat performs the role of sorting and assembling them; it gives life (*l'ame*), makes physical, and demonstrates the *motus* of music's "numberable length."[71] It is the folding point in the various graphs, the relational numeral in the proportional hierarchies, and the animating force that drives the important distinctions. Most significantly, though, the beat is principally a motion. This motion is what lends each system its continuity; it is what organizes the theories of meter in these years.

"Honor Them All": On the Use (and Misuse?) of Meter Theory

Adriano Banchieri began his discussion of the beat in the 1614 *Cartella musicale* with a colorful quip:

> Now, when the devout pilgrim leaves his own beloved country to travel to the Holy House of Loreto, and, having arrived at his first lodging-place, inquires of

70. Loulié, *Éléments*, 81–88.
71. Lippius, *Synopsis musicæ*, Dv.

his host as to the correct path, he receives this answer: "Good men follow that which is beaten [*la battuta*], in order not to go astray."[72]

The Holy House of Loreto, the Virgin Mother's supposed birthplace, was well known in Catholic legend for its miraculous transportations from Israel through various Eastern European locales before finally coming to rest in Italy under the care of angels. It would seem that this destination was a moving target for the devout pilgrim whose only hope was to follow the *battuta*.

Banchieri's playful story mingled the motion-centered construction of the beat (as a beaten path) with the confusion that the topic occasionally caused in his day (just where was the *peregrino* to go, and how best was he to learn?). There have always been disagreements about the beat, and the sixteenth and seventeenth centuries were no exception. Given the proliferation of the systems in which the concept was employed, it should come as no surprise that writers and musicians quibbled over the particularities of its choreography. Incongruities abound in the description of particular aspects of the time-beating practice, such as the part of the body responsible for the action of the beat. Was it the foot (which theorists occasionally mentioned), the finger (as is prescribed in some fifteenth- and sixteenth-century texts), or the entire hand?[73] Others worried about the audibility of the strike. "In singing," Daniel Friderici instructed, "the beat should never be heard, only seen."[74] Then there were the numerous "reprobate errors" listed in Agostino Pisa's treatises. Among his many complaints, Pisa repudiated those authors that described the time-beating practice in reverse, beginning with a raising of the hand and finishing with a lowering.[75] In fact, Pisa complained so much of this practice that his contemporary, Lodovico Zacconi, misunderstood his writings and took Pisa's position to be in line with those who reversed the beat.[76] Added to all of this confusion in direction was the classical problem that occurred in the transplanting of the Greek terms *thesis* and *arsis* into the lexicon of the Latin grammarians, who took the raising involved in *arsis*

72. "Al'hora, che il devoto Peregrino parte dall'amata patria, per transferirsi alla santa Casa di Loreto, et giunto al primo alloggio ricerca l'Ostiero della retta via, ecco gli viene risposto, Huomo da bène seguitate la battuta, che non potete errare." Banchieri, *Cartella musicale*, facsimile ed. (1614; Bologna: Forni, 1968), 33.
73. For a view that finds an important distinction between a "tapped" beat, associated with fifteenth-century music, and a visual beat associated with music of the sixteenth century and onward, see Blachly, "Mensuration and Tempo in 15th-Century Music," (PhD diss., Columbia University, 1995), 207–335; and Blachly, "*Mensura* versus *Tactus*." See also Alyson McLamore, "A Tactus Primer," in *Musica Franca: Essays in Honor of Frank A. D'Accone*, ed. Irene Alm, Alyson McLamore, and Colleen Reardon (Stuyvesant, NY: Pendragon, 1996), 299–321.
74. "Im singen sol der Tact durchaus nit gehöret, sondern allein gesehen, oder wo es müglich, nur observiret und gemercket werden." Daniel Friderici, *Musica figuralis* (Rostock: Johan Richels Erben, 1638); facsimile edition in *Deutsch Gesangstraktate des 17. Jahrhunderts*, ed. Florian Grampp (Kassel: Bärenreiter, 2006), facsimile p. 48.
75. Pisa, *Battuta della musica*, 24, and elsewhere.
76. Walther Dürr, "Auftakt und Taktschlag in der Musik um 1600," in *Festschrift Walter Gerstenberg zum 60*, ed. Georg von Dadelsen and Andreas Holschneider (Wolfenbüttel: Möseler, 1964), 26–36, at 27–28.

to mean a heightening of the voice, or an accentuation.[77] Finally, in the face of such discrepancies, some writers simply expressed a frustration with the doctrines of the past. Lippius, for instance, complained of older meter theories: "On this dimension of sound, the ancients of previous generations wrote frequently and ineptly."[78]

Of course, the differently directed disputes of the earlier ages have found a way to rehearse themselves centuries later, wherein more recent commentators have asserted viewpoints on the beat as varied as: "the word *tactus* has absolutely nothing to do with our concept of meter";[79] and "the whole system of mensural notation rests upon the principle of a fixed, i.e., unchangeable unit of time, the *tactus*."[80] But also, "THE THEORY OF ONE TACTUS OF INVARIABLE SPEED CANNOT BE SUSTAINED."[81] Tellingly, though, the twentieth-century sources are often worried about aspects of the beat rather different to those quarreled over in the centuries previous. These more recent sources question whether or not the beat was variable in pace, its relationship to accent, and the ways in which it is most appropriate to draw from the historical accounts in the context of performance. In any case, we must acknowledge that every attempt to recreate a practice (a performance) of the beat respectful of the historical accounts will, of necessity, represent only one portion of these writings; in a certain sense, each particular view was idiosyncratic. As Banchieri himself said:

> ...diverse opinions are printed in volumes, folios, and discourses, some of which hold that the beat begins with the lowering of the hand and finishes with the raising; others would like to indicate that it begins with the beat and terminates at the top of the motion, and others say that one sings during the motions, and others [during] the stops. I have observed all of these caprices, and I honor them all.[82]

What, then, is the "use" of all of this meter theory? A twenty-first century reader might well wonder what good can come from the study of meter's historical

---

77. On the history of this confusion see Alan Holder, *Rethinking Meter: A New Approach to the Verse Line* (Lewisburg: Bucknell University Press, 1995), 36–37.
78. "Hac in Soni dimensione Veteres ante secuculum multum ineptiebant." Lippius, *Synopsis musicæ*, B5v.
79. "Hier sieht man recht eigentlich, daß das Wort "*tactus*" absolut nichts mit unserm Begriff Takt zu tun hat." Georg Schünemann, "Zur Frage des Taktschlagens und der Textbehandlung in der Mensuralmusik," *Sammelbände der Internationalen Musikgesellschaft* 10, no. 1 (1908–9): 73–114, at 82. Boone also employs this quotation, in "Marking Mensural Time," 26.
80. Willi Apel, *The Notation of Polyphonic Music: 900-1600* (Cambridge, MA: The Mediaeval Academy of America, 1942); 5th ed., rev. and with commentary (Cambridge, MA: The Mediaeval Academy of America, 1961), 146–47.
81. J. A. Bank, *Tactus, Tempo and Notation in Mensural Music from the Thirteenth to the Seventeenth Century*, 259. Capitalization in the original.
82. "...diversi pareri sono alla stampa in volumi fogli e discorsi alcuni tengono, che la Battuta comincia nel calar della mano e finisca nella levata; altri vogliono habbia principio nella Battuta, e termina all'in sù, & altri dicono, che cantino li moti, e chi le quiete, io hò veduti tutti questi I capricci e tutto onoro..." Banchieri, *La Banchierina; overo, Cartella picciola del canto figurato di D. Adriano Banchieri* (Venetia: Alessandro Vincenti, 1623), 14–15.

sources if so many of them disagree on the beat's execution. As much as we ought to give careful attention to those important idiosyncratic distinctions—which caused as many disputes then as there are today—we might also learn something from the grounds on which opinions diverge. These return again and again to the particularities of the beat's motion, as the quotations above and countless other examples illustrate. For Agostino Pisa, those who performed the action incorrectly displayed an ignorance of the nature of time and of being; their errors were, in fact, "contrary to Aristotle."[83] For others, whose relationship to the Aristotelian conception of time was never made explicit, the correct motions would simply have been a matter of avoiding "huge foolishness," and confusion.[84]

The most important point about the disputes, then, is that the topic at stake was a matter of understanding and knowing. Giving these historical sources their due need not entail taking on any of their specific prescriptions for the performance or experience of music. The sound world that emerges from these texts is one in which the beat—no matter its specific execution or particular musical context—was used to understand the numbering and division of duration. Because the beat served a central role in theories of meter—because it coordinated the hierarchy of durational division and served as a physical theorization of time—its execution merited discussion and even, occasionally, debate. Despite the divergent results, the foundations of the various positions (even those that are reflected in the twentieth and twenty-first centuries) bespeak the centrality of its physical motion. The various manners in which writers described these motions provide windows into a certain knowledge on time that was created under one primary analytic: *motus*.

---

83. Pisa, *Breve dichiarazione della battuta musicale*, 6.
84. Friderici, *Musica figuralis*, 48.

CHAPTER Two

The Beat: A Technical History

A Technical and Physical Solution

In their explanations of meter, writings on music from the sixteenth and seventeenth centuries offer us depictions of a physical act that they called the beat. These passages functioned as technical and physical solutions to an ongoing problem in the conceptualization of time: the problem of continuity. Throughout the history of Western thought, the supposed continuity of temporal passage has caused problems for those who seek to theorize it. How can it be that time is continuous and unbroken if it seems to consist of separate instants? This problem is even more obvious in the face of musical notation: how is it that time in music is continuous if we rely on discrete note shapes to represent and communicate it? Writers on music and natural philosophy have attempted countless explications and apologias for these vexing problems, and the physical act of the beat provided one potential (and effective) solution. As such, the beat served as a kind of tool or technique for those who aimed to explain the tenets of practical music theory. A part of the genealogy of temporal conceptualizations in music, the beat is also part of the history of musical technologies.

Technological and material developments have always shaped the writing of music theory. Music treatises betray the era of their creation through the instruments—musical and otherwise—to which they make reference. Organologists have long recognized these references as important historical data and regularly consult music theoretical texts among their primary sources. More recently, Cristle Collins Judd has drawn our attention to the material conditions of music printing and their effect on the making of music theory.[1] These are two ways in

---

1. Cristle Collins Judd, *Reading Renaissance Music Theory* (Cambridge: Cambridge University Press, 2000).

which scholars have thus far understood the intertwined nature of the histories of ideas and of technologies in music.

Yet another is to investigate the techniques and materials to which theorists made explicit reference in the explanation of their most difficult concepts. In the case of many sources on musical meter, these techniques consist of the physical actions of beating time. In the sixteenth and seventeenth centuries, treatises on music described the beat as a lowering and raising of the hand in *thesis* and *arsis*. Conceptualizing this act as a site of technological intervention might seem a bit peculiar insofar as it did not require any mechanical brilliance or manufactured objects; the prescribed action of the beat was patently simple, evidencing none of the complexity of other technological innovations of the period.[2] And yet, the conceptual work that this physical technique accomplished was so effective that the act became part of the basic groundwork of music theory. The beat did what the most successful technologies do: it disappeared.

In this way, the absence of explicit descriptions of the beat as a kind of technology only serves to highlight the act's usefulness. As in Heidegger's analysis of the "handy," or "ready-to-hand" (*zuhanden*) tool, the effectiveness of the beat allowed its role in the conceptualization of time to slip from view.[3] Like Heidegger's famous example of the ready-to-hand hammer, the beat was part of a system of useful techniques only visible when ceasing to function. The "handiness" of properly functioning tools coincides not incidentally with the figure of the hand itself, which was for Heidegger as for the early moderns a supreme instrument in its own right.[4] While the hand was the part of the body to which theorists most frequently referred when describing the beat, it was the action of the beat all told that was "ready-to-hand" in the true Heideggerian sense. The action, in its various implementations, did the work of explaining temporal continuity without explicit acknowledgement.

It is only because the act of beating time has ceased to function in this role that we can now provide an account of the work that it once did. To write a history of the beat in this manner is to write a history of a technique that closely limns the interface between concept and implementation.[5] If the beat solved a

2. Marcel Mauss writes, "I made, and went on making for several years, the fundamental mistake of thinking that there is technique only when there is an instrument. I had to go back to ancient notions, to the Platonic position on technique, for Plato spoke of a technique of music and in particular of a technique of the dance, and extend these notions." Mauss, "Techniques of the Body," trans. Ben Brewster, *Economy and Society* 2, no. 1 (1973): 70–88, at 75.

3. See the analysis in Heidegger, *Being and Time*, trans. Joan Stambaugh (Albany: SUNY Press, 1996), 62–71; and in Graham Harman, *Tool-Being* (Chicago: Open Court, 2002), 15–24.

4. As Heidegger wrote, "All the work of the hand is rooted in thinking. Therefore, thinking itself is man's simplest, and for that reason hardest, handiwork, if it would be accomplished at its proper time." Heidegger, *What Is Called Thinking*, trans. J. Glenn Gray (New York: Harper and Row, 1968), 16–17. Below I explore the ways in which early moderns discussed the hand as an instrument.

5. My historical method here is informed by the work of Lucien Febvre. In particular, see his short but pithy essay "Réflexions sur l'histoire des techniques," *Annales d'histoire économique et sociale* 7, no. 36 (November 30, 1935): 531–35. On Febvre's project within the context of the *Annales* school in general, see Pamela O. Long, "The Annales and the History of Technology," *Technology and Culture* 46, no. 1 (January 2005): 177–86.

problem in the description of time's continuity, it did so in a way that only made sense in action (whether real or imagined). The beat is not simply a concept but a concept with material and physical heft; its descriptions, then, should be read not only as pieces of meter's intellectual heritage but also of meter's technological history. It is part of what Lucien Febvre called a "history of techniques," which must be integrated into the genealogy of ideas on temporality and, more specifically, the history of meter.[6]

Before a closer inspection of this technique, however, it is necessary to review in detail the problem that it was meant to solve. Beginning with Aristotle and continuing directly through late Scholastic and Cartesian thought, anxieties about the continuity of time abounded. The details of these disputations make it clear how the act of the beat would have functioned as one particular technique for overcoming them. Understanding the beat in this way also clarifies the language used and authorities drawn upon in Zarlino's curious chapter "Della battuta" in *Le istitutioni harmoniche*. Medical, philosophical, and potentially abstruse (to modern readers), Zarlino's references in his short chapter on the beat were legible as part of a demonstration of temporal logic.

A Problem of Continuity

The Problem

The technique of the beat was only one solution to a conceptual problem with a long and rich genealogy. Versions of the same issue are found throughout the history of philosophy. The problem is expressed easily enough in one of Zeno's famous paradoxes: if a moving arrow can be located in a fixed, spatial position at any given moment in the arc of its trajectory, how is it that the arrow is moving at all?[7] Put another way: how is the continuum of time composed? Continua in ancient geometry were said to be divisible infinitely.[8] If time is also a continuum, it too should be infinitely divisible. This would indicate that time cannot be built up of discrete units like musical notes. How is it, then, that we come to know time through something like a present moment, or a moment "now"? Is the now a discrete unit? If not, does anything like the present exist at all? Our contemporary editions of Aristotle's *Physics* IV pose the problem thus:

6. Febvre, "Réflexions sur l'histoire des techniques."
7. Aristotle discusses this Zeno paradox in *Physics* 6.9.239b30: "The third [of Zeno's arguments]...claims that a moving arrow is still. Here the conclusion depends on assuming that time is composed of nows; if this assumption is not granted, the argument fails." Aristotle, *Physics*, trans. Robin Waterfield with an introduction and notes by David Bostock (Oxford: Oxford University Press, 1996), 161–62. On this and the related paradoxes, see Bertrand Russell, "The Problem of Infinity Considered Historically," in *Zeno's Paradoxes*, ed. Wesley C. Salmon (New York: Bobbs-Merrill, 1970), 45–58.
8. See Jacob Klein, *Greek Mathematical Thought and the Origin of Algebra*, trans. Eva Brann, 2nd ed. (1968; New York: Dover, 1992), esp. 186–224.

It is necessary that, of everything that is resoluble into parts, if it is, either all the parts or some of them should be when it is. But of time, while it is resoluble into parts, some [parts] have been, some are to be, and none is. The now is not a part, for a part measures [the whole], and the whole must be composed of the parts, but time is not thought to be composed of nows.[9]

This is the second of the three puzzles that open Aristotle's account of time in the *Physics*. This particular puzzle is rooted in Aristotle's commitment to a strict distinction between continuous and discrete quantities. The continuous, according to Aristotle and Aristotelian thought, includes all of those things whose parts "join together at some common boundary," such as a line or a surface.[10] The discrete, by contrast, include those quantities that "have no common boundary at which they join together"—these quantities are composed of separate units.[11] They include numbers as well as other quantifiable and separable entities, such as the syllables of speech. In this scheme, time was included within the category of the continuous, alongside the objects of geometry. Time, however, poses a particular problem for this system, as the quotation above makes clear: it is difficult to say how we experience time. Even though we seem to know time through the present, the present cannot be some fixable quantity of time. If it were, it would be a discrete unit out of which time is composed. Time, after all, "is not thought to be composed of nows," or discrete units. But if the present is not some sort of identifiable unit, how can it be said to exist? It must be that none of time actually exists.

Aristotle's commentators remade and reshaped this problem repeatedly through the sixteenth and seventeenth centuries, making it a vital component of the study of time in natural philosophy. The exposition of time's continuity as a problem suited the *quaestio* and *cursus* forms perfectly, as controversy and argument were the textual procedures through which these texts customarily imparted concepts. To be sure, these later Scholastic texts held steadfastly to the distinction between continuous and discrete quantities on which the issue was based. In fact, to find an excellent early modern version of this Aristotelian distinction, one need look no further than the first book of Zarlino's *Le istitutioni harmoniche*. The continuous, Zarlino writes, includes those things "whose parts are conjoined at a common boundary, like a line, a surface, a body; and in addition to these, time, place, and all other things to which one can attribute magnitude."[12] The discrete, for Zarlino and the Aristotelians, included those things

9. Aristotle, *Physics* 4.10.218a2–8; *Aristotle's* Physics Books III and IV, ed., trans., and with commentary by Edward Hussey (Oxford: Clarendon Press, 1983), 41.

10. Aristotle, *Categories*, chap. 6; as translated in *Aristotle's* Categories *and* De Interpretatione, trans. with notes by J. L. Ackrill (Oxford: Clarendon, 1963), 13.

11. *Aristotle's* Categories *and* De Interpretatione, trans. Ackrill, 12.

12. "La Continoua nominorno quella, le cui parti sono congiunte ad un termine commune; come la Linea, la Superficie, il Corpo; & oltra di queste il Tempo, & il Luogo; & tutte quelle cose, che si attribuiscono alla Grandezza." Zarlino, *Le istitutioni harmoniche* (Venice: Francesco de i Franceschi Senese, 1558), 28; my translation with reference to Lucille Corwin, "*Le istitutioni harmoniche* of Gioseffo Zarlino, Part 1: A Translation with Introduction" (PhD diss., The City University of New York, 2008), 303.

"whose members are not conjoined at any common boundary, but remain distinct and separate, like number, speech, a herd, a crowd, an amount of grain or what have you—all the things to which we can give the name multitude."[13] Zarlino's reproduction of this Aristotelian distinction was meant to clarify the various forms in which quantity comes; it is found in a part of his treatise that is strictly concerned with the nature of quantity.

The place of number in this Aristotelian system is significant. Number is a kind of quantity that is discrete. It is, as Aristotle put it, one form of "that by which we count."[14] We count by numbers. We can also count by other units: cows in a herd, syllables in a sentence, and so forth. Time, like an object of geometry (such as a line), is not composed of units by which we count, but rather is said to be "that which is counted."[15]

Scholastic commentators on Aristotle's *Physics* specifically highlighted the incompatibility of time's now with the quantity indicated by number. The commentaries of Saint Thomas Aquinas, which were important teaching tools in the Scholastic university of the sixteenth and seventeenth centuries, compared the two directly.[16] The 1517 print edition of his commentaries on the *Physics* reads:

> In regard to each divisible thing it is necessary, while it exists, that one or more of its parts exist. But time is not of this nature. For certain parts of time are now past, and other parts are in the future, and no part of time—insofar as it is divisible—exists in act. The now, which exists in act, is not a part of time. Because a part is that which measures a whole, as two is a part of six, or at least that from which the whole is composed, as four is a part of six, not as measuring it, but because four and two together compose six. However, time is not composed of nows, as will be proven below. Therefore, time is not something.[17]

13. "La Discreta dissero esser quella, le cui parti non sono congiunte ad alcun termine commune; ma restano distinte & separate; come è il Numero, il Parlare, una Gregge, un Popolo, un Monte di grano, over di altro, alle quali cose conviene il nome di Moltitudine." Zarlino, *Le istitutioni harmoniche*, 28; Corwin, "*Le istitutioni harmoniche* of Gioseffo Zarlino," 303.
14. Aristotle *Physics*, 4.11.219b1–8; *Aristotle's* Physics *Books III and IV*, trans. Hussey, 44.
15. Aristotle *Physics*, 4.11.219b1–8; *Aristotle's* Physics *Books III and IV*, trans. Hussey, 44.
16. On the importance of a Thomistic Aristotelianism in the early modern era (particularly in Jesuit education) see Paul F. Grendler, "Italian Schools and University Dreams during Mercurian's Generalte," in *The Mercurian Project: Forming Jesuit Culture 1573-1580*, ed. Thomas M. McCoog (Rome: Institutum Historicum Societatis Iesu and St. Louis: The Institute of Jesuit Sources, 2004), 483–522, at 505–6.
17. "Cujuslibet divisibilis existentis necesse est, dum est, aliquam partem esse, vel aliquas: sed tempus non est hujusmodi: quia quaedam temporis partes sunt praeteritae, aliae vero sunt futurae; et nihil temporis, quod sit divisibile, est in actu. Ipsum vero nunc, quod est in actu, non est pars temporis; quia pars est, quae mensurat totum, ut binarius senarium: vel saltem ex qua componitur totum, sicut quaternarius est pars senarii non mensurans ipsum, sed quia ex ipso et binario componitur senarius: tempus autem non componitur ex ipsis nunc, ut infra probabitur: tempus igitur non est aliquid." Saint Thomas Aquinas, *S. Thomas super physica: expositio diui Thome Aquinatis Doctoris Angelici super octo libros Physico[rum] Aristotelis...* (Venetijs: Im pensis domini Luc[a]e Antonij de Giunta Florentini, 1517), 55r. My translation with reference to Aquinas, *Commentary on Aristotle's* Physics, trans. Richard J. Blackwell, Richard J. Spath, and W. Edmund Thirlkel, with an introduction by Vernon J. Bourke (New Haven: Yale University Press, 1963); rev. ed. with forward by Ralph McInerny (Notre Dame: Dumb Ox, 1999), 272–73.

Aquinas places actual numerical quantities in the context of the continuity puzzle in order to foreground the problematic nature of the now as a unit; in comparison to these straightforwardly discrete quantities, the now seems impossibly vague or even nonexistent. Nearly identical statements (using the same numbers) are found in the commentaries of Duns Scotus, Giles of Rome, and in the sixteenth-century *Super octo libros Physicorum Aristotelis quaestiones* of Domingo de Soto.[18] The Coimbria commentaries record a comparison in slightly different terms: "The now does not appear to be a part of time, because all parts must make up a part of the whole, as in a mathematical ratio."[19] These statements of the puzzle conclude in like manner: "It must be that time does not exist."[20]

Solutions

There was no singular solution to the problem of temporal continuity; rather, there have been several solutions over the course of the history of philosophy. In general, the various solutions all shift the problematic need for continuity away from time. In one set of solutions, continuity itself is displaced in favor of a system that can tolerate a time composed of definite units; this type of solution is generally called "atomist," and replaces the problem of continuity with a problem regarding the nature of space and extension (what is the smallest indivisible unit?). Another set of solutions shifts the problem of continuity away from time and attributes time's continuity to the continuity of *motus* (a Scholastic concept that means both motion and change). This solution, adopted in Aristotle's *Physics* and in the Aristotelian commentaries, replaces the problem of constructing temporal continuity with the problem of constructing the continuity of *motus*.

The atomist solution has a heritage in ancient philosophy and was revived again in fourteenth-century thought. Ancient atomists (such as Leucippus, Democritus, Epicurus, and Lucretius) understood the composition of all magnitudes to consist of tiny, indivisible units. This was true for geometric extension as it was for time.[21] During the fourteenth century, this particular way of composing continua saw

18. Johannis Duns Scoti, "In octo libros physicorum Aristotelis," in *Opera Omnia* (Paris: Apud Ludovicum Vivès, 1891), 3:118; Giles of Rome [Aegidii], *Aegid. Columnii in Porphyrii Isagogen, Aristotelis Categorias, & lib. Peri Hermenias...absolutissima commentaria* (Bergomum, 1591), 245; Domingo de Soto, *Reuerendi patris Dominici Soto Segobiensis theologi Ordinis Praedicatorum Super octo libros Physicorum Aristotelis quaestiones* (Salamanca: Andrea de Portonaris, 1555), 69v.

19. "Momentum autem non videtur pars temporis, quia omnis pars quanta alicuius totius, ut apud Mathematicos ratum habetur..." *Commentarii Collegii Conimbricensis e Societate Jesu in octo libros Physicorum Aristotelis Stagiritae*, facsimile ed. (1594; Hildesheim: Georg Olms, 1984), 2:78; See Mário S. de Carvalho, "Time According to the Coimbra Commentaries," in *The Medieval Concept of Time*, ed. Pasquale Porro (Deiden: Brill, 2001), 353–82.

20. As Domingo de Soto put it "Ergo tempus non est." de Soto,...*Super octo libros Physicorum Aristotelis quaestiones*, 69v.

21. *The Stanford Encyclopedia of Philosophy*, ed. Edward N. Zalta, s.v. "Ancient Atomism," by Sylvia Berryman, accessed January 19, 2011, <http://plato.stanford.edu/archives/fall2008/entries/atomism-ancient/>; see also Andrew Pyle, *Atomism and Its Critics: Problem Areas Associated*

renewed popularity among a small group of philosophers.[22] The approach held obvious appeal to writers on music. If notated durations could be said to have some sort of numeric quantity with respect to mensuration, how could they constitute parts of a temporal continuum?

Several fourteenth-century music theorists employed some type of atomism when theorizing duration; unlike true atomists, though, these theorists adopted a distinction between time in general and the division of rhythmic durations in music. Although they universally agreed that time itself was a continuous quantity, these theorists argued that each note shape or rhythmic figure represented a discrete unit of time.[23] As such, their concept of specified duration could be said to resemble one of the often-repeated examples of discrete quantity in Aristotelian thought: the syllables of speech.[24] In these examples, temporal phenomena (notes or syllables) are said to possess numerical quantity in a way that does not correspond to the nature of time as such.

By contrast to the atomists, Aristotle and the Aristotelians dealt with the problem of continuity by reference to *motus*—the guiding principle of temporal philosophy. Time for the Aristotelians was "the number of *motus* with respect to the before and after."[25] Time gained continuity by reference to the continuity of *motus*, since time in their system was logically descended from it. The 1517 edition of Thomas Aquinas's commentary explains the transfer of continuity:

It has been stated that time is something of *motus*, that is, it is consequent upon it. We must ask, then, how time is consequent upon *motus*—that is, in respect to the before and after...

[Aristotle] shows that continuity in time is from motion and magnitude...

He says, therefore, first that everything which is moved is moved from something to something. Among all *motus*, the first is local motion, which is motion from place to place in respect to some magnitude. But time is consequent upon the first motion. Therefore to investigate time it is necessary to consider along with it motion in respect to place. Hence, since motion in respect to place is *motus* from something to something in magnitude, and since every magnitude is continuous, then it is necessary that *motus* is consequent upon magnitude in

with the Development of the Atomic Theory of Matter from Democritus to Newton (Bristol, UK: Thoemmes, 1995), 1–40.

22. John E. Murdoch, "Infinity and Continuity," in *The Cambridge History of Later Medieval Philosophy*, ed. Norman Kretzmann, Anthony Kenny, and Jan Pinborg, with associate editor Eleonore Stump (Cambridge: Cambridge University Press, 1982), 564–91, at 575–84. In connection to music-theoretical atomisims, see Dorit Tanay, *Noting Music, Marking Culture: The Intellectual Context of Rhythmic Notation, 1250–1400*, Musicological Studies and Documents 46 (American Institute of Musicology: Hänssler-Verlag, 1999), esp. 102–5.

23. These theorists and their concern with the continuity of time are the subject of Tanay's *Noting Music, Marking Culture*, particularly 102–45.

24. Aristotle, *Categories*, chap. 6; *Aristotle's* Categories *and* De Interpretatione, trans. Ackrill, 12–13.

25. Aristotle *Physics* 4.11.219b1; *Aristotle's* Physics *Books III and IV*, trans. Hussey, 44; and in the Aristotelian commentaries, for example: "Hoc enim est tempus, numerus motus ratione priorus & posterioris," *Commentarii Collegii Conimbricensis e Societate Jesu in octo libros Physicorum Aristotelis Stagiritae*, 2:81; "Numerus motus secundum prius & posterius," Eustachius, *Summa philosophiae quadripartita* (Leiden: Franciscum Moyardum, 1647), 2:158.

continuity, that is, since magnitude is continuous, *motus* is continuous. And consequently time is also continuous.[26]

It is clear from the presentation of ideas in Aquinas's commentary that time can only be said to have continuity once it has been shown that motions through magnitudes are continuous. In fact, the displacement of the problem is slightly more nuanced than it might appear. In the Aristotelian system, the continuity of *motus* caused none of the problems of the continuity of time. In *motus* there is some object that is undergoing change. This change can be of quality (as in the case of a man becoming musical) or of place (as in the case of a hand moving down and up). The thing undergoing change does not have temporal parts, but is always the same thing.[27] A hand moved is always the same hand, first having the accidental property of being high in the air and then having the accidental property of being on the table. The continuity of *motus*, then, depends upon the fact that the thing undergoing change or motion through a magnitude is continually the same thing.[28] In this solution, the problem of continuity is shifted to the thing undergoing change or motion.

Understood this way, it was clear that time must exist (contrary to the formulation of the puzzle) because changes and motions through magnitudes exist. As one commentator put it, "Motus est: ergo tempus est."[29] Time was said to be the "the number of *motus* with respect to the before and after."[30] A number of change, but not with respect to "that with which we count" (e.g., numbers or units, as outlined above); time instead was "that which is counted": a continuity of noted (counted or numbered) changes with respect to their states before and their states after.[31] Time was simply a way of noting or numbering the changes (in states, over spatial magnitudes, or what have you) that occurred to things.

---

26. "Supposito enim quod tempus sit aliquid motus, consequens scilicet ipsum, restat investigandum, secundum quid tempus consequatur motum, quia secundum prius et posterius…Primo ostendit quod continuitas est in tempore ex motu et magnitudine…Sed inter alios motus, primus est motus localis, qui est a loco in locum secundum aliquam magnitudinem. Primum autem motum consequitur tempus: et ideo ad investigandum de tempore, portet accipere motum secundum locum. Quia ergo motus secundum locum est secundum magnitudinem ex quodam in quiddam: et omnis magnitudo est continua, opertet quod motus consequatur magnitudinem in continuitate; ut quia magnitudo continua est, et motus continuus est, et per consequens tempus etiam continuum est…" Saint Thomas Aquinas, *S. Thomas super physica*, 56v; my translation is a modified version of Aquinas, *Commentary on Aristotle's* Physics, trans. Blackwell, Spath, and Thirlkel, 280.
27. Aristotle, *Physics* 1.7–8; Aristotle, *Physics*, trans. Waterfield, 24–30. On this point see Ursula Coope, *Time for Aristotle* (Oxford: Clarendon), 24–25.
28. Ursula Coope argues that change through magnitude must mean change of place through spatial magnitude. She argues that this must be true because Aristotle denies that there can be infinitely many states within any change of state (as in the example of a man becoming musical). See Coope, *Time for Aristotle*, 50–51.
29. Giles of Rome [Aegidii], *Aegid. Columnii in Porphyrii Isagogen, Aristotelis Categorias, & lib. Peri Hermenias…absolutissima commentaria*, 245.
30. Aristotle *Physics* 4.11.219b1; *Aristotle's* Physics *Books III and IV*, trans. Hussey, 44; and see n25 above.
31. "Time is that which is counted and not that by which we count." Aristotle *Physics* 4.11.219b8; *Aristotle's* Physics *Books III and IV*, trans. Hussey, 44.

This way of solving the continuity of time persisted in the Aristotelian tradition well into the seventeenth century. Its explanatory power was evidently strong enough for Descartes to adopt it; he reproduced the Aristotelian definition nearly verbatim in the *Principia philosophiae*.[32] As Jean-Luc Marion writes of Descartes: "The customary polemic against Aristotle therefore seems, in the definition of time, to undergo a noteworthy cease-fire."[33]

Conceptualizing time as a way of relating the structure of change leads to some interesting conclusions about the nature of temporal passage in the everyday world. Understanding the consequences of this conceptualization is of foundational importance to understanding the writings on meter from this period. If time describes change or motion, then each and every change or motion that occurs in the world creates its own time. As the Scholastics often repeated, "there are as many times as there are motions."[34] But if all changes create equally valid temporal demarcations, then they are all equally useless for telling time.

The Aristotelian solution to this problem was to identify one single change to which all other changes could be compared. The time that measured the *motus* of the stars was the only universal temporal measure.[35] This particular instance of *motus* was perfect for the task because it was uniform and without interruption. The motion of the stars, then, was a cosmic timekeeper that could serve as a kind of standard for all other motions, and the time that described this motion was the standard for all other times. This was the only time that could possess "extrinsic measurement," as Francisco Suárez put it.[36]

With the motion of the stars as the standard, all earthly changes and motions were microcosmographical reproductions of the temporal passage in the heavens. Each change of place or quality on earth was not only a change to be reckoned against these otherworldly changes, but also, in a way, a tiny echo of the grand, continual motion of the cosmos.[37] It is this microcosmographical nature

---

32. "tempus…dicimusque esse numerum motûs…" Descartes, *Principia philosophiae* I, sec. 57, in *Œuvres de Descartes*, ed. Charles Adam and Paul Tannery, rev. ed. (Paris: Vrin/CNRS, 1973), 8:27.

33. Jean-Luc Marion, *On Descartes' Metaphysical Prism: The Constitution and Limits of Onto-theo-logy in Cartesian Thought*, trans. Jeffrey L. Kosky (Chicago: University of Chicago Press, 1999), 184n59. Marion also speculates on the specific Aristotelian sources Descartes may have had in mind, and suggests the Coimbra commentaries (on the authority of Etienne Gilson) and Suzarez's *Disputationes Metaphysicae*. Marion, *On Descartes' Metaphysical Prism*, trans. Kosky, 183n57.

34. "Tot tempora quat motus." In the words of Miguel Angel Granada, this was a "constantly repeated Scholastic adage." Granada, "The Concept of Time in Giordano Bruno: Cosmic Times and Eternity," in *The Medieval Concept of Time*, ed. Porro, 477–505, at 490.

35. Aristotle *Physics* 4.14.223b21–30; *Aristotle's Physics Books III and IV*, trans. Hussey, 44. On this point see Hussey's Introduction to *Aristotle's Physics Books III and IV*, xl.

36. Franciscus Suárez, *Metaphysicarum disputationum* (Paris: Apud Michaelem Sonnium, 1605), 50.10.12, 2:663.

37. Aristotle specifically discusses the relationship between motion on earth and motion in the heavens as a relationship between the microcosm and the macrocosm. Aristotle *Physics* 8.2.252b25; *Aristotle's Physics Book VIII*, trans. and with a commentary by Daniel W. Graham (Oxford: Clarendon, 1999), 5. As the Aquinas commentaries put it: "Hence it is said by some that man is a little world." Aquinas, *Commentary on Aristotle's Physics*, trans. Blackwell, Spath, and Thirlkel, 523.

of all earthly movement—this relationship of resemblance—that we must keep in mind when attempting to interpret the doctrine of the beat in the sixteenth and seventeenth centuries.

The Technē of the Beat

Sixteenth- and seventeenth-century conceptualizations of time were able to understand distinct events as part of a seamless continuum of temporal passage; in order to do so, they conceptualized the continuity of time through the continuity of *motus*. Theories of meter in this period were no different, and employed a local, earthly motion as their primary form of theorizing the divisions in musical duration. They called this motion the beat.

Chapter 1 explored the ways in which the beat structured and organized the hierarchy of duration in sixteenth- and seventeenth-century theories of music. As Giovanni Lanfranco wrote, the beat "governs" the division of time in music.[38] It marshals and makes legible the various systems of note-value indication. More specifically, though, the beat provided a spatial demonstration or a physical theorization of the "before and after" in change, as the Aristotelians would say.[39] Meter, then, is nothing other than the temporal relationship that describes this local, earthly *motus* through spatial magnitude with respect to the before and after. The technique of the beat provided the structure of *motus*, on which the continuity of time could hang like a scrim.

Consider the definition of the beat in Lippius's *Synopsis musicæ*:

> This temporal flux of sound is numbered in musical science by observing a constant musical *tactus* patterned after the heartbeat. This involves a raising and lowering in definite proportion, mainly duple proportion in geometric proportionality.[40]

Lippius's beat is a motion that defines potential divisions in time through the structure of physical change. He describes a motion in "geometric proportionality": a movement through a continuous spatial magnitude such as a path or line traced in geometry. The division of time takes place in accordance with the direction of movement, as motion visually interprets and bisects the passage of time that is, all the while, continuous. This technique of the beat creates a way in which sound is numbered. Importantly, the beat is not said to provide a numerical unit

---

38. Giovanni Maria Lanfranco, *Scintille di musica,* facsimile ed. (1533; Bologna: Forni, 1970), 67.
39. See the various Aristotelian definitions of time above.
40. "Quò hæc Soni fluxio temporanea numeretur Tactus Musicus ad Cordis motum in scientiâ Musicâ observatur constans depreßione & elevatione juxta Proportiones certas præsertim duplas in Proportionalitate Geometricâ." Johannes Lippius, *Synopsis musicæ*, facsimile ed. (1612; Hildesheim: Georg Olms, 2004), B5r. Translation adjusted from Lippius, *Synopsis of New Music*, trans. Benito Rivera (Colorado Springs: Colorado College Music Press, 1977), 16.

(such as might constitute a "number with which we count");[41] rather, the beat shows in space the divisions that are counted in time. The falling and rising of the beat literally puts the divisions of mensural hierarchy into place.

Following on his definition, Lippius explains how the beat interprets the duration of each note shape. The seemingly discrete musical notes are understood in relation to the structure of the beat's local change of place from high to low and back again. The changes of place made in the action of the beat are said to count or to "number" these durations in the "temporal flux of sound."[42]

This passage and others similar to it in music theory texts of the era are descriptions of a practice that was probably a part of performance. They are also music theory's solution to the technical and intellectual problem of temporal continuity. As such, they are techniques or apparatuses that do conceptual work through the manipulation of spatial relations, ideas, and images.[43] These theories gesture outside of the page—they exteriorize continuity in the form of one object undergoing change of place in local motion. But as much as they make reference to an act performed, they also create a space for that physical act within a system of numbers, notational conventions, and concepts of musical organization. They are a piece of *techné* in dialogical relationship with the *epistēmē* of time.[44]

Thinking about the beat in this way explains, in part, why theorists were able to describe it with so many different variations, with different choreographies to be performed with as many different implements. The technique of the beat was as malleable as was the structure of local motion itself. So long as the beat could provide a consistent demarcation of the before and after—so long as it could visually and spatially depict the structure of *motus*—it could provide potential divisions in the continuity of time, thereby creating the framework with which to organize hierarchies of duration. The beat could include one stopping point or many; it could be performed with the hand, the foot, the finger, or what have you. As Banchieri wrote, it could be performed with a "stick or kerchief."[45] All of these actions mark the potential divisions through *motus* and—most importantly—they all include one object (hand, fabric, foot) that remains the same through the incidental changes in location.

There were, however, two particular objects to which theorists of the beat most enjoyed referring: the hand and the heart. They deserve our detailed attention. Theorists consistently depicted these two human instruments in the motions

41. Aristotle *Physics* 4.11.219b8; *Aristotle's* Physics *Books III and IV*, trans. Hussey, 44.

42. Lippius, *Synopsis musicæ*, B4v.

43. Here I make direct reference to Giorgio Agamben's interpretation of the term "apparatus" or "dispositif" in the work of Foucault. See Agamben, "What Is an Apparatus," in *What Is an Apparatus and Other Essays*, trans. David Kishik and Stefan Pedatella (Stanford: Stanford University Press, 2009), 1–24.

44. With reference to Febvre, "Réflexions sur l'histoire des techniques"; and also the central thesis of Bernard Stiegler's three-volume *La technique et le temps*. See Stiegler, *Technics and Time, 1: The Fault of Epimetheus*, trans. Richard Beardsworth and George Collins (Stanford: Stanford University Press, 1998), 1–18.

45. Banchieri has "bacchetta over fazzoletto." Banchieri, *Cartella musicale*, facsimile ed. (1614; Bologna: Forni, 1968), 33.

of falling and rising, or *thesis* and *arsis*. Tellingly, only the reference to one of these—the hand—could have indicated some sort of performance direction, while the motions made with both the hand and the heart were equally suited to the task of visualizing *motus*.

The Hand

The beat owes much to the hand. The tactile origins of the Latin *tactus* and German *Takt* are readily apparent; other terms for the beat such as *battuta* and *Schlag* indicate an action that could have been performed with the hand or the foot. Some authors, such as Zarlino, Mersenne, and Kircher, refer to the term *Plausus*—or "hand clapping"—which they attribute to either Augustine or the ancients.[46] The hand has long enjoyed a high status among the parts of the human body. Its liberation and use in the making of the first technologies is, some would argue, what makes us human.[47] The hand not only produces tools, it is the first example of the tool. Its capability for gesture and for an exteriorization of the self has earned it a revered place in paleoanthropology and in the philosophy of being.[48]

But the vaulted status of the hand is not new, nor is it unique to studies of human origins or existential thought. In *De anima*, Aristotle wrote, "the soul is as the hand, for the hand is an instrument with respect to instruments as the intellect is a form with respect to forms."[49] Like the *Physics*, Aristotle's *De anima* was also transformed and transmitted in various strands of early modern Scholasticism. Thomas Aquinas's commentaries add, "the hand is the most perfect of organs."[50] More significant than the Aristotelian commentaries on *De anima*, though, were the group of texts on anatomy that disseminated knowledge about the human body through the learned world in this period. Chief among these were the works of Galen, which elaborated on the Aristotelian notion of the hand as an instrument. His *De usu partium*, which was copied and cited as an authoritative source on anatomy throughout the sixteenth and seventeenth centuries, begins with a long passage on the wonders of the hand.

---

46. Zarlino; *Le istitutioni harmoniche* (Venice: Francesco de i Franceschi Senese, 1558), 207; Mersenne, *Harmonie universelle*, facsimile ed. (1636–37; Paris: Centre national de la recherché scientifique, 1963), vol. 2, "Livre cinquiesme de la Composition," prop. XI, 324v; Kircher, *Musurgia universalis*, facsimile ed. (1650; Hildesheim: Georg Olms, 1970), 2:52.

47. On this point see André Leroi-Gourhan, *Gesture and Speech*, trans. Anna Bostock Berger (Cambridge, MA: MIT Press, 1993), particularly 25–28.

48. Stiegler reviews the relevant literature in *Technics and Time 1*, 143–54.

49. Aristotle, *De anima* 3.8.432a1–3. Aristotle, *De anima*, in *The Works of Aristotle: Volume III*, ed. W. D. Ross and trans. J. A. Smith (Oxford: Clarendon, 1931), unpaginated.

50. Thomas Aquinas, *Commentary on Aristotle's* De Anima, trans. Kenelm Foster and Silvester Humphries with an introduction by Ralph McInerny, rev. ed. (1951; Notre Dame, IN: Dumb Ox, 1994), lect. XIII, no. 790, p. 235.

Thus man is the most intelligent of the animals and so, also, hands are the instruments most suitable for an intelligent animal. For it is not because he has hands that he is the most intelligent, as Anaxagoras says, but because he is the most intelligent that he has hands, as Aristotle says, judging most correctly. Indeed, not by his hands, but by his reason has man been instructed in the arts. Hands are an instrument, as the lyre is the instrument of the musician, and tongs of the smith. Hence just as the lyre does not teach the musicians or tongs the smith but each of them is a craftsman by virtue of the reason there is in him although he is unable to work at his trade without the aid of his instruments, so every soul has through its very essence certain faculties, but without the aid of instruments is helpless to accomplish what it is by Nature disposed to accomplish...

For though the hand is no one particular instrument, it is the instrument for all instruments because it is formed by Nature to receive them all, and similarly, although reason is no one of the arts in particular, it would be an art for the arts because it is naturally disposed to take them all unto itself. Hence man, the only one of all the animals having an art for arts in his soul, should logically have an instrument for instruments in his body.[51]

For Galen, the hand embodied the technical ability of humanity. His treatises returned again and again to the image of the body as a microcosm. The hand, in *De usu partium*, was yet another form of microcosmography; it was the most complex and yet elegant part of the body, and it represented on a smaller scale the human capacity for reason (the "art for arts"). It was a tiny version of humankind's distinctive qualities. Through the hand, the human became technical.

This view of the hand only intensified in the early modern copying and transforming of Galen's texts. "The hand is an instrument that surpasses all instruments," wrote a sixteenth-century Galenist in the vernacular French.[52] With Galen and Aristotle as their cited authorities, sixteenth- and seventeenth-century anatomists saw the hand as the body's site of agency.[53] It was the meeting point between the body and the world of things to be manipulated, controlled, and mastered.

In theories of meter, the hand was the chief instrument for marking divisions in time. Because this instrument was unchanged as it moved through space, it solved the problem of time's continuity and marked or counted time through the before and after in change. The technique of the beat was the human and earthly way of using spatial motion to number time. The hand was ideally suited for the task because it was a "judge and discerner of touch," as Helkiah Crooke wrote in his anatomy text of 1615. Crooke continues, "For albeit this touching vertue or

51. Galen, *On the Usefulness of the Parts of the Body* 1:4, 6; translated with an introduction and commentary by Margaret Tallmadge May (Ithaca: Cornell University Press, 1968), 1:69–71.

52. Galen, *De l'usage des parties du corps humain*, trans. and ed. Jacques Dalechamps (Lyon: Guillaume Rouillé, 1566), 17.

53. Katherine Rowe writes, "For early modern writers, following Aristotle by way of Galen, the location of agency in relation to the body is the chief intellectual tenor of representations of the hand." Rowe, " 'God's handy worke': Divine Complicity and the Anatomist's Touch," in *The Body in Parts: Fantasies of Corporeality in Early Modern Europe*, ed. David Hillman and Carla Mazzio (New York: Routledge, 1997), 287–309, at 287.

tactive quality be diffused through the whole body both within and without... yet we do more curiouslie and exquisitely feele and discerne both the first and second qualities which strike the Sense in the Hand than in other parts."[54]

The use of the term "discerner" in Crooke's text referred not only to the ability of the hand in distinguishing differences; to "discern" in the early modern era also indicated a physical operation of separating, distinguishing, and dividing. This is the reason the hand held a place of prominence in early anatomy texts that were meant to guide dissections: the hand was the most complex and exemplary part of the body, and it was also the instrument with which the dissection of the body was to take place.[55] The hand, then, was not only the subject of anatomy, but also the supreme dissecting and dividing instrument for it.

The hand was a tool of division. It was used for dividing the continuity of time in the act of the beat. The hand discerned and distinguished the unfolding of music as it implemented—conceptually and visually—the physical structure of *thesis* and *arsis*.

The Heart

The only part of the body as universally cited as the hand, in this period's theories of meter, was the heart. Though the hand took precedence in the prescription of the beat's motion, the explanatory power of the heart would seem to have been more significant. This is evident in the fact that the motion of the hand is often said to be "in imitation of" or "patterned after" the beating of the heart.[56] The most convenient point of comparison between the beat and the heartbeat was the twofold nature of both motions. In their comparisons, theorists often listed the corresponding medical and musical terms for these two parts. The motion of the heart was composed of systole (a tightening of the heart, or "beating") and diastole (the corresponding loosening). Often, these Greek medical terms were brought into comparison with the musical *thesis* and *arsis*. Mersenne (who we can always rely on for a generous explanation) clarified, "it seems as though the measure has taken its time and its regulation from the beating of the heart, or the pulse, or the arteries, for the lowering of the hand corresponds to the *systole*, or the compression and lowering of the heart, and the lifting to the *diastole*, or the dilation and elevation."[57]

---

54. Helkiah Crooke, *Microcosmographia: A Description of the Body of Man* ... (London: Printed by William Iaggard dwelling in Barbican, and are there to be sold, 1615), 730.
55. Rowe, "'God's handy worke': Divine Complicity and the Anatomist's Touch," 296.
56. See Lanfranco, *Scintille di musica*, 67; Lippius, *Synopsis musicæ*, B4v; Zacconi, *Prattica di musica* (Venice: Bartolomeo Carampello, 1596), vol. 1; facsimile ed. (Hildesheim: Georg Olms, 1982), 20v.
57. "Il semble que la mesure ait pris son temps & son reglement du batement du coeur, du poulx, ou de l'artere, car le baisser de la main respond à la *systole*, ou compression & abaissement du coeur, & le lever à sa *diastole*, ou dilatation, & elevation..." Mersenne, *Harmonie Universelle*, vol. 2, "Livre cinquiesme de la Composition," prop. XI, 324v.

It is significant that Mersenne's comparison focuses specifically on the actions of compression and dilation in *systole* and *diastole*, and not on the momentary percussions that mark their boundaries. Here again a comparison with recent theories of meter is instructive. If recent notions of the beat would seem to have more in common with the intervals marked between the pulsations of a heartbeat, the sixteenth- and seventeenth-century theories have more affinity with its process of continual motion. Nowhere was the microcosmographical element of earthly timekeeping more apparent than it was with the perpetual heartbeat. Crooke introduced the heart in his anatomy text as humanity's one bodily timekeeper.

> The busie wit of man observing the perpetuall motions of the heavens, hath long travelled to imitate the same, and in making experiments, hath framed excellent and admirable peeces of workmanship, whilest everyone carried a perpetuall motion about himselfe, which happly hee little remembred or thought upon, and that is the perpetuall motion of the heart, which from the day of birth, til the day of death, never ceaseth, but moveth continually…[58]

Just as the motion of the heavens was said to be perpetual—and thereby the best timekeeper—so too did the "little world of the body of a man" include one perpetual motion in the beating of the heart.[59]

In addition to the fact that the motions of the beat and the heartbeat both resembled the one true perpetual motion in the cosmos, they were also said to resemble one another. The history of this relationship is quite extensive and entangled. Music theoretical sources suggest that the logic of the beat's motion derives from the heartbeat, and it might seem as though these texts theorized the beat with concepts and language borrowed from medicine. In fact, the discourses on these two bodily motions were developed reciprocally.[60] As it was understood in medieval and early modern medicine, the heartbeat as an act was already musical. Medieval texts on anatomy and medicine claimed that the heartbeat was best understood through the rubric of rhythm.[61] One reason for including detailed descriptions of the heartbeat in early medical treatises was that the many different variations of the pulse were said to indicate different temperaments and could even be used to diagnose illnesses. A long tradition of medical sources, citing ancient authorities including Galen, claimed that the best way to understand the proportions and durations of these heartbeats was through the rules of music theory.[62]

---

58. Crooke, *Microcosmographia: A Description of the Body of Man…*, 400.
59. Crooke, *Microcosmographia: A Description of the Body of Man…*, 400.
60. Dale Bonge first explicitly formulated this thesis for the case of Gaffurius. See Bonge, "Gaffurius on Pulse and Tempo: A Reinterpretation," *Musica Disciplina* 36 (1982): 167–74.
61. Nancy Siraisi, "The Music of Pulse in the Writings of Italian Academic Physicians (Fourteenth and Fifteenth Centuries)," *Speculum* 50, no. 4 (1975): 689–710. Siraisi's study, which focuses principally on fourteenth- and fifteenth-century Italy, documents this general trend in medieval and early modern Europe.
62. In fact, some early medical authorities included lengthy and detailed passages of music theory in their discussions of the musicality of the pulse. Peter of Abano, notably, included material

The sources on which medieval medical texts relied included: Galen's four major treatises on the pulse (which, together with his minor works on the topic, identified twenty-seven different varieties of heartbeat); later interpretations of Galen such as Paul of Aegina's *Seven Books on Medicine*; and the Arabic *Canon of Medicine* of the polymath Ibn Sīnā, known in the West as Avicenna.[63] All of these sources described a heartbeat that was composed of two fundamental motions, in which was found "the nature of music" (after Avicenna).[64] The different "rhythms" of the heartbeat described the differences in temporal intervals marked by and between those two motions. "In general, rhythm is, in fact, the ratio of one time to another. In regard to the pulse, it is, according to some, the ratio of the time of motion to the time of rest, as of the systole and diastole to their intermediate time of rest," reads a 1532 edition of Paul of Aegina's *Medici insignis opus divinum*.[65] It is the plethora of different heartbeats that makes the modern assumption about a supposed connection between pulse rate and tempo designation all the more surprising.[66] Anatomists, observing the variety of heartbeats, attempted to explain them with music theory; we should not, therefore, understand music-theoretical references to the heartbeat as references to some sort of basic tempo. If anything, the equation of the two served to demonstrate how varied both could be.

The heavens, the heart, and the hand were nodes in a network that understood motion in space to describe, divide, and number time. All earthly motions created their own times in reflection of the heaven's motion. The hand in the motion of the beat echoed this grand motion as it discerned and divided time. Its twofold, local motion also matched the best imitator of the sky's perpetual movement: the beating of the heart. Writings that were meant to explain and describe the human motions of the beat and the heartbeat, then, borrowed words and

borrowed from Boethius, Augustine, and Guido of Arezzo. See Siraisi, "The Music of Pulse in the Writings of Italian Academic Physicians (Fourteenth and Fifteenth Centuries)," 690–91.

63. Siraisi, "The Music of Pulse in the Writings of Italian Academic Physicians (Fourteenth and Fifteenth Centuries)," 695–96. Not only did Paul of Aegina go by many names in the West (Pauli Aeginetae, Paulus Aegineta) but so did his medical encyclopedia. The sixteenth-century versions consulted for this study were translated and interpreted by Albano Torino Vitodurensis, and published under the title *Pauli Aeginetae medici insignis Opus divinium...Albano Torino Vitodurensi interprete* (Basileae: Andr. Crantandrum et Io. Bebelium, 1532). On Avicenna's name see *Complete Dictionary of Scientific Biography*, s.v. "Ibn Sīnā, Abū cAlī Al-Husayn Ibn cAbdallāh, also known as Avicenna," by G. C. Anawati and Albert Z. Iskandar (Detroit: Charles Scribner's Sons, 2008), 15:494–501, accessed January 28, 2011, <www.gale.cengage.com>.

64. Avicenna, *Liber canonis* (Venetiis: Apvd Ivntas, 1582), 1:47v.

65. "Est vero rhythmus in genere habitudo quaedam, sive proportio temporis ad tempus. Caeterum in pulsu secundum tempora quaedam ipsius motus, ad tempus tranquillitatis, verbi caussa, distentionis & contractionis ad aliquod tempus, quod est medium inter quietem." Paul of Aegina, *Medici insignis Opus divinium*, ed. and trans. Albano Torino Vitodurensi (Basileae: Andr. Crantandrum et Io. Bebelium, 1532), 63. The translation presented here is a modified version of that found in *The Seven Books of Paulus Aegineta*, trans., and with a commentary by Francis Adams (London: The Sydenham Society, 1846), 1:204. Paul of Aegina goes on to say that others disagree, and that the ratio might be taken from one time of motion and rest to the next time of motion and rest; or, it might be taken from one motion to the next.

66. Again see Bonge, "Gaffurius on Pulse and Tempo: A Reinterpretation."

concepts from each other as they attempted to make sense of time's relationship to *motus*. The hand and the heart, as objects in motion, were able to describe change through spatial magnitude and solve the problem of time's continuity. In practice as in theory, these motions were techniques through which musicians and natural philosophers could explain the division of time's continuum.

Rereading Zarlino

It was in an intellectual world filled with ideas connecting time and *motus* that Zarlino wrote—and his contemporaries read—*Le istitutioni harmoniche*. The movement of an object through spatial magnitude solved the problem of temporal continuity, and local motions here on earth (including those of the human body) echoed the one true cosmic timekeeper. Zarlino's explanation of the beat was created with and understood through these conceptual frameworks.

Zarlino paced the opening of his book on counterpoint slowly. The third book in *Le istitutioni harmoniche*, it dwells for thirty-nine chapters on intervals, acceptable progressions, and other rudiments before introducing note-against-note, two-voice counterpoint. From the fortieth chapter onward, the pace of instruction increases; Zarlino introduces "diminished counterpoints" (*contrapunti diminuti*), demonstrating contrapuntal treatment in note values smaller than those of the subject given.[67] Within settings such as these, as Zarlino points out, the student must consider the placement of consonances and dissonances with respect to the temporal division of the subject. Before introducing fugue, then, Zarlino includes a short chapter, "Della battuta" (chapter 48), on the nature of temporal division.

As discussed in chapter 1, Zarlino's "Della battuta" conveys three fundamental points. The first describes the nature of the beat as a motion; the second specifies the fundamental distinction between equal and unequal meter; the third supplies information on the types of durations suited to these two different types of meters. Zarlino focuses the information concerning the beat as an act within his first point of inquiry, or the first twenty-seven lines of text in the chapter.[68]

Opening the discussion, Zarlino makes it clear that the present topic is not a matter of notation but rather the rule that musicians have devised in order to interpret the many "diverse figures of song" that were already described in the second chapter of the book on counterpoint.[69] The beat, then, is not something that notated durations posses but a manner of discerning and orienting them. At this point in the text, what was already a physical topic (by means of its name alone) becomes more explicitly so with the introductions of specific bodily

---

67. Zarlino, *Le istitutioni harmoniche*, 195–99.
68. Zarlino, *Le istitutioni harmoniche*, 207. This is true for both the 1558 edition and the 1562 edition.
69. In "Della inventione delle Chiavi, & delle Figure cantabili," Zarlino, *Le istitutioni harmoniche*, 149.

motions. Zarlino introduces the motions of the hand and the heart simultane-ously, explaining the former by means of the latter. He writes this two-part intro-duction to the motions of the beat with a reference to the past, calling the beat an invention of those *Musici* who had come before. "They imagined that it would be best if such a sign were made with the hand, such that every singer were able to see, and if it were composed of regular movements like the human pulse."[70]

Temporal division is explained with reference to a motion of the hand, which in turn is explained through the perpetual motion of the heartbeat. "Because I cannot imagine another movement [that former musicians] could have found that would be made naturally and that would be able to give them the rule and proportion of [the heartbeat]."[71] Turning away from the signs of notated dura-tions, Zarlino is able to explain the rule of recurring temporal division through a visualization of the body's best microcosmographical motion. He uses the heart-beat as a technique to accomplish conceptual work. He employs this technique not only to help describe the performed actions of the hand, but also to summon the logic of the continuous temporal passage that renders measured song intelli-gible.

Furthermore, Zarlino is able to evoke the technique of the beat in a way that pays respect to tradition and established authority. Immediately upon mention-ing the motions of the hand and the heart, he calls upon Augustine for the term *Plausus* and indicates that his predecessors had also employed the term *battuta* along with *Tempo sonoro*. Paul of Aegina and Galen are two authorities that help to explain the nature of the heartbeat, which "is composed (see Avicenna's second part of book I [of the *Canon of Medicine*]) of two movements and two reposes. The [musical] beat also has two movements, called the *Positione* [fall] and *Levatione* [rise], which are made with the hand."[72]

Zarlino's technique of the beat was more than a simple a set of references to efficacious imagery and Scholastic tradition. It was one particular instantiation of an understanding of time through *motus* that relied upon the logic of local, spatial motion. Indeed, up until this point in the text there had been no need to cite Aristotle directly, though the *Physics* was perhaps the most obvious authority on time. This renders the moment of Zarlino's explicit Aristotle citation all the more interesting, because it arrives when the Italian theorist is forced to explain the only part of the beat that is not composed of motion.

---

70. "Et s'imaginarono che fusse bene, se cotal segno fusse fatto con la mano; accioche ogn'uno de i cantori lo potesse vedere, & fusse regolato nel suo movimento all guisa del Polso humano." Zarlino, *Le istitutioni harmoniche*, 207. My translations from book three with reference to Zarlino, *The Art of Counterpoint*, trans. Guy A. Marco and Claude V. Palisca (1968; repr., New York: Norton, 1976), 116–17.

71. "Percioche non so vedere, qual movimento potevam ritrovare, che fusse fatto naturalmente, che potesse dare a loro regola, & proportione, fuori che questo." Zarlino, *Le istitutioni harmoniche*, 207. Zarlino, *The Art of Counterpoint*, trans. Marco and Palisca, 117.

72. "Esser composto (come vuole Avicenna nel Secondo Fen del lib. 1.) di due movimenti, & di due quiete, delle quali cose similmente la Battuta viene ad esser composta; & prima di due movi-menti, che sono la Positione & la Levatione, che si fa con la mano." Zarlino, *Le istitutioni har-moniche*, 207. Zarlino, *The Art of Counterpoint*, trans. Marco and Palisca, 117.

The resting points of the beat, or the moments of repose between *thesis* and *arsis*, necessitate Aristotelian authority for explication. These portions of the technique are nevertheless a part of the composition of the overall movement "because (according to Aristotle) between such movements, [reposes] are always found."[73] Zarlino refers here to Aristotle's *Physics* 8.8, in which the Philosopher asserts that finite motions in any one direction will eventually have to pause before reversing.[74] The analogy to the heartbeat is all the more meaningful in this case, because it, too, is a microcosmographical motion—even said to be the body's "perpetuall motion"—with its own moments of repose.[75]

The local motions of the hand and the heart did not need to move seamlessly in order to solve the problem of time's continuity.[76] Instead, the function of these motions—these tools of temporal discernment—was to mark a "before and after" with respect to change.[77] With two distinct movements and moments of repose interspersed, the motion of the body's supreme instrument (the hand) and perpetual timekeeper (the heart) could count or number time.

These two bodily motions need not be evenly paced or uniform, as the huge variety of heartbeats would attest. This is why the relationship between the heartbeat and tempo prescription would be rather curious, if it existed at all.[78] For Zarlino's purposes, the heartbeat's non-uniformity itself was helpful in describing the two essential varieties of the beat: the equal (for duple meters) and the unequal (for triple meters). "Similarly, just as the pulse is found in two manners—namely, the equal and unequal (according to the principle, celebrated medical authorities)—the quickness and slowness of notes arises only from this equality and inequality."[79] For early authorities on the pulse this distinction was one among many, but for Zarlino the equal durations of the duple beat and the unequal durations of the triple beat created the extent of the motions required to explain the rule of division for any kind of song.[80]

73. "Percioche (secondo la mente di Aristotele) tra questi movimenti…sempre [quiete] ritrovano." Zarlino, *Le istitutioni harmoniche*, 207. Zarlino, *The Art of Counterpoint*, trans. Marco and Palisca, 117.
74. Aristotle, *Physics* 8.8.262a12–15; *Aristotle's* Physics *Book VIII*, trans. Graham, 25.
75. Crooke, *Microcosmographia: A Description of the Body of Man. . .*, 400.
76. It was on this point that Agostino Pisa so passionately disagreed, in his *Breve dichiaratione della battuta musicale*, facsimile ed., ed. Piero Gargiulo, with extracts from *Battuta della musica* (1611; Lucca: Libreria Musicale Italiana Editrice, 1996); and idem., *Battuta della musica* (Rome: Bartolomeo Zanetti, 1611), facsimile ed. in Pisa, *Breve dichiarazione della battuta musicale* [*sic*], edited by Walther Dürr (Bologna: Forni, 1969).
77. Aristotle *Physics* 4.11.219b1; *Aristotle's* Physics *Books III and IV*, trans. Hussey, 44.
78. Again see Bonge, "Gaffurius on Pulse and Tempo: A Reinterpretation," whose comments are also relevant to Zarlino.
79. "Simigliantemente; si come il Polso si ritrova di due maniere, secondo l'autorità delli commemorati principi della Medicina, cioè Equale, & Inequale: pigliando però solamente quella equalità, & inequalità, che nasce dalla velocità & tardità." Zarlino, *Le istitutioni harmoniche*, 207. Zarlino, *The Art of Counterpoint*, trans. Marco and Palisca, 117.
80. For one exemplary, medical distinction between the even and uneven heartbeat, see Paul of Aegina, *Medici insignis Opus divinium*, ed. and trans. Albano Torino Vitodurensi, 63. This is Paul of Aegina's ninth variety of pulse distinction.

The chapter goes on to describe mensuration signs through the logic of the beat, and offers patterns in poetic feet appropriate for equal and unequal meters.[81] The derivative nature of these topics is clear; they serve to provide the details for the general rule of the beat described above. While the mensuration signs were part of the notational system, the patterns of durations indicated with poetic feet seem to have operated under a different rubric than the temporal division of the beat. There is some evidence to suggest that Zarlino may have considered syllabic emphasis a discrete quantity. After all, the "syllables of speech" served as a prime example of discrete quantity in both Aristotle's *Categories* and in part 1 of *Le istitutioni harmoniche*.[82] Passages in Aristotle's *Poetics*, too, indicate that words are only divisible into their smallest elements (their letters) like all discrete quantities.[83] Syllabic emphasis, then, might have been a kind of quantifiable intensity that musicians could coordinate with duration through the rule of the beat. Only the context of temporal measure, properly considered, was continuous.

Fundamentally, though, if Zarlino's discrete syllables seem hard to reconcile with continuous time, they were no more so than the value-specific durations of musical notes have always been. The problem of accounting for continuity among distinct entities—syllables, feet, notes—has had many potential answers, each with its own strategy. For Zarlino and his contemporaries, the technique of the beat in local motion was able to count continuous time. It was one way to implement *motus*, or to provide a rule of division in time's continuity by which musicians could interpret distinct durations. "From this," Zarlino wrote, concluding the first portion of his chapter, "rhythm and the many proportions of tempo are born."[84]

81. Zarlino, *Le istitutioni harmoniche*, 208. For the details of Zarlino's account, see chapter 1.
82. Aristotle, *Categories*, chap. 6; as translated in *Aristotle's* Categories *and* De Interpretatione, trans. with notes by J. L. Ackrill, 12–13; Zarlino, *Le istitutioni harmoniche*, 28.
83. "The parts of diction in its entirety are as follows: (i) the element [i.e., letter], (ii) the syllable, (iii) the particle, (iv) the conjunction, (v) the name [i.e., noun or adjective], (vi) the verb, (vii) the inflection, (viii) the utterance. (i) the element is an indivisible sound—not every [kind of] sound, but one from which it is natural for a composite sound to arise." Aristotle, *Poetics* 1.1456b20–24; Aristotle, *Poetics*, trans. with notes by Richard Janko (Indianapolis: Hackett, 1987), 26.
84. "Onde si fa il Rithmo, dal quale nasce molti movimenti proportionati." Zarlino, *Le istitutioni harmoniche*, 207–8. Zarlino, *The Art of Counterpoint*, trans. Marco and Palisca, 117–18.

CHAPTER Three

A Renewed Account of Unequal Triple Meter

Equality

From its earliest formulations in writings on music, triple meter has held a special position. Conceptions of triple meter as the perfect mode of temporal division eventually gave way during the sixteenth century to conceptions of triple meter grounded in a basic inequality, connected to the construction of the unequal *tactus* or *battuta*.[1] These accounts, prevalent through the seventeenth century, generally provided for two types of beats: the equal and the unequal. Both types of beats consisted of a lowering and a raising of the hand in the *thesis* and *arsis* of time-beating motion. While duple meters consisted of a lowering and raising of equal length, triple meters consisted of a lowering double the length of the following raise, as shown in figure 3.1, below. In other words, triple meter went from one type of marked case (perfection) to another (inequality). In this second form, triple meter was an unequal meter, similar in nature to the unbalanced meters in five or seven with which we are familiar in the twenty-first century.

In theoretical writings of the past forty years, however, triple meter no longer garners special treatment. It has become, for the most part, an equivalent of duple

---

1. Unfortunately, no current secondary scholarship exists that takes this transition as its specific focus, although a number of sources on the evolution of rhythmic notation, taken together, make it evident. Among the sources on early notation, see Dorit Tanay's *Noting Music, Marking Culture: The Intellectual Context of Rhythmic Notation, 1250-1400*, Musicological Studies and Documents 46 (American Institute of Musicology: Hänssler-Verlag, 1999); on the period following, Anna Maria Busse Berger's *Mensuration and Proportion Signs* (Oxford: Clarendon Press, 1993). Also helpful in this regard is *Oxford Music Online*, s.v. "Notation," by Ian Bent et al., accessed August 21, 2009, <www.oxfordmusiconline.com>; and Ruth I. DeFord, "Tempo Relationships between Duple and Triple Time in the Sixteenth Century," *Early Music History* 14 (1995): 1–51. On an exceptional sixteenth-century source invested in more types of inequalities than those discussed here, see Matthew S. Royal, "Tradition and Innovation in Sixteenth-Century Rhythmic Theory: Francisco Salinas's *De Musica Libri Septem*," *Music Theory Spectrum* 34, no. 2 (2012): 26–47.

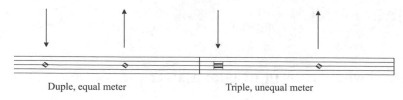

Duple, equal meter   Triple, unequal meter

Figure 3.1 Comparison of duple, equal meter and triple, unequal meter.

meter with a different cardinality (that is, a different number of beats per measure). In these theories, triple meter is an isochronous meter—all of its parts are equal in length. This is the result of recent scholarship's heavy theoretical investment in the properties of equal division and graduated hierarchy.

Conceptualizations of triple meter offer the most extreme case of discord between early modern theories and those of the twentieth and twenty-first centuries. They are not only the most obvious points of disagreement between the rules of the texts in question, they also point up the different ways of knowing and experiencing that these texts presume. Revitalizing the notion that triple meter can be unequal—which dominated accounts of meter in the sixteenth and seventeenth centuries—affords a uniquely distorted lens through which to contemplate the ways of understanding and experiencing music in that period. Viewing triple meter unequally also sheds new light on the surprisingly deliberate evenness of our recent theories of meter. More importantly, it illuminates the foundational assumptions that allow such evenness to appear natural, obvious, and normative.

As noted in previous chapters, recent theoretical writings conceptualize the beat as an abstracted temporal interval. Meter arises from the nested levels of these regular intervals. This basic idea is deployed under the auspices of a great number of theories to analyze a huge variety of repertoire. Within it is lodged the important premise that all division must be division into equal parts within the hierarchy. Contemporary theories motivate for this conclusion using all sorts of vocabularies. In general, though, they emphasize that meter—so conceived—has the infinitely mutable ability to divide a span of music at any sort of evenly spaced interval and replicate some form of this division at higher levels. The theories account for these time intervals as spans of time marked out with durationless points, series of recurring pulses, equal divisions in the listener's consciousness, or simply ways of dividing.[2]

Curiously, the investment in equal division and graduated hierarchy is most apparent in theories that seek to explain the complex relationships between types of divisions themselves. These theories often fall under the rubric of metric

---

2. Representative examples include Fred Lerdahl and Ray Jackendoff, *A Generative Theory of Tonal Music* (Cambridge, MA: MIT Press, 1983), 18; Harald Krebs, *Fantasy Pieces* (Oxford: Oxford University Press, 1999), 23; Carl Schachter, "Rhythm and Linear Analysis: Aspects of Meter," in *The Music Forum* VI, ed. Felix Salzer, Carl Schachter, and Hedi Segel (New York: Columbia University Press, 1987), as reprinted in Carl Schachter, *Unfoldings*, ed. Joseph N. Straus (Oxford: Oxford University Press, 1999), 80, 81.

dissonance, and are interested in rhythmic and metric irregularities. Instead of predisposing them toward the possibility of unequal division, however, this analytical desideratum seems to have prohibited it. The logic of the theories of metric dissonance is that there must be a regular, evenly spaced standard against which some irregularity must find itself in contrast. Each division of their hierarchies represents a division that is made with a consistent duration each time. These are often said to resolve to some common subdivision, which works graphically or numerically to explain the nature of the dissonance.[3]

Early modern theories, as we have seen in the previous chapters, are also concerned with division and hierarchy. But the way in which these theories make division explicable allows for and, indeed, prescribes a different way of understanding regularity. The centrality of the two-part motion in these accounts creates a framework for repetition and recurrence. It also supports forms of hierarchy (particularly microcosmography, as discussed in chapter 2). But the recurrence of the motions in these writings is never limited to equal nested durations. Equality, in this way of understanding division, was far more particular. It was attached to duple meters specifically, and was the characteristic that distinguished duple meters from triple meters.

Not all of our contemporary theories of meter adhere to the paradigm of equal division strictly, however, and some of them describe a kind of division that is not altogether different from the sort imagined in early modern theories. Justin London's theory, as outlined in *Hearing in Time*, offers one point of departure. London's 2004 monograph synthesizes and relates to music theory numerous recent psychological studies on metric attending. The theory presented therein uses circular diagrams called N-cycles to visualize meter, as shown below in figure 3.2. The points on these cycles represent potential subdivisions.[4] London calls the patterns embedded within these cycles "subcycles," and the beat level often corresponds to one of these. Following Lerdahl and Jackendoff's *Generative Theory of Tonal Music*, he provides his own rules for "well-formedness" employing the logic of his diagrams.[5] His rules are called "well-formedness constraints."

London's is one of the most ecumenical of the recent meter theories, and the only one to provide a detailed account of unequal meters—what he refers to, in the more scientific terminology, as non-isochronous meters. London imagines a much more robust landscape of meters than other contemporary scholars, and

3. See for instance Harald Krebs, *Fantasy Pieces*; Richard Cohn, "Complex Hemiolas, Ski-Hill Graphs, and Metric Spaces," *Music Analysis* 20, no. 3 (2001): 295–326; Daphne Leong, "Metric States, Symmetries, and Shapes: Humperdinck and Wagner," *Journal of Music Theory* 51, no. 2 (2007): 211–43; Scott Murphy, "Metric Cubes in Some Music of Brahms," *Journal of Music Theory* 53, no. 1 (2009): 1–56; David Temperley, "Hypermetrical Transitions," *Music Theory Spectrum* 30, no. 2 (2008): 305–25; and Yonatan Malin, *Songs in Motion: Rhythm and Meter in the German Lied* (Oxford: Oxford University Press, 2010), particularly 35–66.

4. Justin London, *Hearing in Time* (Oxford: Oxford University Press, 2004), 68. London and I use the term cardinality in different ways—he employs the term to refer to the total number of points on these cycles.

5. For Lerdahl and Jackendoff's discussion of well-formedness rules, see *A Generative Theory of Tonal Music*, 8–12.

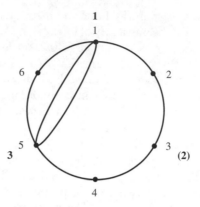

Figure 3.2 Diagram of unequal triple meter after London's N-cycle system, showing six subdivisions (4 + 2).

creates a framework in which some unequal divisions are the rule rather than a departure from it. Nevertheless, though London's theory of meter acknowledges and carefully theorizes inequality, the divisions in early modern triple meters are more unequal than his theory will allow. To begin, he mandates that all points on the cycles are evenly spaced. This rule runs against the spirit of all unequal meters, if not their theoretical existence, in positing that all unequal durations are divided evenly at least in concept.[6] Therefore, a traditional unequal meter such as 5/4 (which London accepts as well-formed) can indeed show its unequal division into parts of two and three beats, but could not show unequal spacing amongst its five beats. A hypothetically constructed unequal triple meter from a cycle with six evenly spaced points (or subdivisions) is impossible under a further rule which applies specifically to unequal meters. This hypothetical triple meter is shown above in figure 3.2. Four points comprise the subdivisions of its first beat, which is twice as long as the second beat (comprised of two points). The problem with this construction is London's stipulation that all meters, equal or no, be maximally even.[7] Maximal evenness is a concept London imports from scale theory.[8] In a maximally even set of elements in a space, elements are positioned as far apart and as evenly as possible. For meters as London conceives them, this means that divisions are as regular as possible. A cycle of six with two subdivisions, such as in figure 3.2, could not include a division into four and two (an unequal triple meter) but would need instead a division into three and three (a duple meter with a triple subdivision) in order to maintain maximal evenness.[9]

6. London, *Hearing in Time*, 72.

7. London, *Hearing in Time*, 103.

8. In particular he cites John Clough and Jack Douthett, "Maximally Even Sets," *Journal of Music Theory* 35, nos. 1–2 (1991): 93–173.

9. Indeed, in London's account this meter not only fails to be maximally even, it also creates ambiguities insofar as doubling the length of the second, short beat yields a duration which should be of a higher-order but is instead the same length as that of the first beat. Thus, even London's

Plate 3.1 Hasty's construction of triple meter through the concept of deferral, from his *Meter as Rhythm* (Oxford: Oxford University Press, 1997), 134. Used by permission of Oxford University Press, USA.

EXAMPLE 9.19 Deferral

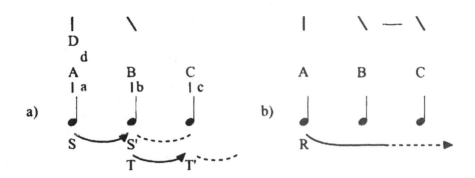

In other words, a cycle of six with a division into two can only ever be an even duple meter in London's system. Triple meter, for London, must always involve isochrony. Even within a theory that specifically aims to grapple with the difficult but pertinent question of unequal division, the rule of isochrony finds some place; there is a limit to the amount of inequality even in this progressive, embracing account of unequal meters.

Another important exception to the contemporary trend and, importantly, to its basic construction of triple meter, is Christopher Hasty's *Meter as Rhythm*. Hasty's account of meter as projection departs substantially from the paradigms and aims of earlier models. It is telling that it is only within his atypical theoretical framework that triple meter emerges as a distinctive, important, and unequal case in twentieth-century music theory.

Hasty's theory of meter is grounded in the ability to project, from a given duration, the durations that may follow. Central to his theorization of triple meter is an acknowledgement of the duple nature built into projection (one thing projects its next, its partner). "Since projection is essentially binary and requires that the two terms be immediately successive," Hasty writes, "and since projection results in equality, a projective account of triple, unequal meter is problematic."[10] If, in triple meter, the second beat prolongs "the activity and presence of the beginning [i.e., the first beat]," then the third beat can do no more than to continue to prolong this same activity (these relationships are shown in the contrast between the vertical line and the diagonal lines that follow in his diagram, reproduced above as plate 3.1).[11] Hence, third beats in Hasty's triple meters deny

revised, flexible formulation of well-formedness constraint six, found on p. 131, would not allow for non-isochronous triple meter.

10. Christopher Hasty, *Meter as Rhythm* (Oxford: Oxford University Press, 1997), 131.
11. Hasty, *Meter as Rhythm*, 131.

the possibility for the beginning of new measures, while they still "make the second beat past."[12] The type of denial that the third beat exhibits is special, since it is not analogous to the work of continuation alone, nor is it a mere denial of the projective potential that begins with the commencement of the measure. Instead, the third beat exhibits what Hasty calls "deferral," since it puts off the beginning of a new measure for yet another beat. The third beat for Hasty works in tandem with the continuation of the second beat, but also enlarges the "projective situation" of the measure as a whole.[13]

This theorization leaves Hasty with a novel account of triple meter. Not only has he theorized an unequal triple meter, his version of this meter is actually the reverse of unequal triple meter as theorists conceived of it in the sixteenth and seventeenth centuries. Where the historical theorists held that triple meter consisted of two parts, the first twice as long as the second, Hasty's triple meter is divided into two with its second part (B and C in plate 3.1 above) twice as long as the first. While he acknowledges the historical names for unequal triple meter, he does not discuss this disagreement in particular.

Paarigkeit

Although Hasty's basic construction of triple meter reverses the historical theories, it shares with them an important relationship to pairing—what Hasty calls "twoness," or the German "*Paarigkeit*."[14] The starting point of his treatment of triple meter is the troubling duple nature of projection. "I cannot deny that the governing hypothesis of projection is grounded in the twoness of immediate succession," Hasty writes.[15]

This twoness is also present in the historical theories, and is also responsible for the unequal nature of their triple meters: these theories have their basis in the two-part nature of the time-beating motion (and the other two-part motions related to it). While in duple meters the two-part motion produced uniformity and equality, in triple meters it took precedence over the cardinality of three and created a measurement unequal in its two parts. Take for example the account given in Martin Agricola's *Musica figuralis deudsch* (1532).[16] Agricola begins his sixth chapter concerning meter with an overall definition: "the beat (*tact*)...is a motion of the hand...by means of which notes are measured in accordance with the [mensuration] signs."[17] This motion has two parts, a lowering and a raising of

12. Hasty, *Meter as Rhythm*, 131.
13. Hasty, *Meter as Rhythm*, 134.
14. Hasty, *Meter as Rhythm*, 103, 135.
15. Hasty, *Meter as Rhythm*, 135.
16. Agricola's is the first unambiguous account of the unequal *tactus*. Ruth DeFord, in "Tempo Relationships between Duple and Triple Time in the Sixteenth Century," 6, credits Nicolaus Wollick, *Enchiridion musices* (Paris, 1509), with the first use of the term *tactus proportionatus*.
17. "Der Tact...ist eine stete und messige bewegung der hand...durch welche gleichsam ein richtscheit, nach ausweisung der zeichen, die gleichheit der stymmen und Noten des gesangs recht geleitet und gemessen wird. . ." Martin Agricola, *Musica figuralis deudsch*, facsimile ed. (1532; Hildesheim: Georg Olms, 1969), G3v.

Plate 3.2 Three versions of unequal triple meter, from Agricola, *Musica figuralis*, facsimile ed. (1532; Hildesheim: George Olms, 1985), G4v.

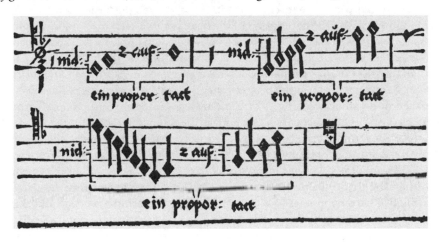

Example 3.1 Adapted from plate 3.2: three versions of unequal triple meter, from Agricola, *Musica figuralis deudsch*, facsimile ed. (1532; Hildesheim: George Olms, 1985), G4v.

the hand. Agricola then provides specifics, and distinguishes between three forms of *tact*: the whole *tact*, the half *tact*, and the *proporcien tact*. The whole and half *tact* are both forms of duple meter, the second twice as quick as the first, which consist of two even motions. The *proporcien tact*, Agricola's triple meter, consists of two motions, the first a lowering of the hand twice as long as the subsequent raising, as shown in his figure above (plate 3.2). The figure depicts three versions of a *proporcien tact*: the first in semibreves, the second in minims, and third in semiminims. These are given in contemporary notation in example 3.1. Agricola demonstrates that the first two-thirds of the durations in each case (two semibreves, four minims, or eight semiminims) is marked with the lowering of the hand or "nidderschlagen" (abbreviated "nid") while the final third (one semibreve, two minims, or four semiminims) is marked with the raising of the hand or "auffheben" (abbreviated "auf"). One *proporcien tact* consists of taking these unequal motions together.[18] In Agricola's account, the two-part definition of the

---

18. Agricola, *Musica figuralis deudsch*, G3v–G4v.

beat took logical and rhetorical precedence over the cardinality of three and the description of triple meter.

Theorists through the seventeenth century followed the basic formula represented in Agricola. The description of the beat as a two-part motion outweighed in space and importance the distinction between equal duple meters and unequal triple meters in, for example, Pisa's Scholastic writings on the beat of 1611.[19] The Italian theorist Lorenzo Penna took a similar approach in *Li primi albori musicali* (1672). Penna first defined the beat in general as a two-part motion, then distinguished in detail between types of triple meters (*maggiore* and *minore*, both of which consist of a lowering twice as long as the following raising of the hand).[20] So, too, Giovanni Maria Bononcini's *Musico prattico* (1673) gives the general two-part definition for the beat before offering similar specifics on triple meters.[21]

William Bathe's *A Briefe Introduction to the Skill of Song* (ca. 1587) presents an interesting case. Bathe uses the universal duple motion of time beating to distinguish between duples and triples, what he calls semibreve time and three minim time. "Semibrefe time is the striking up and downe of the hand equally in length continuing. Three minim time is the striking downe & then up of the hand equally in length, making each latter stroke just halfe the former."[22] Of particular significance in Bathe's formulation is his attention to the equal spatial length of each stroke as opposed to the unequal time applied to the strokes of triple meters. He underscored the basic equality, in twoness and in dimension, of the movement that was different in time for the different meters.

For these authors, the two-part nature of the beat's motion logically determined the unevenness of triple meter. This construction of triple meter was common in the sixteenth and seventeenth centuries. Triple meter was marked with inequality. Although it might seem at first blush that this marking of inequality separated triple meters from the others, in fact it brought them closer to their duple counterparts in forcing them to comply with a uniform law of twoness (and, in some cases, handstrokes equal in length). On closer inspection, it is our recent theories of meter, by contrast, that are more particular and specific regarding each meter; they make room for even meters of two, three, and four beats, and some go so far as to justify the nature of less-common meters. The sixteenth- and seventeenth-century theorists were actually far more generalizing in their definitions; all of their meters fell under the rubric of the binary *thesis* and *arsis* motion. Theorists of this era came to know division through these motions, and conceptualized the division of triple meters through their motions' inequality.

19. See Agostino Pisa, *Breve dichiaratione della battuta musicale*, facsimile ed., ed. Piero Gargiulo, with extracts from *Battuta della musica* (1611; Lucca: Libreria Musicale Italiana Editrice, 1996), 16, and chapter 1.
20. Lorenzo Penna, *Li Primi albori musicali,* facsimile ed. (1684; Bologna: Forni, 1969), 36–37.
21. Giovanni Maria Bononcini, *Musico prattico*, facsimile ed. (1673; Hildesheim: Olms, 1969), 10–23.
22. William Bathe, *A Briefe Introduction to the Skill of Song,* facsimile ed., ed. Bernarr Rainbow (1587; Kilkenny, Ireland: Boethius Press, 1982), B–B2v.

Hasty and the historical theorists both offer theories of unequal triple meter based on the inescapable duple foundations of their systems. While the sixteenth- and seventeenth-century theorists were unapologetic and took this as a matter of course, Hasty expresses concern:

> The reader may have had the suspicion that the preceding account of deferral is an attempt, like Hauptmann's, to fit the round peg of triple meter into the square hole of *Paarigkeit*, or an attempt to reduce triplicity to an underlying duplicity. In defense of this account (or at least to keep the question open), I assure the reader that I would not present the hypothesis of deferral if I did not think it justified primarily on experiential grounds.[23]

Hasty feels the need to present a defense of his account, though it shares its duple bias with many theories of triple meter for which there was never a defense needed. Responding to the prevailing belief in which meter is understood through equal division and hierarchy, Hasty has to motivate for his distinctive theory and assure his readers that he does not intend to "reduce triplicity to an underlying duplicity." By contrast, for the sixteenth- and seventeenth-century theorists, as too for the nineteenth-century theorist Hauptmann, the twoness of meter was more fundamental and basic than the particularity of triples.[24]

Perhaps, then, we might profitably attempt the exercise that makes Hasty defensive: fitting, without apology, "the round peg of triple meter into the square hole of *Paarigkeit*," and taking this misshapenness as our starting point.[25] We might bring to triple meter a renewed perspective of inequality, taking our cue from Hasty but with attention to the particular inequality that the historical theorists had in mind. This distorted view of triple meter has insights to offer our contemporary theories of meter that concern more than a strange way of dividing. It offers an opportunity to reassess a way of knowing meter and understanding division that our contemporary theories have all but evened out of existence.

Inequality

Fore-Dances and After-Dances

Unequal triple meter was a familiar concept for musicians of the sixteenth and seventeenth centuries, and several practical procedures of music making reflect this. One of the more potent examples is the process of deriving a triple meter instrumental after-dance from its duple-meter fore-dance. In many of these derivations, musicians produced triple-meter dances simply through the doubling in duration of the

23. Hasty, *Meter as Rhythm*, 135.
24. For an explication of Hauptmann's system, see Roger Mathew Grant, "Four Hundred Years of Meter: Theories, Ideologies, and Technologies of Musical Periodicity since 1611" (PhD diss., University of Pennsylvania, 2010), 231–63.
25. Hasty, *Meter as Rhythm*, 135. Incidentally, I'm not sure why it isn't a triangular peg.

first half of each *battuta* or *tactus*.[26] This left the players with an unequal triple meter clearly dependent on an equal duple. These after-dances went by many names, including the *rotta*, *espringale*, saltarello, *piva, tourdion*, galliard, *tripla, sciolta*, and *Proportz*.[27] Morley, in *A Plaine and Easie Introduction to Practicall Musicke* (1597), describes this practice in the context of the galliard specifically:

> After every pavane we usually set a galliard (that is, a kind of music made out of the other), causing it go by a measure, which the learned call "trochaicam ratio-nem," consisting of a long and short stroke successivelie, for as the foote *tro-chaeus* consisteth of one syllable of two times and another of one time so is the first of these two strokes double to the latter, the first beeing in time of a semibrefe and the latter of a minime. This is a lighter and more stirring kinde of dauncing than the pavane, consisting of the same number of straines, and looke how manie foures of semibreves, you put in the straine of your pavan, so many times sixe minimes must you put in the straine of your galliard.[28]

Morley describes a type of triple music "made out of" duple music, in which a trochaic construction of the beat results from the doubling of a duple-meter dance's first half-*tactus*. This was a fitting of the round peg of triple meter into the square hole of duple meter in practice, and it was taken as a matter of course.

So foundational was this conception of triple meter that the procedure for turning duple dances into triple dances was sometimes improvised on the spot. Arbeau, in his dance treatise *Orchésographie* (1589), could instruct his student Capriol to find additional basse dances in other volumes, even if the volumes to which he referred contained only dances printed in duple meter.

> CAPRIOL: *I would have liked very much for you to have inscribed five or six pavans and as many basse dances for me.*
>
> ARBEAU: *You can find a great number of these in the books of danceries printed by the late Attaignant, who lived near the church of St. Cosmo in Paris, and in the books of the late Master Nicholas du Chemin, printer in the said Paris, at the sign of the Silver Lion: however, you will have to re-render in triple meter the aforementioned basse dances, which are there set in duple meter.*[29]

---

26. *Oxford Music Online*, ed. Laura Macy, s.v. "Nachtanz," by Suzanne Cusick, accessed August 25, 2009, <www.oxfordmusiconline.com>; Daniel Heartz, "Hoftanz and Basse Dance," *Journal of the American Musicological Society* 19, no. 1 (1966): 21–25.
27. These are the varieties of after-dance listed in Suzanne Cusick's "Nachtanz."
28. Thomas Morley, *A Plaine and Easie Introduction to Practicall Musicke…*(London: Peter Short, 1597), 181.
29. "Capriol: l'eusse bien voulu que m'eussiez mis par escript cinq ou six pavanes, & autant de basse dances. Arbeau: Vous en treuverez assez grand nombre dedans les livres de danceries imprimez par seu Attaignant, qui demeuroit pres l'Eglise sainct Cosme à Paris, & dedans les livres de seu maistre Nicolas du Chemin Imprimeur audit Paris, à l'enseigne du Lion d'argent: Toutefois, il vous fauldra reduire en mesure ternaire lesdictes bass-dances, lesquelles sont mises en mesure binaire." Thoinot Arbeau, *Orchésographie* (Langres: Jehan des Preyz, 1589), 37–38v.

There were several composers, however, who provided notation for these derived, triple-meter after-dances (perhaps because, as Isaac Posch noted in 1618, the practice of improvising them did not always produce the best results).[30] The relationships between these notated triple-meter dances and the duple-meter dances from which they are derived vary. Schein's *Banchetto musicale* (1617) provides examples of pairs with fairly direct relationships. The Allemande and Tripla from this volume's first set of dances are reproduced below as example 3.2. Dotted barlines are added to this example for ease of reading. Each "measure" is equivalent to one full *tactus*.

These two pieces are nearly identical in pitch and differ significantly only in rhythm and meter. In most cases, whatever durations are present within the first minim of each *tactus* in the duple Allemande are exactly doubled in the Tripla (resulting in a dotted-semibreve span for a full *tactus* here). Take for example the first four measures. Everything within the first portion of the Allamande's *tactus* can be found in the first portion of the Tripla's *tactus*, though the latter lasts a full semibreve while the former takes only a minim. The second portion of the *tactus* lasts a minim in both the Allamande and the Triple, and contains more or less the same material. There are some minor changes to this basic pattern; the dotted rhythm in the second measure of the Allamande is smoothed over in the Tripla, for example. The other change works to an interesting effect: Susato prepares the Allamande's third measure suspension with one semiminim of C in the tenor, and manages to supply the same duration of preparation for that suspension in the Tripla as well. He is able to do this by augmenting the preceding D by three times (rendering it a dotted minim). In so doing he preserves the place of the preparation, suspension, and resolution in the measure, which falls on the second part of the *tactus* in both the Allamande and the Tripla. The resulting tenor rhythm in the Tripla is somewhat awkward, and it is perhaps for this reason that Schein does not attempt the procedure when the suspension should be in the soprano (as it is in all of the other cases). Instead he forgoes the suspension altogether. Other minor variations occur throughout, in which dotted rhythms (mm. 2, 6, 10, and 14) and syncopations (mm. 7, 11, and 15) are simplified for the Tripla version. But generally Schein expands the thematic material found in the first minim span of each full *tactus* in the Allemande to the length of a semibreve span in the Tripla. The result is a triple composition that sounds nearly identical in pitch content to its duple model, but very different in feeling and in meter.

Other after-dances capture the feeling of their fore-dances without converting their durations so exactly. The Salterelle (no. 22) from Susato's *Danserye* (1551), for example, does not render anew every note of the Ronde VI (no. 18), its model (these are shown below in example 3.3; dotted barlines are again added for ease of reading). In contrast to Schein's approach, Susato adds rhythmic variety to accomplish the augmentation of the first semibreve span; rather than converting the first two semiminims of the soprano in the third *tactus*

---

30. Cusick, in "Nachtanz," refers to Isaac Posch's preface to his *Musicalische Ehrenfreudt* of 1618.

Example 3.2 Schein, Allemande and Tripla from the first suite of the *Banchetto musicale* (1617).

into minims, Susato instead triples the length of the first to a dotted minim, leaving the second a semiminim. Elsewhere Susato alters the music in order to create a triple meter with an anacrustic tug. Already in the first measure of the Salterelle he adds dominant harmony in the final minim. He repeats this procedure in the ninth measure, and the eighth measure's last minim features a subdominant harmony not present in the Ronde VI. Where the duple-meter Ronde has semibreve spans, Susato adds a rearticulation in the last minim of the triple-meter version (as in the second measure) that further propels the anacrustic motion forward.

These examples illustrate particularly revealing instances of unequal triple meter because we know the duple-meter music from which they were derived. The process of conversion that renders these after-dances triples serves to highlight the particular design of three with which they were constructed; not all beats were created equal, so to speak, in their composition. Their triple meter is closer to our contemporary understanding of other unequal meters—meters in fives and sevens—than it is to our contemporary understanding of triple meter. The unequal way of knowing meter that is integral to their design and is made clear in comparison with their duple equivalents points out the strange flatness

Example 3.3 Susato, Ronde VI (no. 18) and Salterelle (no. 22) from *Danserye* (1551).

Example 3.3 Continued

in our recent theories of triple meter.[31] These pieces provide a perspective on how inequality may have shaped the composition, performance, and experience of triple-meter music. It is clear that this way of knowing is vastly different from the hierarchical weightings our contemporary theories presuppose.

31. A major point here is not to confuse the issue of meter with that of either dance patterns or dance rhythms, both of which contribute to the feel of the pieces that are discussed above (and indeed, the semibreve, minim pair that makes up a good deal of these two pieces in particular is an important constituent of many dance rhythms).

To take just one theory as an example, the dot notation of Lerdahl and Jackendoff's *A Generative Theory of Tonal Music* falls short of accounting for what is at work in the meter of these pieces. Example 3.4 shows two applications of their notation to mm. 17–24 of the Ronde VI and Salterelle from Susato's *Danserye*. The first, *a*, represents the traditional, contemporary conception of meter that their theory prescribes. This interpretation has difficulty in reflecting the organization of the triple Salterelle, especially in that it makes no distinction between the second and third minims. The second application, *b*, represents a modification of the notation for the Salterelle, in which the analysis of duple meter in the Ronde VI is converted into unequal triple meter along with the music. This modified analysis is simply a distorted form of the analysis of duple meter and would not qualify as an acceptable reading or "well-formed" meter for Lerdahl and Jackendoff.[32] Each first beat has been stretched to exactly twice its length, rendering the measure unequal

Example 3.4 a, Traditional Lerdahl and Jackendoff meter analysis for mm. 17–24 of Susato's Ronde VI (no. 18) and Salterelle (no. 22) from the *Danserye*; *b*, a modified version of this analysis for the Salterelle; and *c*, detailed comparison between the Ronde and Salterelle, mm. 17–18.

32. See Lerdahl and Jackendoff, *A Generative Theory of Tonal Music*, 68–74.

Example 3.4 Continued

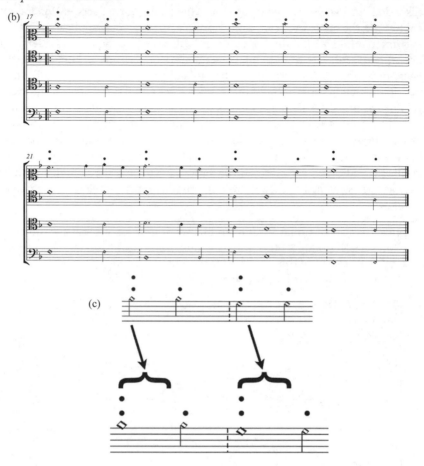

(as shown in *c*). This distorted analysis readjusts the metric hierarchy in order to reflect the process of rendering unequal triple from duple.

The pieces discussed above were the historical manifestations of a way of knowing meter. The always-unequal division of triple meter provided in the two-part motion of the beat was the guiding principle of this and much more music in the early modern era. Apart from suggesting modifications for our theories of triple meter, these pieces also supply models against which we might compare other repertoires. They invite us to envision yet other pieces under the same distorted lens: to see the inequality hiding just behind the surface of music in an otherwise familiar meter, or to be sensitive (at the very least) to the possibility of unequal division in triple settings.

Coherence in Inequality

Triple-meter after-dances reveal a telling coherence in the first part of their unequal measures. As a further example from Schein will demonstrate, this

Example 3.5 a, Schein, second Allemande and Tripla pair from the *Banchetto musicale* (1617), mm. 17–24 (third strain) of both, showing harmonic rhythm and half-*tactus* marks; and *b*, detailed comparison, mm. 17 and 19.

Example 3.5 Continued

(b)

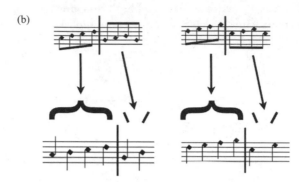

coherence is an integral part of their construction of unequal triple meter. The third strains of the second Allemande and Tripla pair from the *Banchetto musicale* appear below as example 3.5. Dotted barlines are added for ease of reference. Each measure corresponds to a full *tactus*. Two particular points of interest in the musical design of these passages are pertinent to the transformation from duple to triple. The first concerns the patterning of harmonic shifts, or what Walter Piston would eventually name the "harmonic rhythm."[33] In the duple-meter Allemande, the harmony changes at each half-*tactus* point, as marked in the example (a minim in duration). In addition to these shifts, the harmonic rhythm of mm. 18, 20, and 23 features divisions in half of the first minim duration, while m. 22 features a division in half of the second minim duration. In the Tripla, the consistent shift in the harmonic rhythm is located after the first semibreve within each *tactus*, dividing mm. 17, 19, and 21 unequally. Mm. 18, 20, and 23 show divisions in half of this initial semibreve; what was contained in one minim in the duple measures is now spread over two minims. M. 22 is the only unique measure in its treatment of harmonic rhythm—here it is the second half of the duple *tactus* that appears expanded over the second two-thirds of the same *tactus* in the Tripla.

The melodic structure of the strain interlocks with the patterns of its harmonic rhythm. Each measure in which the harmonic rhythm moves only once (mm. 17, 19, and 21) supports a melody of running fusae. Between these measures are two of the measures in which the harmonic rhythm changes twice, mm. 18 and 20; these measures continue the running fusae from the measures that preceded them and conclude the line in a minim cadence, thus thematically bisecting the *tactus* in half. The thematic material in the Tripla bisects the measures unequally, again following on the first semibreve duration. The material from the first minims of the duple measures appears, doubled in duration, in the first semibreves of the triple measures, while the second minims of the duple measures are condensed in the last minim durations of the triple measures (shown in example 3.5b). This is true also for the penultimate measure of the strain. Schein's

---

33. Walter Piston, *Harmony* (New York: Norton, 1944), 41–44.

Tripla sounds characteristically halting, especially because the melodic material in the first portion of many of its measures is identical to its matching Allamande. The minim span that follows consequentially sounds cut off or abbreviated, rushing too quickly on to the next bit of melodic material.

In Schein's Tripla, harmonic and thematic movement create coherence for the first two-thirds of each triple *tactus*. When compared with its duple model, this coherence is evident—the first two-thirds of each triple measure are derived from the first half of the duple measures. But the coherence is a property of the Tripla itself, irrespective of its model; it makes clear and sensible the division of the *tactus* into unequal parts. It is this type of coherence that we might investigate in other instances of triple meters, particularly those instances that are not clearly derived from a duple model.

Such coherence is still evident in triple-meter works of the late seventeenth century. Purcell's triple-meter choruses provide excellent examples. His chorus "Come all and sing" from *The Indian Queen* (1695) is shown below in example 3.6. Again, it is the harmonic and thematic elements in this piece that lend favor to an unequal interpretation of its triple meter. The anacrustic nature of its melodies, initiated from the start, predisposes the thematic material toward a "trochaic" organization (to borrow this use of the term from Morley) within each measure. The quarter notes, on each third beat, often initiate new melodic motion, or depart thematically from the material in the first half note. These thematic shifts—which, as in the Schein Tripla, divide the measure unequally—are supported with harmonic shifts and changes in inversion. Although not derived from any duple model, Purcell's chorus solicits a similar understanding of unequal triple meter.[34]

Clearly, though, not every element of the harmony and thematic material is forever in lock step with this organization, and Purcell's chorus provides a few moments in which the rhythm would seem to cut across the metric grain in syncopation. These moments are excerpted in example 3.7, below. They show an unequal division of the measure that is the opposite of the typical organization; instead of half note plus quarter note, these measures give us organization in an unequal quarter note plus half note form, as in m. 77. Here the melodic material and harmonic rhythm align in an abrupt shift, after a single quarter note on the word "night," for what sounds like a very early "ap-[pear]." The same pattern is present in the measures preceding two strong cadences, the first in m. 87 and the second in m. 93.

Taken together with the material that precedes these measures we have what we today call the cadential hemiola, a technique with a long history of its own.[35]

34. It is important to note here that iamb and trochee work in tandem in this example as they often do in instances of unequal triple meter: viewed from the perspective of the anacrustic melody and its prosody, the passage is an example of iambic organization, which the musical meter organizes in a trochaic fashion with the longer duration on the downbeat. For more on questions related to the difference between downbeat and prosodic accent, see chapter 8.

35. Twenty-first century secondary sources on the history of the cadential hemiola leave much to be desired, but see the early and still important work of Michael Collins, in "The Performance of

Example 3.6 Purcell, "Come all and sing" from *The Indian Queen* (1695).

bright Than thou-sands, than thou-sands, thou-sands, than thou - sands of vic - to - rious days, than

bright Than thou-sands, than thou-sands, thou-sands, than thou - sands of vic - to - rious days, than

bright Than thou-sands, than thou-sands, thou - sands of vic - to - rious days, than

bright Than thou-sands, than thou - - - - sands of vic - tor-rious days, than

thou-sands, than thou - sands, thou-sands, than thou - sands of vic - to - rious days.

thou-sands, than thou - sands, thou-sands, than thou - sands of vic - to - rious days.

thou-sands, than thou - sands, thou - sands, thou-sands of vic - to - rious days.

thou-sands, than thou - - - - sands of vic - to - rious days.

Example 3.7 Excerpts highlighting syncopation from Purcell, "Come all and sing" from *The Indian Queen* (1695).

This particular type of syncopation was familiar to the theorists of the period and did not go unaccounted for; in fact, some proposed the renewed use of the then-antiquated blackening of notes to identify it.[36] To clarify, Penna wrote: "If you come upon some black Breves and some black Semibreves that are positioned to indicate a syncopation, assess these as though they were white," and gave the example that follows below in plate 3.3 (shown in updated notation in example 3.8).[37]

The semibreve and breve in the third measure of Penna's example are blackened even though they are meant to express the same durations they otherwise would if they were open noteheads. The type of blackening Penna's example accounted for was a midpoint in the transformation from unbarred white mensural notation to modern notation. Hemiolas in the earlier forms of notation were blackened in their entirety; take for example the hemiola in the opening of the bass

Plate 3.3 Blackening used to indicate syncopation in Penna's *Li Primi albori musicali* (Bologna: Giacomo Monti, 1684), 37.

Example 3.8 Adapted from plate 3.3: Syncopation in Penna's *Li Primi albori musicali* shown in updated notation.

Sesquialtera and Hemiolia in the 16th Century," *Journal of the American Musicological Society* 17, no. 1 (1964): 5–28; and idem., "The Performance of Coloration, Sesquialtera, and Hemiola (1450–1750)," (PhD diss., Stanford University, 1963).

36. Here and elsewhere I use the term syncopation in its traditional sense to denote a feeling of arriving early or late.

37. "Si trovano alle volte alcune Bervi nere, & alcune Semibervi nere, che sono poste per la sincopazione, queste vagliono, come se fossero bianche," Penna, *Li Primi albori musicali*, 37. On the other hand, Bononcini's account of the same phenomenon dismisses this notational practice, arguing that it is not used by composers of worth (citing Morales, Porta, and Palestrina to make his point). His position confirms that it was, indeed, a practice to be reckoned with at the time of his writing. See Bononcini, *Musico prattico*, 15.

Example 3.9 Josquin, Kyrie I, *Missa l'ami baudichon*, bass.

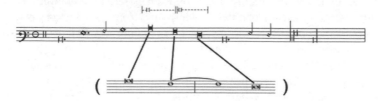

line to Josquin's Kyrie for the *Missa l'ami baudichon* (example 3.9). Here the hemiola is comprised of three blackened, imperfect breves that take the place of two perfect breves.

The technique that Penna felt the need to account for, by contrast, was a remnant of this older type of blackening. In the more updated technique, only the second half of the hemiola pattern was blackened, as in Penna's example above. The reason for the partial blackening was that, although blackening was no longer notationally necessary in the "modern" system, it was still used to mark the way the second half of the hemiola pattern cut across the normative division of triple meter; only the second half of the hemiola, in Penna's example and in many period examples, disturbed the unequal division of the measure by displacing the normal division (instead of breve, semibreve, the second half of the hemiola pattern divides the measure into semibreve, breve).

Exemplary for its use of this updated blackening technique is Claude Gervaise's *Sixième livre de danceries* (1555). Example 3.10 gives the Branle Courante I. Again, the triple meter is organized unequally, and the moments Gervaise departs from this consistent organization are set off neatly in black; these syncopations are, as in the Purcell example above, always the reverse of the predominant pattern (here semibreve followed by breve), and part of a hemiola followed by harmonic closure.

Although the use of this partial (or updated) blackening technique had dwindled by the time Purcell wrote his choruses and Penna published his treatise, the conception of triple meter that supported its logic had not;[38] it is for this reason that Penna must have felt justified in including his example. The unequal organization of triple meter—with the first part of the *tactus* twice as large as the second—was still prevalent, and so it made sense to recognize the practice of marking or blackening those measures that departed from this organization.

A Final Word on the Cadential Hemiola

If triple meter offers an extreme case of the distance between our contemporary theories and those of the early moderns, the cadential hemiola is the point of

---

38. Chapter 5 documents the continued use of this type of blackening in eighteenth-century manuscript copies of sixteenth-century music.

Example 3.10 Gervaise, Bransle Courante I from the *Sixième livre de danceries* (1555).

Example 3.10 Continued

furthest remove. Our contemporary understanding of the cadential hemiola is grounded in the same unspoken ideal of equal division that supports our theories of meter. More to the point, it specifically employs the mutability of this equal division to explain how two measures of three can be understood as three measures of two. The trend is as old as H. H. Wintersgill's classic 1936 identification a phenomenon he called "Handel's two-length bar."[39] More recent analytical studies have expanded the field of inquiry, identifying a variety of different hemiolas in Handel's music—not all cadential—and extrapolating their impact on large-scale structure and thematic design.[40] The final movement of Handel's Concerto no. 2 for Oboe in B-flat, HWV 301, shown in example 3.11, concludes with a classic example from the canon of eighteenth-century literature.[41]

The premise of the analyses that surround works like Handel's Concerto is that the hemiola creates a situation in which duple organization takes over momentarily; the perceived incongruity of the two types of organization is predicated on an understanding of both duple and triple as composed of equal-length parts. But the triple meter of Handel's Concerto shares much with the Purcell, Schein, Susato, and Gervaise works discussed above. This music too can be

39. H. H. Wintersgill, "Handel's Two-Length Bar," *Music and Letters* 17, no. 1 (1936): 1–12.

40. For example, see Channan Willner, "Metrical Displacement and Metrically Dissonant Hemiolas," *Journal of Music Theory* 57, no. 1 (2013): 87–118; Channan Willner, "The Two-Length Bar Revisited: Handel and the Hemiola," *Göttinger Händel-Beiträge* 4 (1991): 208–31; Channan Willner, "More on Handel and the Hemiola: Overlapping Hemiolas," *Music Theory Online* 2, no. 3 (1996), <http://mto.societymusictheory.org/issues/mto.96.2.3/mto.96.2.3.willner.html>, accessed August 28, 2009. David Schulenberg later responded to Willner's *MTO* article, criticizing it for its lack of interaction with the literature on performance practice; Willner responded to Schulenberg, rather creatively, with an essay on semiotics and genre. See David Schulenberg, "Commentary on Channan Willner, 'More on Handel and the Hemiola,'" *Music Theory Online* 2, no. 5 (1996), <http://mto.societymusictheory.org/issues/mto.96.2.5/mto.96.2.5.schulenberg.html>, accessed August 28, 2009; Channan Willner, "Handel, the Sarabande, and Levels of Genre, a Reply to David Schulenberg," *Music Theory Online* 2, no. 7 (1996), <http://mto.societymusictheory.org/issues/mto.96.2.7/mto.96.2.7.willner.html>, accessed August 28, 2009. See also Willner's related piece, "Sequential Expansion and Handelian Phrase Rhythm," in *Schenker Studies* 2, ed. Carl Schachter and Hedi Siegel (Cambridge: Cambridge University Press, 1999), 192–221.

41. As Robert Gjerdingen has noted, the cadential hemiola is most closely associated with what he calls the standard galant clausula, with a bass that rises through scale degrees 3, 4, and 5 before falling to the tonic. See Gjerdingen, *Music in the Galant Style* (Oxford: Oxford University Press, 2007), 168; on the standard galant clausula, 139–42.

known and understood in an unequal framework. The break from the prevailing pattern in m. 37 is reminiscent of Purcell's chorus and prepares the way for the rhythms of the cadence. The harmony on the downbeat of m. 38, occupying the first two quarter notes of that measure, is a momentary return to customary unequal organization before the predominant harmonies bring us to the cadential dominant on the second quarter note of m. 39.

If our contemporary hemiola analyses leave off historical inquiry, they are in one way right to do so: the hemiola patterns of centuries previous were rather different from those that often appear in the analytical literature. The hemiola in example 3.11, for instance, is composed of five vertical sonorities segmented across two measures, whereas the Josquin hemiola in example 3.9, above, consists of three sonorities of imperfect duration that take the place of two perfections. But what the lack of historical interest misses is an extra dimension of richness in hemiolas written in unequal triple meter. As in the other examples above, the sudden harmonic break on beat two of m. 39 in example 3.11 is a syncopation that simply displaces the form of the unequal measure. Following on a pattern of normal triple inequality, this syncopated inversion creates a two-measure pattern outlined abstractly in figure 3.3. A preceding unequal measure of triple meter, with its first part twice as long as its second, then leads to a measure constructed in the reverse, with its second part twice as long as its first.

What was different about hemiolas in unequal triple meter—which was neither in place when the hemiola practice originated, nor is recalled in analytical

Example 3.11 Handel, Concerto no. 2 for Oboe in B-flat, HWV 301, iv, mm. 33–40, showing the traditional cadential hemiola.

Figure 3.3 Normal triple inequality followed by a syncopated inversion.

literature today—was that the first part of many cadential hemiolas was actually the normative division of the measure, as shown in figure 3.3, and in Penna's example. For Penna, as for others who encountered and wrote hemiolas in his time, it was the second part of the hemiola that was marked, potentially blackened, and syncopated. Conceptually, then, the scenario depicted in figure 3.3 could result any time a triple measure hinted at an inversion of its unequal structure, or any time a syncopation such as described in Penna's treatise was included after a measure of unequal organization. This does not mean that such a moment is not a hemiola, but rather that this way of making a hemiola is actually much more than only three iterations of a "two-length bar." It is both a way of organizing duple groupings within a triple context and also a way in which two unequal duple groupings (one trochaic, one iambic) join each other to create a composite, symmetrical phenomenon that is made of four unequal—rather than three equal—parts.

All of this is not to say that every prevalent pattern is actually a meter, or that unequal triple divisions can be found everywhere. Still, our contemporary theories are not always best suited for the analytical work we want them to do. In the case of triple meter, they encourage a way of knowing and experiencing division that is uniform and abstract; they produce a flatness that cannot capture the sometimes distorted inequality of this meter. With the historical practices and theories presented here in mind, we might trouble our dearly held investment in equal division and graduated hierarchy. We might begin to approach pieces in triple meter with a sensitivity to the inequality that was once (in the words of Morley) their most "stirring" characteristic.[42]

42. Morley, *A Plaine and Easie Introduction to Practicall Musicke*, 101.

PART II

CHAPTER Four

Measuring Music

Meter, Measure, and Motion in Eighteenth-Century Music Theory

The long eighteenth century witnessed a dramatic transformation in the theorization of musical meter. The beat, once the basis for an idea of meter grounded in the logic of motion, became conceptually separated from the measure and lost its place of prominence in writings on the subject. Theorists struggled to come to terms with the newly emerging concept of the measure and endeavored to define its properties and attributes. The edifice that had once joined meter with character and tempo began to shatter. Theories of meter reflected a shift in the epistemological grounding of time itself over the course of the century. In this new view, time was no longer a conceptual descendant of motion but was its own conceptual category: a demarcated backdrop against which events were situated. Explained anew, meter was no longer a motion—the beat and the measure finally parted ways over the course of this transition.

No theoretical writing better encapsulates this reconceptualization of meter than Johann Philipp Kirnberger's *Die Kunst des reinen Satzes in der Musik* (1771–79). Kirnberger, a prominent Berlin musician, worked with his student Johann Peter Schulz in collaboration with Johann Georg Sulzer to produce the music articles for Sulzer's aesthetic encyclopedia, the *Allgemeine Theorie der schönen Künste*.[1] Kirnberger's theory treatise was the result of these

---

1. The collaboration of Kirnberger with his student, J. A. P. Schulz and the aesthetician J. G. Sulzer is well known. Just how these three individuals collaborated is less than clear. Schulz himself suggests that Kirnberger's *Die Kunst des reinen Satzes in der Musik* was the result of Kirnberger's teaching relationship to Sulzer; after organizing his thoughts on music theory in order to instruct Sulzer, Kirnberger simultaneously penned the articles on music from A–K for the *Allgemeine Theorie der schönen Künste* along with the first volume of his *Die Kunst des reinen Satzes in der Musik*. If there is influence from another individual in Kirnberger's writings on meter, though, it is more probably Schulz rather than Sulzer. Again according to Schulz's account, the music articles in Sulzer's *Allgemeine Theorie* from S–Z were executed by Schulz under Kirnberger's guidance, without Sulzer's assistance (Schulz and Sulzer collaborated on the music articles from L–S).

collaborations. The reception of this text in recent secondary scholarship perfectly illustrates the interior tensions that are fundamental to it. On the one hand, twentieth- and twenty-first century scholars laud Kirnberger's theory of meter as a transformative landmark in the history of music theory.[2] Kirnberger reconceived of measure division as a result of the accents applied to certain tones in the ongoing flow of time. In order to do so he imagined an endless string of undifferentiated durations, which he depicted as the figure reproduced in plate 4.1. He then imagined the different ways in which one might divide this flow of

Both Kirnberger's treatise and the musical entries from S–Z (including the article *Takt*) were written roughly around the same time. I have chosen to identify Kirnberger as the author of the theory of meter and have chosen to discuss the theory as it is presented in *Die Kunst des reinen Satzes in der Musik* for the following reasons: regarding authorship, Sulzer credits the collaborations of Kirnberger and Schulz for his *Allgemeine Theorie*, while Kirnberger claims sole authorship of his *Die Kunst des reinen Satzes in der Musik*. This suggests that ideas in this theoretical work belonged to Kirnberger, and those that made it to the *Allgemeine Theorie* as well should be understood as primarily his. I focus on the writings in *Die Kunst des reinen Satzes in der Musik* because it is here that the theory of meter is presented in its most developed form. The authorship of *Die Kunst des reinen Satzes in der Musik* and the *Allgemeine Theorie der schönen Künste* was first discussed in J. A. P. Schulz's "Über die in Sulzers Theorie der schönen Künste unter dem Artikel Verrückung angeführten zwey Beispiele. . .," *Allgemeine musikalishe Zeitung* [Leipzig] 2, no. 16 (January 15, 1800): col. 273–80. The best secondary source on this issue remains David Beach, "The Harmonic Theories of Johann Philipp Kirnberger: Their Origins and Influences" (PhD diss., Yale University, 1974), 7–13; additional sources include Danuta Mirka's *Metric Manipulations in Haydn and Mozart* (Oxford: Oxford University Press, 2009), 3–4n3; Claus Bockmaier, *Die instrumentale Gestalt des Taktes* (Tutzing: Hans Schneider, 2001), 256; Nancy K. Baker's partial translation of Heinrich Christoph Koch's *Versuch einer Anleitung zur Composition* as *Introductory Essay on Composition: The Mechanical Rules of Melody, Sections 3 and 4* (New Haven: Yale University Press, 1983), xviin19; and Thomas Christensen, "Introduction," in *Aesthetics and the Art of Musical Composition in the German Enlightenment*, ed. Nancy K. Baker and Thomas Christensen (Cambridge: Cambridge University Press, 1995), 14.

2. Wilhelm Seidel was the first to point out the innovation of Kirnberger and his circle, in *Über Rhythmustheorien der Neuzeit* (Bern: Francke, 1975), 85–134. He returned to this topic again in a later piece, "Division und Progression: Zum Begriff der musikalischen Zeit im 18. Jahrhundert," *Il saggiatore musicale* 2, no. 1 (1995): 47–65. Seidel's ideas on this issue were taken up in Carl Dahlhaus, *Die Musiktheorie im 18. und 19. Jahrhundert. Zweiter Teil: Deutschland*, Geschichte der Musiktheorie 6, ed. Ruth E. Müller (Darmstadt: Wissenschaftliche Buchgesellschaft, 1989), 157–73; Bockmaier, *Die instrumentale Gestalt des Taktes*, 255–60; William Caplin, "Theories of Musical Rhythm in the Eighteenth and Nineteenth Centuries," in *The Cambridge History of Western Music Theory*, ed. Thomas Christensen (Cambridge: Cambridge University Press, 2002), 666–68; Danuta Mirka, *Metric Manipulations in Haydn and Mozart*; Roger Mathew Grant, "Epistemologies of Time and Metre in the Long Eighteenth Century," *Eighteenth-Century Music* 6, no. 1 (2009): 59–75; and Tomas McAuley, "Rhythmic Accent and the Absolute: Sulzer, Schelling and the *Akzenttheorie*," *Eighteenth-Century Music* 10, no. 2 (2013): 277–86. The idea that the conceptualization of meter changed in the eighteenth century more generally is older than all of this literature, and can be traced at least to the writings of Thrsybulos G. Georgiades. See Georgiades, "Aus der Musiksprache des Mozart Theaters," in *Mozart-Jahrbuch* 1950, reprinted in *Kleine Schriften*, ed. Theodor Göllner (Tutzing: Hans Schneider, 1977), 9–32; idem., "Zur Musiksprache der Wiener Klassiker," in *Mozart-Jahrbuch* 1951, reprinted in *Kleine Schriften*, 33–43; and idem., *Nennen und Erklingen* (Göttingen: Vandenhoeck und Ruprecht, 1985). The genealogy traced here bares resemblance to that given in Georgiades's *Nennen und Erklingen*, though our musical sources are quite different.

Plate 4.1 A string of undifferentiated durations, from Kirnberger's *Die Kunst des reinen Satzes in der Musik*, facsimile ed. (1771–79; Hildesheim: Georg Olms, 1968), 2:115.

Plate 4.2 The division of these durations into groups of two, three, or four beats, from Kirnberger's *Die Kunst des reinen Satzes in der Musik*, facsimile ed. (1771–79; Hildesheim: Georg Olms, 1968), 2:115.

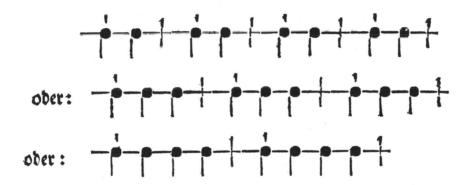

duration: into groups of two, three, or four beats, as he depicted in the figure reproduced as plate 4.2.

Several histories of meter theory view Kirnberger's contributions as transformative, and some scholars have suggested that his dynamic model of meter anticipates twentieth- and twenty-first-century theories of meter.[3] On the other hand, however, many contemporary scholars remember Kirnberger as a conservative bastion of outmoded teachings in the late eighteenth century. His theory of meter, after all, is followed by a twenty-page explanation of meter signatures as arcane and curious as 4/2 and 18/16.[4] Kirnberger's writings on meter, in this view, are an "exception" to the less-baroque theories of his contemporaries;[5]

3. Seidel, *Über Rhythmustheorien der Neuzeit*, 85–134; Dahlhaus, *Die Musiktheorie im 18. und 19. Jahrhundert. Zweiter Teil: Deutschland*, ed. Ruth E. Müller, 157–73; Caplin, "Theories of Musical Rhythm in the Eighteenth and Nineteenth Centuries," in *The Cambridge History of Western Music Theory*, ed. Christensen, 666–68; the later point is made by Mirka in *Metric Manipulations in Haydn and Mozart*. McAuley, in "Rhythmic Accent and the Absolute," focuses on the article "Rhythmus" in Sulzer's *Allgemeine Theorie der schönen Künste*.

4. Johann Philipp Kirnberger, *Die Kunst des reinen Satzes in der Musik*, facsimile ed. (1771–79; Hildesheim: Georg Olms, 1968), 2:117–36.

5. This contextualization in particular belongs to Claudia Maurer Zenck, in her *Vom Takt: Überlegungen zur Theorie und kompositorischen Praxis im augehenden 18. und beginnenden 19. Jahrhundert* (Vienna: Böhlau, 2001), 325. In general, though, see Nicole Schwindt-Gross,

furthermore, this view of Kirnberger's writings accords well with the often-repeated assertion that his teachings were generally conservative, and meant to preserve the lessons of his former teacher, J. S. Bach.[6]

The juxtaposition between the old and the new in Kirnberger's treatise is representative of eighteenth-century meter theory itself. Understanding this apparent contradiction is key to understanding the place of meter in the reconceptualization of time. With the slow separation of the concept of meter from the act of beating time, theorists endeavored to identify the nature of the measure and, eventually, the properties of the various types of measures and meter signatures. Concerned about the waning connections between meter, character, and tempo, theorists of the mid- and late-eighteenth century produced lengthy tracts detailing the legacy of these very associations.[7] The result was what I call a "multiplicity of measures": a proliferation of information on the measure and on every possible meter signature. At the peak of this tradition, certain theorists thought it time to simplify meter and to provide a theory that would account for the generation of all of the diverse signatures. These proposed reforms sought to reign in the unwieldy description of "times" and instead to describe a singular time. Kirnberger provided one such theory. In so doing, he adopted the language of time as an absolute quantity.

Why, in his formulation of one of music's most basic elements, did Kirnberger make recourse to an imagined, unending stream of undifferentiated durations? The recasting of meter in Kirnberger's theory and the imagery that came with it participated in a new understanding of time as an absolute "flow"—a dynamic quantity independent of the events that it had theretofore only measured. This new conception redrew the relationship between time and motion. Whereas in the older doctrine time had measured motion—just as the beat had measured music—now time was its own motion. Discourses on natural philosophy and mathematics—particularly the calculus—divorced time from the category of *motus* and, slowly, disseminated the image of time as an absolute flow. Meter as Kirnberger conceived it, then, was the situation of accents and measure divisions within the ongoing flow of time.

"Einfache, zusammengesetzte und doppelt notierte Takte: Ein Aspekt der Takttheorie im 18. Jahrhundert," *Musiktheorie* 4, no. 3 (1989): 203–22; and also certain portions of Mirka's *Metric Manipulations in Haydn and Mozart*, particularly 10.

6. See, for instance, *Oxford Music Online*, s.v. "Kirnberger, Johann Philipp," by Howard Serwer, accessed March 15, 2010, <www.oxfordmusiconline.org>; and David W. Beach, introduction to Kirnberger, *The Art of Strict Musical Composition*, trans. Beach and Jurgen Thym (New Haven: Yale University Press, 1982), xvi–xviii.

7. By character, I mean the distinctive use of rhythmic, melodic, and or harmonic compositional resources in such a way that would have been legible within eighteenth-century semiotic systems. See for instance Kirnberger's use of the term in *Die Kunst des reinen Satzes in der Musik*, 105ff. In the German tradition, the term character (*Charakter*) eventually became associated with the ability of instrumental music to express the emotions of the composer. This transformation is treated in chapter 8, but see also Richard Will, *The Characteristic Symphony in the Age of Haydn and Beethoven* (Cambridge: Cambridge University Press, 2002), 4–5; and Matthew Pritchard, "'The Moral Background of the Work of Art': 'Character' in German Musical Aesthetics, 1780-1850," *Eighteenth-Century Music* 9, no. 1 (2012): 63–80.

Once wrapped up with the expression of motion, now time had become its own category: an ongoing substrate that existed independently of any and all terrestrial events and beings. It was precisely in its divorce from the measurement of these earthly events that natural philosophers and metaphysicians began to describe time as a motion itself. Alongside this transformation in time, eighteenth-century theorists found new ways of imagining the beat, the measure, and finally, meter.

A Transformation in Time

Kirnberger's theory was written in a Berlin roiled with debates on the nature of time. The Berlin Academy was host to acrimonious disputes on the issue, and the intellectual journals of the day documented each quarrel.[8] The intensity of the debate in the Prussian capital was representative of its impact across the continent, as the learned world grappled with the significance of new developments in natural philosophy and metaphysics.[9] Since the mid-seventeenth century, discourses in natural philosophy had begun to reorganize the network of relationships between time and motion. This change was registered in multiple developments, and took technological as well as material and aesthetic forms.[10] Through the eighteenth century, the name most frequently attached to this restructuring of terms was Isaac Newton.

Newton's own revisionary metaphysical writings on the nature of time and space resulted from his efforts to understand force and geometry.[11] He framed his first attempts to do so against Descartes, the philosopher he countered in much of his speculative and practical writings alike. For Newton, it was Descartes who best represented the continued Scholastic tradition in which time was conceptualized under the rubric of *motus*.[12] In Descartes's view both time and space were

8. The most comprehensive history of the Berlin Academy (The Royal Academy of Sciences and Belles-Lettres) is Adolf von Harnack's massive documentary account and index, the *Geschichte der Königlich preussischen Akademie der Wissenschaften zu Berlin* (Berlin: Reichsdruckerei, 1900); a concise account can be found in Lewis White Beck, *Early German Philosophy* (Cambridge: Harvard University Press, 1969), 314–24.

9. For a summary, see Emily Grosholz, "Space and Time," in *The Oxford Handbook of Philosophy in Early Modern Europe*, ed. Desmond M. Clarke and Catherine Wilson (Oxford: Oxford University Press, 2011), 51–70.

10. Technological and material forms are discussed in chapter 5.

11. For a more detailed treatment of Newton's metaphysics, see Andrew Janiak, *Newton as Philosopher* (Cambridge: Cambridge University Press, 2008), particularly 130–62; Howard Stein, "Newton's Metaphysics," in *The Cambridge Companion to Newton*, ed. I. Bernard Cohen and George E. Smith (Cambridge: Cambridge University Press, 2002), 256–307; and Robert Rynasiewicz, "By Their Properties, Causes and Effects: Newton's Scholium on Time, Space, Place and Motion. II: The Context," *Studies in History and Philosophy of Science* 26, no. 2 (1995): 295–322.

12. This term is impoverished in its English translations, which renders it either "motion," or "change." See chapters 1 and 2.

entirely full of the things that they described, in the sense that they did not exist outside of them.[13] For this reason, Descartes's ideas on space and time can be characterized as *plenist*. Newton, by contrast, attempted to envision time and space as categories distinct from that which they measured: absolute, nonrelative frameworks within which to situate events and bodies. He codified this approach to the nature of time and space in the Scholium on *tempus, spatium, locus*, and *motus* in his *Principia* of 1687.

> Absolute, true and mathematical time [*tempus*], of itself, and from its own nature, flows equably without relation to anything external, and by another name is called duration [*duratio*]: relative, apparent and common [*vulgare*] time, is some sensible and external (whether accurate or unequable) measure of duration by means of motion [*per motum mensura*], which is commonly used instead of true [absolute] time: such as an hour, a day, a month, a year.[14]

In this initial definition for *tempus*, Newton formally articulated the separation of "true" time from motion. Absolute, true, mathematical time is said to unfold "without relation" to external motions, while relative, apparent, common (or vulgar) time is a measure of duration *per motum mensura*. The latter is the quintessence of the Scholastic understanding of time, which persisted in certain strains of thought as late as the writings of Kirnberger's contemporaries in mid-eighteenth-century Berlin.[15]

Newton's separation of time from motion was one articulation of a slow change that took place in the epistemological configuration of time and *motus*. His explicit formulation addressed a problem that had become more obvious with the disintegration of the Aristotelian cosmology: if the cosmos no longer contained perfectly regular celestial motions, then there could be no cosmic *motus* for time to describe. Astronomical observation had dismantled the universal cosmic clock. As Newton wrote further on in the Scholium, "It may be, that there is no such thing as an equable motion, whereby time may be accurately measured."[16]

13. René Descartes, *Principles of Philosophy*, trans. Valentine Rodger Miller and Reese P. Miller (Dordrecht: Reidel, 1983), xxiv. See also Stein, "Newton's Metaphysics," for an account of the relationship between the metaphysical systems of Newton and Descartes.

14. Isaac Newton, *Philosophiae naturalis principia mathematica*, third edition of 1726 with variant readings, ed. Alexandre Koyré and I. Bernard Cohen with the assistance of Anne Whitman (Cambridge: Harvard University Press, 1972), 1:46. Translation modified from Richard T. W. Arthur, "Newton's Fluxions and Equably Flowing Time," *Studies in the History and Philosophy of Science* 26, no. 2 (1995): 323–51, at 324.

15. Specifically the Leibnizians and Wolffians of the Berlin Academy, as discussed below.

16. Newton, *Philosophiae naturalis principia mathematica* translated as *Sir Isaac Newton's Mathematical Principles of Natural Philosophy and His System of the World*, trans. Andrew Motte in 1729, revised translation by Florian Cajori (Berkeley: University of California Press, 1934), 7–8. As Rynasiewicz points out, "The modality here is that of physical possibility, not epistemic uncertainty," since Newton discusses planetary motions that he finds to be regular. Rynasiewicz, "By Their Properties, Causes and Effects: Newton's Scholium on Time, Space, Place and Motion. II: The Context," 142n19. On this point see also Arthur, "Newton's Fluxions and Equably Flowing Time," 344–51.

The classic accounts of Alexander Koyré and Edward Grant narrate the gradual transformation of astronomical knowledge in the seventeenth century, in which the writings of Bernardino Telesio, Giordano Bruno, Pierre Gassendi, and their contemporaries overturned the Scholastic teachings and "opened" the universe.[17] Acknowledging the absence of a single, uniform motion in the cosmos, these seventeenth-century thinkers were forced to conclude either 1) that time described the measure of any motion, and that no motion could describe a universal time (as Bruno held), or 2) that time might not be the measure of any motion at all (as Gassendi and Isaac Barrow indicated).[18] The absence of a universal cosmological timekeeper forced thinkers to choose between the existence of multiple, local "times," or a very different sort of universal time. Setting aside for a moment the matter of innovative priority, the crucial point to remember about the concept of this new, absolute time is that it first gained significant discursive and philosophical traction in the dissemination of Newton's natural philosophy and mathematics. With the astronomical observations of the seventeenth century in place, it was Newton's method and framework—particularly in mathematical topics—that became the basis for the "Newton wars" at the origins of the Enlightenment.[19] It should be no surprise, then, that one of Newton's most hotly debated innovations should also be one of the best examples of time and motion reconfigured: the Newtonian calculus. Even before writing the *Principia*, Newton's flowing, absolute time was already the basis for many of his geometrical and mathematical attainments.[20] This conception of time as a flow is part of a genealogy that stretches through late-eighteenth century Berlin.

Time's Flow and the Newtonian Calculus

For all of the importance attached to the new relationship between time and motion in Newton's redrawn natural philosophy, it might seem odd that he should describe absolute time as a kind of flow. Why would Newton appeal to a

17. Alexandre Koyré, *From the Closed World to the Infinite Universe* (Baltimore: The Johns Hopkins Press, 1957); Edward Grant, *Much Ado about Nothing* (Cambridge: Cambridge University Press, 1981).
18. Milič Čapek examines these choices alongside the incipient articulations of absolute time before Newton in "The Conflict between the Absolutist and the Relational Theory of Time Before Newton," *Journal of the History of Ideas* 48, no. 4 (1987): 595–608.
19. This is the topic of J. B. Shank's monumental study, *The Newton Wars and the Beginning of the French Enlightenment* (Chicago: Chicago University Press, 2008).
20. In particular see Newton's "Methodus serierum et fluxionum," which was first published as *The Method of Fluxions and Infinite Series; with Its Application to the Geometry of Curve-Lines*, trans. John Colson (London: Printed by Henry Woodfall and sold by John Nourse, 1736); an edition and translation of this document is found in Derek T. Whiteside, ed. and trans., *The Mathematical Papers of Isaac Newton, volume III: 1670-1673* (Cambridge: Cambridge University Press, 1969), part I, 2, pp. 32–328; On the relationship of this document to Newton's development of the calculus, see Aleksandar Nikolić, "Space and Time in the Apparatus of Infinitesimal Calculus," *Novi Sad Journal of Mathematics* 23, no. 1 (1993): 199–218; and Arthur, "Newton's Fluxions and Equably Flowing Time."

kinematic image at exactly the moment that he sought to examine time outside of *motus*? In fact, Newton's recourse to flow was integral to his conceptualization of time. It was also an important component of his work's dissemination. Kirnberger, too, in his theory of meter, would make recourse to the same image of flow in his revision of meter theory.

Newton's application of a kinematic and temporal approach to spatial problems in geometry ultimately led to his advancement of the fundamental theorem of the calculus, which would show that the determination of the area under a curve was inverse to the determination of the changing direction of the tangent to the curve.[21] The problems that curves posed for earlier mathematicians had been significant. In the methods of the "ancients," polygons with indefinitely many sides were used to approximate curves. This method was known as the method of exhaustion; it required that at a certain point the squaring process stop, discarding indefinitely small units as occupying—practically—zero space. The unfortunate result, however, was that the entire area under the curve was composed of an amalgam of these zeros, creating the logical problem that it was composed of tiny nothings.[22]

Newton's innovation, which owed much to his predecessors Isaac Barrow and Pierre Gassendi, was to conceptualize the curve of a function (a relationship between two variables, for the purposes of this discussion, $f(x, y) = 0$) as the place of intersection of two lines in motion. Any coordinate point (x, y) on the curve of the function represented an instant in the accretion of quantity within the constant flow of time (see plate 4.3). Newton called these quantities "fluents." He imagined the rate at which these fluent quantities increased or diminished in the same way one would conceptualize the velocity of a point compared against the equable flow of time. He called this rate, or velocity, a "fluxion." With temporal change as a constant flow, Newton understood the variable quantities (x, y) in the function as instantaneous velocities gauged against time's constant flux. What his predecessors had understood as infinitesimally small units, Newton called "moments of fluxions."[23]

In an appendix to the *Opticks*, Newton summarized this kinematic and temporal approach to a geometric problem:

> Mathematical quantities I here consider not as consisting of indivisibles, either parts least possible or infinitely small ones, but as described by a continuous motion. Lines are described and by describing generated not through the

21. Historians and philosophers of mathematics disagree over the importance of Newton's flowing time to his development of calculus and his ontology in general. For a skeptical view, see John Earman, *World Enough and Space-Time* (Cambridge, MIT Press, 1989), esp. 6–7. For the opposite view—the one that I have chosen to represent—see Arthur, "Newton's Fluxions and Equably Flowing Time."

22. For the sake of clarity, I have simplified the description of calculus techniques before Newton. For a more thorough treatment of these, see Carl B. Boyer's carefully written *The History of the Calculus and Its Conceptual Development* (New York: Dover, 1949), esp. 96–186. Another brief and informative account of this history can be found in J. Struik, *A Concise History of Mathematics* (New York: Dover, 1948), 2:150–55, 170–82, and 189–92.

23. Nikolić, "Space and Time in the Apparatus of Infinitesimal Calculus," 205–12; Arthur, "Newton's Fluxions and Equably Flowing Time," 334–35.

Plate 4.3 Example from Newton's "Methodus serierum et fluxionum," showing
the creation of a curve through the motion of line BED. Reproduced here from
Newton, *The Method of Fluxions and Infinite Series*, trans. John Colson
(London: printed by Henry Woodfall and sold by John Nourse, 1736), 23. Image
reproduced with kind assistance from the Beinecke Rare Book and Manuscript
Library, Yale University.

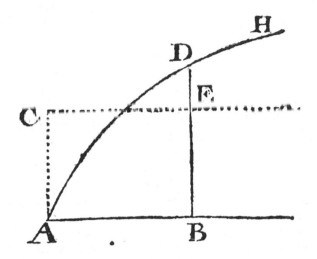

apposition of parts but through the continuous motion of points; surface-areas
are through the motion of lines, solids through the motion of surface-areas,
angles through the rotation of sides, times through continuous flux, and the like
in other cases. These geneses take place in the physical world and are daily
enacted in the motion of bodies visibly before our eyes.[24]

In essence, Newton's fluxional calculus made novel use of time's continuity in
order to solve the problem of the quantity limit. Newton wanted to avoid the use
of numeric quantity to represent the indefinitely small (or "nonzero") spatial
extensions of the calculus. Numeric quantity, for Newton, should not represent a
"part least possible" or an "indivisible" part of extension. These indefinitely small
spatial extensions should instead be represented by a purely continuous quantity: for this purpose, Newton employed his newly conceived "mathematical"—
or absolute—time. In Newton's fluxional calculus, the continuity of absolute time
is used to explain the continuity of numerical quantity and spatial extension.

The strategy described above involves a cunning reversal of terms; it is one of
the most innovative and unique aspects of Newton's calculus. Newton's

24. As edited and translated in Whiteside, ed. and trans., *The Mathematical Papers of Isaac Newton,
    volume VIII: 1697-1722* (Cambridge: Cambridge University Press, 1981), part I, 2, pp. 92–167, at
    107. See also Arthur, "Newton's Fluxions and Equably Flowing Time," 342. Newton's "Tractatus
    de quadratura curvarum" was the second of two documents appended to the first edition of the
    Opticks (London: Printed for Sam Smith and B. Walford, 1704).

distribution of concepts is an inversion of the Scholastic configuration, in which the continuity of motion explains the continuity of time. This was only possible with the reconceptualization of time as an absolute quantity.

Although Newton developed his kinematic approach to the calculus in the late seventeenth century, the approach was widely debated throughout the eighteenth—particularly on the continent. This was due in part to the fact that the learned world began to associate Newton's name with mechanical and mathematical innovation over the course of the eighteenth century.[25] It was also due, however, to the rivalry between his calculus techniques and those of Gottfried Leibniz. Not only did these two quarrel over the invention of the calculus (one of the most storied conflicts in the history of science), they also fundamentally disagreed on the representation of quantity and extension in this grand mathematical technique. Their sensationalized public conflict drew attention to the nature of the spatial and temporal conceptualizations lodged within their mathematics, and incited heated discourse on the topic.

In brief, Leibniz had developed a technique that accomplished roughly the same task as Newton's. His approach, however, made no effort to resolve the problem of the indefinitely small quantities of spatial extension that Newton had explained kinematically. In fact, Netwon's use of temporal continuity in the calculus flew in the face of Leibniz's metaphysics. For Leibniz, spatial extension could not exist outside of the bodies that it described, and time only existed as a measurement of motion.[26] In this sense, he carried forward the Scholastic tradition as Descartes had done before him. (It should be noted that by midcentury the Leibnizian doctrine was regularly equated with Cartesianism and understood in opposition to Newtonianism).[27] For Leibniz (as for Descartes) the world

25. J. B. Shank makes this point in *The Newton Wars and the Beginning of the French Enlightenment*, 505–6. The publication and dissemination of Newton's calculus was slow. His important "Methodus serierum et fluxionum" was published posthumously in 1736, and the most significant document for the continental transmission of his work, Colin MacLaurin's two-volume *Treatise of Fluxions*, was published in 1742. In fact, as Shank has shown, many of the early eighteenth-century conflicts surrounding the calculus did not yet involve Newton's name or reputation. Newton, *The Method of Fluxions and Infinite Series; with Its Application to the Geometry of Curve-Lines*, trans. John Colson; Judith V. Grabiner, "Was Newton's Calculus a Dead End? The Continental Influence of Maclaurin's Treatise of Fluxions," *American Mathematical Monthly* 104, no. 5 (1997): 393–410. See also Niccolò Guicciardini, "Dot-Age: Newton's Mathematical Legacy in the Eighteenth Century," *Early Science and Medicine* 9, no. 3 (2004): 218–56. The classic account of the Newton-Leibniz controversy concerning the "discovery" of calculus is A. Rupert Hall, *Philosophers at War* (Cambridge: Cambridge University Press, 1980).

26. The best demonstration of their conflicting views on space and time is the correspondence that resulted from the dispute between Leibniz and the Newtonian theologian Samuel Clarke. The dispute was published and widely disseminated in the eighteenth century—it appeared in ten editions before 1800. Henry Gavin Alexander, ed., *The Leibniz-Clarke Correspondence* (Manchester: Manchester University Press, 1956). An excellent secondary source on this topic is Henry Gavin Alexander's Introduction to *The Leibniz-Clarke Correspondence*, ix–lvi. See also Emily Grosholz, "Space and Time," in *The Oxford Handbook of Philosophy in Early Modern Europe*, ed. Clarke and Wilson.

27. Shank, *The Newton Wars and the Beginning of the French Enlightenment*, 425–26.

was a *plenum*: space was entirely full of bodies. Leibniz proposed that all extension was an aggregate of indivisible basic substances that he called monads.[28]

The squabble between Newton and Leibniz over the calculus precipitated polarized metaphysical debate that long outlasted their lifetimes, which is the reason that the legacy of the debate reached the music theory of the mid-and late eighteenth century. Nowhere was this more apparent than in the Berlin Academy—the scientific society that Leibniz founded in 1700.[29] The coincidence of the individuals that comprised its membership, together with advances in mathematics, astronomy, and physics, made time and space frequent topics in the Academy's journals and the publications of its members. Because of its founder, the Academy retained an important connection to the monadistic approach to the nature of space, one maintained well into the mid-eighteenth century by the philosopher and mathematician Christian Wolff and others.[30] The polymath Leonhard Euler, the new president Pierre Louis Moreau de Maupertuis, and the sometime member Voltaire were among those who championed the Newtonian view of time and space.[31] Although Voltaire never published in the *Mémoires*, the combined contributions of Euler and Maupertuis comprised a significant portion of the Academy's publications.[32]

The Berlin Academy under Maupertuis was divided into four classes—experimental philosophy (or natural philosophy), speculative philosophy, mathematics, and belles-lettres. These four classes met in plenary sessions each week to hear papers, judge essay competitions, discuss their publications, and conduct the general business of the Academy.[33] Many members made contributions to

28. A useful summary is found in Donald Rutherford, "Metaphysics: The Late Period," in *The Cambridge Companion to Leibniz*, ed. Nicholas Jolley (Cambridge: Cambridge University Press, 1995), 124–75, at 132–43.

29. Beck, *Early German Philosophy*, 314–24. The reorganization of the Berlin Academy is documented in Hans Aarsleff, "The Berlin Academy under Frederick the Great," *History of the Human Sciences* 2, no. 2 (1989): 193–206. Apart from these documents, the publications of the Academy themselves have been an invaluable resource to me. These begin with the *Mémoires* for the year 1745 under the title of *Histoire de l'Académie Royale des Sciences et des Belles-Lettres de Berlin 1745* (Berlin: Chez Ambroise Haude, 1746); the *Mémoires* beginning with the year 1770 were published under the title *Nouveaux Mémoires de l'Académie Royale des Sciences et Belles-Lettres 1770* (Berlin: Chex Chrétien Fréderic Voss, 1772). The publication year and the year that the volume records are usually offset by a few years; the publishing house also changed a number of times during the run of the *Mémoires*. I shall refer to them simply as the *Mémoires* throughout this discussion. It is important to note that most of the official business of the Academy, including its annual publications, was conducted in French, the language of the Prussian court in Berlin at this time.

30. Wolff's most representative work in this tradition is his *Philosophia prima sive ontologia* (Frankfurt and Leipzig: Officina Libraria Rengeriana, 1736).

31. Indeed, Voltaire was instrumental in disseminating the Newtonian views on space and time on the continent in general with his *Elémens de la philosophie de Neuton* (Paris, 1738); and *La métaphysique de Neuton, ou, Parallèle des sentimens de Neuton et de Leibnitz* (Amsterdam: Chez Etienne Ledet & Compagnie, 1740).

32. See Harnack's index in *Geschichte der Königlich preussischen Akademie der Wissenschaften zu Berlin*, 1–294.

33. Aarsleff, "The Berlin Academy under Frederick the Great," 196.

more than one class. Perhaps the best example was Sulzer, Kirnberger's collaborator, who—although now remembered for his work on aesthetics—regularly published contributions in the speculative philosophy and experimental philosophy classes of the *Mémoires*. The nature of the debate on time and space was such that it related to all four classes of the Academy, and rarely was an issue of the *Mémoires* published that did not contain an essay that engaged the topic, even if indirectly. In his widely distributed *Lettres à une princesse d'Allemagne*, Euler would later recall:

> When we talk in company on philosophical subjects, the conversation usually turns on such articles as have excited violent disputes among philosophers.
> The divisibility of body is one of them, respecting which the sentiments of the learned are greatly divided. Some maintain that this divisibility goes on to infinity, without the possibility of ever arriving at particles so small as to be susceptible of no further division. But others insist that this division extends only to a certain point, and that you may come at length to particles so minute that, having no magnitude, they are no longer divisible. These ultimate particles, which enter into the composition of bodies, they denominate *simple beings* and *monads*.
> There was a time when…there was scarcely a lady at court who did not take a decided part in favour of monads or against them. In a word, all conversation was engrossed by monads—no other subject could find admission.[34]

Euler tells of "violent disputes" over the nature of division in which all the learned felt compelled to take a side. The stakes of this debate were clearly significant; Euler couches the controversy in the language of monadology, which, with its metaphysical implications for understandings of the world, meant that the conflicting positions had philosophical ramifications on an awe-inspiring scale.

Perhaps the best testimony to the importance of the debate on the nature of time and space in the Berlin Academy was the essay contest it sponsored. One of the first of these drove at the heart of the controversy over the nature of time and space; in 1747, the members of the Berlin Academy asked whether the "doctrine of monads," or the Leibniz-Wolff conception of space, could be entirely refuted or, on the other hand, shown to account for the nature of force and movement.[35] The judging of these essays proved particularly difficult, with the members of the Academy divided evenly over responses in favor of and against monads.[36] This particular contest generated so much interest that the Academy posed a similar question in 1751 on the philosophical system of Alexander Pope.[37] The controversy over the judging of this second essay competition drove Lessing and Moses

34. Leonhard Euler, to Princess d'Anhalt Dessau, May 5, 1761, in *Letters of Euler on Different Subjects in Natural Philosophy Addressed to A German Princess*, ed. and trans. David Brewster with additional notes by John Griscom (New York: Harper Brothers, 1846), 2:39–40.
35. "Questions Proposées Par L'Académie Pour Les Prix," unsigned article in *Nouveau Mémoires de L'Académie Royale Des Sciences et Belles-Lettres 1770* (Berlin: Chez Chrétien Fréderic Voss, 1772), 22 (this unsigned article in the Berlin Mémoires chronicled the competition questions that the Academy had posed since 1745).
36. Beck, *Early German Philosophy*, 316.
37. "Questions Proposées Par L'Académie Pour Les Prix," 24.

Mendelssohn (the latter a student of Kirnberger's) to accuse the Academy of using Pope's name to disguise a question on the Newton-Leibniz controversy.[38] Twelve years later, Sulzer drafted the 1763 question, which asked if philosophers could prove metaphysical truths with the same evidence as proofs of geometry— a clear reference to metaphysical claims constructed with and through Newtonian geometry and physics.[39]

The Berlin Academy of the mid-eighteenth-century was only one of the many venues in which disputes of this nature played out. At that, it showcased particularly dramatic, and particularly metaphysical arguments. The apparent conflict of viewpoints, however, only demonstrates what was so clear to all involved: the Aristotelian understandings of time and space were no longer accepted. Time could not be understood within the old, Scholastic framework of *motus*; these ideas were wedded to a cosmology that was now hopelessly outdated. With the relationship between time and motion In question, the natural philosophers of the mid-eighteenth century mused—often contentiously—on how they should be reconfigured.

Newton's kinematic conception of absolute time retained intellectual currency at the forefront of debates well into the late eighteenth century. Although in this view time was no longer a measurement of motion, it was thought to have something of a motion itself—an equable, absolute flow. Hence, when Euler wrote, "ideas of time and space have almost always had the same fate," he described the intertwined journey of their epistemological networks and not their interdependence.[40] Time's flow, in Euler's account, was an important part of reconceptualizing time as absolute quantity: an equable motion in relation to nothing external, rather than a measurement of motion. Absolute time's "flow," then, marked the complete separation of time from the Scholastic framework of *motus*.

A Multiplicity of Measures

With time's conceptualization no longer rooted in motion, meter's conceptualization was no longer grounded in the beat. Consider definitions of measure in the eighteenth century. Sébastien de Brossard, compiling his 1703 *Dictionnaire de musique*, felt no need to include an article for *mesure*. He mentioned the term in passing within the alphabetically proximate entry *metron*: "a Greek word, in

38. Gotthold Ephraim Lessing and Moses Mendelssohn, *Pope ein Metaphysiker!* (Danzig: J. C. Schuster, 1755); see also Beck, *Early German Philosophy*, 316. On the relationship between Kirnberger and Mendelssohn, see Laurenz Lütteken, "Moses Mendelssohn und der Musikästhetische Diskurs der Aufklärung," in *Moses Mendelssohn im Spannungsfeld der Aufklärung*, ed. Michael Albrecht and Eva J. Engel (Stuttgart-Bad Cannstatt: Frommann-Holzboog, 2000), 159–93.
39. "Questions Proposées Par L'Académie Pour Les Prix," 26–27.
40. Euler, "Réflexions sur l'espace et le tems," 331.

Latin *Tactus*, or *Mensura*, in Italian *Battuta*, or *Tatto*, in German *Tact*, in French *MESURE*. See, *BATTUTA*."[41] Some sixty-five years later, Jean-Jacques Rousseau wrote the articles that would comprise his own *Dictionnaire de musique* (1768). Not only did Rousseau award *mesure* its own entry, he wrote a four-and-a-half-page essay on the term complete with detailed explanations and appended plates.[42] The difference between these two documents illustrates the proliferation of discourse on the measure that occurred after it could no longer be explained through the rubric of the beat. As chapters 1 and 2 demonstrate, the music theory of the sixteenth and seventeenth centuries conceptualized meter through motion. In these theories, the hierarchy of duration was organized and divided through the motion of beating time. The beat—*tactus, Tact, touchment*, or *battuta*—was the primary mode of description for this division. Time in this system was understood to be the number or measure of *motus*.[43]

In the eighteenth century, this group of knowledge relationships changed forever. *Motus* no longer held the explanatory power it once had in natural philosophy, and theories of meter sought an alternative foundation for their explanations of temporal division. The result was a multiplicity of measures: though Brossard was able to dispense with the term *mesure* in his 1703 dictionary by simply referring his readers to an entry on beating time, Rousseau knew that the concept *mesure* would need careful explanation for his late-eighteenth-century audience. In the period that intervened between them, theories of meter shifted their focus from the motion of the beat to the properties of the measure. The eighteenth century saw a huge expansion of discourse on meter signatures, accent, the relationship between meter, character, and tempo, and the qualities of the newly ubiquitous notated measure.[44] Finally, the multiplicity of measures reached its logical outcomes in the simplification schemes of the midcentury and the late-eighteenth-century retheorization of meter.

Theories of meter participated in redistributing the knowledge relationships of time and motion. A withdrawal from the motion-driven explanations for meter was already at work in the late seventeenth century. The struggle to explain meter outside of time beating led to writings on the relationship between meter signatures, measures, tempo, and character: it led to a multiplicity of measures, a proliferation of "times." With Kirnberger's articulation of a new way of

---

41. "*METRON*. Term Grec, en Latin *Tactus*, ou *Mensura*, en Italien *Battuta*, ou *Tatto*, en Allemand *Tact*, en François MESURE. Voyez, *BATTUTA*." Sébastien de Brossard, *Dictionare de Musique* (Paris: Christophe Ballard, 1703), unpaginated.

42. Jean-Jacques Rousseau, *Dictionnaire de Musique*, facsimile ed. (1768; Hildesheim: Georg Olms, 1969), 278–83. A version of this entry also appeared as Rousseau, "Mesure," in the *Encyclopédie ou dictionnaire raisonné…*, ed. Denis Diderot and Jean le Rond d'Alembert (Paris: Briasson et Le Breton, 1751–65), 10:410–11.

43. Aristotle, *Physics*, 4.11.219b1; cf. commentaries on the *Physics* such as the *Commentarii Collegii Conimbricensis e Societate Jesu in octo libros Physicorum Aristotelis Stagiritae*, facsimile ed. (1594; Hildesheim: Georg Olms, 1984), 2:81; Eustachius, *Summa philosophiae quadripartita* (Leiden: Franciscum Moyardum, 1647), 2:158. See chapter 1.

44. On the evolution of the notated measure itself, see Bockmaier, *Die instrumentale Gestalt des Taktes*.

understanding meter, the relationships between time and motion had been redrawn. Time was now said to have its own equable flow, and meter was a measurement thereof.

Already in the 1696 *Éléments ou principes de musique*, Loulié had distinguished the measure (*mesure*) from the physical act of the beat (*battement*) and its temporal duration (*tems*).[45] While Loulié explained these terms cursorily, later writers took on the challenge of explaining their relationship to one another in detail. When Johann Mattheson did so in his *General-Baß-Schule* of 1735, he felt the need to specifically counter the older conception of meter that needed clarification:

> Once, one said, and wrote happily for the world. *Tact* is **nothing other than a raising and lowering of the hand.** Oh! What beautiful ideas must this not give to those who want to know what sort of thing a *Tact* is. It was still better than nothing.[46]

For Mattheson, as for other writers of his generation, there was a growing concern to document meter, measure, tempo, and character as distinct concepts. The direct and pithy explanations of meter as a physical motion were no longer sufficient. The place of meter in Mattheson's many writings makes this clear.

In *Das neu-eröffnete Orchestre* (1713) and the *General-Baß-Schule* (1735), Mattheson had used the section heading "Vom Takt" for his discussion of meter. In *Der vollkommene Capellmeister* of 1739, the heading "Vom Takt" had disappeared and "Von der Zeit-Maasse" had taken its place.[47] By the time Friedrich Wilhelm Marpurg published his *Anleitung zur Musik* in 1763, the term *Tact* required four separate definitions. Marpurg wrote:

> The word *Tact* is used for four concepts in today's music:
>
> 1. The relation by which a number of notes in the melody is divided into a certain period of time. Such a relationship underlies each composition. It is indicated at the start of the piece next to the key signature, sometimes by numbers, sometimes by a half-circle.
> 2. The period of time itself. The distinction between each period of time and the next is marked with a vertical line between the notes.
> 3. The quantity or the determination of this period of time with respect to length or brevity. According to this determination, the same number of notes can be quicker or slower depending on the character and affect of the piece. This

---

45. Étienne Loulié, *Éléments ous principes de musique* (Paris: Christophe Ballard, 1696), 30–31.
46. "Einer sagte, und schrieb es auch glücklich in die Welt hinein: **Der Tact sey nichts anders, als ein Aufheben und Niederschlagen der Hand.** O! welchen schönen Begriff muß das nicht demjenigen geben, der gerne wissen will, was der Tact für ein Ding sey. Es war doch noch besser, als gar nichts…" Johann Mattheson, *Kleine General-Baß-Schule*, facsimile ed. (1735; Laaber: Laaber-Verlag, 1980), 92.
47. Mattheson, *Der vollkommene Capellmeister*, facsimile ed. (1739; Kassel: Bärenreiter, 1965), 171–74.

modification of the period of time, however, is more correctly indicated with the word *Bewegung* or *Zeitmaß* [tempo] than with the word *Tact*.

4. The sensible discrimination and control of this length or shortness by means of certain movements of the hand.[48]

In Marpurg's midcentury text, the motion of beating time was the fourth, and last, dimension of meter. Beating time did not do the explanatory work it once had. Instead, it now described an action that could regulate tempo—something similar to our twenty-first-century understanding of conducting.[49] At the top of the list, by contrast, Marpurg is quick to point out that meter is simultaneously a kind of temporal division, a relationship indicated by a signature, an element of notation, and a tempo determination. In Galeazzi's *Elementi teorico-pratici di musica* (1791), time beating is separated from meter in concept as well as in print: while time beating is covered in the fourth article "Della Battuta, e delle figure Musicale," the meter signatures are discussed in the eighth article, "De Tempi."[50] With Koch's *Musikalisches Lexikon* of 1802, the physical action of the beat was marginalized to the point of exclusion; Koch's definitions for *Takt* encompass Marpurg's first three only.[51]

While the motion of time beating became increasingly less relevant for discussions of meter, the relationship between meter signatures, characters, and tempi grew more so. Because these concepts had drifted apart from one another, theorists in the eighteenth century had to explicitly detail the many relationships between them in prose. There were pragmatic reasons, also, that theorists thought it wise to specify the tempo indications for each meter: the early musical chronometers (such as Loulié's *chronomètre*) were too large and impractical to do that

48. "Das Wort Tact wird auf viererley Art in der heutigen Musik gebraucht, als 1) für das Verhältniß, nach welchem in der Melodie eine Anzahl von Noten in einen gewissen Zeitraum eingetheilt wird. Ein solches Verhältniß wird bey jedem Tonstücke zum Grunde geleget, und vorne am Schlüssel bald durch Ziffern, bald durch einen unvollkommnen Zirkel angedeutet. 2) Für jeden solchen Zeitraum selbst. Der Unterscheid von einem solchen Zeitraum zum andern, wird durch einen Verticalstrich zwischen den Noten bemerket. 3) Für das Maaß oder die Bestimmung dieses Zeitraums in Ansehung seiner Länge oder Kürze. Nach dieser Bestimmung kann eben dieselbe Anzahl von Noten geschwinder oder langsamer geendigt werden, und selbige hänget von dem Character und Affect eines Tonstücks ab. Diese Modification des Zeitraums aber, wird mit dem Worte **Bewegung** oder **Zeitmaß** richtiger, als mit dem Worte **Tact** ausgedrücket. 4) Für die sinnliche Unterscheidung und Regierung dieser Länge und Kürze vermittelst gewisser Bewegungen mit der Hand." Marpurg, *Anleitung zur Musik überhaupt, und zur Singkunst besonders...* (Berlin: Arnold Wever, 1763), 67–68. Many thanks to Martin Küster for his assistance with Marpurg's prose and ideas.

49. Nicole Schwindt-Gross, "Einfache, zusammengesetzte und doppelt notierte Takte: Ein Aspekt der Takttheorie im 18. Jahrhundert," *Musiktheorie* 4, no. 3 (1989): 203–22, at 212. All of this is not to say that descriptions of time beating disappeared entirely, but rather that they were less foundational to the conceptualization of meter.

50. Francesco Galeazzi, *Elementi teorico-pratici di musica* (Rome: Pilucchi Cracas, 1791), 1:27–30, 32–35.

51. Heinrich Chrisoph Koch, *Musikalisches Lexikon*, facsimile ed. (1802; Hildesheim: Georg Olms, 1964), col. 1472–73.

work, and the recently disseminated Italian tempo terms were not quite precise enough.[52]

The situation resulted in an explosion of lists. Eighteenth-century meter theory was made, in large part, out of lists of the meters signatures that were possible (or had been at one point in history) and the tempi and characteristics to which they related. Discourses on meter from this period almost all included these lists—or "curious inventor[ies]" in the words of Mattheson—of signatures new and old.[53] Even though each meter signature could be associated with a number of different characteristics, styles, and tempi, the discourse on meter in this period makes it clear that each distinct constellation of meter signatures, note values, and characters had the capacity to indicate tempo.

Appendix 2 collects thirty-nine representative treatises from the era that include these inventories. Treatises in this list described as few as ten and as many as thirty-five meter signatures. Some went on to mention still further signatures not recommended for use; Marpurg's 1755 Anleitung zum Clavierspielen names the most, at fifty-six signatures in total. The peak of this listing practice is found in publications of the years between 1740 and 1790, during which time treatises regularly included descriptions of over twenty meters.[54] These lists were often intimately tied to descriptions of the notated measure and its properties (these are discussed below).

Kirnberger's Die Kunst des reinen Satzes in der Musik contained one of the most impressive collections of meters, describing twenty-four useful signatures and mentioning ten more. "All types of meters, newly-contrived and conventional, [should be] described to [the prospective composer], each according to its true nature and its proper execution ... [and] the spirit or character of each meter [should be] defined as precisely as possible," Kirnberger wrote.[55] His treatise codified aspects of the eighteenth-century Affektenlehre, or doctrine of affections, and is often remembered in recent scholarship on musical topics.[56] As he observed about meter, character, and tempo, "the name *Gemüthsbewegung*, which we Germans give to passions or affections, already points to their analogy to tempo [*Bewegung*]."[57] For Kirnberger, as for many other eighteenth-century theorists,

---

52. Some theorists included lists of these tempo terms alongside their lists of meter signatures. See for instance Marpurg, *Anleitung zum Clavierspielen* (Berlin: Haude and Spener, 1765), 16–17; and Galeazzi, *Elementi teorico-pratici di musica*, 35–37. This is the topic of chapter 5.

53. Mattheson, *Kleine General-Baß-Schule*, 77.

54. A late exception to this trend, Augustus Frederic Chrostopher Kollman's *An Essay on Musical Harmony* (London: J. Dale, 1796), draws heavily on Kirnberger.

55. "Daß ihm alle bis ist erfundene und gebräuchliche Arten des Tacktes, jeder nach seiner wahren Beschaffenheit und nach seinem genauen Vortrag, beschrieben werden ... Daß man, so genau es angeht, den Geist oder den Charakter jeder Tacktart, bestimme." Kirnberger, *Die Kunst des reinen Satzes in der Musik*, 2:114.

56. Chiefly in Wye J. Allanbrook, *Rhythmic Gesture in Mozart* (Chicago: University of Chicago Press, 1983), esp. 13–15; but see also Leonard G. Ratner, *Classic Music: Expression, Form, and Style* (New York: Schirmer, 1980), 68–71.

57. "Der Name **Gemüthsbewegung**, den wir Deutschen den Leidenschaften oder Affekten geben, zeiget schon die Aehnlichkeit derselben mit der Bewegung an." Kirnberger, *Die Kunst des reinen Satzes in der Musik*, 2:106.

the particular nature of each meter had the capacity to create a distinct affective experience.

Still, although eighteenth-century theorists tried to solve the problem of tempo and character specification through meter signatures, it had already become clear to some that these signs could never do all of that work. The signature 2/2 is an excellent example. On the one hand this meter signature was associated with the emphatic and learned church style known as the *alla breve* or *alla capella*, sometimes notated ₵. Koch and Kirnberger described it as a meter fit for "fugues and fugal compositions" and "highly developed choruses" ("ausgearbeiteten Chören").[58] By contrast, J. J. Quantz noted, "this meter is used in the gallant style more now than it ever was."[59] Presumably, performers would have discerned the type of 2/2 and the tempo appropriate with reference to the composition in question (this confusing issue is the topic of chapter 6). Some took this as an obvious consequence of meter's inexact notation. "Le goût est le vrai Chronometre," concluded the student in the dialogue of Anton Bemetzrieder's *Leçons de clavecin et principes d'harmonie* (1771).[60] Others were less than satisfied. Rousseau carefully described sixteen meter signatures in his article "mesure." Still, he lamented, "If all these signs are intended to mark so many different sorts of measures, there are too many; and if they are to express the different degrees of tempo, there are not enough."[61]

Kirnberger's collaborator Schulz, writing closer to the end of the century for Sulzer's *Allgemeine Theorie der schönen Künste*, took direct aim against Rousseau's position.

> Other [composers] who, with Rousseau, think that the multiplicities of meter are merely arbitrary inventions and are angry about it, either have no sense of the particular execution of each meter, or deny it, and therefore run the risk of composing things in which the character of the piece (in the meter in which it was written) is quite different than what they intended.[62]

58. This style and its association with the meter signature is the topic of chapter 6. The *alla breve* also counts as a classic topic, as discussed in Allanbrook, *Rhythmic Gesture in Mozart*, 19–23. Kirnberger, *Die Kunst des reinen Satzes in der Musik*, 2:118; Koch, *Versuch einer Anleitung zur Composition*, facsimile ed. (1782–93; Hildesheim: Georg Olms, 1969), 2:293.

59. "Denn diese Tactart ist im galanten Styl itziger Zeit üblicher, als sie in vorigen Zeiten gewesen ist." J. J. Quantz, *Versuch einer Anweisung, die Flöte traversiere zu spielen*, 3rd ed. (1752; Breslau: Johann Friedrich Korn dem ältern, 1789); facsimile ed. (Kassel: Bärenreiter, 1953), 56. Johann Adolph Scheibe also notes this discrepancy in *Ueber die Musikalische Composition: Erste Theil Die Theorie der Melodie und Harmonie*, facsimile ed. (1773; Kassel: Bärenreiter, 2006), 203–4.

60. Anton Bemetzrieder, *Leçons de clavecin et principes d'harmonie*, facsimile ed. (1771; New York: Broude Brothers, 1966), 69.

61. "Si tous ces signes sont institués pour marquer autant de différantes sortes de *mesures*, il y en a un boucoup trop; & s'ils le sont pour exprimer les divers degrés de Mouvement il n'y en a pas assez." Rousseau, *Dictionnaire de Musique*, 282.

62. "andere, die mit Rousseau die Vielheiten der Takte für blos willkührliche Erfindungen halten, und darüber ungehalten sind, haben entweder kein Gefühl von dem besondern Vortrag eines jeden Taktes, oder verläugnen es, und laufen daher Gefahr, Sachen zu sezen, die, weil sie nicht in dem rechten, dem Charakter des Stüks angemessenen Takte gesezt sind, ganz anders vorgetragen werden, als sie gedacht worden." Schulz, "Takt," in Sulzer, *Allgemeine Theorie der schönen Künste* (Leipzig: M. G. Weidmanns Erben und Reich, 1771–74), 2:1133.

The anxiety about meter signatures, which is clear in the quotation above, was attached to the moribund nature of *tempo giusto*: the system in which they were tied to tempo and character.[63] "Today's composers and performers seem to understand so little of these subtleties that they believe, in fact, that such meter signatures were merely a caprice of the ancients," Kirnberger wrote.[64] What the lists of meter signatures tried to codify was exactly what had become less obvious. No longer epistemologically grounded in *motus*, meter found itself surprisingly multiple.

Properties of the Measure

There are many themes that run through the explosion of knowledge that was made on meter in the eighteenth century. One of the most uniform is the focus on the properties of the measure as a unit. This theme emerged alongside the appearance of the notated measure as an aspect of meter itself. As we have seen above, theorists such as Marpurg, Koch, and others identified the unit formed between printed barlines as a basic conceptual component of meter.[65] This new focus on the measure as such resulted in writing on accent and its relationship to the printed barline, as well as writing on the various types of measures and measuring systems contained between those barlines.

Long before the eighteenth century, writings on music examined the relationship between the diversity of meters and the durations that best matched them. Zarlino's chapter on meter in *Le istitutioni harmoniche* contains a catalogue of poetic feet: he enumerated those that would best accord with duple meters and those that would best match triple meters.[66] Mersenne, Matheson, and many others created similar lists.[67] In this quantitative understanding of poetic feet, the indications of long (—) and short (v) were meant to translate into the length and brevity of musical durations. Alongside this tradition, theorists began to

63. This topic is treated in further detail in chapter 5. For a period definition of *tempo giusto*, see Jean-Jacques Rousseau, "Mouvement" in the *Dictionnaire de Musique*, facsimile ed. (1768; Hildesheim: Georg Olms, 1969), 303. The notion of *tempo giusto* used here is not to be confused with the tempo marking that occurs occasionally in Handel's works. For more on *tempo giusto* see *Oxford Music Online*, s.v. "Tempo Giusto," "Tempo and Expression Marks," by David Fallows, accessed November 27, 2011, <www.oxfordmusiconline.org>; and Helmut Breidenstein, *Mozarts Tempo-System* (Tutzing: Hans Schneider, 2011).

64. "Den heutigen Componisten und Pracktikern scheinen diese Subtilitäten so wenig bekannt zu seyn, daß sie vielmehr glauben, dergleichen Tacktbezeichnung sey blos ein Grille der Alten gewesen." Kirnberger, *Die Kunst des reinen Satzes in der Musik*, 2:123.

65. Marpurg, *Anleitung zur Musik*, 67–68. Koch, *Musikalisches Lexikon*, col. 1472–73. See also Mattheson, *Kleine General-Baß-Schule*, 92.

66. Zarlino, *Le istitutioni harmoniche* (Venice: Francesco de i Franceschi Senese, 1558), 208–9.

67. Mersenne, *Harmonie universelle*, facsimile ed. (1636–37; Paris: Centre national de la recherché scientifique, 1963), vol. 2, "Livre Sixiesme de l'art de bien chanter," 374–410. Mattheson, *Der vollkommene Capellmeister*, 160–70. George Houle calls this practice "Rhythmopoeia." Houle, *Meter in Music: 1600-1800* (Bloomington: Indiana University Press, 1987), 62–77.

describe the parts of the measure qualitatively. Different parts of the notated measure were said to have different emphasis. Some theorists described a connection between the location of emphasis within the measure and the structure of the time-beating motion.[68] Wolfgang Caspar Printz called the nondurational quality of emphasis an "inner time-length" in his *Satyrischer Componist* of 1696:

> Furthermore, it should be known that the meter signature [*Zahl*] has a strange force and virtue, which causes notes or tones of the same length to seem longer or shorter... This different length of notes with the same value is called *Quantitas Temporalis Intrinseca*, or the inner time-length.[69]

Printz accounts for the difference in quality among tones as a function of measure position, attributing a perceived difference in length to the work of the meter signature and the barlines. Other treatises used different methods to account for these qualities. In a rather confusing innovation, Scheibe suggested employing poetic feet in order to indicate these nondurational "inner time-lengths." (Effectively, he transposed the notation of a quantitative system meant to indicate rhythms onto a qualitative system meant to indicate stress).[70] Marpurg and Koch later expanded upon Scheibe's suggested correspondence between the accentual

68. Johann Adam Hiller provides an interesting case study. In his *Anweisung zum musikalisch-richtigen Gesange*, Hiller explains that the division of the measure determines the emphasis, or "inner quantities" [*innerlichen Quantität*] of the notes. This, he says, is made evident in notation with barlines and in performance with the action of beating time. Here it is important to note that the action of beating time is conceptually separate from the measure. Hiller, *Anweisung zum musikalisch-richtigen Gesange* (Leipzig: Johann Friedrich Junius, 1774), 47–48. Marpurg, in his *Anleitung zum Clavierspielen*, also relates the "good" and "bad" parts of the time-beating motion—*thesis* and *arsis* respectively—to the parts of the measure. Marpurg, *Anleitung zum Clavierspielen*, 19–20, for example. For a rather different contextualization of the "inner quantity" theories, see Houle, *Meter in Music: 1600–1800*, 78–84. See also Suzanne J. Beicken's commentary in Hiller, *Treatise on Vocal Performance and Ornamentation*, ed. and trans. Beicken (Cambridge: Cambridge University Press, 2001), 73n5.

69. "Ferner ist zu wissen, daß die Zahl eine sonderbare krafft und Tugend habe, welche verursacht, daß unter etlichen, der Zeit nach, gleich-langen Noten oder Klängen, etliche länger, etliche kürzer zu seyn scheinen... Diese unterschiedliche Länge etlicher, der Zeit oder Währung nach, gleich-lange Noten, wird genennet *Quantitas Temporalis Intrinseca*, die innerliche Zeit-Länge." Wolfgang Caspar Printz, *Satyrischer Componist* (Dresden and Leipzig: Johann Christoph Mieth and Johann Christoph Zimmermann, 1696), "Synopsin musices poeticæ," 18. Again see Houle for his discussion of *Quantitas Intrinseca*, in which he quotes and translates this passage. Houle, *Meter in Music: 1600–1800*, 78–84.

70. Scheibe, *Critischer Musikus*, Stücken 37–38, May 12–21, 1739, facsimile ed. (1746; Hildesheim: Georg Olms, 1970), 346–62. This topic is taken up in detail in Martin Küster, "Thinking in Song: Prosody, Text-Setting and Music Theory in Eighteenth-Century Germany" (PhD diss., Cornell University, 2012). Incidentally, there is already a hint of the relationship between metric structure and poetic feet in Thomas Morley's *A Plaine and Easie Introduction to Practicall Musicke*, in which he describes triple meter as "measure which the learned call 'trochaicam rationem.'" Thomas Morley, *A Plaine and Easie Introduction to Practicall Musicke...* (London: Peter Short, 1597), 181. The important difference is that Morley uses the "troche" to describe the actual durations of the motions of the beat, while Scheibe is interested in using poetic feet in analogy with the nondurational stress of measure parts.

properties of the measure and the patterns of poetic feet.[71] These theorists attempted to account for the relationships between phrase structure and cadential accent by reference to quantities of notated durations and the qualities of their measure positions.

All of these various attempts to describe and locate the accentual power of meter were aimed, fundamentally, at a detailed understanding of the measure itself.[72] With the physical act of the beat no longer the primary focus of meter theories, the discourse turned to the space between the barlines. Accent, in these accounts, was described with reference to notational practices; it was understood to be a relationship between the measure and the durations it contained. Employing a multitude of terms and techniques, theorists began to link knowledge on meter with a newly created set of knowledge on the parts of the measure.

Eighteenth-century theorists were keen to explain the many different types of notated measures in detail. Appendix 2 lists the categories used to classify them. Categories concerned with the distinction between duple and triple were carried over from the previous centuries of meter theory. As before, the terms even and uneven described duple and triple respectively.

Added to the traditional distinctions between types of meter, the eighteenth century saw the rise of a completely new set of classifications. This set is best understood through the analytic of 1) simple, 2) tripled, and 3) compounded measures. Though theorists disagreed on the terminology, there was a general consensus that each beat in any measure could be divided into either two or three parts. In the twenty-first century American pedagogical tradition, we call meters with a triple subdivision "compound." This term is problematic for reasons that will become clear below. In the present analytic, it is useful to call them "tripled" measures: each beat in these measures is subdivided into three. The customary examples include 6/8, 9/8, and so on. Eighteenth-century German theorists described yet another type of measure: one in which two smaller measures were written together in the space of one. In these meters, which are here called "compounded," every other barline is missing. 6/4 was often described in this way. Marpurg, Kirnberger, Koch, and others explain that each measure of 6/4 is actually two measures of 3/4 in one.[73] Against the tripled and compounded measures, theorists contrasted the simple measure. Simple measures were typically of two or three beats, but some theorists made room for simple measures of four beats.[74]

---

71. Marpurg, "Theorie des Tacts" of the *Kritische Briefe über die Tonkunst*, Letters XIII–XVI, September 15 and 22, and October 6, 1759, facsimile ed. (1760; Hildesheim: Georg Olms, 1974), 1:97–126. Heinrich Christoph Koch, *Versuch einer Anleitung zur Composition*, 3:13–38. Again see Küster, "Thinking in Song"; and Maurer Zenck, *Vom Takt*, esp. 141–55.

72. For a single revelatory case study, notice that one of Marpurg's central examples in his "Theorie des Tacts" is a piece of music that he understands to be barred incorrectly. Marpurg, *Kritische Briefe über die Tonkunst*, Letter XIV, September 22, 1759; facsimile ed., 1:106–7.

73. Marpurg, *Kritische Briefe über die Tonkunst*, Letter XIV, September 22, 1759; facsimile ed., 1:107; Kirnberger, *Die Kunst des reinen Satzes in der Musik*, 2:132. Koch, *Versuch einer Anleitung zur Composition*, 2:338–39. Non-German theorists who describe these types of measures are drawing on German sources: this is the case for Kollman's *An Essay on Musical Harmony* (which draws on Kirnberger).

74. For instance, in Kirnberger's *Die Kunst des reinen Satzes in der Musik*, 2:122–26.

The terminology theorists used to describe these types of measures is, and was, potentially confusing. Early in the century, tripled measures went by the names *mixtam, composée,* or *zusammengesetzt*. In late eighteenth-century German treatises, however, *zusammengesetzt* indicated compounded measures, and tripled measures were known as either *triplirt* or *vermischt* (see appendix 2). If this was confusing, the relationship between these types of measures and their signatures was even more so. Some theorists maintained that all measures of four beats were a type of compounded measure, while others insisted that some four-beat measures were, in fact, simple.[75] Worse, meters like 6/8 might indicate tripled measures (a tripling of 2/4, as Koch describes) or compounded measures (two measures of 3/8 in one).[76]

What these terminological issues reveal is that it was not only the tempi and characters of meter signatures that required explanation; even the number of beats or measures a meter signature indicated required prose explication in the eighteenth-century system. The multiplicity of measures, the details concerning tempo, the associations with character, the accentual properties of place within

75. Kirnberger falls in the latter category. Kirnberger, *Die Kunst des reinen Satzes in der Musik,* 2:122–26. Eighteenth-century disagreements on the properties of barlines, accents, and compounded measures have found a way to play themselves out again in recent scholarship. Some scholars, such as Claudia Maurer Zenck and Danuta Mirka, take the view that mid-measure cadences indicate the presence of compounded measures, since many eighteenth-century theorists indicate that cadences should fall on downbeats. A good deal of analysis in their scholarship is based on this premise. See Maurer Zenck, *Vom Takt*; and Mirka, *Metric Manipulations in Haydn and Mozart*. Others, such as Floyd K. Grave and William Rothstein, hold that composers only obeyed the rule regarding downbeat cadences in the early and mid-eighteenth century. They find that a new and predominantly German attitude about the relationship between phrase structure and accent developed toward the century's end. In this new view, cadences did not need to be located on downbeats; thus not every mid-measure cadence indicates the presence of a compounded measure. Rothstein proposes that this change in compositional practice was related to the linguistic stress patterns of different European languages: music barred according to the principles of Italian and French must place cadences on the downbeat in order to preserve the linguistic *accento comune* (in Italian) or *accent tonique* (in French). Music barred in this fashion gives rise to end-accented phrase structures, and persists in certain styles well into the nineteenth century. The newer type of barring, which followed the principles of the German language, required no such cadential accents. The phrase structure of this music is typically beginning-accented. As Rothstein indicates, the two types of phrase structure correspond to two different ways of listening that became possible in the late eighteenth century, a topic taken up in the eighth chapter of this book. See William Rothstein, "National Metrical Types," in *Communication in Eighteenth-Century Music,* ed. Danuta Mirka and Kofi Agawu (Cambridge: Cambridge University Press, 2008), 112–59; and Rothstein, "Metrical Theory and Verdi's Midcentury Operas," *Dutch Journal of Music Theory* 16, no. 2 (2011): 93–111; Floyd K. Grave, "Metrical Displacement and the Compound Measure in Eighteenth-Century Theory and Practice," *Theoria* 1 (1985): 25–60; and idem, "Abbé Vogler's Revision of Pergolesi's *Stabat Mater,*" *Journal of the American Musicological Society* 30, no. 1 (1977): 43–71. See also Schwindt-Gross, "Einfache, zusammengesetzte und doppelt notierte Takte: Ein Aspekt der Takttheorie im 18. Jahrhundert"; Markus Waldura, "Marpurg, Koch, und die Neubegründung des Taktbegriffs," *Musikforschung* 53, no. 3 (2000): 237–53; and Breidenstein, *Mozarts Tempo-System,* 75–78.
76. Koch, *Versuch einer Anleitung zur Composition,* 2:322–31. Kirnberger, *Die Kunst des reinen Satzes in der Musik,* 2:132.

the measure, the relationship of measures to barlines: all of these were part of the new discourse that grew up around the concept of meter in the eighteenth century.

Simplification Schemes

Like all conceptual developments, meter's new multiplicity had its defenders and its critics. As noted above, some theorists found the listing of meter signatures imperative, while others such as Rousseau complained that the profusion of signs was ineffective. Rousseau was hardly the first—perhaps only the most outspoken—to suggest a simplification scheme for the multiplicity of meter signatures; one such scheme had already been proposed in Rameau's *Traité de l'harmonie*. Rameau related, "several persons have indicated to me the difficulty they have in distinguishing the different meters by the disposition of numbers that serve to mark them."[77] His proposed solution was to replace all the meter signatures with the numerals 2, 3, and 4 only: "since meter distinguishes only of 2, 3, or 4 beats, no other numerals are needed to indicate it."[78] In order to designate the value of the beat in each meter, Rameau instructed composers to place the appropriate duration to the left of the clef. 3/2 meter, for example, should be indicated with a half note to the left of the clef and the single numeral three in the place of the meter signature. Tempo, instead of according to the signature itself, was in this system linked to the size of the note value given as the beat. Pieces in longer note values were understood to carry a slower tempo, those in shorter values, faster.

Although Rameau's proposed reform aimed to reduce the multiplicity of meters to three basic types, it nevertheless recreated the same multiplicity in different guise. Through his new notational method, Rameau gave examples of four different types of duple meter, four types of quadruple meter, and five types of triple meter. In addition to these, he made room for tripled meters (which were indicated with dotted notes to the left of the clef) and even created a special type of indication for unequal triple meters, or meters of "two unequal beats" (these he indicated with two notes to the left of the clef showing the unequal division of the measure, such as a half note and a quarter note).[79] In total, this left Rameau with thirty-seven distinct varieties of meter.

Though Rameau's system may have been just as intricate as the standard practice, its foundational premise outlined the framework for a simplification of meter signatures. Fundamentally, all of the signatures could be reduced to a few basic categories including duple, triple, and (for Rameau) quadruple meters. In this basic premise the theorists Michel Pignolet de Montéclair and Joseph Lacassagne

77. "Cependant plusieurs personnes m'ayant fait remarquer la difficulté qu'elles avoient à distinguer la différence des mesures par la differente disposition des chiffres qui servent à les marquer." Jean-Philippe Rameau, *Traité de l'harmonie*, facsimile ed. (1722; New York: Broude Brothers, 1965), 151.
78. "...puisque la mesure ne se distingue qu'en 2, 3, ou 4 tems, nous n'avons pas besoin d'autres chiffres pour la marquer..." Rameau, *Traité de l'harmonie*, 151.
79. Rameau, *Traité de l'harmonie*, 156.

followed Rameau's suggested reform. Both preceded their discussion of the simplified system with an explanation of the traditional signatures; Montéclair gave an account of fifteen signatures in the second part his *Principes de musique*, devoted to "all that regards the measure and tempo."[80] His simplification scheme was found in the fourth part of his treatise, alongside other proposed reforms in music notation (his "Abregé d'un nouveau systhême de musique").[81] Here he echoed the complaint about the complexities of meter notation: "There were even masters who established up to 20 signs for measures, some of which were rejected as useless."[82] Montéclair advanced that all meter signatures could be reduced to only the numerals 2 and 3, since "the measure of four beats is nothing other than the measure of two beats doubled." He indicated tripled measures with a stroke through the single numeral of the meter signatures. A cut numeral 2, then, would have indicated a tripled measure of two beats (something equivalent to 6/8). Unlike Rameau, Montéclair was left with only four meter signatures in total.

Lacassagne followed suit in a note inserted well after his description of the traditional signatures in his *Traité général des élémens du chant*. Like Montéclair, he also advocated for the signatures 2 and 3, though he included, in addition, the option of using 2/3 for uneven triple meters.[83] Both Montéclair and Lacassagne felt that tempo terms should do the work of indicating tempo, rather than the signatures themselves or the durations in which the music was composed (as Rameau had suggested). Montéclair asked, "If the 19 signs for measures are necessary to indicate the various tempi of airs, why don't composers use them correctly?"[84]

Rousseau's simplification scheme was similar, though more extreme; it was a part of his project to reform musical notation in an elimination of the staff and note shapes altogether. In his reformed system, pitches were indicated in scale degrees and durations through an elaborate system of barlines and commas which marked individual beats. For Rousseau, the reduction of meter signatures to the lone numerals 2 and 3 was a necessary step in the refinement of what he saw as an ineffectually complex system:

> Musicians recognize no less than fourteen different types of measures in music: the distinction of which can cloud the minds of students infinitely. Yet,

80. Michel Pignolet de Montéclair, *Principes de musique*, facsimile ed. (1736; Geneva; Minkoff, 1972), title page.
81. Montéclair, *Principes de musique*, 99.
82. "Il y a eu même des Maitres qui ont etabli jusqu'à 20 Signes de Mesures, dont quelques uns ont eté rejettés comme inutilles." Montéclair, *Principes de musique*, 116.
83. Incidentally, it seems as though Lacassagne thought it appropriate to indicate all tripled meters as versions of simple, unequal triple. Hence, in his system, a measure of 6/4 "composée" (e.g., tripled 2/4) is notated with the 2/3 signature and barred every three quarter notes. Joseph Lacassagne, *Traité général des élémens du chant*, facsimile ed. (1766; New York: Broude Brothers, 1967), 98–103.
84. "Si les 19 Signes de mesures sont necessaires pour indiquer les differents mouvements des Airs, pourquoy les compositeurs ne les marquent t'ils pas correctement?" Montéclair, *Principes de musique*, 117.

I maintain that all the tempi [*tous les mouvements*] of these different measures can be reduced exclusively to two; namely, a tempo of two beats and a tempo of three beats [*mouvement à deux temps, et mouvement à trois temps*]; and I dare to challenge the most refined ear to find anything natural that cannot be expressed with all the precision possible by one of these two measures. I shall now therefore begin to eradicate all of those bizarre numbers, reserving only the two and the three, with which (as you will soon see) I will express all the possible tempi.[85]

Rousseau included no discussion of the standard meter signatures in the description of his reformed system. Unlike Rameau, Montéclair, and Lacassagne, Rousseau did not introduce his simplification scheme in a general treatise on music but instead as his first presentation to the Paris Academy of Sciences. In this context, his reduction of signs for meter can be understood, within the culture of the Paris Academy, as an effort to find a universal rule that would explain meter's many varieties. It was an attempt to reform the explosion of meter's "times" to a single rule for time. Drawing on the reforms already suggested, Rousseau explained that one principle united the great diversity of meter signatures: they all divided the measure into two or three parts. The legacy of this explanation was significant for Kirnberger's reconceptualization of meter, which came at a moment when meter signatures were many.

Kirnberger's Contribution

That Kirnberger and his collaborators should have envisioned a new way of understanding meter was almost inevitable given the circumstances of their writing. Kirnberger penned *Die Kunst des reinen Satzes in der Musik* in conjunction with his work on the music articles for Sulzer's *Allgemeine Theorie der schönen Künste*, which aimed to elucidate general principles for aesthetics. For musical precedent, Kirnberger and his student Schulz drew—famously—on Rameau's theories. Theses authors undertook their task, meanwhile, in a Berlin riveted by debates on the nature of time, space, and motion.

It should be no surprise, then, that Kirnberger's theory found a way to accommodate the period's multiple meters with the French simplification schemes; indeed, his theory did just this specifically by drawing on the language of time's

---

85. "Les musiciens reconnoissent ou moins quatorze mesure différentes dans la musique: mesures dont la distinction brouille l'esprit des écoliers pendant un temps infini. Or je soutiens que tous les mouvements de ces différents mesures se réduisent uniquement à deux; savoir, mouvement à deux temps, et mouvement à trois temps; et j'ose défier l'oreille la plus fine d'en trouver de naturels qu'on ne puisse exprimer avec toute la précision possible par l'une des ces deux mesures. Je commencerai donc par faire main basse sur tous ces chiffres bizarres, réservant seulement le deux et le trois, par lesquels comme on verra tout-à-l'heure j'exprimerai tous les mouvements possibles." Rousseau, "Projet concernant de nouveaux signes pour la musique, Lu par l'auteur à l'Académie des Sciences, le 22 août 1742," facsimile ed. in Rousseau, *Project Concerning New Symbols for Music*, ed. and trans. Bernarr Rainbow (Kilkenny, Ireland: Boethius, 1982), 15–16.

flow so important to the debates of the day on time and extension. What Kirnberger did was to integrate the two, reconfiguring the epistemological grounding of meter in the same way that time had been re-explained. He used the core premise of Rameau's simplification scheme—that all meters divide the measure into 2, 3, or 4 beats—to generate the full variety of meters from an endless flow of durations.

Although the groundwork had already been laid in the collaboratively written encyclopedia articles "Rhythmus" and "Takt," the new theory received its fullest presentation in the second volume of *Die Kunst des reinen Satzes in der Musik*.[86] It begins with a lengthy figurative exposition:

> If one imagines a melody in which all the notes are given with equal intensity, or all the same stress, and also completely all the same length or duration—as if, for example, this melody were to persist in reiterating only whole notes—it would resemble an equably flowing stream...
>   [the] conversion of a bare stream of notes into a melody similar to speech comes to pass in part through accents that are given to a few notes, and partly through the variance between long and short notes.[87]

The image of the equably flowing stream and the verb for flow (*fließen*) factored importantly in Kirnberger's discussion of meter. They allowed him to describe musical time as an absolute: an ongoing flow that meter then divides into regular groupings through the application of accent (real or imagined). Because theories of meter at the time of his writing were usually constructed in the opposite way, focusing on the properties of the measure itself or the characteristics of each meter signature, Kirnberger could not have begun with the heart of the theoretical discussion itself.

After this figurative introduction, Kirnberger defines meter as "accents that are given to some notes in regularity."[88] Meter for Kirnberger was a division of ongoing musical time into regular parts. This definition is his most concise, but it is still not a complete theorization. The more technical exposition of meter follows this definition by several paragraphs, and again returns to an abstract register:

---

86. "Rhythmus; Rhythmisch" in Sulzer, *Allgemeine Theorie der schönen Künste*, 2:975–85; "Takt," in Sulzer, *Allgemeine Theorie der schönen Künste*, 2:1130–38. On the differences between the theories set out in the *Allgemeine Theorie der schönen Künste* and *Die Kunst des reinen Satzes in der Musik*, see Mirka, *Metric Manipulations in Haydn and Mozart*, 4–5.

87. "Wenn man sich einen Gesang vorstellt, in dem alle Töne mit gleicher Stärke, oder mit einerley Nachdruck angegeben würden und auch durchaus von einerley Länge oder Dauer wären, wie wenn z. B. der Gesang aus lauter ganzen Tacktnoten bestünde, so würde er einem gleichförmig fließenden Strom gleichen... Diese Verwandlung eines blossen Stroms von Tönen in einen der Rede ähnlichen Gesang geschieht eines Theiles durch Accente, die auf einige Töne gelegt werrden [sic], theils durch die Verschiedenheit der Länge und Kürze Töne." Kirnberger, *Die Kunst des reinen Satzes in der Musik*, 2:113.

88. "In der genauen Einförmigkeit der Accente, die auf einige Töne gelegt werden... bestehet eigentlich der Tackt." Kirnberger, *Die Kunst des reinen Satzes in der Musik*, 2:113.

If one hears a series of equal beats that are repeated one after the next with an equal space of time, as in, for example [plate 4.1], experience teaches us that we, in our minds, immediately divide them metrically by arranging them in segments, each containing an equal number of beats. Indeed we do this such that we place an accent on the first beat of each segment or we imagine that we hear it stronger than the other beats. This division can come about in three ways [as shown in plate 4.2], that is to say, we divide the beats into segments of two, or three, or four beats each...

The application of this is easy to make. Instead of the word "beat," one uses time [*Zeit*], and measure [*Tackt* (e.g., meter and/or measure)] instead of "segment," so one can get an idea of what meter is, and how many varieties there are.[89]

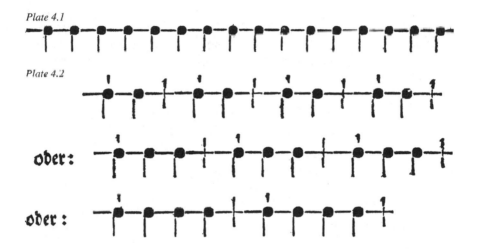

Plate 4.1

Plate 4.2

ober:

ober:

Although it may appear from the first paragraph above that Kirnberger is already setting forth a theory of meter, he does not actually do so in full until the second paragraph quoted above, when he suggests that all he has said theretofore abstractly can be applied to meter. Equal beats divided up metrically "in our minds," for Kirnberger's contemporaries, was quite far from a theory of meter,

89. "Wenn man eine Folge von gleichen Schlägen, die in gleichem Zeitraum nach einander widerholet werden, vernimmt, z. B. [plate 4.1] so lehrt die Erfahrung, daß wir in unsern Gedanken alsobald eine tacktmäßige Eintheilung dieser Schläge machen, indem wir sie in Glieder ordnen, die eine gleiche Anzahl Schläge in sich fassen, und zwar so, daß wir auf den ersten Schlag eines jeden Gliedes einen Accent legen, oder ihn stärker als die übrigen Schläge zu vernehmen glauben. Diese Eintheilung kann auf dreyerley Art geschehen, entweder also: [plate 4.2] nemlich, wir theilen die Schläge in Glieder von zwey, oder drey, oder vier Schlägen ein...Die Anwendung hievon ist leicht zu machen. Statt dem Worte Schlag setze man Zeit, statt Glied Tackt, so hat man einen Begrif von dem, was der Tackt, und wie vielerley er ist." Kirnberger, *Die Kunst des reinen Satzes in der Musik*, 2:114–16. Here I have decided to employ some elements of the Beach-Thym translation in the first half, while departing sharply from their translation in the second. Note that Beach and Thym interpret the German *Zeit* as "beat." This leads them to translate *Schläg* as pulse, in order to differentiate between pulse and beat. I have chosen to interpret the ambiguities in these terms differently, leaving *Zeit* as time. See Kirnberger *The Art of Strict Musical Composition*, trans. Beach and Thym, 383–84.

nor would they have recognized it as such until the point at which he suggests the application, to meter, of all that he had written above.[90] So when Kirnberger writes, "If one hears a series of equal beats that are repeated one after the next with an equal space of time," he is still writing figuratively. He uses this abstract register to describe a scene of sensuous cognition, in which an individual attempts to parse one of the world's natural phenomena—in this case, an unending flow of duration—into intelligible parts.[91] The components of this scene resonate with the period's aesthetic traditions, in which our experiences of art mediating nature excite our attentions and sentiment. In Kirnberger's theory of meter, the crucial point of the encounter is the application of accent "in our mind." We do this, he tells us, "such that we place an accent on the first beat of each segment." The accent is the point of contact between the flow of duration and our understanding of it. It should not be understood to be a prescription for the performance of meter or an explanation of a notational practice but rather a description of our encounter with musical material. The accent here is something like a peak of our attention's energy and does not require a special articulation on the part of the performer: "we *imagine* that we hear it stronger than the other beats [emphasis added]."[92] Kirnberger's theory takes us quite a distance from the sixteenth- and seventeenth-century motion-driven logic of the beat, in which duration is

90. Shifting constructions of listening and the listener, although outside the scope of this chapter, were certainly a part of shifting temporal conceptualizations. Kirnberger's references to the mind of the listener in his theory are an important part of his relationship to Rameau, on the one hand, and to Sulzer's aesthetics on the other. The definitive account of the new relationship to listening and the listener in Rameau's theories can be found in Jairo Moreno's *Musical Representations, Subjects, and Objects* (Bloomington: Indiana University Press, 2004), 85–127. See Matthew Riley's rather different treatment of the same topic with regard to Sulzer in his *Musical Listening in the German Enlightenment* (Aldershot: Ashgate, 2004). Also of relevance here are the alternative historiographies of temporal philosophy that are available: McAuley, for instance, notes a crucial distinction between the Newtonian conception of flowing time and its subsequent development in the writings of Kant and Schelling, which he argues is of great significance for the intellectual heritage of the absolute. See McAuley, "Rhythmic Accent and the Absolute."

91. I use the phrase "sensuous cognition" to place Kirnberger in a genealogy of aesthetic thought alongside Sulzer and following on Baumgarten. Baumgarten famously defined aesthetics as a "science of sensuous cognition." Sulzer made an important distinction between cognition (*Erkennen*) and sensation (*Empfinden*), and believed music uniquely capable of evincing a heightened form of sensation, in which we "become aware of a modification within ourselves." Meters, in Kirnberger's view, had the powerful capacity to depict specific passions and sentiments. Alexander Gottlieb Baumgarten, *Meditationes philosophicae de nonnullis ad poema pertinentibus* (Halle: Grunert, 1735), §cxv; modern ed., ed. Benedetto Croce (Naples: Vecchi, 1900), 41; Sulzer, "Sinnlich," in the *Allgemeine Theorie der schönen Künste*, 2:673; Kirnberger, *Die Kunst des reinen Satzes in der Musik*, 2:105 and 113. On the role of music in Sulzer's aesthetics see Matthew Riley, "Civilizing the Savage: Johann Georg Sulzer and the 'Aesthetic Force' of Music," *Journal of the Royal Musical Association* 127, no. 1 (2002): 1–22; and Riley, *Musical Listening in the German Enlightenment*.

92. The idea of attentional energy has affinities not only with Sulzer's aesthetics but also twenty-first century theories on the cognition of meter. In particular see Mari Jones, Heather Moynihan Johnston, and Jennifer Puente, "Effects of Auditory Pattern Structure of Anticipatory and Reactive Attending," *Cognitive Psychology* 51, no. 1 (2006): 59–96, particularly 61–62. Although

rendered explicable through a real or imagined motion. Here, the independent motion of unending flow is what needs to be parsed and divided through the imagined application of regular accent in sensuous cognition. For Kirnberger, meter was a way of attending to the ongoing flow of time.

The image of flow and Kirnberger's theoretical succession of equal beats did the work of presenting the basis for his theory of meter. They allowed him a way to present meter in its general form before distinguishing between the different kinds of meters that were possible. Engaging Rameau's essential principle for meter's organization, Kirnberger presented a universal theory with which one could dynamically generate any of the meters from his exhaustive list; the unending flow of time could be divided any number of ways within the basic categories he set out.

Kirnberger generalized the logic of his multiple meters in the form of a universal theory. The activity of attending creates the unit of the measure, which his contemporaries had taken as their starting point. Accent was no longer an attribute of the notated measure or the durations it contained, it was now a relationship between the unfolding of duration and mind of the listener. Meter could now be understood as a general rule that operated within absolute time to create the specific "times" of the multiple meters in the eighteenth-century doctrine. His abstract description of meter in general is followed by all of the specifics: a detailed description of twenty-four different useful meters (including explanations of *triplirt* and *zusammengesetzten Tacktarten*) supplemented with fifty-eight examples.[93] He explains how our parsing of musical duration renders explicable the variety of meters, each of which will impart its characteristic affect as we listen.

But why did Kirnberger depend so heavily on the specific kinetic images—the flowing stream and the undifferentiated beats—prevalent in his discussion? Why would he have chosen to reconceptualize meter, to depart from the theories of his predecessors, specifically through these metaphors? Kirnberger's figurative introduction to his theory of meter did more than simply prepare the way for a theory that would depart from long-held traditions. His "equably flowing stream" of undifferentiated pitches situated his theory alongside the epistemological reconfiguration of absolute time.[94] Kirnberger, like his contemporaries in natural philosophy, participated in rewriting the relationship between time and motion, attributing motion or flow to time itself and discarding the older conception of time as a measurement of motion.

Kirnberger's imagery in his explication of meter reproduced, in a different form, the notion of the fluxion and flowing time in geometry. The "series of equal beats…repeated one after the next" (plate 4.1, reproduced above) in his theoretical

---

not mentioned in Mirka's *Metric Manipulations in Haydn and Mozart*, this is the type of correspondence her book so skillfully highlights.

93. Fifteen of these are included in one large composite example at the head of the chapter. Kirnberger, *Die Kunst des reinen Satzes in der Musik*, 2:107–11. I discus this example and those like it in chapter 5.

94. Kirnberger, *Die Kunst des reinen Satzes in der Musik*, 2:113.

exposition employed both line and point, just as the explication of fluxions in the calculus employed curve and point. Kirnberger's abstract example presented these points on a line to explain the ongoing absolute flow of a temporal phenomenon; the series of beats (or points) on his line (and it is important to note here that it is not a staff) serves to elucidate the same epistemological grounding of time that the motion of points along a curve would have done in the Newtonian calculus.

Newtonian absolute time is a concept that is easy to oversimplify. In the twenty-first century, many of our colloquialisms about time depict a seemingly absolute temporal substrate within which events are located (events are said to be "in" time or are visualized on timelines that appear to express the "emptiness" of time, and so forth). But this particular oversimplification of Newtonian time misses its importantly dynamic, flowing aspect; it fails to understand just how different from our own understanding of "absolute" time this eighteenth-century concept is. It was this aspect that afforded, in Kirnberger's theory of meter, a conceptualization that shares affinities with Christopher Hasty's theory of projection in *Meter as Rhythm*.[95] As in Hasty's theory, Kirnberger accounts for the diachronic unfolding of events and our capacity to sensibly parse them. Indeed, this resemblance is what gives Danuta Mirka license to link Hasty's theory to the eighteenth-century theories she discusses in *Metric Manipulations in Haydn and Mozart*.[96]

Yet the important historical difference between these recent retellings of meter's dynamism and Kirnberger's theory is the relationship that his theory held to the conceptualizations of time and meter that preceded it. Without positing that Kirnberger's theory of meter was somehow a direct transposition of the changes that occurred in eighteenth-century mathematics or natural philosophy, we should understand that a shared and significant change was expressed in all these discourses.[97] The reorientation of the concepts of time and motion made possible the full separation of the measure from the physical act of the beat. This

---

95. Hasty, *Meter as Rhythm* (Oxford: Oxford University Press, 1997), 84–95; nonetheless, in Hasty's account "absolute" time is an objectionable framework for music analysis: "Absolute time thus presents us with the opportunity to view process as a fait accompli, its phases fixed in an immutable order and available for synoptic inspection, like the notes of a score." Hasty, *Meter as Rhythm*, 10.

96. Mirka, *Metric Manipulations in Haydn and Mozart*, 28–30.

97. One could make a claim, however, for a direct line of transmission through any number of individuals to Kirnberger personally. It is clear, for instance, that Kirnberger knew Euler and his work and supported him in his musical pursuits. There is also evidence to suggest that he came into close contact with many members of the Berlin Academy: Moses Mendelssohn studied with him, and his relationships with Sulzer and, above all, with Princess Anna Amalia suggest that he would have socialized in the Berlin Academy circles. Nevertheless, I have not attempted to make such connections or to prove any such lines of transmission. Instead, I want to emphasize that Kirnberger's work was one piece of a broad shift in discourses on time, and as much a symptom of this shift as all of his contemporaries' writings. On Kirnberger's relationship to Euler, see Martin Vogel, "Die Musikschriften Leonhard Eulers," in *Leonhardi Euleri Opera Omnia* (Turici: Societatis Scientiarum Naturalium Helveticae, 1960), ser. 3, vol. 11, lvii–lviii; on his relationship to Moses Mendelssohn, see see Laurenz Lütteken, "Moses Mendelssohn und der Musikästhetische Diskurs der Aufklärung"; on his relationship to Anna Amalia, see Tobias Debuch, *Anna Amalia von Preußen* (Berlin: Logos, 2001), 84–102.

rendered the measure itself a topic of increasing interest in eighteenth-century music theory. Through the course of the century, writings on meter began to list and codify the waning connections between meter, note values, character, and tempo, all the while attempting to explain the properties of the measure and its many forms. Kirnberger and his circle provided one theory that would account for the generation of these diverse measures, drawing at once on the need for simplification and a new understanding of time as an absolute flow of duration. In their theory, the beat and the measure had become so distinct as to allow for the one to create the other. Meter, a special kind of attending that divided beats into measures, was now a general, theoretical concept based on the continuity of absolute time.

CHAPTER Five

Techniques for Keeping Time

The Problem of Tempo

The problem of precise tempo indication troubled eighteenth-century musicians. With the slow conceptual separation of the beat from the measure, it had become evident that musical notation lacked a certain type of specificity in its attempt to encode the unfolding of musical events. Theorists began to worry that printed music did not communicate tempo effectively: although the note shapes provided the durations relative to each other, there was no way of ensuring that the correct tempo of a piece could be understood from the meter signature and note values alone. The system sometimes known as *tempo giusto* had begun to fall apart.

Tempo giusto gives name to the idea that the meter signature, note values, and character of any piece can indicate its natural or "just" tempo.[1] Although meter signatures were not always explicitly associated with particular tempi or characters or note values—and they certainly were not limited to one configuration of these—they were understood to have the capacity to reference this network of ideas and were often called upon to fulfill it. Eighteenth-century writers on music began to realize that tempo was a particularly elusive component of this system; there were few ways to capture tempo in notation with any kind of dependable translatability. Fearing the immanent collapse of this function of meters, the musicians, theorists, and inventors of the era resorted to a set of techniques that they hoped would preserve and communicate their tempi. Among these techniques were the early musical chronometers; predecessors to the metronome, these devices were one version of an attempt to provide a regular, reliable, and external method for indicating time in music. But no significant system of tempo

---

1. For a period source, see Jean-Jacques Rousseau, "Mouvement" in the *Dictionnaire de Musique*, facsimile ed. (1768; Hildesheim: Georg Olms, 1969), 303. This notion of *tempo giusto* is not to be confused with the tempo marking that occurs occasionally in Handel's works. For more on *tempo giusto* see *Oxford Music Online*, s.v. "Tempo Giusto," "Tempo and Expression Marks," by David Fallows, accessed November 27, 2011, <www.oxfordmusiconline.org>.

specification would rely on any of these instruments until well into the nine-teenth century, when Maelzel patented and disseminated the most effective musical chronometer.

Before that moment—and during the heart of the eighteenth-century's tempo anxieties—theorists and musicians made recourse to a technological solution not customarily remembered as such. In the final decades of *tempo giusto*, they cre-ated elaborate taxonomies in their theories of meter, attempting to codify and document the connections between meters, note values, characters, and tempi. These taxonomies mark the final moment in the effort to use *tempo giusto* as a prescriptive tool. Their great quantity and the huge proportion of space they received in the centuries' treatises attest to their aspirations of exactitude—aspi-rations they shared with the century's advanced clockwork mechanisms. It may have been that distant goal of chronometric measurement that prompted Johann Forkel to equate music's rhythms to the division of days into hours and minutes. "In this regard," he mused, "the partitioning of rhythm into measures and phrases with barlines—the marks that express them—is to be seen in like manner to the hour hand, indicating to us the musical relationship of time that every musical phrase has to pass through."[2]

The truth of the matter—as Forkel and his eighteenth-century contempo-raries were all too aware—was that the current notational practices made no use of the contemporary chronometric technologies. There was no way to specify the rate of Forkel's barlines using the hands of any clock, even as the two were under-stood to operate in a similar manner. Rousseau captured these frustrations suc-cinctly in his dictionary article on musical chronometers:

> It is much to be wished that such an instrument might be had, to fix with preci-sion the time of each measure in a piece of music: one could conserve very easily by this means the true tempi of airs, without which they lose their character, and which one cannot know after the death of their authors except by a sort of tradi-tion very subject to change or extinction. It is already a complaint that we have forgotten the tempi of a great number of airs, and it is to be believed that we have slowed them all down.[3]

---

2. "In dieser Rücksicht sind die Abtheilungen des Rhythmus in Takte und Sectionalzeilen, mit ihren äußern Zeichen, den Taktstrichen, gleichsam als Stundenweiser anzusehen, wodurch uns das musikalische Verhältniß der Zeit angedeutet wird, die ein jeder musikalischer Satz zu durchlaufen hat." Johann Nikolaus Forkel, *Allgemeine Geschichte der Musik*, facsimile ed. (1788; Laaber: Laaber-Verlag, 2005), 1:27n16.

3. "Il seroit fort à souhaiter qu'on eût un tel Instrument pour fixer avec precision le tems de chaque Mesure dans une Pièce de Musique: on conserveroit par ce moyen plus facilement le vrai Mouvement des Airs, sans lequel ils perdent leur caractère, & qu'on ne peut connoître, après la mort des Auteurs, que par une espèce de tradition fort sujette à s'éteindre ou à s'altérer. On se plaint déjà que nous avons oublié les Mouvemens d'un grand nombre d'Airs, & il est à croire qu'on les a ralentis tous." Rousseau, "Chronomètre," in *Dictionnaire de musique*, facsimile ed. (1768; Hildesheim: Georg Olms, 1969), 99–100. Throughout his article "Chronomètre" Rousseau relies heavily on ideas and language borrowed from Diderot's "Projet d'un nouvel Orgue" of 1748. See Diderot, "Projet d'un nouvel Orgue," [1748] in *Mémoires sur différens sujets de mathématiques* in *Œuvres philosophiques et dramatiques de M. Diderot* (Amsterdam, 1772), 16:267–75.

Rousseau writes of a "tradition very subject to change or extinction," which characterizes the kind of knowledge contained in *tempo giusto*. His anxieties about its end were representative of the era's overarching preoccupation with timekeeping practices. After the opening of the universe and the loss of cosmological motion as the universal timekeeper, natural philosophy was forced to recognize that all temporal measurements were equally relative, and therefore equally useless for the specification of a universal temporal measure. The universal clock had been dismantled. Concomitantly with these developments, though, the technologies of time measurement grew increasingly more accurate, reliable, portable, and affordable. The authority of time measurement had passed from the universal to the particular in natural philosophy as in everyday life. The new availability and dependability of the mechanical clock made even the smallest units of temporal measure accessible to a broad public.[4] It was during this same period that musicians, theorists, and others began to voice their concerns over musical notation's ability to do the work of the clock—to prescribe tempo precisely and with reference to a widely available standard.

The period's writings on this topic are threaded through with the language of loss and anxiety. Treatises on music consistently depicted the potential to specify duration and tempo through the opposite: the possibility of forgetting or misunderstanding them. Many, like Rousseau, worried that the process of forgetting had already begun, and that a great deal of tempi were already misunderstood. Worse, this process was said to be ongoing and even intensifying, rendering tempo preservation an urgent affair. In this sense, the documentation produced on meter and tempo in the eighteenth century tells a story of loss; it narrates the anxieties of an age newly aware of the possibilities for temporal exactitude and the potential failure of musical notation to live up to the challenge.

Timekeeping Two Ways: 1. Chronometers

By the time Forkel related the work of musical notation to that of the clock's moving hour hand, the analogy was no longer new. As early a theorist as Lodovico Zacconi (in the 1592 *Prattica di musica*) could suggest a similar correspondence, and references to clock time in writings on music appeared sporadically during the seventeenth century.[5] For Forkel, though, the mechanical clock occupied an entirely

4. Of the classic literature on society and timekeeping, see E. P. Thompson, "Time, Work-Discipline, and Industrial Capitalism," *Past and Present* 38, no. 1 (1967): 56–97; Jacques Attali, *Histoires du temps* (Paris: Fayard, 1982), particularly 154–73; Samuel L. Macey, *Clocks and the Cosmos: Time in Western Life and Thought* (Hamden, CT: Archon, 1980); David Landes, *Revolution in Time* (Cambridge, MA: Belknap, 1983), particularly 114–87; and also more recent qualifications of this literature, such as Michael J. Sauter, "Clockwatchers and Stargazers: Time Discipline in Early Modern Berlin," *American Historical Review* 112, no. 3 (2007): 685–709.

5. Lodovico Zacconi, *Prattica di musica*, facsimile ed. (1596; Hildesheim: Georg Olms, 1982), 20v; Christopher Simpson, *The Principles of Practical Musick* (London: Will. Godbid for Henry Brome, 1665), 23; see also Rosamond E. M. Harding's "The Metronome and it's Precursors" [sic], in *The Origins of Musical Time and Expression* (Oxford: Oxford University Press, 1938); subsequently republished as a stand-alone monograph, *The Metronome and it's Precursors* [sic] (Oxfordshire: Gresham Books, 1983), 1–8.

different place in thought and everyday life than it had for earlier theorists. The Europe in which he prepared his 1788 volume of the *Allgemeine Geschichte der Musik* for publication was one that had been completely transformed by the clock's new ubiquity.

Just the year before Forkel's volume was published, the Berlin Academy had installed a large, public clock in its building on Unter den Linden that was to be "set daily...so that all city clocks [could] be set by it."[6] The Academy clock epitomized a new form of public temporal awareness burgeoning in the mid-eighteenth century. A new "clockwatching public" had become increasingly concerned with the accuracy of the timekeepers that regulated daily activities, and they saw the Academy clock as the answer to the problem of horological standardization in Berlin at the time of its installation.[7]

The Academy clock was not the first large, public instrumental standard of its type. In Berlin it was preceded by the instrument in the Domkirche which, with its central location, regulated the other church clocks in the city.[8] Clocks in church towers that disseminated the local time to those in their surrounds constituted a tradition at least four centuries old by the time the Academy chose to install its own public instrumental standard. These early church clocks, the Domkirche's included, were for the most part of the pendulum variety and required frequent adjustment to account for the time they lost. This did not pose much of a problem until the new clockwork mechanisms far surpassed the accuracy of these older timekeepers, creating the possibility and eventual demand for clocks that did not lose their accuracy so easily. Even mid-seventeenth-century instruments lost nearly fifteen minutes over the course of one day. With the development and improvement of the escapement mechanism, however, the eighteenth-century public could expect clocks to lose no more than ten seconds daily.[9] The ability to capture and fix those previously ephemeral minutes proved useful and intoxicating.[10]

In addition to improved accuracy, the eighteenth century saw the development of more affordable, widely available, and smaller clocks than ever before. The growth of pocket watch popularity over the course of the century testifies to an increasingly intimate and exigent relationship with timekeeping.[11] The pocket watch brought the technologies of time to a most extreme form of localization and the closest proximity to the individual. By the end of the century more than

---

6. Ewald Friedrich von Hertzberg, *Historische Nachricht von dem ersten Regierungs-Jahre Friedrich Wilhelm II. Königs von Preussen*...(Berlin, 1787), 19, as cited and translated in Michael J. Sauter, "Clockwatchers and Stargazers: Time Discipline in Early Modern Berlin," 689.

7. I have borrowed the phrase "clockwatching public" from Sauter, "Clockwatchers and Stargazers," 692.

8. Sauter, "Clockwatchers and Stargazers," 696–701.

9. Macey, *Clocks and the Cosmos*, 41.

10. See in particular Lewis Mumford's remarks in his *Technics and Civilization* (New York: Harcourt, Brace and Company, 1934), 12–18.

11. Thompson, "Time, Work-Discipline, and Industrial Capitalism," 64–70; Sauter, "Clockwatchers and Stargazers," 690–91.

400,000 were produced in Europe each year.[12] They were incorporated into the fashion of the era (worn against the body) and made the central object of public timekeeping practices, serving as the personal standards against which to judge the accuracy of other timekeepers.[13]

The smaller, more accurate, and more available timepieces generated a populace that was critical of the public clocks that had once been their only frame of reference. In Berlin, this led the Academy to construct its new clock, which would appease the pocket watch-carrying critics and ultimately set the civic standard. Moreover, the growth of the public sphere in cities like Berlin afforded a venue in which to compare and discuss the merits of these instruments. The dissemination of print media and the institutions for collective conversation created the spaces in which a new kind of talk about timekeeping was born.[14]

The increasing pervasiveness of the clock in the eighteenth century also changed quotidian understandings of temporality. The new availability of accurate, affordable, and portable timepieces allowed a wider range of individuals the opportunity to envision their daily routines in the equable flow of time. Earlier timekeepers, with their physical ties to one immovable location, kept the public conception of time grounded in "socio-spatial markers": natural occurrences, daily routines, or meetings of social organizations in proper, fixed places.[15] The public fascination with accurate timekeeping provided something of a formalization for time, or an abstracted experience of temporal passage. The clock machine, then, was integral to the experience of time discipline.

The ability to quantify the diachronic unfolding of events in dependable, universal measurements not only altered civic life but also provided a new appreciation for location in the world. Responding to a classic problem of navigation, eighteenth-century clockmakers attempted to produce seaworthy (hence, non-pendulum) instruments accurate enough to employ in the calculation of longitude. By midcentury the independent efforts of John Harrison and Pierre Le Roy led to the mass production of what were then known as marine chronometers, which kept their time within seconds even over transatlantic crossings. With the problem of longitude solved, one could envision the most remote destinations within the universal coordinates of time and space. The marine chronometer demystified the giant expanse of the world.[16]

The particular configuration of timekeeping and distance that the marine chronometer produced was only the latest manifestation of a long-standing

12. Landes, *Revolution in Time*, 287–88.
13. Sauter, "Clockwatchers and Stargazers," 691–96.
14. This is one of the central points of Sauter's "Clockwatchers and Stargazers."
15. Anthony Giddens, *The Consequences of Modernity* (Stanford: Stanford University Press, 1990), 17; J. Peter Burgess, "European Borders: History of Space/Space of History," *CTheory*, article a013 (1994), accessed November 30, 2011, <www.ctheory.net/articles.aspx?id=55>.
16. Some, like Jacques Attali, would go so far as to say that it "accompanied, made possible and accelerated the industrial revolution." Attali, *Histoires du temps*, 173.

relationship between the temporally and geographically distant; the idea of temporal precision had long played a role in imaginations of the forgotten and far away. It is no coincidence that the two were conflated in one of the first early modern recommendations for a musical chronometer. Found deep within Mersenne's *Harmonie universelle*, the description of this hypothetical instrument arrives in the midst of a discussion about the precautions one might take "if one were to send a piece of music from Paris to Constantinople, Persia, China, or elsewhere."[17] Mersenne's first concern was to specify the starting pitch of the music, which one could accomplish by notating the number of string vibrations in the time of one measure. The following prescription of duration for the measure, though, conflates the spatially and temporally distant: "Next it is necessary to explain how one might keep the same measure as was intended by the composer, should he be dead or absent," Mersenne writes.[18] His proposed pendulum—marked off at the correct length—would supply the time of the measure for either a new destination or a future performance.

Mersenne's very early and hypothetical chronometer could have supplemented notation's ability to communicate outside of its historical and geographical milieu. As the age of the mechanical clock unfolded, theorists began to express the need for such an instrument much closer to home. The eighteenth century saw a process by which techniques for time discipline in music encroached on local and current practices. Concerns about tempo specification were no longer only an issue for great distance.

Eighteenth-century descriptions of musical chronometers do not often recall Mersenne's passing suggestion but instead refer to the *chronomètre* of Étienne Loulié, first described in the 1696 *Éléments ou principes de musique*.[19] The central component of Loulié's instrument was a pendulum of variable length that was hung against a long vertical rule for measure. Musicians could adjust the pendulum with reference to the spatial units marked on this board (in *pouces*) and could use their measurement to denote a given tempo. "The *chronomètre*," Loulié explained, "is an instrument by means of which composers of music can henceforth mark the true tempo of their compositions; their airs, marked according to this instrument, can be executed in their absence as if they themselves were beating the meter."[20] Loulié thought his specifications useful for more proximate performances than Mersenne had imagined. His primary example concerned the transmission of a new composition to Italy where—once united with one of his

17. "Si l'on envoyoit une piece de Musique de Paris à Constantinople, en Perse, à la Chine, ou autre part…" Mersenne, *Harmonie universelle*, facsimile ed. (1636–37; Paris: Centre national de la recherché scientifique, 1963), vol. 3, "Livre Troisiesme des Instrumens à chordes," 147.

18. "Il faut encore expliquer comme l'on peut garder la mesme mesure suivant l'intention du mesme Compositeur, quoy qu'il soit mort ou absent." Mersenne, *Harmonie universelle*, vol. 3, "Livre Troisiesme des Instrumens à chordes," 149.

19. Étienne Loulié, *Éléments ou principes de musique* (Paris: Christophe Ballard, 1696), 81–88.

20. "Le chronomètre est un Instrument par le moyen duquel les Compositeurs de Musique pourront deformais marquer le veritable mouvement de leur Composition, & leurs Airs marquez par rapport à cet Instrument se pourront executer en leur absence comme s'il en battoient eux-mêmes la Mesure." Loulié, *Éléments ou principes de musique*, 83.

instruments—was sure to be performed correctly. The numbers of the *chronomètre* were a safeguard against misinterpretation. They provided "a sure means of understanding the true tempo," he wrote, "particularly for those who live in the provinces, who may want to know exactly the true tempo of all the works of Monsieur de Lully."[21] What was for Mersenne a concern for intercontinental communication had become an intra-European matter at the opening of the eighteenth century.

A few years after the publication of Loulié's *Éléments*, the acoustician Joseph Sauveur pointed out a significant disadvantage in the *chronomètre*'s design. There was no relationship between Loulié's increments of length and the units of the clock. "The times of the vibrations of his pendulum are for the most part incommensurable with a second," Sauveur wrote.[22] His contribution consisted of a redrawn scale for the musical chronometer that would allow for a correspondence between clock time and *chronomètre* indication. Each beat was to be measured in units of a *tierce*, or on sixtieth of a second.[23]

As the century wore on theorists referred back to Loulié and Sauveur, either lauding their efforts or suggesting mechanical modifications to the basic *chronomètre* design. Louis-Léon Pajot d'Ons-en-Bray—concerned to "fix the duration of the measures and tempi of airs" so that they would "thereby retain their beauty and agreement"—created a dial interface for the apparatus and greatly increased its precision.[24] William Tans'ur advocated for the use of several pendulums at once in order to visualize multiple levels of subdivision.[25] Others designed and demonstrated novel machines that accomplished the chronometer's work in a different fashion, some building their instruments in the manner of music boxes and some fully mechanizing Loulié's basic pendulum design.[26]

No matter how they chose to combat the issue, the innovators of the eighteenth-century musical chronometers all complained that—despite their

---

21. "Un moyen seur pour en connoître le veritable mouvement, particulierement ceux qui demeurent dans les Provinces, lesquels pourront sçavoir a juste le veritable mouvement de tous les Ouvrages de Monsieur de Lully." Loulié, *Éléments ou principes de musique*, 88. For a fascinating theoretical and historical study along these lines, see Theodore M. Porter, *Trust in Numbers: The Pursuit of Objectivity in Science and Public Life* (Princeton: Princeton University Press, 1995).

22. "Les temps des vibrations de son Pendule sont la plupart incommensurables avec une Seconde." Joseph Sauveur, "Système General des Intervalles des Sons, et son Application à tous les Systèmes et à tous les Instruments de Musique," *Histoire de l'Académie Royale des Sciences Année 1701* (Paris: Gabriel Martin, Jean-Baptiste Coignard, & Hippolyte-Louis Guerin, 1704), 299–366, at 322.

23. In this connection see Jimena Canales, *A Tenth of a Second: A History* (Chicago: University of Chicago Press, 2009), on temporal divisions smaller than one second.

24. "Il est très-important, comme nous avons dit, de constater & de fixer la durée des mesures & des temps des différents Airs de Musique…& conserveront par-là leur beauté & leurs agréments." Louis-Léon Pajot d'Ons-en-Bray, "Description et usage d'un Métromètre ou Machine pour batter les Mesures et les Temps de toutes sortes d'Airs," *Histoire de l'Académie Royale des Sciences Année 1732* (Paris: De L'Imprimerie Royale, 1735), 182–195, at 190.

25. William Tans'ur, *A New Musical Grammar*, rev. ed. (1746; London: Robert Brown for James Hodges, 1756), 47–51.

26. *Oxford Music Online*, s.v. "Metronome (i)," by David Fallows, accessed December 4, 2011, <www.oxfordmusiconline.org>; Harding, *The Metronome and it's Precursors* [sic].

efforts and those of their predecessors—no single device had been able to find an established place in musical notation and practice. Not only did these authors take issue with the lack of specificity in the inscription of musical duration, they also disparaged the tempo terms composers had begun to employ. Diderot, taking his place among the critics of tempo notation, lamented: "The words *allegro, vivace, presto, affettuoso, soavemente, piano,* etc. which musicians use will always be vague until we relate them to a fixed term of speed or slowness which can be agreed upon. As one may observe today, people complain that the tempi of many of Lully's arias are lost."[27] Jean-Baptiste Davaux used this same concern to generate interest in his newly devised *chronomètre*, writing to the *Journal de Paris* in 1784, "The inadequacy of these terms and their vague significations have been recognized for too long. It has been demonstrated clearly that the words *allegro, andante,* and so on are susceptible to an infinity of nuances in their tempi, and one can never fix the intention of the author in a precise manner."[28]

Toward the century's end, the language of uncertainty and loss was applied to the present. Composers and commentators worried that notation no longer spoke to anyone with an acceptable degree of accuracy despite their temporal or spatial proximity. A newspaper report on the *rhythmomètre*—a device in competition with Davaux's—specifically commented on the failure of the score: "…lacking such a regulator, [pieces] are almost never performed with the expression characteristic of their tempo and of their printing."[29] The existing practices of inscription required some additional technique.

Still, none of the eighteenth century's many musical chronometers found a place in practice or in print. Large pendulum apparatuses such as Loulié's were ungainly and inconvenient; reconstructing them meant tackling the problem of spatial measure, which was incredibly varied across Europe.[30] Other machines were never produced in any significant quantity or never made in the first place— only proposed as hypothetical tools. A general lack of consensus for any one of

27. "Les mots *allegro, vivace, presto, affettuoso, soavemente, piano,* &c. dont se servent les Musiciens, seront toujours vagues, tant qu'on ne les rapportera point à un terme fixe de vîtesse ou de lenteur dont on sera convenu. Aussi voit-on aujourd'hui des personnes se plaindre que le mouvement de plusieurs airs de Lully est perdu." Diderot, "Projet d'un nouvel Orgue," [1748] in *Mémoires sur différens sujets de mathématiques,* 16:268.

28. "L'insuffisance de ces termes & leur signification vague sont reconnues depuis trop longtemps; il est démontré évidemment que les mots d'*Allegro,* d'*Andante,* &c. étant susceptibles d'une infinité de nuances dans leur mouvement, ne peuvent jamais fixer d'une manière précise l'intention de l'Auteur." Jean-Baptiste Davaux, "Lettre de M. Davaux, aux Auteurs du Journal," *Journal de Paris* 129 (May 8, 1784): 559–61, at 560.

29. "…& qui, faute d'un pareil régulateur, ne son presque jamais exécutés avec l'expression que le propre de ce mouvement est de leur imprimer." Unsigned article, "Rhythmomètre, inventé & exécuté par le sieur Dubos, horloger-méchanicien, qui a eu l'honneur de la présenter au Roi & à la Reine, le 13 Janvier 1787," *Journal général de France* 80 (July 5, 1787): 319.

30. On the work of rectifying this problem, see Kathryn M. Olesko, "The Meaning of Precision: The Exact Sensibility in Early Nineteenth-Century Germany," in *The Values of Precision,* ed. M. Norton Wise (Princeton, Princeton University Press, 1995), 103–221; and idem., "Precision, Tolerance, and Consensus: Local Cultures in German and British Resistance Standards," in *Archimedes* 1, ed. Jed Z. Buchwald (London: Kluwer Academic, 1996), 117–56.

these machines reinforced their overall ineffectiveness. As Quantz so frankly noted of Loulié's *chronomètre*, "this machine can hardly always be carried by everyone, which is to say nothing of the fact that it is almost entirely forgotten, for, as far as one can know, no one has made use of it. This immediately gives rise to doubt as to its efficiency or adequacy."[31]

But it was not predominantly because these instruments were difficult to make or carry that they never took hold. Instead, eighteenth-century musicians and theorists believed that the solution was better accomplished otherwise. The meter signatures, notated durations, and characteristics of a piece could still perform the work of specifying tempo, even if they were not as precise and even though many worried that they had become somewhat illegible in this endeavor. As much as the early musical chronometers promised precision in tempo specification, they also threatened to collapse the system of *tempo giusto*. It was possible, for instance, that the use of these machines would render tempo specification completely unmoored from meter, notation, character, and the sensitivity thereto that musicians had worked to cultivate. Even though Rousseau and Diderot both expressed a need for musical chronometers and extolled the virtues of exact tempo specification, they nevertheless both understood that the eighteenth-century efforts to create such a machine would be futile. The chronometer's promise of invariance cost too much if it also meant insensitive performance. Rousseau's remarks on musical chronometers, quoted above, ultimately conclude with dissatisfaction.

> No matter what instrument one might find for regulating the duration of a measure it will be impossible—even if it should have the easiest execution—that it will ever be used in practice. Musicians, a confident set of people, and making, like many others, their own taste the rule of what is good, will never adopt it. They will neglect the chronometer, and will only rely on the true character and the true tempi of airs.[32]

Even if the waning of *tempo giusto* was the cause for nervous prose in these years, it was still somehow effective enough to serve as the best answer for the problem of tempo. Though the clock-machine and the chronometer played important

---

31. "Inszwischen wird diese Maschine doch schwerlich von einem jeden immer bey sich geführet werden können: zu geschweigen, daß die fast allgemeine Vergessenheit derselben, da sie, so viel man weiß, niemand sich zu Nutzen gemacht hat, schon einen Verdacht, wider ihre Zulänglichkeit und Tüchtigkeit, erreget." J. J. Quantz, *Versuch einer Anweisung, die Flöte traversiere zu spielen*, 3rd ed. (1752; Breslau: Johann Friedrich Korn dem ältern, 1789); facsimile ed. (Kassel: Bärenreiter, 1953), 261.

32. "J'ajoûterai que, quelque Instrument qu'on pût trouver pour régler la durée de la Mesure, il seroit impossible, quant même l'exécution en seroit de la dernière facilité, qu'il eût jamais lieu dans la pratique. Les Musiciens, gens confians, & faisant, comme bien d'autres, de leur propre goût la règle du bon, ne l'adopteroient jamais; ils laisseroient le *Chronomètre*, & ne s'en rapporteroient qu'à eux du vrai caractère & du vrai mouvement des Airs." Rousseau, "Chronomètre," in *Dictionnaire de musique*, 100. As noted above, throughout this article Rousseau relies heavily on ideas and language borrowed from Diderot's "Projet d'un nouvel Orgue" [1748], in *Mémoires sur différens sujets de mathématiques*.

roles in the conceptualization of music's temporal precision, they were neither ideal standards nor the only solutions.

Timekeeping Two Ways: 2. Taxonomies of Meter

"Imagine an assemblage of many component charts that together form a single large one." So begins Diderot's *Encyclopédie* article titled "Chronologique (machine)." It continues:

> The height of this larger chart is hardly a foot; its length must therefore be very considerable. However long, it is divided into small equal parts, alternately black and white, such as those marking out the degrees on the great circle around the globe. There are as many of these parts as there are years that have elapsed from the creation of the world until today. Each of these sections marks one year of the existence of the world... As for the multitude and variety of facts, it is immense and includes everyone of any importance mentioned in history, from the founding of an empire to the invention of a machine; from the birth of a potentate to that of a skilled workman.[33]

Diderot describes an immense machine—a record in paper. His imagined chronological chart is a location for the preservation, notation, and ordering of events. It employs a visual and inscriptive technique for keeping an extraordinarily diverse group of times organized. Like the other timepieces described in the *Encyclopédie*, Diderot's "Chronologique (machine)" responded to the time discipline of its day, but without the pendulums or spring escapements of those instruments. This device used print.

While eighteenth-century musicians and theorists fretted over the inadequacy of their chronometers, they were simultaneously at work on print responses to the problem of tempo. As discussed in chapter 4, the eighteenth century saw an outpouring of information on the connections between tempo, character, and meter signatures. This information most often took the form of exhaustive lists detailing the properties of each meter and the details of the measures associated with it. Theorists accounted for as many as fifty-six different meter signatures in

---

33. "Imaginez un assemblage de plusieurs cartes partielles qui n'en forment qu'une grande. La hauteur de cette grande carte n'est guere que d'un pié; sa longueur ne peut manquer d'être très-considérable. Quelle qu'elle soit, elle est divisée en petites parties égales, alternativement blanches & noires, telles que celles qui marquent les degrés sur un grand cercle de la sphere. Il y a autant de ces parties, qu'il s'est écoulé d'années depuis la création du monde jusqu'aujourd'hui. Chacune de ces parties marque une année de la durée du monde... Quant à la multitude & à la variété des faits, elle est immense; elle comprend tous ceux de quelque importance, dont il est fait mention dans l'histoire, depuis la fondation d'un empire jusqu'à l'invention d'une machine; depuis la naissance d'un potentat jusqu'à celle d'un habile ouvrier." Diderot, "Chronologique (machine)," *Encyclopédie ou dictionnaire raisonné...*, ed. Diderot and Jean le Rond d'Alembert (Paris: Briasson et Le Breton, 1751–65), 3:400.

their tracts on this subject, and took up dozens of pages explaining the system of *tempo giusto*.

In addition to all of their words, theorists applied another technique. Many of their lists and descriptions of meters were accompanied by lengthy sets of musical examples. These taxonomies of notation were often even more impressive than the texts they were bound with. Some example sets stretched for more than ten pages on their own, reproducing copious amounts of music; others employed shorter examples but in huge quantity, numbering over one hundred different examples in some cases.[34] Within the printed space of this technique, meter signatures met note shapes and characteristic composition in order to explain the emergent property of tempo. These taxonomies were in dialogue with the eighteenth century's exhaustive compilations of compositions in every key or every useful meter, but they were both more directly instructive and also, in certain cases, quite a bit more abstract.[35] These taxonomies were meant to stage the interaction of notational elements in order to build, reaffirm or comment on the sensibilities of *tempo giusto*.

Appendix 2 catalogues treatises that contain lists of meters from Bononcini (1673) to Momigny (1821). More than half of these thirty-nine treatises include an accompanying set of examples, and fourteen of these sets contain over twenty examples each (some well over that number). It is clear that there was an appetite for coherent excess in discussions of meter.

It is not enough to understand these charts as a part of the Enlightenment project to order knowledge. They were undoubtedly apiece with the period's fascination for system and tabulation, and some of these meter taxonomies were even located within the larger alphabetic organizations of the period's dictionaries and encyclopedias—taxonomies within taxonomies. But quite apart from these trends, the meter taxonomies responded to the messy and confused situation of eighteenth-century notation and style. It was not because of the potential for neat organization that theorists brought so many examples together in their treatises, but rather because of the unmanageable and untamed diversity of music that they realized they had to explain.[36] Their extensive documentation in the last moments of *tempo giusto* offers an exceptional glimpse of a fading practice. A close inspection of four representative meter taxonomies will provide a better

---

34. Charles Antoine Vion's examples, in *La musique pratique et theorique* (Paris: Jean-Baptiste-Christophe Ballard, 1742), stretch from 21–32; Joseph Lacassagne, in the *Traité général des élémens du chant*, facsimile ed. (1766; New York: Broude Brothers, 1967), includes 158 different exercises in his description of the different meter signatures.

35. J. S. Bach's *Das Wohltemperierte Klavier* is only the most famous example; another to consider in this light is Kirnberger's *Recueil d'airs de danse caractéristiques* (ca. 1777).

36. As Lorraine Daston and Peter Galison have written about the compilers of the period's atlases, "Eighteenth-century atlas makers were not free of all epistemological anxieties. Their fears centered, rather, on the untamed variability, even monstrosity of nature." Daston and Galison, *Objectivity* (New York: Zone Books, 2007), 67. This is related to the theoretical point made in Umberto Eco's *The Infinity of Lists from Homer to Joyce*, trans. Alastair McEwen (London: MacLehose, 2009), see esp. 15.

sense of this timekeeping technique's diversity, the forms it took, and how it was said to have worked.

Vion, La musique pratique et theorique (1742)

Vion called his taxonomy of meter a "Modele des differens Degrés de Mouvement, pour toutes sortes de Mesures": a working model or a chart of tempi for all varieties of measures.[37] The pages of his treatise positively explode with examples: his taxonomy occupies roughly an eighth of his entire printed book, and explains seventeen meter signatures with seventy examples of music.[38] Vion's examples are distinctive in their abundant use of contemporary musical excerpts, all of which are identified. These draw heavily on the music of Lully but also include works of Nicolas Bernier, Hotteterre, Robert Valentine, Corelli, and Couperin. Like so many French texts of his era Vion's was printed by the Ballard family and—as was their custom—featured typeset examples with the diamond-shaped noteheads of earlier printed music. These hearty prints take up a great amount of space on the page and thus present themselves as a formidable set of objects for the reader of the treatise to contemplate.

Vion dispenses quickly with the tempo terms that sometimes accompany the "composed signs" of meter, organizing his taxonomy around the signatures themselves and the tempi they denote.[39] His meter of four beats is "lentement," for example, while the meter marked with a simple "2" is "ordinarily fast: one employs it in overtures of opera, marches, ballets, branles, bourées, etc."[40] His sets of examples for the signatures 3/2 and 3/8 are given below in plates 5.1 and 5.2, respectively. In order to demonstrate the "slow three beats" of 3/2, which are useful for "tender airs such as *cantates* and *plaintes*," Vion reproduced six characteristic excerpts. These included the opening of the aria "Vous par qui tant de miserables," an *air serieux* from Nicolas Bernier's cantata *Les nymphes de Diane* and the first-movement adagio from Robert Valentine's six trio sonatas op. 4, no. 1.[41] For 3/8, by contrast, he aimed to show the characteristics of "light airs, like canaries [and] passepieds." Appropriately he reproduced the passepied (no. 1) from act three of André Cardinal Destouches's opera *Issé* and the allegro from Valentine's op. 4, no. 3, among his six examples.

Vion's *modele* combined minimal text with a characteristic taxonomy to create a tool or index of *tempo giusto*. Each of his examples worked to signal a set of qualities commonly shared by works written in the same signature. In this way his *modele* is also like a library—an archive or repository of the typical stylistic associations of each meter. Vion curated the excerpts most representative of their meters from the complicated diversity of everyday practice.

---

37. Vion, *La musique pratique et theorique*, 21.
38. Vion, *La musique pratique et theorique*, 21–32.
39. Vion, *La musique pratique et theorique*, 21.
40. Vion, *La musique pratique et theorique*, 21, 22.
41. Vion misattributes "Fils de la nuit," an aria from Campra's *Les femmes*, to Bernier.

Plate 5.1 Vion's collection of excerpts for 3/2. Vion, *La musique pratique et theorique* (Paris: Jean-Baptiste-Christophe Ballard, 1742), 25. Image reproduced with kind assistance from the Irving S. Gilmore Music Library, Yale University.

Marpurg, Anleitung zum Clavierspielen *(1755)*

Like Vion, Marpurg gave over a good deal of his treatise's space to the explanation of meter. The most striking difference between their two taxonomies is their size relative to the amount of text they work in conjunction with. By contrast to Vion's terse explanations, Marpurg lavishes textual commentary on each meter. In his lengthy discussion he accounts for a total of fifty-six possible signatures (though he treats only thirteen in depth) and spends a considerable amount of text on the properties of each type of measure. Where Vion spared no expense in the reproduction of excerpts for his taxonomy, Marpurg places his examples together at the back of the book in a tidy, engraved plate (see plate 5.3).

A closer look at Marpurg's taxonomy reveals another important difference. Instead of collecting characteristic excerpts, Marpurg composed a set of examples for the purpose of illustrating the meters he described. The first example is set in ₵ and meant to show the *grössere Allabrevetact* or 4/2 meter;[42] it contains a simple

---

42. This meter and those related to it are taken up in detail in chapter 6.

Plate 5.2 Vion's collection of excerpts for 3/8. Vion, *La musique pratique et theorique*, 26. Image reproduced with kind assistance from the Irving S. Gilmore Music Library, Yale University.

tune in C major. Marpurg resets this tune in 4/4 (indicated C), 2/2 (indicated ₵), and 2/4, diminuting the note values and readjusting the barlines appropriately. Here Marpurg is specifically highlighting the relationship between meter signatures and note values by keeping the melodic material constant. A different C major melody undergoes the same procedure for 3/2, 3/4, and 3/8; out of the tail end of this melody Marpurg develops yet another set in 12/4 and reset in 12/8, 6/4, and 6/8. A final melody accomplishes the same work for 9/4 and 9/8.[43]

Marpurg's taxonomy functioned differently than Vion's, though the two worked toward the same goal. In the French theorist's treatise the burden of explanation is placed on the repertoire of the taxonomy itself, which clarifies the system of *tempo giusto* through precedent. In Marpurg's, however, the burden of explanation is left to the text. Within the taxonomy, the minimal variance of the melody demonstrates the ways in which the prospective composer achieves different affects through the application of meter signatures alone.[44] Marpurg's

43. This accounts for thirteen of Marpurg's examples, the final five illustrate the use of two meter signatures together and the use of tuplets.
44. Kirnberger has a similar moment in his treatise, using a single melody with appropriately different durations in both 2/4 and 4/4. See Kirnberger, *Die Kunst des reinen Satzes in der Musik*, facsimile ed. (1771–79; Hildesheim: Georg Olms, 1968), 2:118–19.

Plate 5.3 Marpurg, *Anleitung zum Clavierspielen* (Berlin: Haude and Spener, 1755), table I, nos. 25–35, 42–45.

taxonomy did not collect exemplars from the world of practice to better refine meter theory, but rather offered a way of highlighting meter's diverse affectual capacities in an idealized context, with other parameters equalized. This approach had the added advantage of demonstrating the different durational equivalences under different meter signatures. By contrast to Vion's characteristic taxonomy, Marpurg offered a generic taxonomy.[45]

Kirnberger, Die Kunst des reinen Satzes in der Musik *(1771–79)*

In addition to his innovative theory, Kirnberger also included an impressive meter taxonomy in his *Die Kunst des reinen Satzes in der Musik*. His treatise employs prose and representative examples in a detailed explication of thirty-four different meter signatures and the properties of their measures. A less conventional use of printed music, though, is to be found in the opening pages of his chapter on meter. Shortly following his introduction to the topic of tempo, Kirnberger includes a lengthy, composite taxonomy (reproduced below as plate 5.4). Containing no identifying information, the patchwork figure quoted an amalgam of fifteen incipits in four different meters: four examples each in 4/4, 3/4, and 6/8, and three examples in 3/8. Kirnberger introduced this five-page digression: "Each of these excerpts distinguishes itself from the others through a characteristic motion that is felt primarily through the differences found in

45. The abstract examples in Marpurg's taxonomy should be understood along the lines of what Lorraine Daston and Peter Galison have called the "reasoned image." See Daston and Galison, *Objectivity*, in particular 60.

Plate 5.4 Kirnberger, *Die Kunst des reinen Satzes in der Musik*, facsimile ed. (1771–79; Hildesheim: Georg Olms, 1968), 2:107–11.

tempo and meter and—for those in which the same tempo and meter is found— the differences in note values in which the melody is composed."[46]

46. "Jedes dieser Beyspiele unterscheidet sich von den übrigen durch eine charakterisirte Bewegung, die erstlich durch die Verschiedenheit des Tempo und der Taktart, und bey denen die von ein- erley Tempo und Taktart sind, durch die Verschiedenheit der Notengattungen, aus denen die

Plate 5.4 Continued

Kirnberger's odd collage demonstrated the contrasts in notational practice, character, and tempi between and among some of the more widely used meter signatures of the period. For instance, although both the Allemande and Corrente from J. S. Bach's sixth Partita (the last excerpt in C and the last excerpt in 3/8, respectively) contain many thirty-second notes, the C meter signature and Allemande character of the former affords a slower tempo than is appropriate for the 3/8 signature and syncopated character of the latter. Beyond this type of relationship, though, the set is useful for understanding the many types of measures possible within a

Melodie zusammengesetzt ist, fühlbar wird." Kirnberger, *Die Kunst des reinen Satzes in der Musik*, 2:111.

Plate 5.4 Continued

single signature. François Couperin's 6/8 "La Diligente" (the third and last excerpt in 6/8) demonstrates the use of a "tripled" measure. The meter of this piece should be understood to be 2/4 with each beat subdivided into three. The preceding example in the taxonomy, however, contains mid-measure cadences and demonstrates the "compounded" 6/8 meter: each measure contains two smaller measures of 3/8.

The other examples used in Kirnberger's discussion of meters are either explicitly identified or clearly generic, but his large composite taxonomy—with its lack of identifying information—operates somewhere between these two modes. Like Vion, Kirnberger cultivated a library of excerpts in order to suggest a coherent picture of typical use. Nevertheless, the lack of identification on the examples leaves them abstracted, requiring the lengthy explication he provides later on in his treatise with the listing of meter signatures and the properties of their measures. Standing at the opening of that lengthy discourse, Kirnberger's taxonomy provides a hybrid model for the charting of *tempo giusto*.

Galeazzi, Elementi teorico-pratici di musica *(1791–96)*

An elegant match of examples for explanation distinguishes the taxonomy of meters in Galeazzi's *Elementi teorico-pratici di musica* (plate 5.5). Unlike the three theorists discussed above, Galeazzi closely correlates the thirteen examples of his taxonomy to the twelve meters described in his text. His taxonomy can be said to resemble Marpurg's in that its music was composed especially for the task of exemplification and located at the back of the text in a single plate. But the Italian theorist's abstract examples work differently. If Marpurg attempted to neutralize the element of melody in order to highlight the work of the meter signatures, Galeazzi pushed the role of melody a step further. His melodies are neither so varied as to appear representative of contemporary compositions nor are they so uniform as to employ literal replication across meter signatures (as in Marpurg's treatise). Galeazzi's melodies are closely related to each other but varied enough to reflect the characteristic durations and rhythmic patterns of each meter.

The taxonomy begins with the only meter for which Galeazzi provided two examples: the simple duple meter that he calls *Dupla Maggiore* or *Tempo a Cappella* has one example in the signature ¢ and one with the signature 2.[47] These are said to be equivalent and their simple C major melodies are identical in duration and very close in character. The melody for 2/4 is no great departure from these melodies, though for this tune Galeazzi uses a playful eighth-note figure. The example for 2/8 is a bit longer at five measures and includes a sixteenth-note flourish at its close. The rest of the example set continues in this fashion; the weighty 3/1 example opens with ponderous whole notes in succession, for instance, while the lively 3/8 passage includes syncopation and a sixteenth-note run. Nevertheless, all of these C major melodies are related to each other in their nearly uniform opening ascents, gradually accelerating rhythms, and well-prepared tonic cadences.

47. For Galeazzi's prose description, *Elementi teorico-pratici di musica* (Rome: Pilucchi Cracas, 1791), 1:34.

Plate 5.5 Galeazzi, *Elementi teorico-pratici di musica* (Rome: Pilucchi Cracas, 1791), vol. 1, table II.

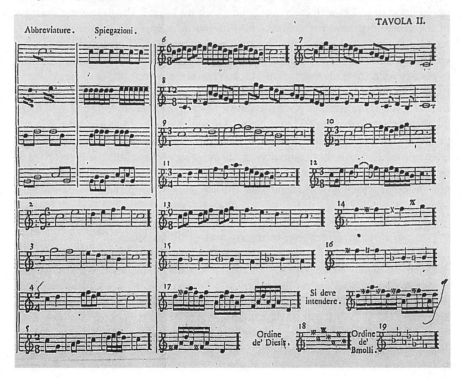

Galeazzi's generic taxonomy portrayed an idealized system of *tempo giusto*. His examples focused so exactly on the nature of each meter that they could surpass existing music. His taxonomy collected the quintessential melodies that existed nowhere—for his purpose these were better examples than could be found in reality.

The Perfect Library

There is something about all of these taxonomies that stands outside of practice and the confusing world of hybridity, change, and irregular use. These were no ordinary examples. Their conspicuous number and consistent implementation across a range of treatises warrants a reconsideration of their role as simple illustrations of the text. Instead they should be thought of as powerful sites at the intersection of knowledge and the implementation of time practices, most specifically the *tempo giusto*. They were wielded—as other tools or instruments are—in order to combat a particular problem, which was in this case the problem of tempo.

The eighteenth-century meter taxonomy, with its focus on temporality, is a distinctive music-theoretical hybrid of a clock and a map: a printed chrono-chart for exacting musical execution. These taxonomies were somewhat like lookup tables, specialized calendars, or even geographical maps; general plans that laid out the groundwork of temporal possibilities for music.[48] They were dictionaries of time, if you will, that had a didactic life in performance outside of the page. Sitting at the intersection of music theory, book history, and technology, these example sets were also analyses of a sort. They worked to cultivate their own sort of time discipline associated with the knowledge of *tempo giusto*. If eighteenth-century theorists couldn't prescribe the exact durations of their compositions with a machine, they could at least aim to give the most exhaustive account of the meter signatures and the tempi they indicated on paper. The practices of collecting the characteristic excerpts and composing the better-than-extant exemplars aspired to the dream of the perfect library: the imaginary archive in which every possibility has already been taken into account. This dream pervaded eighteenth-century thought in general, as the conceptualization of the library itself expanded to include printed compilations, periodicals, and encyclopedias aspiring to universal coverage.[49]

But for all of their potential usefulness, the taxonomies of meter were techniques exposed.[50] They are at once the best explanations of *tempo giusto*'s semiotic system and also the herald of its end. Their very visibility—their prominence, their size, and their voraciousness for detail—betrays the worry that *tempo giusto* was no longer effective. In this sense, taxonomies of meter were repositories for the potentially forgotten. Their pages were the physical locations in which theorists managed the anxiety of loss attending tempo. "It is already a complaint," Rousseau told us, "that we have forgotten the tempi of a great number of airs."[51] In this, they were entirely in keeping with the unachievable dimension of the perfect library dream. The library as a collection of knowledge would always have to choose between comprehensiveness and epitome. Within this process was lodged a belief that the perfect library would be responsible for preserving thought. As Diderot wrote in the introduction to his massive taxonomy, "May the Encyclopedia become a sanctuary, where the knowledge of man is protected from time and from revolutions."[52] The fact that we have such excellent records of

---

48. Here, the idea of a map is to be understood in a figurative sense; these taxonomies do not provide information about spatial relationships.

49. Roger Chartier, *The Order of Books: Readers, Authors, and Libraries in Europe between the Fourteenth and Eighteenth Centuries*, trans. Lydia G. Cochrane (Stanford: Stanford University Press, 1992), 61–91. See also Alberto Manguel, *The Library at Night* (New Haven: Yale University Press, 2008).

50. I mean to refer again to Heidegger, as in chapter 2. See Heidegger, *Being and Time*, trans. Joan Stambaugh (Albany: SUNY Press, 1996), 62–71; see also Graham Harman, *Tool-Being* (Chicago: Open Court, 2002), 15–24.

51. Rousseau, "Chronomètre," in *Dictionnaire de musique*, 99–100.

52. "Que l'Encyclopédie devienne un sanctuaire où les connoissances des hommes soient à l'abri des tems & des révolutions." Denis Diderot, "Discours preliminaire," to the *Encyclopédie ou dictionnaire raisonné*, 1:xxxviii.

the *tempo giusto* system from the late eighteenth century is the result of its impending decline.

The eighteenth-century meter taxonomy was constructed under the sign of loss. This dimension of the meter taxonomies was intertwined with their role as a useful technique for the problem of tempo; after all, imagined destinations—far away and in the future—had never stopped playing a part in the anxiety about tempo communication. Theorists only added to these in their concern that *tempo giusto* was no longer understood or already forgotten in their local and immediate contexts. The material manifestation of their response to this problem took on printed form. It thus spoke to the centrality of loss in the European experience of the book.[53] Aspiring to the perfect library of tempo memory, taxonomies of meter allowed for forgetting by safeguarding against it. They worked against their own best interests.

The perversity of inscribing in print a response to a problem of notation reflects the basic internal conflict of the meter taxonomies. Implemented correctly, the taxonomies were techniques for building and refining tempo intuitions. Their ordered tabulation coordinated the meter signatures with notational practices and characteristic gestures in such a way that the prescribed tempo became fairly evident. But one always needed some intuition, in the end, to guess at the right tempo. The tempo, of course, was the one thing that the taxonomies could never show exactly in notation (lacking any useful chronometer). The impossibility of writing it necessitated the taxonomy in the first place. But if tempo was a problem because of inscription, it could never have been fully resolved in a system on the page. So long as some prior sonic experience, or some former aural teaching, or some nearly forgotten intuition had to close the last distance between the meter and the tempo, this technique of *tempo giusto* would not offer enough. Thus the late eighteenth century, the golden age of *tempo giusto*'s documentation, was also the sunset of its efficacy. Produced in its final, anxious moments, taxonomies of meter offer us a glimpse of what was already lost, and testify to one way of keeping it.

53. See Richard Yeo, *Encyclopaedic Visions: Scientific Dictionaries and Enlightenment Culture* (Cambridge: Cambridge University Press, 2001), 84.

CHAPTER Six

The Eighteenth-Century *Alla Breve*

A Rather Vague Indication

One of the terms most frequently discussed in the proliferation of information on meters and measures in the eighteenth century was the *alla breve*. In the twenty-first century we associate the *alla breve* with duple meter—almost invariably ₵—and the *stile antico*. From the late seventeenth century and consistently through the eighteenth, treatises included the term in their lengthy lists of meter signatures. The *alla breve* was a "quick, duple meter used in the *Capellstyl*," as Marpurg put it, often employed in "fugues and other contrapuntal pieces."[1] The term simultaneously indicated a meter, a style, and a tempo; it was often connected to the notational conventions and compositional practices of sixteenth-century counterpoint.

Theorists, however, were inconsistent in their descriptions, and exactly what was understood about the *alla breve* is less than clear in an examination of the theoretical treatises alone. While some claimed that the *alla breve*'s ₵ was twice as fast as its counterpart C (4/4), others asserted that its long note values required a grave and sedate performance.[2] Even more confusingly, some authorities claimed that the misunderstandings surrounding the meter had led to improper use. As Hiller wrote, composers "often set in 4/4 what by its nature is an *alla breve*."[3] The ambiguities surrounding the "rather vague" meter and its ₵ sign have continued to

---

1. "Allabreve, wird von einer geschwinden geraden Tactart im Capellstyl gebraucht"; ". . .und wird nur meistens in Fugen und andern contrapunctischen Sachen gebraucht." F. W. Marpurg, *Anleitung zum Clavierspielen* (Berlin: A. Haude and J. C. Spener, 1755), 17, 19.
2. Quantz, *Versuch einer Anweisung die Flöte traversiere zu spielen*, facsimile ed. (1752; Wiesbaden: Breitkopf und Härtel, 1988), 56. Carlo Gervasoni, *La scuola della musica*, facsimile ed. (1800; Bologna: Forni, 1969), 1:165.
3. "Da sie offt zu einem Viervierteltacte machen, was seiner Natur nach ein Allabreve oder Zewyvierteltact ist." Hiller, *Musikalische Nachrichten und Anmerkungen* (Leipzig: In Verlag der Zeitugs-Expedition, 1770), vol. 1; January 15, 1770, 20–21.

the present day, with some secondary sources asserting that its tempo is without exception double that of C, and others insisting that its relationship to the *stile antico* "require[s] a slower tempo and a more solemn style of execution."[4]

At first blush it would seem as though the meanings of the *alla breve* were nothing other than contradictory. The sign and term indicated an extremely quick tempo but also a weighty slowness reserved for only the most dusty exercises in antiquated compositional technique. But the coexistence of these two meanings and the preponderance of confusion are important legacies of a particular moment in meter's history. The vagaries surrounding them tell a fascinating story about eighteenth-century music theory's engagement with the past and meter's connections to tempo and notation.

In the eighteenth century, the length of the notes employed in *stile antico* counterpoint (half notes, whole notes, and sometimes breves: "white" or "void" notes) would have indicated a slow tempo.[5] Note shapes still carried an important relationship to tempo at this time, and while short notes prescribed a quick pace, long notes meant just the opposite. The *alla breve*, associated as it was with *antico*, long-note music, indexed both the stylistic connotations of sixteenth-century counterpoint and the doubling of speed that would have been required to bring this long-note music into accord with the shorter notes of the eighteenth century. Nevertheless, because the meter retained both meanings (one relating to antique style, the other to quick tempo) the two were used independently of each other just as much as they were used in conjunction.

The confusion caused by the *alla breve*—both then and today—is indicative of its distinct position in the changing network of relationships that connected meter to tempo and character. Its multiply directed meanings capture a final moment in the history of meter's ability to signify style and character, and the relationship that moment held to the inscription of duration and tempo. The story of the *alla breve* in the eighteenth century is one that exposes the cracks in eighteenth-century music theory's elaborate taxonomic edifice. It is an account that cautions against any neutral interpretation of meter's signs.

Long-Note Music in the Eighteenth Century

The *alla breve* was a part of a thriving culture of long-note music in the eighteenth century. Sixteenth-century counterpoint—particularly the works of

4. Johann Adolph Scheibe describes the *alla breve* as "sehr unbestimmt" in *Ueber die Musikalische Composition*, facsimile ed. (1773; Kassel: Bärenreiter, 2006), 1:203. The second quotation in this sentence is from Wye J. Allanbrook, *Rhythmic Gesture in Mozart* (Chicago: University of Chicago Press, 1983), 15. Among those who disagree with Allanbrook's interpretation, see Clive Brown, *Classical and Romantic Performing Practice: 1750-1900* (Oxford: Oxford University Press, 1999), 313–35; and Frederick Neumann, *Performance Practices of the Seventeenth and Eighteenth Centuries* (New York: Schirmer, 1993), 57–63.

5. *Oxford Music Online*, s.v. "Notation, §III, 4: Mensural notation from 1500," by Geoffrey Chew and Richard Rastall, accessed August 29, 2011, <www.oxfordmusiconline.org>.

Palestrina—had a vibrant life in the eighteenth century, disseminated in manuscripts, print editions, and theoretical treatises.[6] Palestrina's works themselves had become identified with contrapuntal excellence, so their perceived importance stemmed not only from their representation of the musical past but also from their pedagogical value. In addition to the survival of this older repertoire, eighteenth-century composers attempted their own imitations, replicating the older music's long note values in their compositional exercises.

That Palestrina's counterpoint held an important place in eighteenth-century musical culture has long been documented by scholars of both Renaissance and Enlightenment musical traditions.[7] Chapel masters in Catholic countries were well acquainted with the *stile antico* tradition, and by 1725 Fux's *Gradus ad Parnassum* had codified this legacy in print.[8] The Protestant North was also familiar with Palestrina; we know that J. S. Bach, in particular, came into contact with his music in Weimar and Leipzig.[9] In addition to the adoption of a "Palestrina style," performances of the sixteenth-century repertoire itself were an important part of the tradition. In some locales, such as Rome and Vienna, Palestrina and other sixteenth-century contrapuntalists enjoyed continued performance.[10] In England, where Palestrina's music was heard regularly, secular institutions supported the performance of sixteenth-century music. The Academy of Ancient Music, the Madrigal Society (the meetings of which reportedly included lectures from Zarlino's *Le istitutioni harmoniche*), and other groups such as the Gentlemen's Catch Club performed and archived the music of Palestrina and his contemporaries.[11]

---

6. For comprehensive bibliographic data on these last two, see Clara Marvin, *Giovanni Pierluigi da Palestrina: A Guide to Research* (New York: Routledge, 2002), 13–77.

7. The classic study is Karl Gustav Fellerer, *Der Palestrinastil und seine Bedeutung in der vokalen Kirchenmusik des achtzehnten Jahrhunderts: Ein Beirag zur Geschichte der Kirchenmusik in Italien und Deutschland* (1929; repr., Walluf bein Wiesbaden: Sändig, 1972). More recent work includes Jen-Yen Chen, "Palestrina and the Influence of 'Old' Style in Eighteenth-Century Vienna," *Journal of Musicological Research* 22, nos. 1–2 (2003): 1–44.

8. Paul R. Laird, "Catholic Church Music in Italy, and the Spanish and Portuguese Empires," in *The Cambridge History of Eighteenth-Century Music*, ed. Simon P. Keefe (Cambridge: Cambridge University Press, 2009), 29–58; and Chen, "Catholic Sacred Music in Austria," in *The Cambridge History of Eighteenth-Century Music*, ed. Keefe, 59–112.

9. On Palestrina in Bach's Weimar, see Barbara Wiermann, "Bach und Palestrina: Neue Quellen aus Johann Sebastian Bachs Notenbibliothek," *Bach-Jahrbuch* 88 (2002): 9–28. On Bach's relationship to Palestrina and sixteenth-century counterpoint in general, see Christoph Wolff, "Bach and the Palestrina Style," in *Bach: Essays on His Life and Music* (Cambridge, MA: Harvard University Press, 1991), 84–104. See also Gabriel M. Steinschulte, "Palestrina und Deutschland," in *Atti del II Convegno Internazionale di Studi Palestriniani*, ed. Lino Bianchi and Giancarlo Rostirolla (Palestrina: Fondazione Giovanni Pierluigi da Palestrina/Centro di Studi Palestriniani, 1991), 615–23.

10. Peter Ackermann, "Die Werke Palestrinas im Repertoire de Cappella Sistina," in *Collectanea II. Studien zur Geschichte der päpstlichen Kapelle. Tagungsbericht Heidelbert 1989*, ed. Bernhard Janz (Vatican City: Biblioteca Apostolicae Vaticana, 1994), 405–30; Jen-Yen Chen, "Palestrina and the Influence of 'Old' Style in Eighteenth-Century Vienna," 2.

11. Sir John Hawkins, *A General History of the Science and Practice of Music*, rev. ed. (1776; London: Novello, Ewer & co., 1875), 2:887; Thomas Day; "A Renaissance Revival in the Eighteenth Century," *Musical Quarterly* 57 (1971): 575–92.

Less documented in this eighteenth-century reception history are the notational transformations that the ancient music underwent in the hands of scribes, copyists, printers, and editors. The original notation, which was written in parts (rather than score), often in obsolete ligatures, and certainly without barlines, needed updating for its new audiences. Copyists and editors took care to render the music newly intelligible: they rewrote the parts into score and added the consistent barlines that their readership would have expected from eighteenth-century polyphony.

The most interesting decision of these individuals, though, was something they chose not to do. Despite the other changes they effected on the music, they left its durations intact. This meant not only preserving the disproportionate length of the notes (which would have looked strikingly void next to the mostly black music of their era) but also its ligatures. Their choice often proved difficult to uphold, especially because it was at odds with the desire to clarify the notation for eighteenth-century musicians and—most significantly—to provide barlines.

The transmission of Palestrina's *Missa Ecce sacerdos magnus* serves as an interesting example in this regard. First published in the 1554 *Missarum liber primus*, this mass uses mensuration signs for diminution and augmentation. In the Agnus Dei III, the superious and altus begin in O (a simple triple meter), the tenor is written in long notes with the signature Φ used for diminution, and the bassus is written in short notes with the signature ℭ used for augmentation. All voices eventually transition to C, bringing their note values into accord with each other and the meter to duple.

Eighteenth-century manuscript copies of this mass preserve not only the mensuration signs but also the specific note shapes, including the ligatures, blackened notes for hemiola, and "non-colored" or void quarter notes.[12] The opening of the Agnus Dei III, as transcribed in a manuscript copy of the *Missarum liber primus* in Princess Anna Amalia's library (D-B AmB 278) is shown below in plate 6.1.[13] Rather than bring the durations into accord with the barlines (which reflect the triple meter in these opening measures), the scribe instead copies the note shapes exactly as they appear in the 1554 print and adds clarifying numerals above them. While the first whole note in the soprano at m. 2 is held for one beat,

---

12. Void quarter notes (semiminims) derive from an older model of mensural notation in which the semiminim was distinguished from a mimin by means of a flag attached to the stem instead of a blackened or filled head as we do today. An entire series of smaller, void durations was possible in the sixteenth century and distinguished from the blackened notation in the addition of another flag. See Chew and Rastall, "Notation."

13. The Amalien-bibliothek represents the collection of Princess Anna Amalia and Kirnberger. See Eva Renate Blechschmidt (Eva Renate Wutta), *Die Amalien-Bibliothek* (Berlin: Merseburger, 1965); and Eva Renate Wutta, *Quellen der Bach-Tradition in der Berliner Amalien-Bibliothek* (Tutzing: H. Schneider, 1989); D-B AmB 278 is nearly a complete copy of the *Missarum liber primus*—the "Missa Ad coenam Agni" is left incomplete. This manuscript should not be confused with the other eighteenth-century Berlin copies of this mass (D-B AmB 275, D-Bsa SA 424/ZC 629, D-B Mus. Ms. 16695, and D-B Mus. Ms. 16700), which also preserve the original durations. D-Bsa SA 424/ZC 629, and D-B Mus. Ms. 16695 are described and partially reproduced in Wiermann, "Bach und Palestrina." For more information on D-B AmB 275 and 278, see Blechschmidt (Wutta), *Die Amalien-Bibliothek*, 176–77.

Plate 6.1 Palestrina, "Missa Ecce Sacerdos Magnus," Agnus Dei III, opening, in D-B AmB 278, 31r. Reproduced by kind permission of the Staatsbibliothek zu Berlin—Preußischer Kulturbesitz, Musikabteilung mit Mendelssohn-Archiv.

the second is held for two (as indicated with the numeral); the first whole note in the bass, however, is held for three beats in accordance with the ₵ augmentation; the scribe adds a numeral three for clarification. Whole notes stand for three different durations in these opening four measures.

A manuscript copy of the *Missarum liber primus* in the British Library (GB-Lbl MS. Add. 5045), transcribed by director of the Academy of Ancient Music Henry Needler, also preserves the durations exactly as they appear in the 1554 print.[14] In this manuscript, the effort to preserve the original durations is even more extreme. Instead of employing the use of ties (as done in D-B AmB 278), Needler draws barlines directly down the middle of durations that would otherwise straddle them (see plates 6.2 and 6.3). Everywhere in the manuscript crashes with barlines abound. Where a dotted duration would carry on into the next measure, Needler places the notehead in the first and the dot in the second. As in the Amalien-bibliothek manuscript, the ligatures, blackening, and void quarter notes are preserved, and identical note shapes carrying non-identical durations sit one atop the next in a deceivingly modern score format.

Crashes like those found in the Needler manuscript are found in other eighteenth-century copies of sixteenth-century music, both on the continent and in England.[15] In one British Library manuscript (GB-Lbl MS. Add. 31407, shown below in plate 6.4, probably from the hand of John Immyns) a stunning effort to preserve the durations in Victoria's "O Quam Gloriosum," resulted in ligatures stretched over three measures. The bizarre stretching of these note shapes

---

14. In fact, BL Ms. Add. 5045 reads: "Transcribed by Henry Needler from the 1572 Print edition, *Missarum liber primus* (Rome: apud Heredes Aloysii Dorici, 1572)." There is no difference from the 1554 edition in the notation of the Agnus Dei III.

15. For example, in the British Library: GB-Lbl MS. Add. 5040; GB-Lbl MS. Add. 5036; GB-Lbl MS. Add. 5037 and many others. In the AmB collection: D-B AmB 218.

Plate 6.2 Palestrina, "Missa Ecce Sacerdos Magnus," Agnus Dei III, opening. © The British Library Board, GB-Lbl Ms. Add. 5045, 48.

Plate 6.3 Palestrina, "Missa Ecce Sacerdos Magnus," Agnus Dei III, showing barline crashes, preserved ligatures, and blackening. © The British Library Board, GB-Lbl MS. Add. 5045, 50.

dramatized the uncomfortable fit of the antiquated notation in its updated format. It was apparently important enough to preserve these original shapes in the act of copying to render the newly intelligible score format almost unintelligible again.[16]

16. Marpurg was apparently familiar with this type of notation, and described noteheads cut by barlines as an antiquated way of notating a syncopation. Marpurg, *Des critichen Musicus an der Spree*, facsimile ed. (1750; New York: Georg Olms, 1970), 1:82.

Plate 6.4 Victoria, "O Quam Gloriosum," mm. 1–6. © The British Library Board, GB-Lbl Ms. Add. 31407, 18r.

The consistent preservation of the long note values and the crashing of note shapes with barlines were acts of knowledge production. These transcriptions were theorizations of notational history left on top of the copied music. They relate, above all, a deliberate investment in the shapes of the historical notes. Copyists of sixteenth-century counterpoint expressed a certain reverence for the musical text in the case of its durations—a reverence they did not extend to other elements of the music's notation.[17] These updated versions of the antiquated counterpoint set the newer forms of notation into sharp relief, highlighting the changes that had taken place in the interim. The barlines, then, were modern intrusions on the older music, forcing at the least a proliferation of ties and in some cases a strangely protracted process of crashing. Here, the new collided with the old.

This eighteenth-century reverence for the durations of sixteenth-century counterpoint manifested itself in other ways as well. Print editions of the older music, such as those found in Burney's edited collection, *La musica che si canta annualmente nelle Funzioni della Settimana Santa nella Cappella Pontificale*, adopted a technique similar to that of the cleaner manuscripts, preserving the durations (without barline crashes) and converting the music into score format.[18] In addition to Burney's volume, prints of Palestrina and his contemporaries

17. One can almost see a proto-romantic idea of the musical work emerging in these copies, as their eighteenth-century scribes fastidiously preserved note shapes that would have been difficult for contemporary audiences to interpret, emphasizing fidelity to the work as it was originally created.

18. *La musica che si canta annualmente nelle Funzioni della Settimana Santa nella Cappella Pontificale*, ed. Charles Burney (London: R. Bremner, 1771).

appeared in theoretical treatises through the eighteenth century, rendered in score with their durations preserved.[19]

Eighteenth-century counterpoint treaties are particularly interesting sites for the investigation of long-note music in this period. In these documents the spirit of preservation was explicit. Fux's *Gradus ad Parnassum* sought to emulate "the glorious light of music, Palestrina," and others following in his tradition adopted the numinous tone.[20] For Johann Georg Albrechtsberger, Fux had become the oracle in a kind of second-order veneration.[21] Padre Martini's reverence for the past came in a more tangible form. His fascinating two-volume document, the *Esemplare o sia saggio fondamentale pratico di contrapunto sopra il canto fermo*, was both a large compendium of sixteenth-century works and a treatise on counterpoint. Within its pages, Martini reproduced the music of Willaert, Victoria, Palestrina, and many of their contemporaries. These eighteenth-century books on counterpoint wanted to preserve both a set of practices and a group of repertoire.

Although these books included musical examples in many meters and in a variety of note shapes, the preponderance of music in the counterpoint treatises discussed above were in ₵ and written in long note values.[22] Especially representative were the given materials—the *cantus firmi* or *Choräle*—which almost always consisted of a series of whole notes given in ₵ (this tradition extends into the twenty-first century, with *cantus firmi* in texts by Parks and Salzer and Schachter given in whole notes).[23] Fux dispenses with other meters quickly in his lesson on the second species: "We have yet to speak of ternary time here; in this case three notes are set against one. Because this is an easy affair and of little import, I do not think it worth while to arrange a special chapter dealing with it."[24] The absorption of this preference for duple meter is clear in the choices Martini and Albrechtsberger

19. These include Antonio Eximeno y Pujaver, *Delle origini e delle regole della musica colla storia del suo progresso, decadenza, e rinnovazione* (Rome: Michel'Angelo Barbiellini, 1774); Giuseppe Paolucci, *Arte pratica di contrappunto* (Venice: Antonio de Castro, 1765–72); Johann Georg Albrechtsberger, *Gründliche Anweisung zur Composition* (Leipzig: Johann Gottlob Immanuel Brietkopf, 1790); and Giovanni Battista (Padre) Martini's *Esemplare o sia saggio fondamentale pratico di contrapunto sopra il canto fermo* (Bologna: Lelio dalla Volpe, 1774–75), 2 vols., discussed below.

20. "Clarissimum illud Musicæ lumen Prænestinum." Johann Joseph Fux, *Gradus ad parnassum* (Vienna: Johann Peter van Ghelen, 1725), unpaginated preface.

21. Albrechtsberger, *Gründliche Anweisung zur Composition*, 48.

22. This was particularly true for the learning of the basic rules and the species; once the treatises reached free counterpoint there was more flexibility in the types of durations included. Other writings on counterpoint, such as those of Kirnberger and Momigny, for example, began with half note durations instead of whole notes. Johann Philipp Kirnberger, *Die Kunst des reinen Satzes in der Musik*, facsimile ed. (1771–79; Hildesheim: Georg Olms, 1968), 1:141–89; Momigny, *Cours complet d'harmonie et de composition* (Paris: The author and Bailleul, 1806), 49ff. On the different approaches to the contrapuntal doctrine, see Ian Bent, "*Steps to Parnassus*: Contrapuntal Theory in 1725: Precursors and Successors," in *The Cambridge History of Western Music Theory*, ed. Thomas Christensen (Cambridge: Cambridge University Press, 2002), 554–602.

23. Richard S. Parks, *Eighteenth-Century Counterpoint and Tonal Structure* (Englewood Cliffs, NJ: Prentice-Hall, 1984); Felix Salzer and Carl Schachter, *Counterpoint in Composition*, new ed. (1969; New York: Columbia University Press, 1989).

24. "Hîc quoque dicendum esset de Tempore Ternario, ubi tres Notæ contra unam ponuntur. Quia autem ob rei facilitatem parvi est momenti res, operæ pretium non arbitror, peculiarem eâ causâ

made for their examples. In an extraordinary feat of consistency, every single one of the fifty-seven compositions printed in Martini's first volume of the *Esemplare* are in ¢ with breve-length bars.[25] Many use the antiquated C. O. P. ligature.[26]

The counterpoint treatises of Fux, Martini, and Albrechtsberger, then, can be understood to have had a role in the preservation of the sixteenth-century repertoire and notation while simultaneously reinforcing a strong connection between this repertoire and the ¢ sign, specifically. Furthermore, contrapuntal exercises—like the repertoire they were intended to model—were made in the long notes that set the older repertoire apart from the new. These treatises bear witness to a network of relationships that grew up around long notes, duple meter, and contrapuntal composition.

Not surprisingly, the new music composed in the style these treatises described was an eighteenth-century form of long-note music. Masses written in the *stile antico* were a vital component of eighteenth-century sacred music, and were heard regularly during the seasons of Lent and Advent, during which time the performance of concerted music was prohibited.[27] Antonio Salieri, Joseph Haydn, and many others wrote masses in this vein (the opening of Haydn's *Missa sunt bona mixta malis* appears below in example 6.1).[28] Like the sixteenth-century contrapuntal compositions they were meant to imitate, these works feature melodies in whole notes, half notes, and a few quarter notes; their final cadences are in breves. An emphasis on melodic writing in all parts and, of course, imitative excellence are their most distinguishing characteristics. In addition, the music was set apart by its note values. As Mattheson already remarked in 1713, the maxima, long, and breve were "hardly found elsewhere anymore but in the *Stylo Ecclasiastico*…principally in *allabreve*."[29] The visual appearance of this music—its durations and choice of meter—sent a strong signal about the style it represented.

Long Notes and Tempo

A further wrinkle in the story of sixteenth-century counterpoint's eighteenth-century life is the relationship that the note values held to tempo. Despite the presence of all

Lectionem statuere." Fux, *Gradus ad parnassum*, 63; my translation with reference to *The Study of Counterpoint from Johann Joseph Fux's* Gradus ad Parnassum, ed. and trans. Alred Mann, rev. ed. (1943; New York: W. W. Norton, 1971), 49.

25. The single exception consists of twenty-five measures of Palestrina's "Gaudent in coelis" that are written in triple meter, on pages 127–28.

26. Or the *ligatura cum opposita proprietate*. See *Oxford Music Online*, s.v. "Ligature (i)," by Peter Wright, accessed September 6, 2011, <www.oxfordmusiconline.org>.

27. Chen, "Palestrina and the Influence of 'Old' Style in Eighteenth-Century Vienna."

28. What we have today of Haydn's *Missa sunt bona mixta malis* is only the Kyrie and the Gloria through the phrase "Gratias agimus tibi." See Haydn, *Missa Sunt bona mixta malis*, ed. H. C. Robbins Landon and David Wyn Jones (Paris: Editions Mario Bois, 1992).

29. I understand Mattheson's use of the term *Stylo Ecclesiastico* to be the rough equivalent of *stile antico*. "…daß sie niemahls anderswo als im Stylo Ecclesiastico statt gefunden haben, und zwar, wie leicht zu erachten, ihrer ungeheuren Länge wegen; wiewol noch jetzund, vornemlich aber im allabreve…" Mattheson, *Das neu-eröffnete Orchestre*, facsimile ed. (1713; Laaber: Laaber, 2002), 90.

Example 6.1 Joseph Haydn, *Missa sunt bona mixta malis*, mm. 1–14.

of the long-note music discussed above, eighteenth-century musicians evidently retained the belief that longer notes indicated slower tempi. Perhaps the most visible corroboration of this continued belief were Rameau's efforts to reform the system of metric notation (discussed in chapter 4). If meter signatures did a poor job of indicating tempo, Rameau suggested relying on the note shapes:

> Nothing could be more proper in order for us to distinguish slowness or quickness than the value of the notes with which each measure may be filled. Once one knows that the tempo of the whole note is slower than that of the half and likewise the half to the quarter…who would not immediately understand that a meter in which the whole note is worth one beat will be slower than one in which the half note is worth one beat, and accordingly the half note to the quarter etc. The meter in which the whole note is worth one beat will be the slowest of them all.[30]

30. "Rien ne seroit plus propre à nous faire distinguer sa lenteur & sa vitesse, que la valeur des Nottes dont chaque mesure peut être remplie; car sçachant que le mouvement de la Ronde est plus lent que celui de la Blanche, & ainsi de la Blanche à la Noire, de la Noire à la Croche, & de la Croche à la double-Croche; qui est-ce qui ne comprendra pas sur le champ, qu'une mesure où la Ronde ne vaudra qu'un tems, sera plus lente que cell où la Blanche vaudra un tems, & ainsi de la Blanche à la Noire, &c. La mesure où la Ronde ne vaudroit qu'un tems, seroit la plus lente de toutes." Rameau, *Traité de l'harmonie* (Paris: Jean-Baptiste-Christophe Ballard, 1722), 2:151–52.

The idea that shorter notes should be performed faster grates against our modern sensibilities because we are familiar, in the twenty-first century, with so much music that employs extremely short note values and therefore necessitates a moderate speed. This was not the case in the eighteenth century. For Rameau, the correlation between long notes and slow tempo was so evident as to render the tempo indications of the meter signatures themselves superfluous. Was all of the important, long-note counterpoint to be performed slowly, then?

Many theoretical sources addressed this issue directly, advocating for long-note counterpoint to be brought up to speed with the use of the ₵ signature. Fux chose to tackle the confusing situation in a series of examples (shown below in plate 6.5). Toward the conclusion of *Gradus ad Parnassum* in a section on the variety of fugue subjects, he demonstrates that a long-note, imitative piece in "Tempus binarium," or ₵, translates into C with its durations halved and a marking of *Presto*. A further diminution of the note values in half again merits the slower tempo of *Adagio* in C. In order for all three versions of the duet to sound the same, the shortest note values require a slower tempo indication while the longest are set in ₵. Riepel employs a similar equivalence in his *Anfangsgründe*

Plate 6.5 Johann Joseph Fux, *Gradus ad Parnassum* (Vienna: Johann Peter van Ghelen, 1725); reproduced by arrangement with Broude Brothers from *Monuments of Music & Music Literature in Facsimile*, ser. 2, vol. 24 (New York: Broude Brothers, 1966), 238.

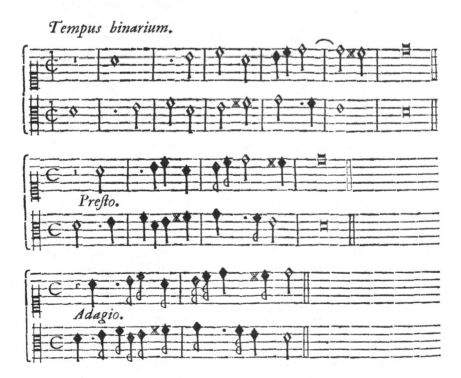

Plate 6.6 Joseph Riepel, *Anfangsgründe zur musicalischen Setzkunst…De Rhythmopoeïa, oder von der Tactordnung* (Regensburg and Vienna: Emerich Felix Bader, 1752), 1:28. Image reproduced with kind assistance from the Irving S. Gilmore Music Library, Yale University.

zur musicalischen Setzkunst of 1752. Explaining the properties of various meter signatures in his chapter on "Tactordnung," Riepel demonstrates how a short-note melody in 2/4 is equivalent in tempo to the same melody with doubled note lengths in ₡. He goes on to set the melody in C (4/4) using the short note values of the 2/4 version; in this instance each measure is a compounded, double measure and includes within it two measures of the 2/4 melody (see plate 6.6).

For Fux and Riepel, the *alla breve* ₡ meter sped up the long notes, undoing the connotations of slowness these notes still had in the eighteenth century. Kirnberger explained the situation thus:

> The 2/2 or—better—*alla breve* meter, which is always indicated with ₡ or 2, is most often used in church pieces, fugues, and highly developed choruses. Of this meter it should be noted that it is very serious and emphatic, however it is to be performed once more so fast as its note values indicate, unless the tempo is specified with an accompanying word such as *grave, adagio,* etc.[31]

31. "Der Zweyzweytel oder besser der Allabrevetackt, der durchgängig mit ₡, oder auch mit 2 bezeichnet wird, ist in Kirchenstücken, Fugen und ausgearbeiteten Chören von dem vielfältigsten Gebrauch. Von dieser Tactart ist anzumerken, daß sie sehre schwer und nachdrücklich, doch noch einmal so geschwind, als ihre Notengattungen anzeigen, vorgetragen wird, es sey denn, daß die Bewegung durch die Beywörter *grave, adagio* &c. langsamer verlangt wird." Kirnberger, *Die Kunst des reinen Satzes in der Musik*, 2:118. See also Kirnberger, "Alla Breve," in the *Allgemeine Theorie der schönen Künste*, ed. J. G. Sulzer, 2nd printing (1771–74; Leipzig: Weidmannschen Buchhandlung, 1792), 1:76, which delivers the same message and includes an example similar to the examples of Fux and Riepel reproduced above. A curious remark of Kirnberger's might seem at first to indicate a contradiction: "In Ansehung der Taktart find die von größeren Zeiten, als der Allabreve…von schwerer und langsamerer Bewegung, als die von kürzeren Zeiten." *Die Kunst des reinen Satzes in der Musik*, 2:106. In light of his other—more specific—instructions on the *alla breve* and 2/2, "langsamerer" here must indicate

All of the gravity that the *stile antico* required was no doubt a feature of the *alla breve*, but the sign and the term also worked to rid long notes of the lugubrious tempi they otherwise might have connoted.[32] This created a system of special relationships among the long notes, the long-note style, and the halving of value that the stroke through the C could imply. By the end of the century the relationship was established enough for Jean-Louis Castilhon, writing in the first volume of Framery's *Encylopédie méthodique* of 1791, to judge that short notes had no place in the *alla breve* under any circumstances. "The *alla breve* has a very quick tempo, such that the quarter notes pass as quickly as the eighth notes in an ordinary allegro; this is why sixteenth notes are not admitted."[33]

It was a particular concatenation of circumstances in the history of meter that allowed for a concept such as the *alla breve* to exist. Note values were not yet freed from tempo indications during the eighteenth century, but nevertheless a distinctive style of composition (and theory teaching) had emerged that employed much longer note values than were customarily found in the music of the period. Associated as it was this style, the *alla breve* simultaneously worked to bring the long-note music up to speed while it also indexed its distinguishing *antico* features.

Still, the relationships between these signs and practices were tenuous. The late eighteenth century saw the final moments of the *tempo giusto* tradition; the power of meter signatures to indicate style and tempo had already begun to diminish. The ₵ sign was associated with more than just *antico* composition and long note values. The *alla breve*, newly effective but also increasingly vague, could point toward style, tempo, or duple meter, but not any consistent combination thereof.

something about the affect and not the tempo. If nothing else, Kirnberger's remarks about the *alla breve* demonstrate just how confusing the issue must have been. The words "noch einmal so geschwind" are also used in Daniel Gottlob Türk, *Klavierschule, oder Anweisung zum Klavierspielen*, facsimile ed. (1789; Kassel: Bärenreiter, 1962), 109.

32. Clive Brown comes close to suggesting this when he writes, "It seems to have been the case with many Continental composers of the late eighteenth century and early nineteenth century, including Haydn, Mozart, Beethoven, Spohr, Schubert, and Mendelssohn, that, though they accepted a notional 2:1 relationship between C and ₵, this was modified in practice by the influence of the note values. Thus, the greater weight of the larger note values in ₵ held back the tempo and prevented it attaining double speed." Brown and I here take differing opinions on the same phenomenon. Rather than the notes holding back the speed of the meter, I would argue that the meter was used to undo the tempo that the note shapes implied. Brown, *Classical and Romantic Performing Practice: 1750-1900*, 319. For an interesting seventeenth-century precedent to the sources gathered here, see Michael Praetorius, *Syntagma musicum*, 2nd printing (1618; Wolfenbüttel: Elias Holwein, 1619), 3:50–51.

33. "L'alla brève a le mouvement très vif, de façon que les noires y passent aussi vite que les croches dans un allegro ordinaire; c'est pourquoi les doubles croches n'y sont point admises." Jean-Louis Castilhon, "Alla breve," "Alla Capella," in *Encylopédie méthodique...: Musique*, ed. Nicolas-Étienne Framery, Pierre-Louis Ginguené, and Jérôme-Joseph de Momigny (Paris: Panckoucke, 1791), 1:65.

Long Notes in Eighteenth-Century Music

Part of the confusion surrounding the tempo of the *alla breve* has its roots in the broad acceptance of its connection to serious and exalted styles. Even if in practice the ₵ sign was used indiscriminately, the term *alla breve* was employed more exclusively in the context of learned music. Composing in strict, long-note imitation of sixteenth-century counterpoint—the narrowest definition of the *stile antico*—was only one form that this music could take.[34] Often, the *alla breve* was attached to a learned style partially invested in these older ideals but mixed with updated techniques. The fact that the ₵ sign could work for both antiquated and modern styles was what put its special relationship with note values and tempo into question. This flexibility of the ₵ signature heralded the end of its ability to signify with the *tempo giusto* system. Its problematic plurality is what created the conundrum of the *alla breve* in the eighteenth century and the reason it continues to this day; it represents the challenges that the inscription of meter and tempo faced at the end of *tempo giusto*.

When Marpurg and Koch offered an example of the *alla breve* in the music of their contemporaries, they both recalled a single movement from C. H. Graun's celebrated oratorio *Der Tod Jesu*. The fugal movement, "Christus hat uns ein Vorbild gelassen," is scored for four voices and instruments *colle voci*. In the 1760 print it bears the ₵ signature and the marking *alla breve*. With a text on the topic of Christ's example for humanity, this is the most learned movement in Graun's diverse work. He chose to use long durations for the movement, but the melody is comprised mostly of half notes and quarter notes—not the whole notes of Haydn and Salieri's *antico* masses. Graun's fugal writing in the movement is strict and expertly deployed, involving augmentation and stretto. Other aspects depart from these consciously *antico* choices. Below the voices Graun included a separate basso continuo line with figured bass numerals, casting the vocally conceived polyphony above as successions of vertical sonorities. This line follows the vocal basses closely, but at certain moments it almost seems as if both of these low parts serve a basso continuo function in contrast to the vocal independence and melodic shape of the upper parts (see mm. 8–10 in example 6.2, for instance). The close of the movement also shades toward a homophonic texture (example 6.3). Although the movement is written in a strict, *antico* style, many of its features are borrowed from more recent practice.

Graun's inclusion of figures in the otherwise imitative bass was not without precedent in the context of the learned style. Fux wrote specifically on the use of the organ to accompany masses in *stylus a Capella*, and Graun's written-out

---

34. For a specific definition of the eighteenth-century *stile antico*, see Christoph Wolff, *Bach: Essays on His Life and Work* (Cambridge, MA: Harvard University Press, 1991), 99. On the "learned style" and its relationship to the galant style, see Elaine Sisman, "Genre, Gesture, and Meaning in Mozart's 'Prague' Symphony," in *Mozart Studies 2*, ed. Cliff Eisen (Oxford: Clarendon Press, 1997), 27–84, esp. 64; and Sisman, *Mozart: The "Jupiter" Symphony* (Cambridge: Cambridge University Press, 1993), 69–74.

Example 6.2 Graun, "Christus hat uns ein Vorbild gelassen," from *Der Tod Jesu*, mm. 1–10.

Example 6.3 Graun, "Christus hat uns ein Vorbild gelassen," from *Der Tod Jesu*, mm. 76–81.

basso continuo may have been a reference to this procedure.[35] Instances of learned style compositions that include basso continuo can also be found in the chamber music of the period. An excellent example is the *alla breve* movement from Handel's Sonata for flute and continuo in B minor, op. 1, no. 9 (HWV367[b]) (see example 6.4). This movement stands out from all of the others in the sonatas of op. 1. It was the only movement to receive the designation *alla breve* in the first printing of these sonatas (by John Walsh ca. 1730), and it delights in imitative writing, sequences, and long chains of descending suspensions. Here more than in any other movement of the twelve sonatas in this opus, the basso continuo emerges as an equal partner to the soloist. Nevertheless, the contrapuntal writing is loosely imitative rather than strict, and although the bassline is conceived to answer the soloist well, it is also occupied with the harmonic support indicated in the figures. Even in this imitative context it retains the work of supplying the vertical sonorities that would be otherwise missing from this contrapuntal duet. The movement concludes with feints toward homophony, and the bassline comes

35. Fux, *Gradus ad parnassum*, 243.

Example 6.4 Handel, Sonata for flute and continuo in B minor, op. 1, no. 9, HWV367^b, mm. 1–11.

to a pause on the dominant at m. 74. Intriguingly, it is here that the early eighteenth-century Walsh print employs the most archaic notational practices: instead of using two tied whole notes for this pause in the bassline motion, it employs a single breve straddling the seventy-fifth barline.[36] At the end of the movement, homophony finally wins out: the soloist brings the *alla breve* to a close with a cadenza. The long durations of the ensuing final cadence are set in whole notes and breves with barlines added irregularly (see plate 6.7; it is almost as though the organization has switched to breve-length measures here, though the anti-penultimate and penultimate barlines do not line up in the two parts). The intersection between the final homophonic texture and the antiquated notation—the ¢ signature, *alla breve* indication, the use of long notes, and crashing barlines—captures this movement's intriguing hybridity. Invested in the contrapuntal ideals of an older style, this *alla breve* also showcased the textures of recent music.

Another way of using basso continuo in an imitative movement is to remove it from the structure of imitation altogether. The *alla breve* movement in Quantz's Trio Sonata in C major, QV 2.anh 3, is an interesting example. The movement opens with a slowly ascending, long-note melody in the second flute. This melody is not accompanied by a countermelody but instead by a traditional bassline with figures. After the opening few measures the character of flute writing begins to change. Quantz includes shorter durations and repeated notes, moving away from the vocally conceived ideals of imitative melody (example 6.5). The first flute provides an answer beginning on the fifth scale degree in m. 11. Following this entry, the bass participates briefly in the imitation (beginning in m. 21) but after six short measures the three-part polyphony morphs into figurative homophony. In the interior of the movement the flutes take turns joining forces

36. Even as late a treatise as Daniel Gottlob Türk's 1789 *Klavierschule* would mention notes "through which a barline is drawn, which cuts them, as it were, equally in two." Türk went on to clarify: "This manner of notation…still occurs in the so-called strict style." ("Ganz anders verhält sichs mit denenjenigen Noten, durch welche ein Taktstrich gezogen ist, wodurch sie gleichsam zerschnitten werden…Diese Schreibart…kommt noch in dem so genannten gebundenen Style vor.") Türk, *Klavierschule*, 72.

Plate 6.7 Handel, Sonata for flute and continuo in B minor, op. 1, no. 9, HWV367[b], *alla breve* (London: John Walsh, ca. 1730), 47.

with the basso continuo in long stretches of arpeggios. This movement is on the opposite end of the spectrum from Graun's. Although the writing is mostly imitative and—like Handel's—contains sequences and chains of suspensions, it also contains large swaths of figuration in all three parts. Quantz's *alla breve* movement brings portions of long-note melody and contrapuntal treatment into dialogue with the galant. Like Handel, Quantz uses the *alla breve* designation to play with the boundaries between archaic references and updated techniques.

Which Alla Breve?

Although these three movements all bear the marking *alla breve* and the ₵ meter signature, they explore the stylistic connotations of the term in rather different ways. Further, they implement different versions of metrical structure. While Graun's "Christus hat uns ein Vorbild gelassen" uses measures of breve length, the Handel and Quantz movements use measures of whole-note length. Their divergences point to the wealth of *alla breve* types in the eighteenth century, and the many ways in which single movements could explore its style. Within the multiplicity of meters that theorists described and composers used, the *alla breve* was itself rather multiple.

In certain ways, the term and its related signs were at the center of the proliferating discourse on the uses and meanings of meters. German theorists in particular took extra care to describe and discriminate among the many meters that could have been called *alla breve*. Like any meter in the eighteenth century, the *alla breve* could have indicated simple measures (in this case, of two beats) or

Example 6.5 Quantz, Trio Sonata in C major, QV 2.anh 3, mm. 1–34.

compounded measures (which join two simple measures for a total, in this case, of four beats between barlines).[37] In addition to this duality, theorists accounted for the fact that some composers used measures of whole-note length for the meter, while others used measures the length of a breve. These different categories created the possibility for *alla breve* music in a) simple measures, one breve in length, of two whole-note beats (2/1); b) compound measures, one breve in length, with a total of four half-note beats between barlines (4/2); and c) simple measures, one whole note in length, of two half-note beats (2/2).[38]

As was their want, many of the theorists disagreed. Scheibe identified a difference between whole-note- and breve-length measures, calling the former the "small or common *alla breve*" ("kleine oder gemeine Allabrevetakt") and the latter the "large *alla breve*" ("große Allabrevetakt").[39] He insisted that the large *alla breve* was frequently misunderstood, and should be treated as a "two semibreve meter," or a simple meter of two beats only—never a compounded meter, and specifically never 4/2. In order to further distinguish this particular version of *alla breve*, he recommended using the signature 2/1 or, instead of ¢, using a ₵.[40] Kirnberger also acknowledged the existence of a simple meter made of two whole notes and written in breve measures. Like Scheibe, he called this meter the "large *alla breve*," or 2/1, but in a strange historical reappropriation thought it wise to indicate it with the sign Φ (a renaissance sign for triple meter).[41] Turning to the literature to provide an example, Kirnbeger wrote "I know of only one Credo by the older Bach in the large *alla breve* meter of two semibreves," referring to the *stile antico* Credo of J. S. Bach's Mass in B minor (example 6.6).[42] The movement, which contains breve-length bars and expertly deployed counterpoint, is marked with ¢ in most editions.

Marpurg, on the other hand, consistently wrote of the "large *alla breve*," as a compounding of two duple measures (each a whole note in length for a total of four half-note beats between barlines). He identified this meter with the

---

37. These and other types of measures are treated in chapter 4.
38. Compounded measures, one whole note in length, of four quarter note beats between barlines (4/4) would not have fallen under the *alla breve* rubric given their short note vales.
39. Scheibe *Ueber die Musikalische Composition*, 202, 196. On this distinction and on 3/2 *alla breve* see Helmut Breidenstein, *Mozarts Tempo-System* (Tutzing: Hans Schneider, 2011), 31–34.
40. Scheibe, *Ueber die Musikalische Composition*, 199. Türk also recommends the use of ¢ for the large *alla breve* or 2/1. Türk, *Klavierschule*, 94.
41. Kirnberger, *Die Kunst des reinen Satzes in der Musik*, 2:117–18.
42. "Von dem alten Bach ist mir nur ein Credo in dem grossen Allabrevetackt von zwey Semibreven bekannt." Kirnberger, *Die Kunst des reinen Satzes in der Musik*, 2:118. Kirnberger's views on the large and small *alla breve* meters are fairly complicated. In his system, meters could be simple or compounded; simple meters could have two, three, or four beats (he was one of few eighteenth-century theorists to advocate for simple meters of four beats). Kirnberger discusses the possibility of the large *alla breve* of two beats (2/1 or φ) and mentions the possibility of a large *alla breve* of four beats (4/2) indicated with the renaissance sign O. The latter would have been some version of his simple quadruple meter (4/4) with half note beats instead of quarter note beats. In any case, he advises against the use of this large, quadruple *alla breve*, recommending that the composer employ the term *grave* in conjunction with the meter signature 4/4. Kirnberger, *Die Kunst des reinen Satzes in der Musik*, 2:122.

Example 6.6 J. S. Bach, Credo from the Mass in B minor, mm. 1–8.

numerals 4/2, but also endorsed the use of ₵ to distinguish this large *alla breve* from the small.[43] Koch seems to have agreed with Marpurg on this issue, and offered Graun's "Christus hat uns ein vorbild gelassen" as an example of the compounded meter.[44] Graun, for his part, does not make any distinction between the midpoint of his measures and the downbeat. He locates subject entries and cadences alike on the first and third half notes, suggesting that his ₵ measures contain two smaller measures of 2/2 each.[45] This movement can be said to be in Marpurg and Koch's 4/2 meter.

Compounded or no, the large *alla breve* sparked creativity in notation, as composers and theorists worked to set it apart from its smaller counterpart. The ₵ seems to have been at least somewhat useful in this regard. Albrechtsberger, reproducing a G minor fugue of Fux, used the ₵, thereby reflecting the piece's

43. Marpurg, *Anleitung zum Clavierspielen*, 19; idem., *Kritische Briefe über die Tönkunst*, facsimile ed. (1760; Hildesheim: Georg Olms, 1974), 1:109.

44. Heinrich Christoph Koch, "Alla Breve," in *Musikalisches Lexicon*, facsimile ed. (1802; Hildesheim: Georg Olms, 1964), 129; idem., *Versuch einer Anleitung zur Composition*, facsimile ed. (1787; Hildesheim: Georg Olms, 1969), 2:334.

45. On compounded measures see Floyd K. Grave, "Metrical Displacement and the Compound Measure in Eighteenth-Century Theory and Practice," *Theoria* 1 (1985): 25–60; Nicole Schwindt-Gross, "Einfache, zusammengesetzte und doppelt notierte Takte: Ein Aspekt der Takttheorie im 18. Jahrhundert," *Musiktheorie* 4, no. 3 (1989): 203–22; Claudia Maurer Zenck, *Vom Takt: Überlegungen zur Theorie und kompositorischen Praxis im augehenden 18. und beginnenden 19. Jahrhundert* (Vienna: Böhlau, 2001), 141–250; and Markus Waldura, "Marpurg, Koch, und die Neubegründung des Taktbegriffs," *Musikforschung* 53, no. 3 (2000): 237–53. See also chapter 4.

breve-length measures.[46] The sign also appears in copies of Bach's Fugue in E major from the second book of *The Well-Tempered Clavier*. Two British Library manuscripts of that fugue (GB-Lbl Ms. Add. 14330 and GB-Lbl Ms. Add. 65973) use the ¢ marking, as does an early nineteenth-century Parisian print.[47] Kirnberger's revival of Φ for duple use was transmitted later in the Paris Conservatory's textbook, the *Principes élémentaires de musique arrêtés par les Membres du Conservatoire, pour servir à l'étude*. In this treatise, Φ translated to 2/1 specifically, while O indicated 4/2.[48] Later, Schubert would mark the breve-length measures in his G-flat major Impromptu (op. 90, no. 3) with ¢¢, thinking perhaps of the ¢ that his predecessors used.[49]

Defined in opposition to the proliferation of marks for the large *alla breve*, the small *alla breve* was, as Scheibe put it, the more "common" of the two.[50] It could be marked with ¢ or even ₵ as Kirnberger mentions, and always contained measures a single whole note in length. Michael Praetorius's seventeenth-century name for the small *alla breve* is perhaps the most fitting: it was, after all, really an "alla semibreve."[51]

If the large *alla breve* was associated with more signs and signatures, the small *alla breve* was mixed with more styles. The many uses for ¢ made the implementation of the stylistic characteristics of the *alla breve* in "*alla semibreve*" measures a tricky affair. These measures looked just like measures of 4/4, so *alla semibreve* music could easily give way to music in other styles (and even with other metric structures).[52] By contrast, the longer measures of the large *alla breve* made it difficult to import updated styles in any transformative way.

These conditions may have encouraged composers and theorists to experiment more with the signs and signatures for the large *alla breve* than the small. As ¢ began to mean more things (and, therefore, to lose its specificity), there may have been an urge to affix new symbols to the archaic practices associated with the large *alla breve*'s long-note counterpoint. What better than a changed or reinterpreted renaissance mensuration sign to indicate archaism?

46. Albrechtsberger, *Gründliche Anweisung zur Composition*, 220–22. This G-minor fugue appears in Fux, *Gradus ad parnassum*, 213–14.

47. GB-Lbl Ms. Add. 14330 is a copy of Bach's *Wohltemperirte Klavier* by Samuel Wesley; GB-Lbl Ms. Add. 65973 contains an arrangement of the E-major fugue for four voices by "C. Stokes," 6r–8v. J. S. Bach, *Vingt-quatre preludes et fugues dans tous les tons et demi-tons du mode majeur et mineur pour le clavecin ou piano-forte* (Paris: Richault, 1828).

48. *Principes élémentaires de musique arrêtés par les Membres du Conservatoire, pour servir à l'étude*, ed. Agus, Catel, Chérubini, Gossec, Langlé, Lesueur, Méhul, and Rigel (Paris: A l'imprimerie du Conservatoire de Musique, Paubourg Poissonniere, 1800), 1:40–41. Türk also uses O for 4/2 in the *Klavierschule*, 95; as does Augustus Kollmann, in *An Essay on Musical Harmony* (London: J. Dale, 1796), 74. The new, duple uses of these signs continued into the nineteenth century with Gottfried Weber. See Weber, *Versuch einer geordneten Theorie der Tonsetzkunst*, rev. ed. (1817–21; Mainz: B. Schott's Söhne, 1830–32), 1:93, 114.

49. See Chew and Rastall, "Notation."

50. Scheibe, *Ueber die Musikalische Composition*, 202.

51. Praetorius, *Syntagma musicum*, 3:49.

52. The practice of shifting meters without changing the meter signature is a major topic taken up in Danuta Mirka's *Metric Manipulations in Haydn and Mozart* (Oxford: Oxford University Press, 2009).

By contrast to these experimental signs, the long-established ₵ was asked to do more work. Not only could it accommodate *alla breves* both large and small, but it was also affixed to music written entirely in the new styles. This was particularly true in France, where theoretical treatments of the *alla breve* were less common. Charles Vion's *La musique pratique et theorique*, with its extensive example sets, breezes past the ₵ signature without ever mentioning counterpoint. Instead, Vion describes the use of ₵ in "entreés, marches, ritornellos, [and] preludes."[53]

For an example of truly galant writing in ₵, one needs look no further than Stamitz's symphonic movements. The opening of his Symphony in E-flat, op. 4, no. 4 (Wolf E-flat 4) is given below in example 6.7. Here, ₵ indicates the two-beat nature of each measure, serving in its role as simple duple meter. But beyond its duple indication, this relic of the old mensural system imports nothing of its stylistic connotations into Stamitz's work.

The Alla Breve *and the End of* Tempo Giusto

By the middle of the century, theorists had observed—and openly deplored—the lack of specificity surrounding the *alla breve* and the ₵ signature. In 1752, Quantz remarked that the signature 2/2 was increasingly associated with the galant.[54] Scheibe, writing on the *alla breve* slightly later, elaborated on the difficulties:

> Today this meter appears in all sorts of writing—even in theatre pieces, in chamber pieces, and all kinds of instrumental works. Truthfully its proper place is the church, where it would be used splendidly for choruses, fugues, and highly developed pieces; the fact alone that it is now also used for other types of pieces means that one must get used to finding it therein. But this makes it all the more necessary that in every situation the tempo required by the piece, whether an aria, symphony, allegro, or concerto allegro, and so on, be indicated. In any case, since the operas and symphonies have mastered it, and it is often used in the very fastest and most fiery compositions where its old grandeur and seriousness find no place, so has it almost assumed an entirely different character; for it is now as preeminently beloved in the galant style as it was previously in the church style.[55]

53. Charles Vion, *La musique pratique et theorique: réduite à ses principes naturels* (Paris: De L'Imprimerie de Jean-Baptiste-Christophe Ballard, 1742), 23.
54. J. J. Quantz, *Versuch einer Anweisung, die Flöte traversiere zu spielen*, 3rd ed. (1752; Breslau: Johann Friedrich Korn dem ältern, 1789); facsimile ed. (Kassel: Bärenreiter, 1953), 56.
55. "diese Taktart heute zu Tage in allen Gattungen der Schreibarten vorkommt, und auch wohl auf dem Theater, in der Kammer, wie auch in allerhand Instrumentalsachen erscheinet. Es ist wahr, ihr eigentlicher Sitz ist die Kirche, wo sie vorzüglich in Chören, Fugen und gearbeiteten Sachen zu gebrauchen wäre; allein da sie nun auch zu andern Sachen gebrauchet wird; so muß man sich darein finden; aber um desto mehr ist es nöthig, dass jederzeit die Bewegung angezeiget wird, die der Satz es sey nun eine Arie, eine Sinfonienallegro, oder ein Concertenallegro u. d. g. erfodert. Da sich ohnedieß die Opern und die Sinfonien dieser Taktarten gar sehr bemeistert haben, und sie oft zu den allergeschwindesten und feurigsten Satzen gebrauchet wird, wo ihre alte Würde und Ernsthaftigkeit keine Statt findet: so hat sie bey nahe einen ganz andern

Example 6.7 Stamitz, Symphony in E-flat, op. 4, no. 4 (Wolf E-flat 4), i, mm. 1–7.

As chapters 4 and 5 argue, the anxieties that surrounded *tempo giusto* resulted in a proliferation of discourse and exemplification on the multiplicity of meters. Because theorists worried that meters no longer did a decent job of indicating tempo and character, they worked harder at explaining the different tempos and characters with which the different meters might be associated. Quantz, Scheibe,

Charakter angenommen; denn sie wird nunmehr in der galanten Schreibart eben so vorzüglich geliebet, als sie vorher im Kirchenstyl venerabel war." Johann Adolph Scheibe, *Ueber die Musikalische Composition*, facsimile ed. (1773; Kassel: Bärenreiter, 2006), 1:203–4.

Example 6.8 Mozart, Symphony no. 41, K. 551 ("Jupiter"), iv, mm. 1–8.

and others were quick to point out that these could include contradictory indications.

Something different happened with the *alla breve*, though, that made its position in all of these changing notational practices distinctive. The ₵ sign with which the term and the long-note counterpoint were associated not only worked for galant writing in addition to *stile antico*, it worked for galant music mixed with—and written on top of—*stile antico*. In other words, the use of the signature for various styles did not create a deadlock of confusion but instead increased the flexibility of its application. The ₵ sign was welcoming enough to long-note counterpoint and fast-moving gallantry that composers could use the two in conjunction with each other.

The most celebrated example of this intersection is the finale of Mozart's "Jupiter" symphony, but other symphonic finales of the period made use of this combination: the final movements of Michael Haydn's Symphonies in C, P. 31, and in D, P. 43, and of Joseph Haydn's Symphony in F, Hob. I:40, are among them (all four symphonies' openings are shown in examples 6.8–11).[56] Together with the finale of Mozart's K. 551, these works form a group with many common features. All written in ₵, they combine long-note themes with lighter—and shorter—material. Consider the opening of Michael Haydn's Symphony in C. The subject begins with two repeated whole notes on the tonic before the leap of a sixth sends the melody tumbling into a faster descent. With the addition of eighth notes in the fifth measure the tune has become

56. The relationship between Michael Haydn's Symphonies and Mozart's "Jupiter" symphony is discussed in A. Peter Brown, "Eighteenth-Century Traditions and Mozart's 'Jupiter' Symphony K.551," *The Journal of Musicology* 20, no. 2 (2003): 157–95.

Example 6.9 Michael Haydn, Symphony in C, P. 31, iii, mm. 1–7.

Example 6.10 Michael Haydn, Symphony in D, P. 43, iii, mm. 1–21.

almost playful. The subject of the learned counterpoint, then, has undergone a transformation even before any of the contrapuntal procedures have commenced. What appeared at first to be the subject of a learned fugue proves to be multifaceted. Mozart's finale also makes use of a chameleon-like subject, though he separates the learned and galant portions with a clearer break (an

Example 6.11 Joseph Haydn's Symphony Hob. I:40 in F, iv, mm. 1–16.

actual rest in the fifth measure). Joseph Haydn uses a theme that alternates between whole notes and quarter notes as if in indecision; the establishment of this pattern will prove useful later on in various contrapuntal combinations. These hybrid subjects are quite distant from the strictly whole-note melodies of the period's *stile antico* masses, many of which were written by the very same composers. The potential awkwardness of a melody that can include both whole notes and sixteenths—as Mozart's does—has rightfully garnered commentary in the recent past. It is not coincidental that Lerdahl and Jackendoff single out the "Jupiter" theme in their chapter on metric structure, noting that its second half requires many new levels of subdivision within the metric hierarchy (see plate 6.8).[57]

As though it were not enough to hybridize the very subjects of strict imitation, these three composers also experimented with vertical combinations of learned and galant. All four of the above-mentioned finales begin with whole

57. Fred Lerdahl and Ray Jackendoff, *A Generative Theory of Tonal Music* (Cambridge, MA: MIT Press, 1983), 73.

Plate 6.8 Opening melody from Mozart's "Jupiter" Symphony, as analyzed in Lerdahl and Jackendoff, *A Generative Theory of Tonal Music* (Cambridge, MA: MIT Press, 1983), 73. © 1982 Massachusetts Institute of Technology, by permission of The MIT Press.

4.8

notes in the themes accompanied by shorter durations in the other voices. Michael and Joseph Haydn use quarter-note basses in a manner that calls to mind the Credo of Bach's Mass in B minor (shown above in example 6.6) or the *alla breve* movement of Quantz's Trio Sonata in C major (example 6.5). Although some might interpret these basslines as countermelodies of a sort, they closely resemble basso continuo lines and often lack melodic interest. Their presence from the outset puts the texture into question; as is the case in the Quantz Sonata discussed above, these basslines tug the otherwise polyphonic organization into homophonic verticalities.

Mozart's movement begins with an outright galant accompaniment that doesn't even attempt to approximate a countermelody. While the long notes spin out, this second voice creates interest, sustaining attacks at the eighth-note level until the melody reaches its faster durations. The opening accompaniment is almost a commentary on the melody, providing a verdict that the long notes need updating and continued movement in order to be held for their required length. The continuo-like basslines in the other finales do similar work, running along at four times (or even eight times) the speed of their subjects. Kirnberger recognized the importance of faster durations in such contexts, recommending that composers use countermelodies "when a fugue [subject] begins very slowly in whole measures, because such an interlude relieves the tune's tediousness."[58] What the repertoire of the period bears out is, of course, not quite what Kirnberger had in mind. The fact that late eighteenth-century composers felt that they could use short-note accompaniment patterns instead of countermelodies speaks to the fragmenting of tempo, character, and notational practice.

Not only the openings of these movements are mixed; a look at their interiors reveals that all three movements thematize the disjuncture of learned counterpoint and lighter composition throughout. When the subject of Michael Haydn's Symphony in D, P. 43, returns in the secondary area, it is set in stretto and accompanied by an almost glib line in quarter and eighth notes (example 6.12). This combination then gives way to a fully galant closing area, complete with dotted

---

58. "Auch ist ein Gegensatz nöthig, oder doch sehr gut, wenn eine Fuge mit ganzen Takten und sehr langsam anfängt, da denn ein solches Zwischenspiel das Langweilige des Gesanges unterbricht." Kirnberger, "Gegensatz," in the *Allgemeine Theorie der schönen Künste*, ed. Sulzer, 2:337.

Example 6.12 Michael Haydn, Symphony in D, P. 43, iii, mm. 77–84.

rhythms and unison runs. Folding to the pressure of formal closure, Haydn interrupts his contrapuntal design with the rules and durations of another stylistic practice.[59]

The combinations and recombinations in the "Jupiter" finale are best known in this context, if only by virtue of their number, intensity, and complexity. Though Mozart presents us with the long-note theme at the very opening, he does not actually treat it imitatively until thirty-six measures into the movement. Before the arrival of this second, and properly learned opening (shown below in example 6.13), Mozart had already fit the melody against two different galant accompaniments. The imitation in this second entry is strict, but before the fifth entry is complete, Mozart abandons the process. The texture shifts abruptly in m. 53 and the music redirects our attention, in m. 56, to a short, galant ascending passage treated imitatively to a repeated-note accompaniment. The counterpoint

---

59. This clash of styles and durations also calls to mind the final movement of Mozart's String Quartet in G major, K. 387, where the learned and comic styles meet. For an account of the tensions between fugue and symphonic form in the eighteenth century, see James Currie, "Disagreeable Pleasures: Negotiating Fugal Counterpoint in Classical Instrumental Music," (PhD diss., Columbia University, 2001), particularly 74–150; see also Elaine Sisman, *Mozart: The "Jupiter" Symphony*, 74–79.

Example 6.13 Mozart, Symphony no. 41, K. 551 ("Jupiter"), iv, mm. 36–64.

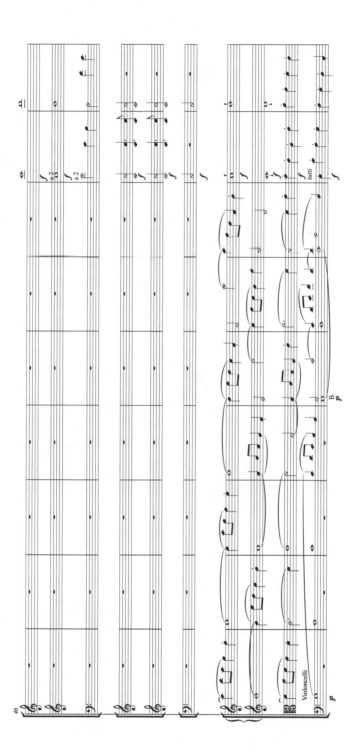

Example 6.13 Continued

in this new passage is significantly different in character and execution from the fugato that precedes it. Elaine Sisman suggests that this type of writing might be called "galant counterpoint," in order to account for its admixture of learned, difficult technique with playful melodic material and eighteenth-century texture.[60] Mozart's finale spans the gamut of contrapuntal engineering, featuring imitative settings of both its learned and galant melodies, and a virtuosic synthesizing of all of the important themes in the coda, which features double fugue and five-part invertible counterpoint.

The great advantage and the great downfall of the ₵ signature was that it could afford a home to all of these styles and all of their respective uses of duration.[61] The long notes from these four finales' themes were appropriate for the signature and the rubric of the small *alla breve* with which it was associated. The sign, the durations, and the learned counterpoint worked together as they did in the strictest church compositions of the day. But galant homophony and very short durations were also welcome in ₵, and moreover the two were free to comingle with long-note counterpoint, as they did in these finales.

With this complex situation in mind, it is easy to understand how confusing the *alla breve* might have been. If the term and the ₵ sign were sometimes associated with the doubling of speed that long-note counterpoint required, then the mixture of short-note galant with long-note music under the sign of ₵ negated this instruction. The four symphonic finales above needed no speeding up, despite the fact that they use long notes under contrapuntal control and bear the ₵ signature. Their long-note music had already been reconciled with contemporary practice through mixing of styles. As Kirnberger reminds us, the short-note music "relieves the tune's tediousness."[62]

In many ways the question of the *alla breve* was a microcosm of the questions all meter theory had to face as the eighteenth century progressed. To what extent did meter explain, and to what extent did it need explaining? Meter signatures were still asked to do the work of indicating tempo and style (at least theoretically), even though in practice they were used to indicate many different metric structures (to speak nothing of their characters and tempi). If the *alla breve* served a special need in an age of preserved long notes when duration could still compel a performer's choice of tempo, composers nevertheless used the term and the sign for galant and mixed works with many short notes. Above all else, this flexibility neutralized the meter signature, blanching out the particularity of its associations with tempo and affect. Scheibe put it best when he wrote: "this makes it all the more necessary that in every situation the tempo required by the

60. Sisman, "Genre, Gesture, and Meaning in Mozart's 'Prague' Symphony," 49; ibid., *Mozart: The "Jupiter" Symphony*, 69–74.

61. As Allanbrook writes of the situation more generally, "the practice necessitated the choice of a flexible, chameleonlike time signature, harmonious not just with one affect but with a particular handful of them." Allanbrook, *Rhythmic Gesture in Mozart*, 24. On this point see also Mirka, *Metric Manipulations in Haydn and Mozart*, 33.

62. Kirnberger, "Gegensatz," in the *Allgemeine Theorie der schönen Künste*, ed. Sulzer, 2:337.

piece...be indicated."[63] The tone of resignation in his words admits defeat over the change in practice.

The eighteenth-century *alla breve* was caught between two systems, one of which was reliant upon the semiotic ability of the meter signatures and note values to indicate character and tempo, and one of which would relinquish that ability. The *alla breve*'s confusing location at this nexus dramatizes the need for critical interpretive work in our twenty-first century understandings of meter's signs, and our obligation to think through the historical evolution of its ability to signify. Despite all of the eighteenth-century's efforts to codify, explain, and tabulate the characteristics and tempo indications of every meter signature (and, in some cases, because of the contradictory information these practices revealed), musicians of that era began to realize that they could not rely on meter signatures to communicate anything consistently. Composers would have to effect a new system in order to indicate their tempi. The story of what unfolded from this set of conditions is told in the following chapters.

---

63. Scheibe, *Ueber die Musikalische Composition*, 1:203.

PART III

CHAPTER Seven

The Reinvention of Tempo

A New Chronometer?

In December of 1812 the Parisian *Moniteur Universel* reported on a new invention of composer Jean-François Despréaux: a pendulum chronometer designed to "fix with precision the time of each measure."[1] Despréaux's new chronometer was met with great enthusiasm, publicized widely, and described alongside the other significant scientific inventions of its day in the *Archives des découvertes et des inventions nouvelles* of 1813.[2] Joachim Le Breton heralded the instrument as "a regulator missing from music which is quite necessary," and a remedy to the vagaries and ineffectiveness of tempo notation.[3] By contrast to the system of *tempo giusto* and the Italian tempo terms—which, according to Le Breton, had "almost no power of direction"—Despréaux's chronometer promised to be an instrument "of mathematical precision."[4] In the judgment of the Institut Impérial

1. "…un instrument qui pût fixer avec précision le tems de chaque mesure." Unsigned article, "Notice sur les travaux du Conservatoire impérial de musique et de déclamation, et sur les objets d'invention ou de perfectionnement qui ont été renvoyés à son examen, pour l'année 1812," *Le Moniteur universel* no. 552, December 17, 1812, 1592–93, at 1593.
2. In addition to the report in the *Moniteur*, see "Notice sur les travaux du Conservatoire impérial de musique et de déclamation, et sur les objets d'invention ou de perfectionnement qui ont été renvoyés à son examen, pour l'année 1812," *Esprit de journaux Français et étrangers par une société de gens de lettres*, February 1813, 2:132–48; Joachim Le Breton, "Notice des travaux de la Classe des beaux-arts de l'Institut impérial de France, pour l'année 1813," *Magasin encyclopédique ou journal des sciences, des lettres et des arts*, November 1813, 6:5–53, at 32–33; and "Chronomètre du Conservatoire," in *Archives des découvertes et des inventions nouvelles, Faites dans les Sciences, les Arts et les Manufactures, tant en France que dans les Pays étrangers, pendant l'année 1813* (Paris: Treuttel et Würtz, 1814), 225–27.
3. "En adoptant l'usage d'un chronomètre, le Conservatoire donne un régulateur qui manquait à la musique, et qui lui est très-nécessaire." Le Breton, "Notice des travaux de la Classe des beaux-arts de l'Institut impérial de France, pour l'année 1813," 32.
4. "Les mots d'adagio, d'allegro, de larghetto, sont si vagues, qu'ils n'ont presque aucune puissance de direction. Le chronomètre est un régulateur, d'une précision mathématique, pour fixer le temps de chaque mesure." Le Breton, "Notice des travaux de la Classe des beaux-arts," 32–33.

de France, the easiest way to universalize tempo indication would be to adopt the inexpensive and easily constructed device that Despréaux had invented.[5]

The early enthusiasm for Despréaux's "invention" conveniently overlooked the fact that his chronometer was nothing more than an update on the instrument that Mersenne had proposed nearly two hundred years earlier in *Harmonie universelle*—the same sort of device that Loulié eventually developed at the close the seventeenth century.[6] An uncomplicated pendulum, its basic mechanics were the stuff of centuries-old science and outdated music theory in Despréaux's era. The keen reception of his proposal speaks to a renewed urgency regarding the quantification of tempo in the early nineteenth century. Something, it would seem, had compelled a reinvention of the musical chronometer.

Between the age of Mersenne and that of Despréaux, the relationships connecting time, motion, and number were fundamentally rearranged. No longer a measurement of motion, time was now its own conceptual category and was said to "flow" independently of the events it measured. Devices that provided the units of temporal measure—mechanical clocks and other chronometers—had become so precise that their units were comprehensible across the Western world. Tempo, once a component of a system that involved the unique properties of meter signatures, note values, and characters, was increasingly treated to a special kind of scrutiny in texts on music.

Toward the end of the eighteenth century and into the nineteenth, theorists and musicians began to understand meter as a way of attending to the flow of time, and tempo as its rate. Thinking in universally applicable terms, they could understand any of music's many meters to be the result of our mind's regular division, while they could—potentially—specify any rate with which that division was to take place using some universally translatable unit of time. Finding a medium to accomplish this work unconnected to *tempo giusto* and yet still widely intelligible constituted a huge project for music theory. Musical chronometers were not new in this period, but the attitude toward them was.

Despréaux was hardly alone in his reinvention. For at least two decades preceding the announcement in the *Moniteur Universel*, the musical journals of the day had been publishing advertisements for new chronometers, positions pieces about them, and hints of new chronometric innovations in great number. The real and imagined machines of the period were as diverse as they were many; they included mechanically elaborate clockwork devices and basic variations of simple pendulums. No matter the technical sophistication of the machines

5. "Notice sur les travaux du Conservatoire impérial de musique et de déclamation, et sur les objets d'invention ou de perfectionnement qui ont été renvoyés à son examen, pour l'année 1812," *Le Moniteur Universel* no. 552, December 17, 1812, 1593; and "Notice sur les travaux du Conservatoire impérial de musique et de déclamation, et sur les objets d'invention ou de perfectionnement qui ont été renvoyés à son examen, pour l'année 1812," *Esprit de journaux Français et étrangers par une société de gens de lettres*, February 1813, 2:225.

6. Mersenne, *Harmonie universelle*, facsimile ed. (1636–37; Paris: Centre national de la recherché scientifique, 1963), vol. 3, "Livre Troisiesme des Instrumens à chordes," 149; Étienne Loulié, *Éléments ous principes de musique*, facsimile ed. (1698; Ann Arbor: University Microfilms, 1964), 81–88. See also chapter 5.

described, though, it was clear that a consistent set of issues surrounding tempo and number were of huge concern to the community that called for them. Their writings on musical chronometers form a much-overlooked corpus of theoretical discourse on tempo in the last decade of the eighteenth century and early decades of the nineteenth. These documents reveal a world invested in the universal translatability of tempo. They are documents of music theory insofar as they chart a process by which tempo became dissociated with the numerals of meter signatures and associated, instead, with the numbers of more widely recognized and reproducible systems of spatial and temporal measure. Tempo has a significant corpus of its own music theory, and these documents comprise one of its most important parts.

In the end, it was the universal translatability of clock time that would supply the ultimate standard for tempo inscription, and it was Maelzel's metronome that became the preferred machine for measuring it. Its units based on the number of beats per minute, the metronome promised to provide an authoritative and universally intelligible medium for the communication of tempo across languages, borders, and generations. Whether enthusiastic or horrified about his machine, the period's commentators recognized that its growing popularity had signaled a change in the relationship between tempo and notation. From this point on, the technique of tempo indication employed the powerful mediating abilities of chronometric numbers. This was nothing short of a reinvention of tempo itself.

Tempo in late eighteenth- and early nineteenth-century music—particularly the music of Beethoven—is a well-trod topic.[7] There is scarcely a generation of music scholars that have not had their say about the appropriate tempi for the music written during this period. Still, for all of the ink spilled on this subject it is surprising that very little has been written about the period's own discourses on the technologies of musical timekeeping. If tempo prescriptions are lacking in what follows, it is because there is yet another fascinating story to be told

---

7. The bibliography surrounding tempo and performance practice in Beethoven's music is rather extensive, though work pertinent specifically to the metronome is more limited in scope. See in particular Alexander Evan Bonus, "The Metronomic Performance Practice: A History of Rhythm, Metronomes, and the Mechanization of Musicality" (PhD diss., Case Western Reserve University, 2010); Claudia Maurer Zenck, Vom Takt (Vienna: Böhlau, 2001); Clive Brown, "Historical Performance, Metronome Marks and Tempo in Beethoven's Symphonies," Early Music 19 (1991): 247–58; Rudolph Kolisch, "Tempo and Character in Beethoven's Music," trans. Arthur Mendel, The Musical Quarterly 29, nos. 1–2 (1943): 169–87, 291–312, reissued in The Musical Quarterly 77, nos. 1–2 (1993): 90–131, 268–342; Rosamond E. M. Harding, "The Metronome and it's Precursors" [sic], in The Origins of Musical Time and Expression (Oxford: Oxford University Press, 1938); subsequently republished as a stand-alone monograph, The Metronome and it's Precursors [sic] (Oxfordshire: Gresham Books, 1983) (I will refer to the monograph version throughout); and David Fallows's Grove articles on the metronome and tempo: Oxford Music Online, ed. Laura Macy, s.v. "Metronome," "Tempo and Expression Marks," and "Tempo giusto," by David Fallows, accessed November 16, 2008, <www.oxfordmusiconline.com>. While scholars such as Zenck, Brown, Kolisch, and others have concentrated on the content of Beethoven's metronome markings and their difference from modern performance practices, theoretical scholarship on the discourses surrounding the instrument is notably scarce.

concerning the changes in the very conceptualization of tempo during this same period.

Meter, Tempo, Number

Meter as Universal System

The reinvention of tempo began with the growing dissatisfaction of Italian tempo terms and the impending dissolution of the *tempo giusto* system at the end of the eighteenth century. During this time, theorists and musicians began to conceptualize both meter and tempo in ways that were universally applicable and no longer so bound up with each other. Writing in that century's final years, the theorist and composer Daniel Gottlob Türk had trouble articulating the relationship between these two concepts. He hesitated over the definition of meter (*Takt*) in his *Klavierschule* of 1789: although the term was used to describe meter signatures, it was also associated with the space between the printed barlines and was "sometimes, though not quite correctly, understood as the tempo [*Bewegung*]: for example, this phrase has a very quick meter."[8] The formulation evidently gave Türk some pause, because a nearly identical passage in his *Kurze Anweisung zum Klavierspielen* of 1792 provides an important reformulation: "[meter] is sometimes, though not correctly, understood as the tempo."[9] More properly, in Türk's account, meter should be understood as a way of measuring music without regard to tempo.

Late eighteenth- and early nineteenth-century theorists like Türk increasingly dissociated meter from the system of *tempo giusto* in which its signatures had once proliferated. The heavy weight of meter's multiplicity within this nuanced system had grown too great by the conclusion of the eighteenth century. Theorists searched for a method of explanation that—like Kirnberger's—would account for the many different types of meters and measures in a single theoretical system. They appealed to the burgeoning discourses on aesthetics, which understood the contemplation of art as a scene of sensuous cognition.[10]

---

8. "Außerdem wird das Wort Takt noch in mancher andern Bedeutung genommen. Man versteht nämlich darunter...3) wird zuweilen, wiewohl nicht ganz richtig, die Bewegung darunter verstanden, z. B. dieser Satz hat sehr geschwinden Takt." Daniel Gottlob Türk, *Klavierschule* (Leipzig and Halle: the author [Leipzig: Schwickert; Halle: Hemmerde & Schwetschke], 1789), 89. Compare Türk's definition to Marpurg's in the *Anleitung zur Musik überhaupt, und zur Singkunst besonders*... (Berlin: Arnold Wever, 1763), 67–68.

9. "...wird zuweilen, wiewohl nicht richtig, die Bewegung darunter verstanden." Türk, *Kurze Anweisung zum Klavierspielen* (Leipzig: Schwickert; Halle: Hemmerde & Schwetschke, 1792), 55.

10. Alexander Gottlieb Baumgarten, *Meditationes philosophicae de nonnullis ad poema pertinentibus* (Halle: Grunert, 1735), §cxv; modern ed., ed. Benedetto Croce (Naples: Vecchi, 1900), 41; Sulzer, "Sinnlich," in the *Allgemeine Theorie der schönen Künste*, (Leipzig: M. G. Weidmanns Erben und Reich, 1771–74), 2:673; Kirnberger, *Die Kunst des reinen Satzes in der Musik*, facsimile ed. (1771–79; Hildesheim: Georg Olms, 1968), 2:105, 113. See the discussion of Kirnberger's theory of meter in chapter 4.

Meter could be thought of as an activity of the mind responding to the unfolding regularities in the raw material of musical sound. Meter was in these theories a way of attending to the ongoing, independent flow of time, construed broadly enough to account for any type of regular dividing scheme at any tempo.

Ultimately for Türk it was our capacity to distinguish regular patterns of accentuation that comprised "the sensation [Gefühl] that we call meter."[11] Koch likewise located our capacity to partition musical time in "the nature of our senses and our imagination."[12] Some theorists continued to advocate for a simplification scheme that would reduce all meters to the basic categories of duple and triple. Momigny in particular made a case for simplification on the basis of our ear's capacity to judge the segmentation of music into either two or three beats.[13] Others followed Kirnberger and began their theoretical treatment of meter with the depiction of a theoretically endless stream of durations that our mind divides into equal segments. "These divisions we shall call bars," Logier suggested, "we... unconsciously lay a stress upon the first note of each bar, but not on the second."[14] Something in our mind did the work of identifying the moments marked for attention within the endless flow of duration. As Gottfried Weber put it, "our internal sentiment overlays something of its own."[15] The act of adducing this particular relationship to musical duration was meter.

Thus understood, "our senses and our imagination" could divide the flow of duration in any way whatsoever, so long as it was regular. Meter, then, was a broad aesthetic category with universal systematicity; the many, oddly specific meter signatures were subcategories thereof and no longer required the careful unpacking that earlier theorists had provided them. The idea that they indicated tempo was, as Türk had it, "not entirely correct," or even "not correct." Meter could be understood as its own conceptual category.

What these universal theories of meter lacked was any significant theorization of tempo. Weber's account was unabashedly equivocal on this subject;

11. "...das Gefühl, welches wir Takt nennen." Türk, Klavierschule, 88.

12. "Die erste Ursache warum er dieses auch mit Vorsaz nicht bewerkstelligen kann, scheint mir nicht sowohl in dem, schon an Tactbewegung gewöhnten Gefühle des Tonkünstlers, sondern hauptsächlich in der Natur unserer Sinnen und unserer Vorstellungskraft enthalten zu seyn." Koch, Versuch einer Anleitung zur Composition (Leipzig: Adam Friedrich Böhme, 1782–93), 2:277–78.

13. Jérôme-Joseph de Momigny, Cours complet d'harmonie et de composition (Paris: the author and Bailleul, 1802–1806), 2:408–16. In Momigny's account there is an added problem concerning our relationship to notation: our ears judge division at the moments that are marked by the barlines, and we should therefore understand all that comes before the barline (any anacrustic material) as the "first" beat. The "second" and subsequent beats consist of the material that falls after the barline. For more on Momigny's anacrustic theory of meter, see chapter 8.

14. Johann Bernhard Logier, A System of the Science of Music and Practical Composition (London: J. Green, 1827), 259.

15. "...unser inneres Gefühl fügt noch etwas Eignes hinzu." Gottfried Weber, Versuch einer geordneten Theorie der Tonsetzkunst 2nd ed. (1817–21; Mainz: B. Schotts Söhne, 1824), 1:99.

reviewing the differences between the various duple meters (2/1, 2/2, 2/4) in his *Versuch einer geordneten Theorie der Tonsetzkunst*, he concludes:

> Looking back at the meter signatures thus far passed over, one finds that all the varieties—the 2/1 meter, 2/2 meter, 2/4 meter, and so forth, are in fact one and the same thing in various configurations and manners of presentation...Therefore it even appears, in the end, a matter of indifference which mode of writing one chooses.[16]

Although Weber was well aware of the tempo connotations that meter signatures and durations carried, he ultimately viewed their differences as matters of notation alone. "The difference," he explained, "lies only in idea."[17] The possibility that meter was a relationship between musical material and sense perception—a matter for the determination of "our senses and our imagination," following Koch—predisposed theorists to see meter's many signatures as little more than notational variants of each other. Toward the end of the eighteenth century and at the beginning of the nineteenth, the elaborate taxonomies of *tempo giusto* faded from view, their utility put into question.

The Numeric Mediation of Tempo

It had once seemed improbable that there could be any other way of setting tempo than to trust in the judgment of the trained musician to discern it from the Italian tempo term, meter signature, note values, and character of a piece. But at the turn of the nineteenth century, attitudes toward the once-dismissed musical chronometers shifted. The proposal gained a new sort of viability alongside the universally applicable theories of meter. At the end of *tempo giusto* and before Maelzel advertised his metronome, writings on music made it clear that the right chronometer could provide a universally intelligible way of indicating and explaining tempo through the translatable properties of number.

In the mid-eighteenth century, Rousseau believed the project of tempo quantification futile. He concluded his dictionary article on musical chronometers in great dissatisfaction: "No matter what instrument one might find for regulating the duration of a measure it will be impossible—even if it should have the easiest execution—that it will ever be used in practice. Musicians...will neglect the chronometer."[18] But when Rousseau's article was reprinted in the first volume of Nicolas-Étienne

16. "Ueberblickt man die bisher durchgangenen Taktarten, so findet man, dass alle graden, der 2/1-Takt, der 2/2-, der 2/4-Takt u. s. w. im Grunde nur Eines und Dasselbe, unter verschiedenen Gestalten oder Darstellungsformen sind...Eben darum scheint es am Ende wohl gar gleichgiltig, welche Art zu schreiben man wähle." Weber, *Versuch einer geordneten Theorie der Tonsetzkunst*, 2nd ed., 1:97–98.
17. "Der Unterschied liegt nur in der Idee." Weber, *Versuch einer geordneten Theorie der Tonsetzkunst*, 2nd ed., 1:113.
18. "J'ajoûterai que, quelqu'instrument qu'on pût trouver pour régler la durée de la mesure, il seroit impossible, quand même l'exécution en seroit de la dernière facilité, qu'il eût jamais lieu dans la pratique. Les musiciens, gens confians, & faisant, comme bien d'autres, de leur propre goût la

Framery's *Encylopédie méthodique* of 1791, it was followed by a serious reassessment from Framery himself. "It is upsetting to find such a joke in a work like [Rousseau's] *Dictionnaire de musique*," he wrote.[19] Framery thought Rousseau's midcentury dismissal of the chronometer completely unfounded, and provided a point-by-point reprisal of the older theorist's dissatisfactions more than twice the length of Rousseau's original article.[20] One of Rousseau's principal objections concerned the ability of a machine to capture and convey the "true character and true tempi of airs."[21] For Rousseau, the execution of just tempo necessitated a musician's application of cultivated taste and experience. Decisions regarding the codification and performance of the right tempo should be left to the musicians themselves. Framery saw things quite differently. In his view, it was the musicians who were suspect. The very passions that stirred them to make judgments about tempo were the cause of their errors: excited by well-executed passages, thrown off by mistakes, taken in by the interest and tenderness of phrases, musicians frequently distorted the tempi of musical works. Conductors too often subjected their orchestras to the flippancy of their moods. "It is not their talent that one should be suspicious of," he qualified, "but the human constitution, which constantly varies."[22] No matter how refined their sensibilities, musicians were in need of a regulator for their erratic states; they required a technique to ensure a baseline of correct communication between unreliable human interlocutors. The chronometer would provide this regulation through number. Its ability to quantify tempo would allow composers "to transmit their idea from one country to another, and to conserve it when they are no more."[23] The chronometer and its indications could be trusted.

If *tempo giusto* was already suspect in the years around the turn of the century, it was nowhere more so than in the process of musical travel. The translation of music across geographical and linguistic boundaries presented *tempo giusto* with a challenge it ultimately could not meet. Faced with the possible

règle du bon, ne l'adopteroient jamais; ils laisseroient le *chronomètre*, & ne s'en rapporteroient qu'à eux du vrai caractère & du vrai mouvement des airs." Rousseau, "Chronomètre," in *Encylopédie méthodique…: Musique*, ed. Nicolas-Étienne Framery, Pierre-Louis Ginguené, and Jérôme-Joseph de Momigny (Paris: Panckoucke, 1791), 1:279–80, at 280. As noted in chapter 5, Rousseau relies heavily on ideas and language borrowed from Diderot's "Projet d'un nouvel Orgue," [1748] in *Mémoires sur différens sujets de mathématiques*, in *Œuvres philosophiques et dramatiques de M. Diderot* (Amsterdam, 1772), 16:267–75.

19. "On est fâché de rencontrer des plaisanteries de ce genre dans un ouvrage comme le Dictionnaire de Musique." Framery, "Chronomètre," in *Encylopédie méthodique…: Musique*, ed. Nicolas-Étienne Framery, Pierre-Louis Ginguené, and Jérôme-Joseph de Momigny (Paris: Panckoucke, 1791), 1:280–82, at 280.

20. Acknowledging that Rousseau's article relies on Diderot's writings, Framery takes on Diderot by name as well.

21. Rousseau, "Chronomètre," in *Encylopédie méthodique*, 1:280.

22. "…ce n'est pas de leur talent qu'on se défie, mais de la constitution humaine, qui varie sans cesse." Framery, "Chronomètre," in *Encylopédie méthodique*, 1:282.

23. "…il resteroit encore au *chronomètre* cet avantage, de servir au compositeur à transmettre son idée d'un pays à l'autre, & à la conserver quand il ne sera plus." Framery, "Chronomètre," in *Encylopédie méthodique*, 1:282.

abstractions of legibility at real or imagined distances, musicians were unhappy relying on the nexus of Italian tempo terms, meters, note values, and characters to communicate tempo. The promise of invariance across distance became a trope in the period's literature on musical chronometers. Just a year after the commotion about Despréaux's reinvented chronometer, a lengthy, unsigned opinion piece appeared in the Leipzig *Allgemeine musikalische Zeitung* (hereafter *AmZ*) bemoaning the state of tempo communication and advocating for the adoption of some chronometric device in music. The worst of the trouble, it would seem, concerned the huge variation that attended the cosmopolitan circulation of musical works.

> There are inventions that, although everyone will concur on their usefulness, are so unused that it is as if they did not even exist. What a long litany a German physicist could list here! Musicians have such a list of their own, albeit a short one. Included in this list is a proposal, often made in years past, of ascertaining a composer's specific tempo for a piece of music using the degree of movement of an instrument, such that, with its help, the tempo could be indicated even in the most remote locations. The advantages of such an instrument have always been obvious…
>
> To cite only one example: I heard Mozart's Overture to *Don Giovanni* rehearsed by the master himself with the former Guardasonischen Gesellschaft in Prague; I then also heard it, among other places, in Paris, Vienna and Berlin. In Paris the Adagio was taken but an inconsiderable amount slower, in Vienna, faster by a huge margin, and in Berlin, almost twice as fast as Mozart. In all three locations the Allegro was more or less faster than his.[24]

This *AmZ* contributor was able to marshal authority on the basis of access to a rehearsal in which Mozart himself had set the tempi. Comparisons with the Paris, Vienna, and Berlin performances, then, were only available to this well-traveled insider, but the apparent observation (true or no) was worrying. Without Mozart's personal authority the tempi did not translate well, even to the musical capitals of Western Europe. From the time of the musical chronometer's inception, imagined destinations had played a role in its descriptions— Mersenne's hypothetical device, discussed in chapter 5, was to accompany music on journeys to Constantinople, Persia, or China—but late eighteenth- and early

---

24. "Es giebt Erfindungen, von deren Nützlichkeit jedermann überzeugt ist, in deren Lobe alle Welt übereinstimmt, und die doch so unbenützt bleiben, als wären sie gar nicht da. Welch eine lange Litaney könnte hier der deutsche Physiker anstimmen! Auch der Tonkünstler hat Stoff zu einer, obgleich kürzern. In diese gehört auch der Vorschlag, der schon vor mehrern Jahren, und oft gethan worden, den Grad der Bewegung eines Musikstücks durch ein eigenes Instrument so zu bestimmen, dass mit dessen Hülfe auch in den entferntesten Orten und Zeiten ein jeder im Stande ist, gerade da selbe Tempo zu fassen, das der Componist haben wollte. Der Vortheil, den ein solches Instrument bringen musste, war einlenchtend…Ich hörte, um nur Eins anzuführen, Mozarts Ouverture zum D. *Giovanni*, vom Meister selbst mit der ehemaligen Guardasonischen Gesellshaft in Prag einstudirt; ich hörte sie dann, unter andern Orten, auch in Paris, Wien und Berlin. Das Adagio nahm man in Paris um ein Unbeträchtliches langsamer, in Wien um ein Beträchtliches schneller, in Berlin fast noch einmal so schnell, als Mozart: das Allegro an allen drey Orten mehr oder weniger geschwinder, als er." Unsigned miscellaneous contribution, Leipzig *AmZ* 15, no. 18, May 5, 1813, 305–7, at 305–6.

nineteenth-century sources were concerned with much more proximate distributions.[25]

The chronometer proposals at the turn of the century were unequivocal in their concern for translatability of every sort. To geographical translation, Gottfried Weber added historical. It was clear to him that an Allegro tempo today could be much faster, and an Adagio much slower, than these had been for musicians living fifty or one hundred years previous. "What is certain is at least this: we no longer know—for it is impossible to know—how fast or slow they took [these tempi]."[26] With historical determinations of any certainty out of the question, prescriptions for the future seemed all the more necessary. For theorists of the period, the imagined translations in geography and temporality took on the characteristics of linguistic confusion. Weber worried that music's lack of a standard chronometric unit would lead to a "Babylonian confusion of tongues."[27]

The solution to the problem of translation was a universal language. Tempo would have to find a universally applicable rule, just as meter had, in order for the diversity of its signs to transcend the imagined geographies and temporalities they would travel. For Weber, the answer was found in an uncomplicated pendulum. "Everyone can easily make for themselves a simple pendulum from some twine and a plumb, every composer can mark his compositions accordingly, [and] every reader will understand this universal language."[28] Despréaux's reinvented chronometer also held this appeal. Advocating for the device, Le Breton noted that in order for any machine to overcome the problem of tempo translation, it would need to be "universally adopted and, consequentially, easy to construct and of a modest price."[29] Despréaux's instrument fit the bill perfectly.

Pendulum devices like Weber's and Despréaux's made up the majority of "new" musical chronometers in the era before Maelzel's metronome. Some inventors (like Despréaux) touted these chronometers as truly new innovations while others (like Weber) simply advocated for a more widespread adoption of these uncomplicated devices.[30] In addition to these, the period saw the development of

25. For another example see G. E. Stöckel, "Über die Wichtigkeit der richtigen Zeitbewegung eines Tonstücks," Leipzig AMZ 2, nos. 38 and 39, June 18–25, 1800, 657–66, and 673–78, at 677; and Thiémé, Nouvelle théorie sur les différens mouvemens des airs, 56–57. This topic is also taken up in chapter 5.

26. "…und gewiss ist wenigstens dieses, dass wir nicht mehr bestimt wissen, ja unmöglich wissen können, wie geschwind sie jenes nahmen, wie langsame dieses." Weber, Ueber chronometrische Tempobezeichnung (Mainz: B. Schott, 1817), 1.

27. "…unfehlbar eine babilonische Sprachverwirrung entstehen müsste." Weber, Ueber chronometrische Tempobezeichnung, 2.

28. "…ein einfaches Pendel aber kann jeder sich selbst leicht anfertigen aus einem Stückchen Bley und Zwirnfaden, jeder Tonsetzer kann sein Tonstück leicht darnach bezeichnen, jeder Leser diese Universal-Sprache verstehen." Weber, "Ueber die jetzt bevorstehende wirkliche Einführung des Taktmessers," Leipzig AmZ 16, nos. 27–28, July 6–13, 1814, col. 445–49 and 461–65, at 448.

29. "Pour produire son effet, il faut le rendre d'un usage universel, par conséquent facile à construire, et d'un prix modique." Le Breton, "Notice des travaux de la Classe des beaux-arts de l'Institut impérial de France, pour l'année 1813," 33.

30. In addition to the literature cited above on Despréaux's instrument, pendulum devices are described or advocated for in William Tans'ur, A New Musical Grammar: or the Harmonical

a small number of elaborate machines for the regulation of tempo. Stöckel, for example, thought that the beat was best kept with a bell or some other audible marker, while F. Guthmann promised to deliver an appropriate mechanism the size of a pocket watch.[31] The pendulum devices, though more clumsy, had a distinct advantage over these other gadgets. Pendulums were constructed and calibrated with units of spatial measure, essentially converting units of distance into units of tempo. Other machines of the era relied on their own system of temporal gradations, and thus could be of no real use unless some consensus or convention developed around the units they employed. The problem was not so much how these machines conveyed the tempo—whether or not they could produce a sound or fit in your pocket—but how translatable and accessible their units of measure turned out to be.

The challenges of tempo translation were part of an ever-stronger desire for a *translatio imperii* in the notation of tempo. The documents on tempo from the

Spector (London, 1746), 41–46; Türk, *Klavierschule*, 112; Abel Bürja, *Beschreibung eines musikalischen Zeitmessers* (Berlin: Petit und Schöne, 1790); Framery, "Chronomètre," in *Encylopédie méthodique*...; Augustus Frederic Christopher Kollman, *An Essay on Musical Harmony* (London: J. Dale, 1796), 72; Frédéric Thiémé, *Nouvelle théorie sur les différens mouvemens des airs* (Paris: Laurens jeune, 1801), 49–61; Antide Janvier, *Étrennes chronométriques, pour l'an 1811, ou précis de ce qui concerne le tems, ses divisions, ses mesures, leur usages, etc.* (Paris: Chez Antide Janvier, ou Palais des Arts; J. J. Paschoud; et à Genève, chez le meme Libraire, 1810), 152–56; Unsigned miscellaneous contribution, Leipzig *AmZ* 15, no. 18, May 5, 1813, 305–7; Franz Sales Kandler, "Rückblicke auf die Chronometer und Herrn Mälzels Neuste Chronometerfabrik in London," Vienna *AmZ* 1, nos. 5–8, January 30–February 20, 1817, col. 33–36, 41–43, 49–52, 57–58; Nikolaus Zmeskall von Domanovecz, "Tactmesser, zum Praktischen Gebrauch Geeignet," Vienna *AmZ* 1, nos. 35 and 36, August 28–September 4, 1817, col. 293–300, 305–8; the numerous writings of Gottfried Weber on this topic, including "Noch Einmal ein Wort über den Musikalischen Chronometer oder Taktmesser," Leipzig *AmZ* 15, no. 27, July 7, 1813, col. 441–47; Weber, "Ueber die Jetzt Bevorstehende Wirkliche Einführung des Taktmessers," Leipzig *AmZ* 16, nos. 27–28, July 6–13, 1814, col. 445–49, 461–65; Weber, "Über ein Chronometrische Tempobezeichnung, Welche den Mälzel'schen Metronome, so wie Jede Andere Chronometer–Machine Entbehrlich Macht," Vienna *AmZ* 1, no. 25, June 19, 1817, col. 204–9; Weber, "Mälzel's Metonome Überall Umsonst zu Haben," Vienna *AmZ* 1, no. 37, September 11, 1817, col. 313–14; Weber, *Ueber chronometrische Tempobezeichnung*; Weber, "Chronometer," in the *Allgemeine Encyclopädie der Wissenschaften und Künste*, ed. Johann Samuel Ersch and Johann Gottfried Gruber (Leipzig: J. F. Gleditsch, 1813–89), 17:204–9; and in the various editions of Weber's *Versuch einer geordneten Theorie der Tonsetzkunst*. For additional bibliographic information, see Bonus, "The Metronomic Performance Practice"; Fallows, "Metronome"; and Harding, *The Metronome and it's Precursors [sic]*.

31. Stöckel, "Über die Wichtigkeit der richtigen Zeitbewegung eines Tonstücks"; idem., "Noch ein Wort über den musikalischen Zeitmesser," Leipzig *AmZ* 6, no. 4, October 26, 1803, col. 49–55; Guthmann, "Ein neuer Taktmesser, welcher aber erst erfunden werden soll," Leipzig *AmZ* 9, no. 8, November 19, 1806, col. 117–19. In addition to these machines there was also the chronomètre developed in tandem by composer Jean-Baptiste Davaux and the clockmaker Breguet: Davaux, "Lettre de M. Davaux, aux Auteurs du Journal," *Journal de Paris* 129, May 8, 1784, 559–61, at 560; the plexichronomètre of the harpist Renaudin: "Variétés: Chronomètre & Plexichronomètre," *Mercure de France* no. 24, June 12, 1784, 85–89; Dubos' Rhythmomètre: Unsigned article, "Rhythmomètre, inventé & exécuté par le sieur Dubos, horloger-méchanicien, qui a eu l'honneur de la présenter au Roi & à la Reine, le 13 Janvier 1787," *Journal général de France* 80, July 5, 1787, 319; and assuredly many others.

turn of the century demonstrate the inclination to transfer the authority of tempo from meter signatures to some universal form of measurement. The problem with *tempo giusto* was that it used notation in an unverifiable and inexact way—it was no longer thought to survive translation. Within that system, the numerals of meter signatures had acted like names or nominal numbers for tempo. They provided a badge or identifying label for the characteristics and qualities of a given piece, linking indexically to the tempo appropriate for it. By contrast, the numerals that musical chronometers would provide were to act as cardinal numbers for tempo, specifying an exact amount within a preexisting standard of measure.

The writings on musical chronometers at the turn of the century imagined a new technique for tempo that coupled a cardinal numeric indication with the use of some machine. This hybrid technique mediated tempo through the universal translatability of numbers. As Stöckel had it, they were to provide tempo with the "cipher" of "a clear, established, unmistakable language."[32] Technologies of distance, numbers were the natural vocabulary of the period's precision rhetoric.[33] The impersonality of their signifying mechanism was equated with their purported objectivity and truth-value over distance and history.[34] Numbers were the missing desiderata of previous notational systems, and hence the object of Weber's impassioned frustration: "My God! Had only Handel, Bach, and Graun set one or two [chronometer] numbers for their works, they would not today be performed with misunderstood, incorrect tempi, defiled, and abased by so many of my colleagues!"[35] From Weber's vantage point, the numbers of musical chronometers were our best hope for the music of the future, even if they were already too late for the music of the past.

Numeric tempo indications might seem far too cold and rigid for their work, threatening to render the execution of tempo a mechanical affair. Some of the contributors to the body of writing on musical chronometers felt that just the opposite was true. Numbers in these writings—as in the period's natural philosophy—were imbued with great authority, trust, and power.[36] Paired with a pendulum device or a machine that would interpret them, they provided a necessary

32. "...dass durch dasselbe, wenn es nur erst eingeführt ist, über alles, was unter die Rubrik Zeit in der Musik gebracht werden kann, eine Allen verständliche, feststehende, und untrügliche Sprache möglich wird, do dass z. B. jeder Komponist durch eine Chiffre, seinem Werke vorgesetzt, gewiss seyn kann, es werde in der ganzen musikalischen Welt in dem Tempo vorgetragen, in welchem er es vorgetragen haben will." Stöckel, "Noch ein Wort über den musikalischen Zeitmesser," col. 49.

33. Theodore M. Porter, *Trust in Numbers: The Pursuit of Objectivity in Science and Public Life* (Princeton: Princeton University Press, 1995), ix; M. Norton Wise, "Precision: Agent of Unity and Product of Agreement: Part I—Traveling," in *The Values of Precision*, ed. M. Norton Wise (Princeton, Princeton University Press, 1995), 92–100.

34. Porter, *Trust in Numbers*, 74.

35. "Mein Gott! hätten doch die Händel, die Bache und Graune eine oder zwey solche Ziffern vor ihre Werke gesetzt: diese würden nicht in jetzigen Zeiten von so manchen meiner Collegen in missverstandenen, unrichtigen Zeitbewegungen aufgeführt, entweiht und geschändet!" Weber, "Noch Einmal ein Wort über den Musikalischen Chronometer oder Taktmesser," 447.

36. Wise, "Precision: Agent of Unity and Product of Agreement."

regulation for tempo's affective qualities, safeguarding the music against incorrect execution and human error. As the announcement of Despréaux's reinvented chronometer explained:

> It is necessary to regulate man even in the midst of pleasures, and the most pure emotions of the soul will receive more charm in attaching themselves to the law of constant motion discovered by Galileo—this mysterious division of time that we need above all in music.[37]

The prevalent opinion was that the chronometer's universal numeric mediation would not render tempo lifeless, but rather that its numbers had the power to translate musical affect. The chronometer as a mathematical instrument—linked in the *Moniteur*'s account to Galilean authority—was better suited to the task of tempo communication than the musicians themselves.[38] As Framery would remind us, musicians were subject to a human disposition that constantly varied, requiring that they submit their passions to the refining precision of the chronometer.[39] This meant that the hybrid technique of chronometric mediation for tempo gave over to numbers a somewhat surprising capability to hone pure emotion through the "mysterious" law of division. Numeric mediation was strangely musical.

Like the universal theories of meter, the universal technique for tempo held an important relationship to the period's aesthetics. The idea that musical sentiment could be perfected when submitted to abstract, numeric rule shares much which the thought of Friedrich Schiller in particular. Schiller, whose aesthetic doctrine psychologized Kantian principles, theorized a mode of aesthetic experience resulting from the harmony of sensuous perception and formal law.[40] His 1795 *Letters on the Aesthetic Education of Man* describe humanity's two basic impulses: the first responds to the immediacies of sensation and feeling—a sensuous drive. The second responds to the rationality of unity and order—a formal drive. The ultimate goal of the aesthetic life is to effect a harmony between the two through a third impulse, which Schiller called a play drive. "These drives necessitate limits," Schiller wrote, "and insofar as they are thought of as energies,

---

37. "Il faut un régulateur à l'homme jusque dans le sein des plaisirs, et les plus pures émotions de l'ame recevront un charme de plus à se rattacher à cette loi constante du mouvement, découverte par Galilée, à cette division mystérieuse du tems dont on a sur-tout besoin dans la musique, où son retour périodique est un des élémens du rhythme et de la cadence." "Notice sur les travaux du Conservatoire impérial de musique et de déclamation," 1593. Similar ideas are found in Stöckel, "Über die Wichtigkeit der richtigen Zeitbewegung eines Tonstücks"; Le Breton, "Notice des Travaux de la Classe des beaux-arts de l'Institut imperial de France, pour l'année 1813"; and Janvier, *Étrennes chronométriques*, 152–56.
38. According to Kollman, chronometers were "sold by the mathematic instrument makers." Kollman, *An Essay on Musical Harmony*, 72.
39. Framery, "Chronomètre," in *Encylopédie méthodique*, 1:282.
40. On the relationship between Schiller and Kant, see Gayatri Chakravorty Spivak, *An Aesthetic Education in the Era of Globalization* (Cambridge, MA: Harvard University Press, 2012), 13–25; and Paul de Man, "Kant and Schiller," in *Aesthetic Ideology*, ed. and with an introduction by Andrzej Warminski (Minneapolis: University of Minnesota Press, 1996), 129–62.

they need tempering."[41] The sensuous and formal drives mutually activate and limit each other. Just as thinking should be tempered by feeling, so too sentiment and sensation should be tempered through reason and form. The period's discourses on musical chronometers characterized the work of numeric mediation in just this way: the numbers of the chronometer were to provide a universal rule or law that would only perfect the raw sentiment of feeling. As Schiller put it, "this tool is art" ("Dieses Werkzeug ist die schöne Kunst"): it was aesthetic mediation itself.[42]

Even before Maelzel patented his metronome, the discourse on musical time-keeping had reinvented tempo. A new relationship to number—the age's best tool of distance—was to offer tempo a universal language. The many possible types of numeric mediation proposed to use chronometers or other machines in order to provide a widely legible unit of measure for music that would regulate the sentiments of its interpreters. Through this technique, tempo would translate across distance and history. All that was left to do was to agree on the units, the machine, and the way that this mediation was to occur.

Length into Duration, Duration into Length: A Crisis of Measures

The universal translatability of the new chronometer devices depended on a wide recognition of their numerical units of measure. In this context the spatial measures of the pendulum devices were better suited to translatability than any newly devised scale, but not by much. When Weber wrote that the Rheinish inches he recommended were known in "all civilized lands," he was distorting the reality of the situation.[43] Not only were these units problematic for communication outside of Europe, they would have required complicated conversions in order to be useful even in his neighboring states. Making reference to spatial measurement standards, the reinvented chronometers of the late eighteenth and early nineteenth centuries attempted to reach outside of themselves with the language of numbers in order to ground their indications in the terms that were already established with some authority. They did so, however, at a time in which natural philosophy was renegotiating those terms under the very same sign of translatability that informed the reinvention of tempo. In a complex twist, the musical chronometers tried to borrow from spatial measures for tempo just while natural

41. "Beide Triebe haben also Einschränkung, und insofern sie also Energien gedacht werden, Abspannung nötig." Friedrich von Schiller, "Über die ästhetische Erziehung des Menschen in einer Reihe von Briefen," in *Gesammelte Werke,* ed. Reinhold Netolitzky (Gütersloh: Sigbert Mohn Verlag, 1961), 5:319–429 at 365.
42. "Dieses Werkzeug ist die schöne Kunst, diese Quellen öffnen sich in ihren unsterblichen Mustern." Schiller, "Über die ästhetische Erziehung des Menschen in einer Reihe von Briefen," in *Gesammelte Werke,* ed. Netolitzky, 345.
43. Weber, "Ueber die Jetzt Bevorstehende Wirkliche Einführung des Taktmessers," col. 448.

philosophers contemplated the transposition of chronometric seconds into new measures for space. The only constants in this kaleidoscopic rearrangement of terms were the units of clock time.

At the end of the eighteenth century, standards for measure were drastically varied across Europe. In pre-revolutionary France alone there were more than 700 different metrical units in use; because each of those varied locally, the total number approached a staggering 250,000.[44] Efforts to standardize this unruly system met with difficulty in France as elsewhere. Maintaining the local specificity of measurements for commerce and exchange was a symbol of power and local sovereignty in small municipalities, and relinquishing that control was no trivial matter.[45] Nevertheless it had become clear by the end of the eighteenth century that the local specificity of measurement standards not only impeded commerce at the regional level but also stymied the efforts at national and international systematization, organization, and scientific study.

In a 1790 address to the French national assembly, the natural philosopher and statesman Charles Maurice de Talleyrand opined, "The innumerable variety of our weights and measures and their bizarre denominations necessarily throws confusion into our ideas and embarrassment into our commerce."[46] The Paris Academy of Sciences had appointed Talleyrand their spokesperson to the national assembly in a bid to address the plurality of local measurements.[47] The Academy proposed an entirely new set of units based on one easily determined measurement: the length of the "seconds pendulum," or what the Academy defined as a simple pendulum that would swing for exactly one second from end to end when set into motion. All other measurements of volume and weight were to be derived from this unit of length, making the seconds pendulum the basis of a logical and reproducible hierarchy.[48] In addition, the determination of the exact length of the pendulum was to be an international affair. In order for the measurement to gain

---

44. Ken Adler, "A Revolution to Measure: The Political Economy of the Metric System in France," in *The Values of Precision*, ed. Wise, 39–71, at 43; see also Roland Zupko, *French Weights and Measures Before the Revolution: A Dictionary of Provincial and Local Units* (Bloomington: Indiana University Press, 1978).

45. Porter, *Trust in Numbers*, 25; Witold Kula, *Measures and Men*, trans. Richard Szreter (Princeton, NJ: Princeton University Press, 1986), 111–13.

46. "L'innombrable variété de nos poids & de nos mesures & leurs dénominations bisarres jettent nécessairement de la confusion dans les idées, de l'embarras dans le commerce." Charles Maurice de Talleyrand-Périgord, *Proposition faite à l'Assemblée nationale sur les poids et mesures* (Paris: De l'imprimerie nationale, 1790), 3.

47. John Lewis Heilbron, *Weighing Imponderables and Other Quantitative Science Around 1800* (Berkeley: University of California Press, 1993), 258. Known through the eighteenth century as l'Académie royale des sciences, the institution was dissolved in 1713 and reopened as La première classe de l'Institut national des sciences et des arts. It retained this name until 1816, at which time the Académie des sciences gained its autonomy though still under the organizational framework of the Institut de France. I will refer to this institution as the Paris Academy throughout.

48. Talleyrand-Périgord, *Proposition faite à l'Assemblée nationale sur les poids et mesures*, 14–15. In order to account for the variation that would occur based on location in the world, the seconds pendulum was to be calculated at the forty-fifth parallel of latitude.

wide recognition, representatives from Britain, Spain, and the United States were invited to join in the experimentation and ceremony of its calculation.[49]

It so happened that the British were simultaneously considering a new standard of measure based on the seconds pendulum. John Riggs Miller, a champion of weights and measures reform and a member of the British parliament, spoke with passion to that body on the need for a universal basis of measure, "a permanent, unalterable foundation, *whence invariable Standards might be obtained*, *to which all nations might refer*, and with which they might compare their respective measures, and *reduce them* to one invariable, universal *denomination, for the mutual convenience and benefit of all mankind*."[50] The reform was to have a worldwide impact, and required of its new units the ability to transcend national, linguistic, and geographic constraints. For Miller the choice for a new foundation was clear. In addition to its simple structure, the seconds pendulum had a crucial political advantage: "[it] does not belong to rival nations," he explained.[51]

These early French and British proposals underscore the universal translatability of the chronometric second at the turn of the century. Both Talleyrand and Miller were drawn to the seconds pendulum for its straightforward design and well-known units. Unlike other lengths, the basis of this spatial unit in clock time meant that it lacked any political or national allegiances. The second was already an international unit of measure, unattached to any locality.[52] Although the definitive establishment of the seconds pendulum's length would require precision calculation—accounting even for the latitude at which it was determined—its basis in temporal measure would ensure the ease of its reproducibility and translatability.

With the French revolution in the background, both the Paris Academy and the British parliament eventually reconsidered their collaboration, and plans for an international effort to determine the precise length of the seconds pendulum were set aside.[53] The Paris Academy eventually went on with an alternative proposal for a new measurement standard based on one ten-millionth the distance from the pole to the equator.[54] In 1799 they objectified the result of their efforts—the new French meter—in a platinum bar with the inscription, "À tous les temps, à tous les peuples."[55] Though their visions for this device of translation and power

49. Adler, "A Revolution to Measure," 51.

50. John Riggs Miller, *Speeches in the House of Commons upon the Equalization of the Weights and Measures of Great Britain* (London: J. Debrett, 1790), 48. Emphasis in original.

51. Miller, *Speeches in the House of Commons upon the Equalization of the Weights and Measures of Great Britain*, 49.

52. Even though the local time varied from one municipality to the next, the duration of the second was a well-established and easily accessible standard in the early nineteenth century. On this topic see the narrative provided in David Landes, *Revolution in Time* (Cambridge, MA: Belknap, 1983), 114–87.

53. As Heilbron has it, "The rationale must be sought, not in the requirements of measurement, but in the circumstances into which the Revolution propelled the Academy." Heilbron, *Weighing Imponderables and Other Quantitative Science Around 1800*, 259.

54. Heilbron, *Weighing Imponderables and Other Quantitative Science Around 1800*, 260; Alder, "A Revolution to Measure," 52.

55. Martin H. Geyer, "One Language for the World: The Metric System, International Coinage, the Gold Standard, and the Rise of Internationalism, 1850-1900," in *The Mechanics of*

were grand, the reign of Napoleon ultimately forestalled the definitive adoption of the metric system until well after the revolution of 1830.[56]

Before that time, new efforts to calibrate spatial measure against the length of the seconds pendulum were underway in the German states. The astronomer Friedrich Wilhelm Bessel led a joint effort of the Prussian government and the Berlin Academy to reform the systems of measure that had been left in disorder following the Napoleonic wars.[57] Bessel brought a fresh approach to the construction of the seconds pendulum. His model involved many subsidiary instruments designed to more closely monitor the pendulum's physical conditions. Barometers, micrometers, thermometers, and the like were included in the apparatus, and Bessel accounted for the local idiosyncrasies in temperature, pressure, gravity, and human error that came to bear on his observations.[58] His system submitted the determination of spatial measure to an unprecedented amount of precision and systematicity, making his seconds pendulum and attendant method the new models for physical investigations and quantifications of length. Bessel's observations formed the new standard for the Prussian foot, or *Urmass*.[59]

Through all of the political tumult, destruction, and warfare of the years between Talleyrand's proposal and Bessel's experiments, chronometric minutes and seconds remained reliable constants. As the efforts to scrutinize and universalize spatial measure developed, experimenters and politicians began to depend on the invariance of these units. Their perceived reliability in an age preoccupied with quantification and precision measurement demonstrates that not every numeric mediation was capable of the same work. Numbers were an important site of power and authority. They were seen in many cases as the constituents of an ideal language. But powerful though they all were, certain types of numbers were able to overcome the particularities of their local and immediate contexts in a way that others were not. The numbers of clock time had the dual advantage of speaking with the vocabulary of mathematics and referring to a standard already in widespread use.

In the age of measurement reforms, the concept of time reached an extreme in its disentanglement from spatial motion. The role of the seconds pendulum demonstrates the new arrangement of terms that had once composed the Scholastic rubric of *motus*. Within that framework, change in spatial location had the power to explain temporal passage. Time was conceptually descended

Internationalism: Culture, Society, and Politics from the 1840s to the First World War, ed. Martin H Geyer and Johannes Paulmann (London: German Historical Institute; Oxford: Oxford University Press, 2001), 61.

56. Alder, "A Revolution to Measure," 61.

57. Kathryn M. Olesko, "The Meaning of Precision: The Exact Sensibility in Early Nineteenth-Century Germany," in *The Values of Precision*, ed. Wise, 103–34, at 122.

58. Friedrich Wilhelm Bessel, *Untersuchungen über die Länge des einfachen Secundenpendels* (Berlin: Kgl. Akademie der Wissenschaften, 1828).

59. Drawing on his observations with the seconds pendulum, Bessel constructed the *Urmaass* with the Berlin mechanic Thomas Baumann between 1835 and 1837. The unit finally became law in Prussia in 1839. See Olesko, "The Meaning of Precision," 122–23.

from motion. By contrast, the new work asked of the seconds pendulum made plain that temporal units now had the power to measure spatial extension. The universal ticking of the second was seen as a suitable basis and groundwork for length. This rearrangement of terms underwrote new uses for timekeeping devices and their numeric indications in a landscape of dramatic measurement diversity and growing translation anxieties.

The concurrence of this conceptual reconfiguration with the growing interest in a universal standard for the measurement of tempo afforded the great variety of ways in which musicians imagined tempo's numeric mediation. Pendulum devices for tempo, though easy and straightforward, attempted to use numbers based on units of distance that were themselves involved in processes of standardization. Tempo looked to spatial measure just as spatial measures looked to time. The footing was constantly shifting. In exasperation, the unsigned opinion piece in the *AmZ* of May 1813 concluded with a strongly worded recommendation for composers to mark their works with durations in clock time. "Would it be such a great and arduous task... for [composers] to look twice at the clock and write, for example, Allegro: duration: eight minutes?"[60] After all, clocks were accessible enough to have facilitated such markings—it would not have been so difficult. But the frustration of the commentary's conclusion suggests that something more was wanting. Composers should have a way of harnessing the power of the clock's numbers directly. The desire to mediate tempo in number ultimately meant an investment in the units of the clock. Like spatial measure, tempo needed recourse to a consistent, reproducible lexicon of numeric terms based on the universal translatability of clock time.

Maelzel's Metronome

The Indispensible Machine

Only a few months after the anonymous *AmZ* contributor implored composers to take note of their clocks in the prescription of tempo, the pages of the same journal announced the invention of an instrument that had the ability to do that work for them. Like many older devices, this reinvented chronometer was based on the simple motion of a pendulum. Its only truly distinctive feature was its use of a set of units calibrated against the minute. This was the first announcement of Maelzel's new metronome; in its earliest incarnation it bore little resemblance to the device commonly associated with that name. Already in this first announcement Maelzel's shrewd marketing and merchandizing tactics were in full effect. The announcement tells of enthusiasm for the device from Beethoven and Salieri,

---

60. "Wäre es denn ein so Grosses und Beschwerliches, dass die Liebe zu ihrem Stück es nicht aufwiegen könnte, zweymal seinetwegen die Uhr anzusehn und dann hinzuschreiben—z. B. Allegro: Dauer: acht Minuten?" Unsigned miscellaneous contribution, Leipzig *AmZ* 15, no. 18, May 5, 1813, 307.

and goes on to report that the latter had already begun to affix Maelzel's metronome markings to the compositions of Gluck, Handel, Haydn, and Mozart.[61]

A confluence of important factors led to the widespread adoption of Maelzel's machine. Among these were his keen business sense and skill for self-promotion. In 1815 he began a publicity tour for his reinvented chronometer, and it was during this tour that he met the inventor Diederich Nikolaus Winkel in Amsterdam. Winkel, who had also crafted a new musical chronometer, imparted crucial insights to Maelzel concerning the design of his central vibrating mechanism. Nevertheless it was Maelzel who patented the improved device in London and Paris later that year. As soon as production of the instruments began, Maelzel sent two hundred metronomes to influential composers across Europe, a clever move that cemented the metronome's popularity, availability, and ubiquity in notational practices.[62]

In addition to its well-known mechanism and conveniently small size, Maelzel's metronome promised the ultimate translatability for the numbers of tempo. Unlike the other devices, the metronome offered numeric mediation in units derived from the most universal standard available. "The metronomic scale is *founded on the division of time into minutes*," he explained in his promotional material. "The minute being thus, as it were, the element of the metronomic scale, its divisions are thereby rendered intelligible and applicable in every country: an *universal standard measure for musical time* is thus obtained."[63] This description was repeated across Europe in advertisements, short histories, and opinion pieces concerning the metronome in the years that followed.[64] The metronome had met the goals of numeric mediation and convenience while simultaneously skirting the problem of spatial measure.

Maelzel's metronome quickly took center stage in the discussions on musical timekeeping. Whether excited by, indifferent to, or upset about his invention, the theorists and musicians of the era knew that they had to address its growing impact. Endorsements from high-profile composers and pedagogues heaped on even more attention. In April of 1816 the *Mercure de France* published a letter endorsing the metronome signed by Cherubini, Catel, Pleyel, and many others.[65] A British contingent, including Attwood, Clementi, Cramer, Kalkbrenner, and still others, followed suit in letters to the *London Times* and London *Morning*

---

61. Unsigned announcement, Leipzig *AmZ* 15, no. 48, December 1, 1813, col. 784–88.

62. Fallows, "Metronome"; *Oxford Music Online*, ed. Laura Macy, s.v. "Winkel, Diederich Nikolaus," by Arthur W. J. G. Ord-Hume, accessed November 16, 2008, <www.oxfordmusiconline.com>.

63. Maelzel, *The Metronomic Tutor* (London: Chappell and Clementi, ca. 1816), as quoted in "Review of New Musical Publications," *The New Monthly Magazine* 4, no. 36, January 1, 1817, 534.

64. In addition to *The New Monthly Magazine* article of 1817, this description appears in Franz Sales Kandler, "Rückblicke auf die Chronometer und Herrn Mälzels Neuste Chronometer fabrik in London," Vienna *AmZ* 1, nos. 5–8, January 30–February 20, 1817, col. 33–36, 41–43, 49–52, and 57–58, at 36; "Maelzel's Metronome," *Quarterly Musical Magazine and Review* no. 11 (1821): 302–5; and "History of Music, Theoretical and Practical," in the *Encyclopaedia Londinensis, or Universal Dictionary of Arts, Sciences, and Literature*, compiled, digested, and arranged by John Wilkes (London: Printed for the proprietor, 1819), 16:395.

65. Untitled article of correspondence "Au rédacteur du *Mercure de France*," *Mercure de France* 66, no. 25, April 1816, 416.

Chronicle in July of the same year.[66] In February of 1818, the authoritative names of Beethoven and Salieri officially endorsed Maelzel's machine in the Viennese *AmZ*.[67] Musical periodicals also issued lists of tempi indications given in the numbers of Maelzel's metronome; the most famous of these, published in the Leipzig *AmZ* of December 1817, provided the tempi for Beethoven's first eight symphonies.[68] The machine also garnered mention in other advertisements: Ricordi used the announcements of his newest publications to herald the adoption of Maelzel's metronome numbers therein.[69] According to Franz Sales Kandler, the metronome had captured "the attention of the entire cultivated world."[70] In the space of a few short years it had become an "indispensable" machine, creating a lasting impact on the notational practices of and theory behind tempo.[71] In an article on the device for his own *Revue musicale*, Fétis contemplated the force of tradition that the instrument had managed to defy. "Despite the power of custom," he wrote, "this machine has gained popularity quite rapidly."[72] For some period witnesses, the metronome had replaced the system of *tempo giusto* entirely.[73]

Fear of the Metronome

Not everyone was so enthusiastic about Maelzel's new invention and the technique of tempo indication that went along with it. Some felt that they could do even better: new proposals for musical chronometers attempted to do even more regulatory work than the metronome could. Andrea Christian Sparrevogn's "Taktur," reproduced below in plate 7.1, took the metronome's connection to clockwork a step further.[74] In addition to a scale based on clock time, the *Taktur*

---

66. Untitled letter to the editor, *London Times* no. 9888, July 16, 1816, col. 14; Untitled letter to the editor, *The Morning Chronicle* no. 14728, July 16, 1816, col. 11. Both of these British letters also included the names of Viennese and Parisian supporters of the device.

67. Ludwig van Beethoven and Antonio Salieri, "Erklärung," Vienna *AmZ* 2, no. 7, February 14, 1818, col. 58–59.

68. "Bestimmung der Tempos aller Symphonien von Beethoven, nach Mälzel's Metronom," Leipzig *AMZ* 19, no. 51, December 17, 1817, col. 873–74. Another example are the tempos given for J. B. Cramer's *Etudio per il Pianoforte*, oder *Exercises pour le Pianof*. Unsigned miscellaneous contribution, Leipzig *AmZ* 19, no. 37, September 10, 1817, col. 633–36.

69. "Foglio d'Annunzj," *Gazzetta di Milano*, no. 326, November 22, 1819, 1590; Unsigned advertisement for the "Biblioteca di musica moderna," *Gazzetta di Mantova*, no. 11, March 11, 1820, 153.

70. Kandler, "Rückblicke auf die Chronometer und Herrn Mälzels Neuste Chronometerfabrik in London," 36.

71. "Invenzioni—Il metronomo," *Teatri arti e letteratura* 7, no. 291, November 12, 1829, 45–46, at 46.

72. "Les avantages du métronome ont même été si généralement sentis que, malgré la puissance de la routine, cette machine s'est assez rapidement popularisée." Fétis, "Sur le métronome de Maelzel," *Revue Musicale* 1, vol. 2, no. 25 (August 1827): 361–64, at 364.

73. Philippe De Geslin, *Cours analytiques de musique* (Paris: Chez l'auteur, rue Grenelle-Saint-Honoré, no. 37, 1825), 221–23.

74. Unsigned article, "Andrea Christian Sparrevogns Taktur," Leipzig *AmZ* 19, no. 14, April 2, 1817, col. 233–44.

Plate 7.1 Andrea Christian Sparrevogn's "Taktur," Leipzig *AmZ* 19, no. 14, April 2, 1817, unpaginated plate.

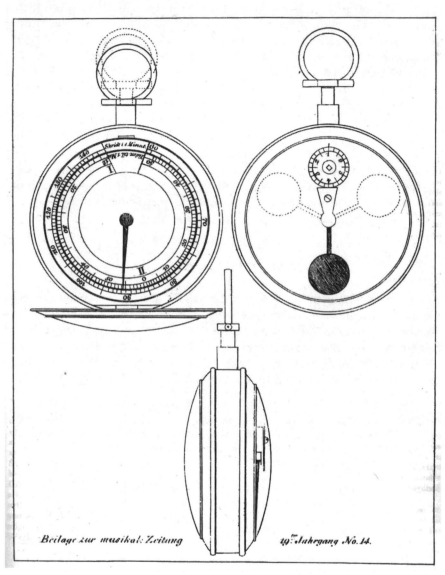

had the shape, form, and size of a pocket watch. Sparrevogn's proposal thus performed the technological impulse of time discipline, affording an even more portable, more intimate relationship to the exact tempo. Giovanni Finazzi's "plessimetro," on the other hand, was focused on the mediation of different metric types. Finazzi complained that Maelzel's metronome was unspecific with regard to meter, since the uniform clicks made no distinctions among beats. Finazzi's

Plate 7.2 Weber's conversion table showing equivalences between Maelzel's numbers and pendulum lengths in Rheinish inches and French centimeters, in "Mälzl's Metonome Überall Umsonst zu Haben," Vienna *AmZ* 1, no. 37, September 11, 1817, col. 313.

Mälzl Metron.	Rheinl. Zolle.	Centi-mètres.	Mälzl Metron.	Rheinl. Zolle.	Centi-mètres.
50 =	55 =	143	92 =	16 =	42
52 =	50 =	132	96 =	15 =	38
54 =	47 =	122	100 =	$13\frac{2}{3}$ =	35
56 =	44 =	114	104 =	$12\frac{3}{4}$ =	32
58 =	41 =	106	108 =	$11\frac{1}{4}$ =	30
60 =	38 =	99	112 =	11 =	28
63 =	34 =	90	116 =	$10\frac{1}{4}$ =	26
66 =	31 =	81	120 =	$9\frac{1}{2}$ =	25
69 =	29 =	75	126 =	$8\frac{3}{4}$ =	22
72 =	26 =	68	132 =	$7\frac{3}{4}$ =	20
76 =	24 =	62	138 =	$7\frac{1}{4}$ =	18
80 =	21 =	55	144 =	$6\frac{1}{2}$ =	17
84 =	19 =	50	152 =	6 =	15
88 =	18 =	46	160 =	$5\frac{1}{3}$ =	13

chronometer offered a better regulatory apparatus, delivering a distinct stroke for the downbeat of each measure.[75]

By contrast, a great many critics feared that the metronome mediated tempo too successfully. Perhaps the most outspoken of these was Weber, who worried that Maelzel's metronome markings would travel further and wider than his machines. Although the numbers of Maelzel's metronome were pegged to a chronometric standard, they were nevertheless difficult and awkward to interpret without his device. Acknowledging the rapid acceptance of the machine, Weber made it his business to explain to as wide a readership as possible how to construct simple pendulum devices in its stead.[76] For this purpose his articles and treatises included lengthy equivalence tables correlating Maelzel's metronome numbers to units in the Rhenish, French, and English systems of spatial measure (shown in plates 7.2 and 7.3). These were meant to ease the "laborious

75. Giovanni Finazzi, "Nuovo stromento per battere la musica, chiamato plessimetro, *del medico Finazzi*," in *Propagatore ossia raccolta periodica delle cose appartenenti ai progressi* (Torino: Alliana e Paravia, 1824–28), 3:387–95.
76. Weber, "Über ein Chronometrische Tempobezeichnung, Welche den Mälzel'schen Metronome, so wie Jede Andere Chronometer–Machine Entbehrlich Macht," Vienna *AmZ* 1, no. 25, June 19, 1817, col. 204–9; idem., "Mälzel's Metonome Überall Umsonst zu Haben," Vienna *AmZ* 1, no. 37,

Plate 7.3 Weber's conversion table showing equivalences between Maelzel's numbers and pendulum lengths in Rheinish inches, French meters, and English inches, in his article, "Chronometer," in the *Allgemeine Encyclopädie der Wissenschaften und Künste*, ed. Johann Samuel Ersch and Johann Gottfried Gruber (Leipzig: J. F. Gleditsch, 1813–89), 17:207.

Mälzel.	Rh. Zoll.	Metrisch.	Inchs.
76 =	23,679 =	0,6188 =	24,385
80	21,369	0,5585	22,007
84	19,383	0,5065	19,961
88	17,661	0,4615	18,188
92	16,156	0,4225	16,638
96	14,839	0,3878	15,283
100	13,677	0,3574	14,085
104	12,645	0,3305	13,022
108	11,725	0,3064	12,075
112	10,903	0,2844	11,228
116	10,164	0,2656	10,467
120	9,498	0,2482	9,781
126	8,615	0,2251	8,872
132	7,848	0,2051	8,083
138	7,181	0,1877	7,396
144	6,595	0,1723	6,792
152	5,918	0,1547	6,096
160	5,342	0,1396	5,502
(168	4,845	0,1266	4,990)
(176	4,415	0,1154	4,547)
(184	4,039	0,1056	4,159)
(192	3,709	0,0969	3,820)

and time-consuming calculations with the most difficult fractions" that had been associated with the pendulum chronometers.[77] They did the work of converting the units for their users, rendering them a rather unexpected place to turn in one's library in order to find the equivalences of various European standards of

September 11, 1817, col. 313–14; idem., *Ueber chronometrische Tempobezeichnung*; idem., "Chronometer," in the *Allgemeine Encyclopädie der Wissenschaften und Künste*, ed. Ersch and Gruber, 17:204–9; and in the various editions of Weber's *Versuch einer geordneten Theorie der Tonsetzkunst*.

77. Ingaz Franz von Mosel explained, "The musical chronometer with the silk chord [the pendulum device]…has its basis in measures of length. Because of the differences between Viennese and Rheinish inches, French centimeters, or above all the measures of length in music's birthplace, Italy—where they are not only different in every province but very nearly in every town—these measures do not allow for a quick, general comprehensibility. Only after laborious and time-consuming calculations with the most difficult fractions can one find the equivalence." ("Der Zeitmesser mit der Seidenschnur, diese mag nun auf einem Zollstabe oder durch Knötchen geregelt werden, hat seine Basis auf dem *Längenmasse*, das, wie die gegenseitige Verschiedenheit

measure. Still, even though they may have expedited some math, they rehearsed a roundabout translation of temporal measures into spatial measures into new temporal measures (Maelzel metronome markings into pendulum lengths into tempi).[78] Weber's frustration with the situation was clear. Concerned that even these tables of equivalence might not be enough to catch up with Maelzel's metronome, he proposed another alternative:

> For those who cannot make use of markings in inches or might not have such measures immediately at hand, one could print a ruler on the page, rendering the matter of different measurements in Rhenish or Parisian inches, English inches, or French meters immaterial. Then, compositions could bring with them, wherever they go, their own measure of time, together with the scale of inches employed in its designation.[79]

Weber imagined a world in which notation brought with it a standard of its own temporal measure; a practice in which the score could designate tempo without reference to any external source of validation. Ultimately Weber wanted to fold the indication of tempo back into the system of easy legibility produced in the inscriptions of the page. His imagined ruler system was an attempt to bypass the steps of mediating work that would otherwise have to be done by the numbers of spatial measure or the numbers of Maelzel's metronome.

The older system of legibility that had once joined tempo with meter signatures, note values, and character had not entirely disintegrated at the end of *tempo giusto*, though the panic expressed in the writings of Weber and others might suggest otherwise. Crucially, the residue of these connections and the perceived ability of tempo to communicate affect created even more anxiety about the metronome's potential success. There had to be a dimension of tempo communication that numbers could not capture, or tempo would turn out to be a purely mechanical and quantifiable affair. Pietro Lichtenthal's entry on the metronome for his 1826 *Dizionario e bibliografia della musica* gave voice to these

des Wiener und des rheinländischen Zolles, des französischen Centimetres, vor Allem aber der Längenmassen in dem Geburtslande der Musik, in Italien, beweiset, wo sie nicht nur in jeder Provinz, sondern beynahe in jeder Stadt von einander abweichen, nie ein schnelles, allgemeines Verständniss zulässt, sondern erst mit mühsamen und zeitfördernden, in die schwierigsten Brüche auslaufenden Annäherungs-Rechnungen gefunden werden kann.") Mosel, "Herrn Johann Mälzels Metronome," Vienna *AmZ* 1, no. 48, November 27, 1817, col. 405–10, at col. 407.

78. In fact, Beethoven's friend Nikolaus Zmeskall von Domanovecz suggested the pendulums themselves should incorporate demarcations of units in Maelzel's metronome numbers. Zmeskall von Domanovecz, "Tactmesser, zum Praktischen Gebrauch Geeignet," Vienna *AmZ* 1, nos. 35 and 36, August 28–September 4, 1817, col. 293–300, 305–8.

79. "Zum Überfluß könte man für diejenigen, welche vielleicht das gebrauchte Zollmaß nicht kennen, oder es nicht gleich bei der Hand haben, einen Zollstab dabei mit abdrucken lassen. Alsdann ist es sogar ganz gleichgiltig, ob man rheinische, oder Pariser Zolle, engländische Inchs, französische Mètres, oder was sonst für ein Maß gebrauchen will: denn ein also bezeichnetes Tonstück bringt, überall, wohin ein Exemplar davon gelangt, seinen Taktmesser samt dem Zollmaße dazu gleich selber mit." Weber, "Chronometer," in *Allgemeine Encyclopädie der Wissenschaften und Künste*, ed. Ersch and Gruber, 207.

reservations. No matter how accurate Maelzel's machine, tempo would always remain "subject to certain gradations that the metronome cannot mark and that the ear of a man of taste appreciates well." Musicians should consider the performance contexts, including the acoustics of the hall, and furthermore should have the liberty to draw on the "impulses of affect," in order to find the true tempo for each performance. "Sentiment will find the just tempo [*il movimento giusto*]," he insisted.[80] The idea that the metronome could take over this work was troubling.

Part of what upset Lichtenthal and others was the idea that metronome markings might not only indicate an unnecessarily precise pace but also a stark uniformity with which to execute it—that musicians would begin to play along with the metronome and perform like it. This second, related fear is evidenced in the many statements that specifically protest against this way of using musical chronometers.[81] Fétis was sure to clarify that the metronome was useful "principally for the transmission of tempi," because "if one were to use it as a regulator for the measure, one would destroy any notion of expression and eloquence in performance."[82] Even as the metronome's technique of tempo indication solved a problem in communication, it threatened to encroach on aspects of live performance that had long been entrusted to musical sensibility.[83]

Critics of Maelzel's popular machine did not so much fear that musical expression would be destroyed with the use of its numbers. Instead, they were more fearful of the strange power those numbers somehow possessed that allowed them to create one of music's most affective dimensions. There was (and remains) something distinctly uncanny about the ability of numbers to produce tempi.[84] Numbers were thought to be universal, translatable, impersonal: devoid of sentiment and signification. And yet, in the technique of tempo indication that coupled numbers with the metronome machine, they gave rise to music that spoke with force. Their abstract quality was exactly what allowed them to create feeling.

As in Schiller's aesthetics, musical sense tempered metronome law in the moment that musicians were asked to play. No one assumed that the metronome's technique of tempo indication and the rigidity of its mechanism could replace musical sensibility entirely. But the metronome achieved what the late eighteenth

---

80. "Si osservi inoltre che ogni movimento, quantunque determinato dal Compositore, è però soggetto a certe gradazioni che il Metronomo non può marcare, e che l'orecchio dell'uomo di gusto sa ben apprezzare. Il sentimento fa trovar il movimento giusto." Pietro Lichtenthal, *Dizionario e bibliografia della musica* (Milan: Antonio Fontana, 1826), 2:39–40, at 40.

81. In addition to Lichtenthal, see for instance, Framery, "Chronomètre," in *Encylopédie méthodique*, 281–82; and Thiémé, *Nouvelle théorie sur les différens mouvemens des airs*, 56.

82. "Au reste, il est bon de remarquer que c'est principalement pour la transmission des mouvemens qu'elle est utile; car, si l'on en faisait usage comme régulateur de la mesure, on détruirait toute idée d'expression et de verve dans l'exécution." Fétis, "Sur le métronome de Maelzel," 364.

83. This is a major topic of Bonus's "The Metronomic Performance Practice: A History of Rhythm, Metronomes, and the Mechanization of Musicality," particularly 112–78.

84. I am drawing here on a notion of the uncanny borrowed from Freud. Sigmund Freud, "The Uncanny," trans. Alix Strachey in *Studies in Parapsychology*, ed. Philip Reiff (New York: Collier, 1963), 19–60; see also Terry Castle, *The Female Thermometer* (New York: Oxford University Press, 1995), 3–20.

century most wanted. It provided musical notation with a tool for the universal mediation of tempo; in providing this assistance it trespassed on the territory of the sensible, carving out a space for the reinvented law of communication that would, eventually, find widespread adoption.

The musicians of early nineteenth-century Europe were simultaneously drawn to and repelled by the metronome's reinvented, uncanny technique of tempo indication. Some celebrated it, some distanced themselves from it; still others did both or simply tried to ensure that musicians in far away and future destinations could understand their tempi. The documents they produced on the uncomfortable bond between quantification and tempo signal the slow and painful uncoupling of tempo from meter, note values, and character. Still vaguely associated with this older network of ideas, tempo was reinvented through a numerical, mechanical technique, its indications entrusted to the power of numbers.

The Disappearing Metronome

The metronome was considered so effective by the middle of the nineteenth century that musicians thought its mediation would disappear with only a few refinements. Berlioz imagined a metronome that could transmit tempo directly from the conductor's podium to musicians' desks. His imaginary metronome

> ...picks up the conductor's movements without being seen by the audience and conveys them directly *before the very eyes* of each player. It gives the beats of the bar and the various degrees of loud and soft with great precision. The players are thus in instant and immediate communication with the feelings of their conductor and can respond as rapidly as piano keys do to the pressure of the fingers, and the conductor can then truly claim to be *playing* the orchestra.[85]

First described in his 1844 story "Euphonia," this machine was clearly something quite different than the musical chronometers that theorists pined for a century previous.[86] This was the fantastic telos of the metronome dream—its role of mediation finally integrated into the fabric of musical performance so as to disappear within the very structure of the orchestral ensemble. This metronome had become one with its musical environment.

In reality, Maelzel's metronome played at the edge of visibility and invisibility. To this day the technique associated with his device occupies a tricky position in musical performance: if the bodies of performers and their instruments are the media through which we experience musical sound, the metronome's

85. Berlioz, "Euphonia," as cited and translated in *Berlioz's Orchestration Treatise: A Translation and Commentary*, trans. Hugh Macdonald (Cambridge: Cambridge University Press, 2002), 356.
86. In fact, a version of Berlioz's electric metronome was eventually realized by the Belgian inventor Joannes Verbrugghe. See *Berlioz's Orchestration Treatise: A Translation and Commentary*, trans. Hugh Macdonald, 355–56.

technique for tempo mediates their mediation. In this respect the technique's numbers and machines are doubly hidden (left backstage, the metronome is somewhere behind the musicians who are, themselves, behind the sound). This is one reason that it can be easy to forget about the metronome. But in the early nineteenth century the metronome's technique for tempo was both hidden in this way and also very much on display in debates, advertisements, articles, music theory treatises, and the like. It was common for musicians to develop strong opinions on the metronome in the age that reinvented tempo.

The same dimensions of the metronome's technique that were the cause for celebration and aversion were also the cause of its eventual disappearance. The numbers of Maelzel's metronome promised the best mediation for tempo, which is why some loved them and others hated them. For better or worse, numbers were the universal language to which late eighteenth- and early nineteenth-century thought aspired. The period's natural philosophy was heavily invested in the ability of numbers to describe and explain the world. Like musicians, experimentalists relied upon instruments to provide these ciphers to natural philosophy.[87] In the case of the world's measurement, Bessel's seconds pendulum created the possibility for a uniform system of quantification. Numbers tamed the wild variability of nature with cool, impersonal precision. Condillac, reinterpreting Locke, found in these abstract signs an impetus to rebuild philosophical language entirely. "Here is the advantage that algebra will have: it will allow us to speak like nature," he wrote.[88] Numbers were so successful at providing information about the world that they dissolved into it; they become the natural language for nature—nature's voice itself.

The metronome was never naturalized into performance in the way that Berlioz imagined, but like the numbers of the period's precision measurement it disappeared from view within the nature of tempo. Once the debates about tempo quantification cooled off, it was easy for the metronome to remain hidden in the way that all useful tools do.[89] Its labor performed offstage, the metronome continued to make possible the new relationships among meter, note values, character, and tempo, though it is principally recalled in connection with only the last of these. What might not be so apparent anymore is that the technique of the metronome left behind it the legacy of an uncomfortable allegiance between number, tempo, and feeling that persists in the twenty-first century. That is why we can still be drawn to and repelled by the metronome when we look too closely.

87. Wise, "Precision: Agent of Unity and Product of Agreement."

88. "Voilà l'avantage qu'aura l'algèbre; elle nous fera parler comme la nature." Condillac, *La langue des calculs* in *Œuvres Philosophiques de Condillac*, ed. Georges le Roy (Paris: Presses Universitaires de France, 1948), 2:435. Derrida quotes this passage in *The Archeology of the Frivolous*, trans. and with an introduction by John P. Leavy Jr. (Lincoln, NE: University of Nebraska Press, 1987), 37.

89. Heidegger, *Being and Time*, trans. Joan Stambaugh (Albany: SUNY Press, 1996), 62–71; Graham Harman, *Tool-Being* (Chicago: Open Court, 2002), 15–24. See also chapter 2.

CHAPTER Eight

The Persistent Question of Meter

The Measure as Mystery

"The measure," Jérôme-Joseph de Momigny tells us, "is one of the greatest mysteries of music."[1] So begins the provocative discussion of meter in the *Cours complet d'harmonie et de composition* of 1806. Momigny thought the current understandings of meter were literally backward, relying too heavily on the visual information of the notated measure and not enough on the sonorous information of the music as it was heard. "It is unimaginable that [the measure] has been as well sensed as it has been poorly understood, and that no one has yet to define it well," he wrote.[2] Momigny's solution, according to the doctrine that follows, was to give over our understanding of musical meter to the judgment of our ears.

We have been asking questions about the nature of meter since the birth of musical discourse. But what we ought to realize in the twenty-first century is that we are still asking these questions in the way that the theorists of the late eighteenth and early nineteenth centuries formulated them. Since that time, meter has been something that we tend to evaluate under the rubric of listening. Where do we feel emphasis? Which durations sound accented? Can we hear the validity of a particular analysis of the meter? These are questions that often dominate the scholarly literature on rhythm and meter in the twenty-first century, and they have their intellectual roots in different though intimately related questions that were first posed by theorists at the turn of the nineteenth.

When Momigny set out to write the *Cours complet d'harmonie et de composition*, meter was already in the midst of the conceptual transformation that

---

1. "La Mesure est un des plus grands mystères de la Musique." Jérôme-Joseph de Momigny, *Cours complet d'harmonie et de composition* (Paris: the author and Bailleul, 1802–6), 2:408.
2. "Il est inimaginable qu'étant si bien *sentie* elle soit si mal *connue*, et que personne enfin n'ait su encore la bien définir." Momigny, *Cours complet d'harmonie et de composition*, 2:408.

entailed the dissolution of the *tempo giusto* system and the reformulation of time as an endless flow unrelated to physical motion. This was the age that was increasingly anxious about the prescription of tempo without meter signatures. It was also an era in which composers had begun to explore the possibility of using a single meter signature to designate more than one way of measuring. Musicians began to experiment with meter as a way of attending to the ongoing flow of duration that was malleable in the moment; they played with ways of switching between simple and compounded meters without changing the meter signature; they theorized the ways in which meter could be organized in durations larger than the notated measure—what Edward T. Cone would later call hypermeasures—and explored how these different types of organizations could be established and then departed from;[3] finally, they broke with notational and stylistic conventions in changing the notated meter signature mid-composition without disrupting the musical fabric.

I call the last type of compositional innovation an integrated metric shift: a change in meter without a concurrent change or break in the texture, tempo, or overall character of the music. Integrated metric shifts introduced new meter signatures onto the page but did not signal a new set of relationships between note values, character, and tempo. They could do so because the system that had once tied them together had worn its effectiveness thin. The nexus of all of these developments took shape alongside a continual reformulation and rearticulation of the idea—outlined in Kirnberger's *Die Kunst des reinen Satzes in der Musik*—that meter could be a way of attending to the ongoing flow of time. For Momigny and his contemporaries like Gottfried Weber, describing exactly how that attending occurred was the object of meter theory.

Although theorists agreed that the explanation of meter should be relocated from the written page to the listener's ear, they by no means concurred on the way in which hearing was supposed to dictate its division. Weber, for instance, heard metric accent associated with the beginnings of musical segments and phrases, whereas Momigny heard the beginning of musical phrases leading to the accents that were located around their cadences, at the end. These two opposing positions on the operation of metric hearing—beginning accentuation and end accentuation respectively—have persisted since the age of Weber and Momigny, and they continue to shape the way we investigate meter both analytically and historically.[4] The longevity of their mutual coexistence, however, is demonstrative of the underlying conceptualization that has been in place since their differences were first made apparent: if meter is simply a way of attending to the ongoing flow of time—no matter how—then there are many different ways in

---

3. Edward T. Cone, *Musical Form and Musical Performance* (New York: Norton, 1968), 79.
4. On this topic see especially Samuel Ng, "Phrase Rhythm as Form in Classical Instrumental Music," *Music Theory Spectrum* 34, no. 1 (2012): 51–77; William Rothstein, "Metrical Theory and Verdi's Midcentury Operas," *Dutch Journal of Music Theory* 16, no. 2 (2011): 93–111; Rothstein, "National Metrical Types," in *Communication in Eighteenth-Century Music*, ed. Danuta Mirka and Kofi Agawu (Cambridge: Cambridge University Press, 2008), 112–59; David Temperley, "End-Accented Phrases: An Analytical Exploration," *Journal of Music Theory* 47, no. 1 (2003): 125–54.

which one can formulate a description or theory of the manner in which this comes to pass. This same conceptualization of meter as attending is what allowed for composers and theorists to describe meter at durations other than the notated measure, and also what allowed them to envision rapid transitions into and out of meters. Different meter signatures would no longer necessarily signal different combinations of character, note values, and tempo. Instead, these different components became independent variables that could be changed without consequence to the others. Meters could shift rapidly, note values could be chosen at will, and the tempo could be set, eventually, with Maelzel's metronome. Character, then, required more explanation in paratextual markings and was understood to emerge from the listener's relationship to musical experience. Meter, finally, was exclusively an action of our minds—a way of attending, an aesthetic activity.

The Reconceptualization of Metric Accent

Like meter, we have never really known what accent is, but the particular way in which we now come to this disheartening realization has persisted from the end of the eighteenth century through to the present day. When Kirnberger reconceptualized meter it was through the elusive power of the imagined accent: we come to know meter when we divide a series of equal beats "in our minds," he tells us, "such that we place an accent on the first beat of each segment or we imagine that we hear it stronger than the other beats."[5] The accent in Kirnberger's theory is a way of parsing the ongoing flow of undifferentiated time. It names the peak of attentional energy that we "place" on certain beats when we "imagine" hearing them "stronger than the other beats." Accent for Kirnberger is a relationship between the listener and the unfolding of the musical material.

Of course, there are many ways in which one can imagine hearing a particular beat strong than another. Kirnberger does not lay out specific criteria in his definition, he simply locates the work of accent in the mind and the imagination rather than on the page. This ambiguity of accent is even more pronounced when hierarchies larger than the most basic, obvious units are involved. Take, for example, a simple melody from the first movement of the Mozart Clarinet Quintet, K.581 (mm. 65–79), shown in example 8.1. The ¢ meter of this melody from the closing area of the exposition would suggest that we hear every other half-note beat stronger, and most performances of the piece render that assertion true. Still, with the melody and accompaniment offset by a half measure it is difficult to say when the first moment of higher-order emphasis arrives. Is it on the melody's first dotted quarter note on the downbeat of m. 66, just after the two quarter-note anacrusis? Or is it at the bottom of the melodic arc, on the downbeat of the following measure, where the pace of articulation in the cello slows? More generally: do we hear emphasis after each set of melodic anacruses, on the

5. "daß wir in unsern Gedanken alsobald eine tacktmäßige Eintheilung dieser Schläge machen, indem wir sie in Glieder ordnen..." Johann Philipp Kirnberger, *Die Kunst des reinen Satzes in der Musik*, facsimile ed. (1771–79; Hildesheim: Georg Olms, 1968), 2:115.

Example 8.1 Mozart, Clarinet Quintet K. 581, i, mm. 65–79.

downbeats of mm. 66, 68, 70, and so forth? Or do we hear them at the momentary reposes and cadences, such as the downbeats of mm. 67, 69, and 71? The melody of this example is dispositioned in such a way that it affords both readings—in this respect it is typical of many eighteenth- and nineteenth-century melodies from both instrumental and vocal music.[6] The questions it raises pertain to the

6. Rothstein, in "Metrical Theory and Verdi's Midcentury Operas," argues that the predominant opinion to the contrary (the notion that this out-of-phase arrangement is atypical) is a result of a bias toward German instrumental music in writings on meter since the 1980s.

relationship between metric accent and grouping. Both the beginning and ending of groups seem fitting locations to direct our attention, and both seem to be the types of moments one might imagine hearing stronger than others.

The tug between beginning accentuation and end accentuation that this short passage from the Mozart Clarinet Quintet demonstrates has haunted writings on meter since Kirnberger's time. Edward T. Cone once explained the dichotomy with the image of a ball thrown into the air: musical phrases, he asserted, are accented at beginnings with the energy of their initiation and at their conclusions with the force of cadence.[7] But Cone's embracing view, which skewered the dichotomy, is exceptional.[8] It has been far more common, in the nineteenth, twentieth, and twenty-first centuries, to take a position for either beginning accentuation or end accentuation. More recently scholars have characterized these two positions on the basis of the types of thinkers that have traditionally held them: the former is said to be an American approach while the latter is German; the two can also be characterized as Schenkerian and Riemannian, respectively.[9] At the birth of the discourse on accent as a way of hearing, though, these two positions were best represented by the contrast between Gottfried Weber, who heard musical groups accented at their beginnings, and Momigny, who heard them accented at their ends.

Momigny

The basis of Momigny's attempted reform of meter was a reorientation of the means by which we assess it. He asserted that musicians, in speaking about meter, "follow their eyes and not their *tact*, or their judgment, or their ear. What makes them reason poorly in this regard is that they believe that the measure is enclosed between two barlines."[10] Essential to Momigny's understanding of meter was a separation between the notational properties of the measure and our experience of accentuation. In order to explain what meter measures, Momigny described the accentuation of musical segments, which he called "propositions." A proposition is accented at its end or cadence, often located just after a barline. These propositions were not contained within barlines, then, but rather straddled them. The barlines cut through the propositions instead of framing them.[11] The measure, or

---

7. Edward T. Cone, *Musical Form and Musical Performance*, 26–27.

8. However, in this connection see also Ng, "Phrase Rhythm as Form in Classical Instrumental Music"; and, of a much earlier time, Thrasybulos G. Georgiades, "Zur Musiksprache der Wiener Klassiker [1951]," in *Kleine Schriften*, ed. Theodor Göllner (Tutzing: Hans Schneider, 1977), 33–43.

9. Rothstein, "National Metrical Types"; and idem., "Metrical Theory and Verdi's Midcentury Operas."

10. "Les Musiciens en parlent d'après leurs yeux et non d'après leur tact, ou leur jugement, ou leur oreille. Ce qui les fait mal raisonner à cet égard, c'est qu'ils croient qu'une Mesure est renfermée entre deux Barres." Momigny, *Cours complet d'harmonie et de composition*, 2:409–10.

11. This characterization of the difference belongs to Riemann, in the *Musikalische Dynamik und Agogik* (Hamburg: Rahter, 1884), 240, unnumbered footnote. See also the discussion and quotation from Riemann in Rothstein, "National Metrical Types."

means for counting these propositions, should therefore not begin at a barline but should end there. In Momigny's simplest formulation each proposition is composed of two parts: an antecedent and a consequent. The antecedent comprises the first beat of the proposition and the consequent the second. Musicians should start counting the first beat with the antecedent no matter where it begins, which is often in mid-measure. This puts the musician in the position of counting the antecedent, beat one, in the middle of the measure and the consequent, beat two, just after the barline on the "downbeat." Momigny anticipated the objections.

> What! The first beat is the upbeat and not the downbeat? Though it may scandalize you, this is not only the case in my opinion but in reality, and it cannot be otherwise. Yes, that which you call the first beat is the second, and that which you call the second or the last is the first of the two.[12]

In order to better understand this system, consider the passage from the Mozart Clarinet Quintet discussed above, which is reproduced below in example 8.2. In Momigny's terms the proposition begins on the second half of m. 65; together, the two quarter notes of the melody are the antecedent, and we are to count them as the first beat. The consequent arrives on the melody's dotted quarter note just after the following barline, and we are to count this arrival as the second beat. Although the numbers of these beats are reversed from their traditional sequence, Momigny explains that the first beat—occurring mid-measure—is the upbeat (*levé*) and the second the downbeat (*frappé*).[13] Thus the barline still marks the location of the downbeat and of metric emphasis. Momigny's main provocation concerns beginnings; since the proposition begins mid-measure, Momigny directs us to start our counting there as well. His theory understands meter's measurement anacrustically.

More important than the idiosyncratic order in which Momigny would have musicians count is the way in which he conceptualizes the nature of this counting. For Momigny, "the measure truly is not the prisoner we see enclosed between two barlines."[14] The measure is not the collection of durations our eye finds in the

---

12. "Quoi! Le premier temps de la *mesure* seroit le levé & non pas le frappe? Malgré que cela vous scandalise, il en est pourtant ainsi, non dans mon opinion seulement, mais dans la réalité, & sans qu'il en puisse être autrement. Oui, ce que vous appelez le premier temps est le second; & ce que vous nommez le second temps ou le dernier, est le premier des deux." Momigny, "Mesure (Théorie de J. J. de Momigny.)," in *Encyclopédie méthodique…: Musique*, ed. Nicolas-Étienne Framery, Pierre-Louis Ginguené, and Jérôme-Joseph de Momigny (Paris: Panckoucke, 1818), 2:132–42, at 133.

13. In order for his theory to work for triple meters, Momigny must rely on the notion that triple meters are essentially unequal. In this view, still present in the eighteenth and early nineteenth centuries to a certain extent, triple meters were said to be composed of two parts, the first twice as long as the second (see chapter 3 on this issue). For Momigny, though, the shorter beat (the upbeat or *levé*) is the "first" beat, while the longer beat (the downbeat or *frappé*), which falls after the barline, is the second.

14. "La mesure véritable n'est donc pas cette prisonnière que l'on voit renfermée entre deux barreaux." Momigny, "Mesure (Théorie de J. J. de Momigny.)," in *Encylopédie méthodique…: Musique*, ed. Framery, Ginguené, and Momigny, 2:134.

Example 8.2 Mozart, Clarinet Quintet K. 581, i, mm. 65–79, analysis after Momigny.

notation, but rather the process through which our ear determines regularity. The measure is a way of understanding, a mode of engagement, and way of feeling the order and emphasis of a proposition. The references to counted numerals and imagined actions in the raising and lowering of a hand help to distinguish meter from the proposition it measures. These numerals and imagined actions, such as the beating of the heart, are each in a "grand analogy with the measure"—a way of parsing the periodic reposes that are "regularly felt."[15]

Momigny's theory marks a point of remove from the eighteenth-century focus on the properties of the notated measure and the meter signatures. For Momigny, the focus on notation was precisely what prevented musicians from understanding the true nature of meter. His frequent recourse to the motions of time beating, by contrast, place his theory into closer affinity with those of the sixteenth and seventeenth centuries, though in Momigny's account the burden of discernment is clearly on the ear; the *levé–frappé* model is a supplement to his perceptual interpretation. In fact, it would seem from his analyses that for Momigny the process of counting the measure was entirely divorced from written music. In some of his analyses beats are not of uniform duration. Propositions were in some cases smaller than the length of the notated measure and in other cases larger, indicating that Momigny's conceptualization of meter itself involved the ability to listen on multiple hierarchic levels with corresponding beat lengths.[16] For Momigny, all levels of division are simultaneously available to the listener as musical duration unfolds.[17] In emphasizing the role of the ear he distanced the concept of meter from explanations related to the notated measure, offering instead a theory of meter grounded in the "judgment of sense."[18]

Weber

Like Momigny, Weber developed a theory of meter heavily invested in the work of the listener.[19] His *Versuch einer geordneten Theorie der Tonsetzkunst*—published in three different editions of 1817–21, 1824, and 1830–32—offers a scene of sensuous cognition in order to describe the measurement of musical duration.[20]

---

15. Momigny, "Mesure (Théorie de J. J. de Momigny.)," in *Encylopédie méthodique…: Musique*, ed. Framery, Ginguené, and Momigny, 2:134; idem., *Cours complet d'harmonie et de composition*, 2:414.

16. Especially in the examples contained within Momigny, "Mesure (Théorie de J. J. de Momigny.)," in *Encylopédie méthodique…: Musique*, ed. Framery, Ginguené, and Momigny, vol. 2, particularly those on 137. See also Momigny's writings in his later *La seule vraie théorie de la musique* (Paris: the author, 1821), 112–23. On this topic see Justin London's assessment of Momigny's theories in London, "Phrase Structure in 18th- and 19th-Century Theory: An Overview," *Music Research Forum* 5 (1990): 13–50, at 21–23.

17. "They work in regularity together," he explained, describing a system in which faster and slower levels of division are united under the rule of a higher-order regularity. "Elles marchent ici régulièrement ensemble, parce qu'elles sont toutes placées sur un cadencé général & commun sur lequel le cadencé particulier est combiné." Momigny, "Mesure (Théorie de J. J. de Momigny.)," in *Encylopédie méthodique…: Musique*, ed. Framery, Ginguené, and Momigny, 2:137.

18. "Tact, qui est le jugement des sens…" Momigny, *Cours complet d'harmonie et de composition*, 2:426.

19. On the period's relationship to listening and the construction of the listener in Weber in particular, see Jairo Moreno, *Musical Representations, Subjects, and Objects: The Construction of Musical Thought in Zarlino, Descartes, Rameau, and Weber* (Bloomington: Indiana University Press, 2004), 128–59.

20. I will refer to the 1824 edition throughout because it is the earliest edition to include the full extent of his writings on meter.

The symmetry of the equally divided lengths of beats is not alone what creates the essence and particular charm of the rhythmic order: rather our internal sentiment overlays something of its own. Specifically we place, as if instinctively, more inner weight on one beat of every smaller or larger group than on the following beat or following two beats, such that a symmetrical sequence of equal beat lengths conforms to a symmetrical alternation of greater and lesser inner weight of beats, which gives the whole a certainty, life, and meaning.[21]

The notational equivalence of beats is not what creates meter's regular division, but rather something our inner sentiment habitually overlays—a kind of internal weight unrelated to duration. Weber's description shares much with Kirnberger's theory, particularly the image of the sequence of equal beats conforming to a sequence of alternating emphases in our detection of inner weight (itself a notion redolent of the *quantitas intrinseca* tradition).[22] It also shares a great deal with Momigny's theory in its assessment of a basic alternation in "every smaller or larger group," and in the belief that we hear accent (or "inner weight") on the beat directly following the barline.

Where Weber does not follow Momigny, however, is in determining the disposition of musical groups in relation to metric accent. For Weber, the emphasis of the barline marks the initiation of the musical group—the first part of each segment is where our sentiment overlays more attentional energy. Weber's musical segments are beginning-accented. This results in a different system of higher-order meter and a different relationship to the musical phrase.

In Weber's theory the perceptual act that overlays accent on duration is not tied to the length of the notated measure—a "higher rhythm" is detectable at durations longer than the measure.[23] This pattern is "altogether similar to the construction of measures only on a larger scale."[24] Again, the theoretical grounding of this higher-order regularity is not at all different from Momigny's, though its implementation in music analysis is. Weber explains, for instance, how the opening two measures of the "Jupiter" Symphony's first movement form a larger measure (see example 8.3). He goes further: the first four measures in the passage taken together form a larger measure still, as do the entire first eight measures considered as a unit. These higher-order measures also contain musical segments

---

21. "Die Symmetrie der genau gegen einander abgemessenen Länge der Zeiten ist es aber nicht allein, was die Wesenheit und den eigenthümlichen Reiz der rhythmischen Ordnung ausmacht: sondern unser inneres Gefühl fügt noch etwas Eignes hinzu. Wir legen nämlich, gleichsam unwillkürlich, auf die eine Zeit jeder kleinern oder grössern Gruppe, innerlich mehr Gewicht, als auf den folgenden, oder auf die zwei folgenden Zeittheile, so dass der symmetrischen Folge gleicher Zeitlängen, eine symmetrischer Wechsel grösseren und geringern inneren Gewichtes der Zeiten entspricht, welcher dem Ganzen Bestimmtheit, Leben und Bedeutung giebt." Gottfried Weber, *Versuch einer geordneten Theorie der Tonsetzkunst*, 2nd ed. (1817–21; Mainz: B. Schotts Söhne, 1824), 1:99.

22. These topics are taken up in chapter 4.

23. Weber, *Versuch einer geordneten Theorie der Tonsetzkunst*, 2nd ed., 2:101–2.

24. "Die Gliederung der grösseren Rhythmen ist eine mehr ins Grosse gehende Symmetrie, übrigens der des Taktbaues völlig ähnlich, nur Alles nach grösserem Maßstabe." Weber, *Versuch einer geordneten Theorie der Tonsetzkunst*, second edition, 1:102–3.

Example 8.3 Mozart, Symphony no. 41, K. 551 ("Jupiter"), i, mm. 1–8, analysis of phrase components and "higher rhythm" after Weber.

of identical length. The first in Weber's analysis consists of the material in the first two measures, which is itself part of the larger segment of four measures, contained within the eight-measure phrase. In this context the higher-order measures line up exactly with the phrase segments they measure.[25] Each musical segment is accented at its beginning, and the counting begins just after the barline. Analyzing the passage under Momigny's theory, the accentuation should be detected at the conclusion of the musical segments where they come to momentary pauses and cadences. In this view, the higher-order measures and the musical segments they measure are offset from each other by the length of one notated measure. Here we come to the basic conflict between the theories of Weber and Momigny.

Hypermeter, Or, How Meter Moved from the Page to the Ear for Good

Momigny and Weber both attempted to account for the particularly tricky phenomenon that we now call hypermeter. In twenty-first century discourse, hypermeter gives name to the activity of metrically attending to durations longer than the notated measure. Hypermeter is difficult because it is, by definition, never inscribed in the traditional sense. Its identification therefore requires

---

25. It is this sort of design that contributes to what Edward T. Cone called the "tyranny of the four-measure phrase." It is what William Rothstein calls the "Great Nineteenth-Century Rhythm Problem," which he defines as "the danger, endemic in 19th-century music, of too unrelievedly duple a hypermetrical pattern, of too consistent and unvarying a phrse structure." Rothstein's rhythm problem is the result of an overwhelming regularity in which phrase structures and hypermeter are aligned. See Cone, *Musical Form and Musical Performance*, 74–75; and Rothstein, *Phrase Rhythm in Tonal Music* (New York: Schirmer Books, 1989), 184–85.

some subjective analytical decisions. Momigny and Weber made their decisions differently, and they did so to different ends. Whereas Momigny was concerned to liberate the measure from the prison of the notated barlines, Weber used the perceptual explanation of higher-order meter to confront a difficulty in notational practice. Specifically, Weber was concerned to account for the existence of the compounded measure: the notational convention in which two measures were written together as one, with every other barline missing.

Unlike Momigny, Weber introduced the concept of hypermeter—or what he called "higher rhythm"—to fold the compounded measure into a universally applicable theory of meter. His discussion of hypermeter is interposed between his description of simple measures and his explanation of how simple measures are sometimes compounded into one.

> Just as…several measures group themselves into a higher rhythm in the way that measure-parts group themselves into a measure, so [the former] in the same way is itself a measure of higher order or larger species; one sometimes actually writes them in the form of larger or compounded [*zusammengesetzten*] measures: that is, instead of placing a barline after every simple measure, one places a barline only after two or more measures, and leaves the intervening barlines out.[26]

Weber's historical observation in this passage is both obvious and profound: compounded measures were already hypermeasures. His remarks are a more developed form of an attitude introduced in Kirnberger's *Die Kunst des reinen Satzes in der Musik*. Kirnberger suggested that measures fast enough to be felt as a single beat ought to be grouped together into one compounded measure without barlines between them.[27] This practice, in which theorists and musicians were able to conceptualize the measure as a compoundable entity, already signaled the slow process of the separation between meter as a perceptual phenomenon and meter as a notational practice.[28] In the twenty-first century the theories of Momigny and Weber look much more like theories of hypermeter than those of the earlier theorists who first dealt with the compounding of measures, but what Weber makes clear is that even the earliest theories of the compounded measure were, in a way, already theories of hypermeter—ways of conceptualizing meter as a process that occurs outside of inscription. Though their intended ends and actual implementations differed greatly, this is the aspect that unites the theories of the compounded measure with those of both Momigny and Weber.

---

26. "Eben weil…mehrere Takte sich zu einem höherer Rhythmus gruppiern, wie Takttheile zu einem Takte, jener also gleichsame ein Takt höherer Ordnung, oder grösserer Gattung ist, so schreibt man ihn zuweilen auch wirklich in Gestalt eines grossen oder zusammengesetzten Takts: d. h. statt nach jedem einfachen Takt einen Taktstrich zu setzen, setzt man einen solchen nur je nach zwei, oder mehreren Takten, und lässt die dazwischen liegenden Taktstriche aus." Weber, *Versuch einer geordneten Theorie der Tonsetzkunst*, 2nd ed., 1:104.

27. Kirnberger, *Die Kunst des reinen Satzes in der Musik*, 2:131.

28. This is a different way of looking at the same transition traced in Rothstein, "National Metrical Types"; and, more generally, Georgiades, "Aus der Musiksprache des Mozart Theaters [1950]," in *Kleine Schriften*, ed. Theodor Göllner (Tutzing: Hans Schneider, 1977), 9–32.

It is no coincidence that the discourse on what we now call hypermeter was born at the same moment that theories of meter relied less on the page and more on the ear—or sentiment, or feeling, or the act of overlaying that extra "something," that "internal weight," in Weber's words—to do the work of explaining meter. The ability to codify hypermeter was the result of this slow intellectual shift. Though Weber has been called the "father of hypermeter," he is rather late in announcing its arrival.[29] Conceptually, meter had already begun to move off of the page with the first description of the compounded measure. Momigny and Weber only made explicit what the previous generation of theorists had written towards and what Kirnberger had attempted to capture: meter is an activity, a way of attending to the ongoing flow of duration that is independent of notation.

To be sure, Momigny and Weber almost certainly had different bodies of musical repertoire in mind when they penned their theories. Momigny was no doubt thinking of French vocal melodies (his examples make this explicit); his theory accommodates the end accentuation characteristic of French and Italian verse. In the verse meters of these languages the heaviest accent is typically located on the penultimate or final syllable. This accent is known in Italian as the *accento comune* and in French as the *accent tonique*. Composers of the late eighteenth and early nineteenth centuries often aligned these poetic end-accents with melodic cadences when writing vocal music.[30] For Momigny these cadences were not only harmonic arrival points with textual emphasis, they were also the peaks of our metric attention. Weber, by contrast, used many examples of instrumental music and music with German texts, in which no such textual accents exist and cadences often arrive mid-measure. For Weber the harmonic pull of a cadence was not as perceptually pertinent as the initiation of new material. But more than styles of composition, the contrasting views of Momigny and Weber reflect divergent modes of engagement on the part of the listener; they demonstrate two different ways of locating the momentary "something" that creates metric accent.

The legacy of this moment in music theory is abiding in the twenty-first century and vital to the way we understand the cognition of meter. Metric accent in the melodies of this period can be heard in a variety of ways. As David Temperley cautions, "The disagreement on the issue of normative meter-grouping alignment should serve as a warning: the perception of meter and grouping can be quite subjective."[31] Indeed, the subjectivity of metric perception is the foundation on which the dual perspectives of beginning and end accentuation are based, and it is the principle that makes them both simultaneously possible. The distinction between them arose at the same moment that the determination of meter began not with the page, but with the ear.

If, like Momigny, we take seriously the notion that the measure is not simply the notes that are imprisoned within the barlines; and if, like Weber, we

29. London, "Phrase Structure in 18th- and 19th-Century Theory: An Overview," 24.
30. The existence of a linguistically based difference in the conceptualization of meter, grouping, and accent on these grounds is one of the core points in William Rothstein, "National Metrical Types"; and idem., "Metrical Theory and Verdi's Midcentury Operas."
31. Temperley, "End-Accented Phrases: An Analytical Exploration," 128–29.

take seriously the notion that each compounded measure actually contains two distinct measures, then the earlier, eighteenth-century compounded measure begins to look very much like the twenty-first century hypermeasure. That a concept approximating hypermeter existed in eighteenth-century thought is demonstrable in the specific warnings against its use. In particular, German theorists warned against situations in which single measures could be heard as individual beats, and groups of notated measures as single measures. The hypermeter they prohibit is composed of measures separated with barlines—in eighteenth-century terms, a sort of compounding of measures without notational impact. "In this case," Koch wrote, "the result is actually not any kind of meter; thesis and arsis, the two main parts of each measure, are separated from each other by the barline and appear in the external form of two measures."[32] He referred to the situation as a "mistake one encounters almost daily in modern compositions."[33] Kirnberger found the phenomenon problematic on similar grounds. In his view, the presence of the barlines in this situation would result in "a melody of only strong beats, owing to the required weight of the downbeat. This would be as contrarious as a sentence of speech comprised of nothing but one-syllable words, each of which had an accent."[34] Despite the efforts of these eighteenth-century theorists to describe a measure-like entity larger than the notated measure—and thus allowing for a type of measure outside of notation—they nevertheless dismissed the idea on the basis of the notation itself. The presence of notated barlines within their imagined hypermeasures suggested an unacceptable relationship to accent.

The notion of measures larger (or at a higher level) than the notated measure was perhaps the most conceptually significant point of confrontation between two moments in the history of meter theory. On the one hand, the idea of a measure freed from notational constraints is at the heart of hypermeter. The idea of reconceptualizing measures as beats and groups of measures as single measures is reliant upon the idea that our sentiment and hearing do the work of determining the meter. If we determine measures with our ears, what should it matter if these segments include barlines within them? But on the other hand, neither Kirnberger nor Koch could accept meter as a concept entirely divorced from notation. Even in segments of our mind's own arranging the existence of a barline would somehow have to indicate downbeat accent.

32. "… in diesem Falle bekömmt man eigentlich gar keine Tactart, sondern die beyden Haupttheile eines jeden tactes, Thesis und Arsis sind durch den Tactstrich von einander getrennt, und erscheinen in der äusserlichen Gestalt zweyer Tacte." Koch, *Versuch einer Anleitung zur Composition*, 2:302.

33. "Ein Fehler den man baynahe täglich in den modernen Tonstücken antrifft." Koch, *Versuch einer Anleitung zur Composition*, 2:319.

34. "Denn wenn dieses Zusammenziehen nicht geschähe, so würde man, wegen der nothwendigen Schwere des Niederschlages, eine Melodie von lauter schweren Schlägen bekommen, welches eben so wiedrig wäre, als eine Periode der Rede, die aus lauter einsylbigen Wörten bestünde, deren jedes einen Accent hätte." Kirnberger, *Die Kunst des reinen Satzes in der Musik*, 2:131. In addition to these prohibitions Riepel would seem to have described the phenomenon. Joseph Riepel, *Anfangsgründe zur musicalischen Setzkunst…De Rhythmopoeïa, oder von der Tactordnung* (Regensburg and Vienna: Emerich Felix Bader, 1752), 1:52.

For Momigny and Weber, the situation was different. The strange persistence of notation's importance to Kirnberger and Koch in the case of hypermeter is symptomatic of a broader situation in which meter and character drifted slowly apart. In order for each meter to be distinctive affectively and stylistically as it once had been, its notation had to matter. Barlines, durations, and the choice of the numerals in the signature itself were all at stake. Barlines, therefore, had to be of some consequence to Kirnberger and Koch. But something had changed by the time that Momigny and Weber wrote. Something that allowed them to see an unimprisoned measure—a way of understanding meter that was not as attached to its previous notational commitments, though nevertheless still mysterious. Momigny and Weber wrote with some historical distance from the music that was composed in Koch and Kirnberger's time. They wrote in a musical environment that already demonstrated the disconnection between meter and notation—music in which the meter could change without an alteration to character.[35]

Meter as Attention, Activity, Aesthesis

The Dissolution of a System

In the third volume of his celebrated *Versuch einer Anleitung zur Composition* of 1793, Koch discusses the connection and expansion of melodic phrases and the manner of combining these small forms into larger compositions. "If one is to connect melodic sections," he begins, "one must, then, decide beforehand if they are even fit for joining."[36] The first two of Koch's minimal qualifications concern the uniformity 1) of the key, and 2) of the meter and tempo of the phrases to be connected. These first two rules seemed so self-evident to him that they received no elaboration or justification in his treatise.

"It would be unnecessarily lengthy to give rules intended to treat the first two of the matters just mentioned, namely, on the unity of the key and the consistency of the metric type [*Tactart*], which phrases suitable for connecting must exhibit. Through practice in vocal or instrumental music, the prospective composer should already be educated well enough that he could never violate rules of this kind."[37] The uniformity of meter, as a minimal qualification for the joining

---

35. As Danuta Mirka tells us, "The fact that changes of metre do not always go together with changes of topics testifies to the new status of metre in the late eighteenth century." Mirka, "Metre, Phrase Structure and Manipulations of Musical Beginnings," in *Communication in Eighteenth-Century Music*, ed. Mirka and Kofi Agawu (Cambridge: Cambridge University Press, 2008), 83–111, at 106.

36. "Will man melodische Theile verbinden, so muß man zuvor entscheiden...daß sie schicklich zu einem Ganzen verbunden werden können." Heinrich Christoph Koch, *Versuch einer Anleitung zur Composition* (Leipzig: Adam Friedrich Böhme, 1782–93), 3:3.

37. "Es würde ohne Noth zu weitläusig verfahren seyn, wenn man über die beyden ersten der genannten Gegenstände nemlich über die Einheit der Tonart, und über die Gleichheit der Tactart, in welcher verbindungsfähige melodische Theile eingekleidet seyn müßen, Regeln geben wollte. Schon durch die Uebung in der Vocal- oder Instrumentalmusik muß der

of small forms into a larger composition, was for Koch indisputable. Not even a beginner would break such a rule.[38]

In fact, Koch's contemporaries regularly wrote music that did just that. In the late eighteenth century composers were able to violate this rule in a rather subtle way when they changed meters mid-composition without changing meter signatures. As Danuta Mirka has shown, these nuanced changes occurred when composers shifted between compounded meters and the simple meters that share the same signature. Example 8.4 below illustrates Mirka's analysis of one such moment at the opening of the second movement from Haydn's "Frog" Quartet, op. 50, no. 6. Although it is written with a 6/8 meter signature the placement of cadential formulae signals a compounded meter in which each measure contains two small measures of 3/8. The barlines can be said to mark the hypermeasures. The first cadence, in the middle of the second notated measure, arrives in this view on the downbeat of the fourth (little) measure. After four notated measures the pace and shape of the music change as the harmonic rhythm slows and the register broadens. The third cadence falls on the downbeat of the tenth notated measure, and it is clear at this point that the meter has switched from a compounding of two small 3/8 measures to a single, simple measure with two beats. The barlines now mark the measure level. Haydn seamlessly changes the meter through a skillful reworking of materials without altering the meter signature or the overall character of the writing.

The metric agility of this passage from Haydn's "Frog" Quartet is representative of the shifts between compounded and simple meters in the repertoire of the era, and it demonstrates the indistinctiveness of the particular meter signatures involved.[39] If both compounded 3/8 and simple 6/8 can coexist in the same passage without any significant consequences for the character and resultant affect of the music, then meter might not be part of the system of characteristics and affectual qualities after all. If the notation is also indifferent to this change, then perhaps meter is best explained without reference to its written codifications. These subtle shifts in meters are historically significant in the way that they highlight the end of *tempo giusto* and the need for an explanation of meter untethered from the notated measure. Even before Weber and Momigny published their first treatises there were already compelling reasons to believe that meter

angehende Tonsetzer so weit gebildet seyn, daß er wieder Regeln dieser Art nicht verstoßen kann." Koch, *Versuch einer Anleitung zur Composition*, 3:6.

38. Although he would seem to have prohibited it in the passage quoted above, Koch later describes the practice (outlined below) in which composers were able to switch between compounded and simple meters that shared the same meter signatures, therefore shifting the meter without changing the locations of the barlines or the length of the measures. Koch, *Versuch einer Anleitung zur Composition*, 2:384, 3:223–25. See Danuta Mirka's discussion of this phenomenon in *Metric Manipulations in Haydn and Mozart* (Oxford: Oxford University Press, 2009), 209–17; and, more generally, Claudia Maurer Zenck, *Vom Takt: Überlegungen zur Theorie und kompositorischen Praxis im ausgehenden 18. und beginnenden 19. Jahrhundert* (Vienna: Böhlau, 2001).

39. Mirka notes that changes from simple meters to compounded meters present additional challenges. Specifically, the composer must be sure not to begin simple measures in the middle of a notated measure. Mirka, *Metric Manipulations in Haydn and Mozart*, 214.

Example 8.4 Haydn, Quartet in D major, "The Frog," op. 50, no. 6, ii, mm. 1–10. Analysis of Danuta Mirka.

might be a phenomenon independent of character, tempo, notated durations, and even barlines.

More extreme than the shifts of meter that did not involve a new notated meter signature are those that did. An early, unusual example is found in Mozart's finale to the second act of *Die Entführung aus dem Serail*. In this quartet the two male leads Blemonte and Pedrillo question the fidelity of their respective partners, Konstanze and Blonde. The women protest, horrified with their lovers' lack of confidence. After the men attempt an apology, the four join together in a beautiful pastoral hymn that requires a sudden change of meter and tempo. This first change in meter is typical in eighteenth-century opera and involves a reconfiguration of character, note values, tempo, and the notated meter. Though rapid, it nevertheless conforms to a system in which all these are linked. The pastoral hymn brings together a chorale texture with a 6/8 meter and sicilliano rhythms, and for fifteen measures the couples seem to have reconciled. Blonde, however, is not satisfied. At the conclusion of the hymn, Pedrillo launches into a declaration of his faith in her fidelity, establishing an allegretto ₵ with a clear break from the hymn's character, shown below in example 8.5. At this point the notation of meter takes an unexpected turn. Blonde interjects in order to rebut Pedrillo, singing over everyone else in 12/8—a meter reserved for her line of the score alone.[40] For twenty-two measures the four singers and orchestra remain in this configuration with Blonde singing against the subdivision before finally acquiescing and accepting Pedrillo's apology.

Mozart could easily have written the same music with triplet subdivisions in Blonde's part alone for the same two-against-three effect. But the liberty that he took in writing her part in 12/8 on top of ₵ music suggests that the notational qualities of that meter did not, in fact, necessitate an entirely different configuration of character, tempo, and note values. On the whole, these twenty-two measures are in a duple meter; for Belmonte, Konstanze, Pedrillo, and the orchestra, that duple meter is a gavotte-like ₵ with barlines every two half notes. For Blonde, the duple meter is a 12/8 with barlines every two dotted half notes. Notation in this case works to accomplish a rhythmic, rather than metric, end. The availability of alternate methods for notating the passage indicates that the meter is not necessarily what is given on the page. The meter is the way we divide this passage into its duple groupings. Our determination of it relies not on notation but on our ears, or our attention. In an age when composers felt comfortable shifting freely between meters with the confidence that they could preserve the overarching affect of a passage, it eventually became more apparent that the specific notational properties of the music did not hold as much stylistic significance as was once believed.

Integrated Metric Shifts

Haydn's "Frog" Quartet and Mozart's scene from *Die Entführung aus dem Serail* demonstrate metric shifts that exploit the mutability of the meters involved. Haydn plays on the dual interpretations of the notated 6/8 meter signature, writing music that moves from compounded 3/8 to simple 6/8. Mozart accomplishes something similar, though with different notational consequences. Superimposing ₵ and 12/8, Mozart takes advantage of the binary basis that these two meters share. Both of these strategies push the flexibility of notated meter to an extreme.

---

40. I find this shift evocative of the kind of immediacy—the here-and-now—that Georgiades discusses in "Aus der Musiksprache des Mozart Theaters."

Example 8.5 Mozart, *Die Entführung aus dem Serail*, act II, no. 16, Quartet, mm. 205–36, from the conclusion of the hymn passage through Blonde's 12/8 measures.

In the early nineteenth century that flexibility was pushed even further. Composers began to create integrated metric shifts: sudden and significant changes in the meter that were fully enmeshed in the stylistic continuity of the music. These shifts do not build on the dual nature of a single meter as the examples above do, but they nevertheless manage to preserve the tempo and character of the passage while simultaneously altering the number of beats per measure and often the notated meter signature. The transition into and out of these changes is usually unexpected and the result is a seamless slip into a different way

Example 8.5 Continued

of measuring. Because of the overarching musical continuity they are embedded within, these changes in meter are difficult to hear until after they have taken place. They have been woven into the design of the phrase, the arc of the melody, and the affective quality of the composition.

The Scherzo of Beethoven's "Eroica" Symphony includes two of these shifts in rapid succession—the transitions into and out of the celebrated measures in ₵, shown in example 8.6. Beethoven's tightly controlled thematic material prepares this moment at the end of the Scherzo, and when it finally arrives it is as if the

Example 8.5 Continued

possibility of measuring the music in this way had been hanging in the balance for the entire movement, only to be realized just before its conclusion.[41] The ₵ measures are located in the repeat of the Scherzo's A section, and their presence

41. Indeed, at the opening of the movement—before the arrival of the theme—we are likely to hear the pairs of alternating pitches suggest a duple meter; the ₵ measures are in a certain sense the fulfillment of this unrealized duple potential. I thank Rick Cohn for sharing this observation with me.

Example 8.5 Continued

transforms a cadential tag that appears twice in this music. At the opening of the movement both presentations of this tag are—like the rest of the opening—in 3/4 meter; they are rhythmically identical, featuring sforzandi on the second beats of the triple measures. There is quite a bit of rhythmic potential and metric ambiguity built into the original, triple meter iterations of the tag. In addition to the beat-two sforzandi, the sudden alteration from iambic to trochaic rhythm in the fourth measure is further destabilizing. When the A section returns after the

Example 8.5 Continued

trio, only the first presentation of this tag remains in 3/4. The second finds itself in a stretched-out ₵, the iambic and trochaic rhythms converted into shocking spondees. For just these four measures, the triple meter of the movement gives way to a completely different metric organization with an altogether different and incommensurable number of beats. At the conclusion of the tag the music

Example 8.6 Beethoven, Symphony no. 3 ("Eroica"), op. 55, iii, n:m. 366–87.

Example 8.6 Continued

returns to 3/4 as quickly as it had left, with the duple pulse momentarily haunting the experience of the triple meter.

The rapid shifts into and out of ₵ are all the more provocative because they are so neatly folded into the surrounding material. Beethoven does not effect these changes of meter in order to achieve different tempi or create different characters or even to use different note values for the beat. Instead, the ₵ passage should be understood as an escape into an alternative method of measuring for just a moment; a transformation of a passage heard many times already. The movements into and out of it are integrated metric shifts.

Beethoven's handling of this ₵ passage differs significantly from other swift changes of the prevailing meter in his music and in the music of his contemporaries. Many sudden shifts were un-integrated; the onset of new meters—albeit sometimes unexpected—in these cases also meant a reorientation in the note values, character, and tempo of the music. Consider the first movement of Beethoven's op. 130 string quartet. The first shift in meter from the Adagio 3/4 to the Allegro C is like many found in movements with slow introductions. The new meter signature brings with it a new tempo, texture, character, and set of musical ideas. Op. 130 is distinctive in its many sudden returns to the 3/4 material, the first of which occurs already in m. 20 after only five measures of C Allegro. In this first movement, each shift in meter also signals a reorientation in tempo and character. These are un-integrated shifts; they resemble the kinds of quick changes in affect found in the opera of the period, or the parade of characters heralded by as many meter signatures in keyboard toccatas of the century previous.[42] Though the difference between integrated and un-integrated shifts is by no means altogether clear in every case, the distinction can serve as a useful heuristic for describing the relationship—or lack thereof—between the notated meter and the note values, character, and tempo of the music to which it is applied. In the case of the first movement from op. 130, each change in meter alters the continuity of the passage. Like the 6/8 that sits at the opening of the hymn in the scene from *Die Entführung aus dem Serail* discussed above, these changes in meter import with them entire musical worlds. The frequency with which they occurred—particularly in eighteenth-century opera—prepared the ground for metric shifts that were integrated.

Some composers used integrated metric shifts to depart from the prevailing meter for more substantial stretches than the four measures of Beethoven's "Eroica." As early as 1795 Muzio Clementi experimented with one such lengthy deviation in the context of a capriccio published with his op. 34 keyboard works. The piece includes a twenty-measure departure from the C meter into 3/4, integrated on both sides by a constant pattern of running sixteenth notes. The shift is in keeping with the fantasy-like and improvisatory character of the piece in general, and the motion to 3/4 is concurrent with an exploration of distant harmonic regions.

---

42. Take for instance the works contained in Frescobaldi's Second Book of Toccatas of 1627.

Another set of substantial departures in a less fantastic context is found in the Scherzo of Spohr's First Symphony (1811). The movement is rich with metric ambiguities throughout, and Spohr builds on these instabilities to move easily into and out of the prevailing 3/4. After only a few phrases in the short opening section Spohr uses the anacrustic energy of the melodic material to initiate an integrated metric shift into 2/4, shown below in example 8.7. The anacrusis in the violin melody initiates a repeating arpeggio pattern, which, together with the downbeat articulations in the winds, reinforces the new duple meter. Initially this passage sounds hemiola-like, as though it might immediately resolve itself back to 3/4. Spohr further complicates the rhythmic texture in the fifth measure of the 2/4 passage, introducing running triplets into the violin melody against the duplet eighth notes in the bass. At this point the music begins to shade away even from 2/4, hinting at 6/8. But after eight total measures of 2/4, Spohr returns us without ceremony to the original 3/4 for the concluding measures of the opening. These shifts in meter preserve the tempo and overall character of the movement. As part of the opening material the 2/4 section is repeated four times in the movement for a total of eight integrated metric shifts.

Spohr's liberties with the meter of his Scherzo did not go unnoticed. E. T. A. Hoffmann took issue with the 2/4 passage in his *AmZ* review of the work, focusing his critique specifically on Spohr's notation.

> Only nineteen measures before the conclusion of the first half there appears a strange eight-measure passage in 2/4 meter, unrelated to the main theme. Being maybe too piquant the composer has employed many techniques, but none in accordance with just feeling. What the composer wanted has very often been attained by Haydn—without changing the type of meter and with no admixture of the theme in any heterogeneous phrases—merely by displacing the rhythm.[43]

It was not the audible result but rather the means through which Spohr attained it that bothered Hoffmann. In his view the change of notated meter implied an undesirable admixture that so altered the music it seemed strange and out of place. Hoffmann was correct, in a sense, that Spohr could have done without the change in meter and written the half notes and half-note length arpeggios inside of triple measures, tying every third half note across the barline and so forth. For this to work out cleanly, Spohr should have written eighteen beats of displaced music, rather than the sixteen contained in his eight measures of duple. Rewriting this passage in 3/4 would have left him with an extra beat.

---

43. "Streng hält sich der Componist an den zur Durchführung gewählten Gedanken, und nur neunzehn Takte vor dem Schluss des ersten Theils tritt acht Takte hindurch ein ganz fremdartiger, dem Hauptthema durchaus nicht verwandter Satz im 2/4 Takt ein. Um vielleicht recht pikant zu seyn, hat der Componist mehrere Mittel angewandt, aber nach des Rec. Gefühl, ohne Noth. Das was der Componist wollte, hat Haydn sehr oft ohne Veränderung der Taktart, ohne Beymischung eines dem Thema ganz heterogenen Satzes, blos durch Verrückung des Rhythms erlangt." E. T. A. Hoffmann, review of Spohr's First Symphony, *Leipzig AmZ* 13, nos. 48 and 49, November 27–December 4, 1811, col. 797–806 and 813–19, at 815. Thanks are due to Deirdre Loughridge for first drawing my attention to this review.

Example 8.7 Spohr, Symphony no. 1, iii, mm. 39–60.

Example 8.7 Continued

The coexistence of Spohr's music and Hoffmann's reactions to it attest to the messy overlaps of the ways in which meter was conceptualized during this period. Whereas Spohr's music points to an understanding of meter as a phenomenon unrelated to notation, tempo, or character, Hoffmann's commentary would suggest that Spohr's inscription of the passage was more important than the latter might suspect. But both Spohr's implementation of and Hoffmann's commentary on the change in notated meter demonstrate a burgeoning awareness that notation had been rendered unable to tell the full story. For the purposes of his criticism Hoffmann separated "what the composer wanted"—the sounding meter—from the means of achieving it in the score.

There are still other ways that Spohr might have inscribed his eight measures in duple meter. In addition to indicating changes in meter with new meter signatures, composers experimented with shifting meters at the hypermetric level. In these cases single measures were conceptualized and felt as beats and composers changed the number of measures in each unit of higher-level organization, or hypermeter.[44]

A rather celebrated piece of evidence for this type of thinking is the famous inscription Beethoven left in the autograph of the Scherzo to his Ninth Symphony. The triple meter movement bears the indication "ritmo di tre battute" above m. 177, indicating a change that takes place not in the meter but in the hypermetric organization; at this point Beethoven switches from a duple hypermeter to triple, and with the written indication simultaneously draws attention to the organization of measures into larger groups and also the change in the size of those groups. This was an integrated metric shift in hypermeter. The fugal disposition of the Scherzo music is central to its articulation. Following the introduction Beethoven spaces the entries of the thematic material at intervals of four measures, thereby emphasizing the duple hypermeter from the beginning not just in units of two, but also in larger units of four with pronounced changes of texture and the re-entry of melodic material, as illustrated in example 8.8 below.

From the outset there is no ambiguity about the regularity of duple patterning at levels above the measure. This regularity continues in the second theme and in the textural alternation at the opening of the development, keeping the duple-based hypermeter firmly in place until m. 177, where the "ritmo di tre battute" begins (example 8.9). Here, the fugato from the opening returns, but with each entry following in units of three rather than of four. Again, the constant textural changes and the repetition of material make the hypermeter unambiguous. Moreover, triple patterning at yet higher levels is apparent from m. 177 through m. 194, as two nine-measure units contain three fugato entries of three

44. For a set of arguments on the importance of this concept to the analysis of late eighteenth- and early nineteenth-century music, see Zenck, *Vom Takt*. Although Zenck and I are both invested in the analysis of hypermeter—what she calls *Doppeltakt*—and are both concerned to explain Beethoven's interest in the metronome, we nevertheless come to different conclusions on the relationship between the two. Zenck's aim is to explain how an analysis sensitive to *Doppeltakt* and compounded measures can clarify some of the more confusing metronome markings associated with Beethoven's music. See in particular chap. 3, "Beethovens Taktarten, Vortragsbezeichnungen und Metronomangaben," in *Vom Takt*, 93–140.

Example 8.8 Beethoven, Symphony no. 9, op. 125, ii, mm. 9–28.

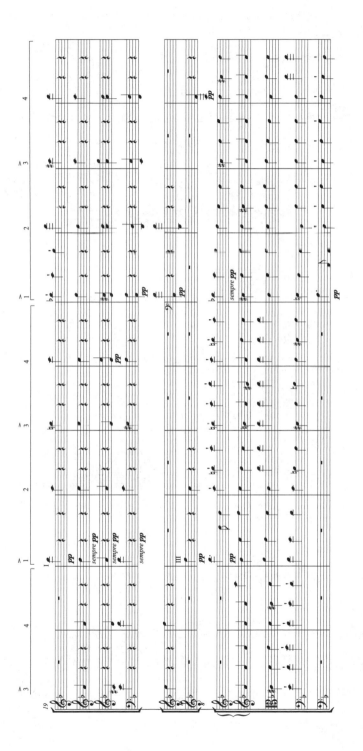

Example 8.9 Beethoven, Symphony no. 9, op. 125, ii, mm. 177–94 (*ritmo di tre battute*).

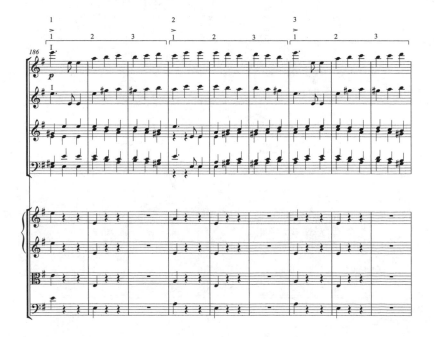

measures each at the same pitch levels, the first three on B, the second three on E. This is the passage that, in the autograph, famously contains Beethoven's two series of numeral markings showing the three groups of three measures each.[45]

The transition back to duple hypermeter, at m. 234 where Beethoven marked "ritmo di quattro battute," is no less dramatic (example 8.10). Again, the burden of the accentual work is left to the textural changes and melodic onsets of the fugato subject, the treatment of which is now accelerated. At m. 234, the upper strings drop out of the texture, leaving only the cellos and basses to sound the characteristic opening of the subject in octaves, echoed a single measure later by the cellos, playing yet another octave higher. The viola entry follows, another measure later, and it is only with the arrival of the second violin entry, yet another two measures later in m. 238, that the duple hypermeter is fully restored. The stretto effect in these measures, although it serves to shift from triple to duple, nevertheless foreshortens the possibility of four-measure organization that the fugato had once evidenced at the opening. The return to "quattro battute" is really a return to *due*. This continual shortening, from four to three to two, is played out again at the close of the Scherzo, shown in example 8.11, where the strings present the fugato subject homorhythmically—first in two four-measure segments, then in eight two-measure segments which finally dissolve into quarter note pairs after a dramatic integrated metric shift in the notated meter to ¢. The trio begins a mere two measures later.

During this period composers also began to experiment with shifts into and out of uncommon meters, such as the uneven meters in fives and sevens. Trials and critiques of quintuples and septuples gradually emerged at the close of the eighteenth century when theorists began to include these meters in their exhaustive lists of every possible signature. During this time composers attempted movements and small pieces in these meters while theorists explained their existence in order to condemn or dismiss it.[46] Particularly noteworthy, though, is the aria "Viens, gentile dame," from Adrien Boieldieu's *La dame blanche* (1825) which incorporates a short section in 5/4 that is surrounded by other meters (example 8.12). The aria begins with the tenor Georges's romantic entreaty in a stately C that contains many triple subdivisions, hinting already at the possibility of a different type of division. A full break intervenes before the new and animated section in 5/4; this transition is not an integrated metric shift but rather accompanies a change in the character of the aria. Boieldieu thematizes periodicity and attending in the fourteen measures that follow, as Georges sings with

---

45. Richard Cohn discusses this element of the autograph in his extensive treatment of the metric organization of this movement in "The Dramatization of Hypermetric Conflicts in the Scherzo of Beethoven's Ninth Symphony," *Nineteenth-Century Music* 15, no. 3 (1992): 190–91. See also Schenker's comments on the autograph in his *Beethoven, Neunte Sinfonie* (1912; repr., Vienna: Universal Edition, 1969).

46. See for example Riepel, *Anfangsgründe zur musicalischen Setzkunst…De Rhythmopoeïa, oder von der Tactordnung*, 1:66–67; Marpurg, *Anleitung zum Clavierspielen* (Berlin: Haude and Spener, 1755), 1:25; Kirnberger, *Die Kunst des reinen Satzes in der Musik*, 2:115; and Augustus Frederic Christopher Kollman, *An Essay on Musical Harmony* (London: J. Dale, 1796), 76.

Example 8.10 Beethoven, Symphony no. 9, op. 125, ii, mm. 231–41.

Example 8.11 Beethoven, Symphony no. 9, op. 125, ii, mm. 396–415.

urgency of his impatience and the beating of his heart in the anticipation of pleasure. At m. 107, in the middle of a textual repetition, Boieldieu changes the meter to 3/4 in an integrated metric shift. The new triple meter also brings with it the return of triple subdivisions in the melody, which are now performed against duple subdivisions in the accompaniment. The aria finally returns to the C meter from whence it came, but only after a convincing cadence in 3/4; Boieldieu brings back the opening line and the original meter almost as an afterthought. The aria thus processes through different meters rather than remaining in one and sampling from another—a notable difference from the integrated metric shifts discussed above.

"Viens, gentile dame" is comparable in certain respects to other multiple-tempo arias of the period; one might draw comparisons to Gernando's

Example 8.11 Continued

aria "Non soffrirò l'offesa" from Rossini's *Armida* (1817), for instance, or to "Vainement Pharaon," sung by the tenor in the titular role of Étienne-Nicolas Méhul's *Joseph* (1807). These arias all include several changes of meter, some of which can even seem sudden. But what sets Boieldieu's aria apart—in addition to its novel use of quintuple meter—is the way in which the shift from 5/4 to 3/4 is put into place. When Rossini, Méhul, and their contemporaries change meters,

Example 8.11 Continued

even mid-aria, it is always with a change in texture and character and often at a pause or cadence (occasionally at an elided cadence, in which the orchestra rejoins the singer after having dropped out of the texture to make way for pre-cadential liberties). Boieldieu's shift is integrated. It does not occur at a cadence, break the texture, or change the overall character of the music.

Example 8.12 Boieldieu, "Viens, gentille dame," from *La dame blanche*, mm. 78–114.

Example 8.12 Continued

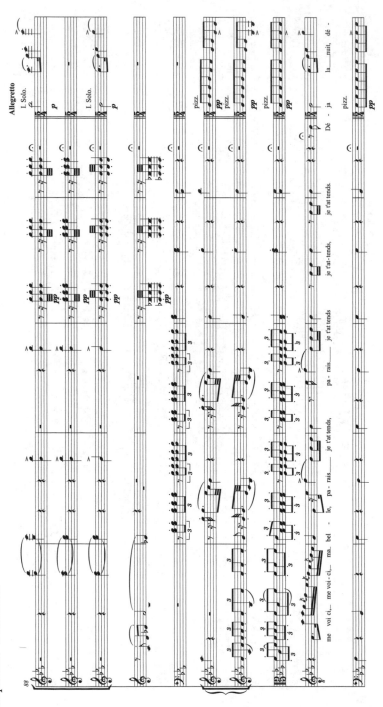

Example 8.12 Continued

What Boieldieu's "Viens, gentile dame" shares with the other integrated metric shifts is the seamless initiation of a new meter built out of an entirely new cardinality: the onset of a new way of measuring ruled by a different number of beats. These examples are representative of what Harald Krebs calls indirect grouping dissonance, which is the experience of incongruity that accompanies rapid changes in the organization of the metric hierarchy.[47] Even as these compositions include notational indications of these shifts—new meter signatures or the "ritmo di tre battute" inscription—they nevertheless demonstrate how compositional continuity was possible in the face of these types of changes. Meter, then, was independent of the other factors that account for these overarching continuities. Shifts in meter no longer had to signal changes in compositional character. These changes were simply alterations in the manner of structuring attention in the ongoing flow of time.

Meter as an Aesthetic Activity

The question of meter's independence from notation, character, tempo, and affect is fundamentally a question about accent. It was this component of meter that was first dislodged from the larger system. When Kirnberger described meter as an activity of the mind that places accents on certain beats such that we imagine hearing them with more emphasis, he was also admitting the theoretical possibility of an irregular or changing application of that activity. Because the flow of time in this model is equable and ongoing, the activity of "placing" an accent on or directing attention to a certain beat could occur in any number of ways that might change in an instant. Newly conceived as attentional energy, accent had escaped from durations, barlines, characters, and tempi. As Momigny would later put it, "the measure truly is not the prisoner we see enclosed between two barlines."[48] Or, we might say, notation no longer imprisons meter.

As the integrated metric shifts demonstrate, meter had become a method of directing attentional energy in order to supply a kind of organization or form to the sensuous information that hits the ears of the listeners. The idea that the method of measurement could change without altering the compositional fabric marks a pivotal moment in the history of theories of meter. Once, the notated meter signature held a clearly representative function. Meter expressed character directly. As Mattheson wrote in *Das neu-eröffnete Orchestre* of 1713, the meter 2/4 "brings forth singing pieces almost by itself."[49] In this conceptualization, meter functioned within an aesthetic system that understood art to imitate the passions, arousing them

---

47. Harald Krebs, *Fantasy Pieces* (Oxford: Oxford University Press, 1999), 30–34 on the difference between grouping and displacement dissonance; on direct and indirect dissonance, see 45–46.
48. "La mesure véritable n'est donc pas cette prisonnière que l'on voit renfermée entre deux barreaux." Momigny, "Mesure (Théorie de J. J. de Momigny).)," in *Encylopédie méthodique…: Musique* ed. Framery, Ginguené, and Momigny, 2:134.
49. Mattheson, *Das neu-eröffnete Orchestre* (Hamburg: the author and Benjamin Schillers Witwe, 1713), 79.

affectually in those who observed, read, or listened. Art was deemed successful if it worked as a natural sign.[50] This aesthetic orientation, made explicit in the writings of the Batteux, Lessing, and many others, underpinned eighteenth-century music theory.[51] It wrapped character up with tempo, meter, note values, and other qualities in order to accomplish the work of representation. As Sulzer explained, "every composition...must have a certain character and awaken in the mind of the listener emotions of a certain kind."[52] Even if representations didn't always work this way in practice, it was generally held that they had the capacity to. Character and affect were, in this understanding, the two poles of an aesthetic relationship that ideally lost nothing in transmission.

But something was happening to character as theorists concomitantly re-examined the nature of accent and meter. As the components of the *tempo giusto* system were wrest further and further apart, character and expression required their own reassessments. In 1795, Christian Gottfried Körner could remark, "what we call character we cannot even perceive directly in the real world or in any work of art, but rather we can only infer it from that which is contained in the attributes of individual situations."[53] No longer a matter of direct representation, character now involved a process of discernment.[54] Körner could not be sure that any particular combination of tones, timbres, and

---

50. David Wellbery makes this point in relation to Lessing's *Laocoön* in particular. Wellbery, *Lessing's Laocoon: Semiotics and Aesthetics in the Age of Reason* (Cambridge: Cambridge University Press, 1984), 7, 191–203.

51. "D'où je conclus 1. Que l'objet principal de la Musique & de la Danse doit être l'imitation des sentimens ou des passions." Charles Batteux, *Les beaux-arts réduits à un même principe* (Paris: Durand, 1747), 267. Lessing's *Laocoön* begins, "Der erste, welcher die Mahlerey und Poesie mit einander verglich, war ein Mann von feinem Gefühl, der von beyden Künsten eine ähnliche Wirkung auf sich verspürte. Beyde, empfand er, stellen uns abwesende Dinge als gegenwärtig, den Schein als Wirklichkeit vor; beyde täuschen, und beyder Täuschung gefällt." Lessing, *Laocoön: oder über die Grenzen der Mahlerey und Poesie*, 2nd printing (1766; Berlin: Christian Friedrich Voß, 1788), 2v. On this moment in the history of aesthetics, see Rancière, *The Politics of Aesthetics*, trans. Gabriel Rockhill (New York: Continuum, 2004), 21–22; Wellbery, *Lessing's Laocoon*; and M. H. Abrams, *The Mirror and the Lamp* (Oxford: Oxford Unviersity Press, 1953), particularly 30–46.

52. "Jedes Tonstük, es sey ein würklicher von Worten begleiteter Gesang, oder nur für die Instrumente gesetzt, muß einen bestimmten Charakter haben, und in dem Gemüthe des Zuhörers Empfindungen von bestimmter Art erweken." Sulzer, "Ausdruk in der Musik," in the *Allgemeine Theorie der schönen Künste*, ed. Sulzer, 2nd printing (1771–74; Leipzig: Weidmannschen Buchhandlung, 1792), 1:271.

53. "Was wir Charakter nennen, können wir überhaupt weder in der wirklichen Welt noch in irgend einem Kunstwerke unmittelbar wahrnehmen, sondern nur aus demjenigen folgern, was in den Merkmalen einzelner Zustände enthalten ist." Christian Gottfried Körner, "Ueber Charakterdarstellung in der Musik," *Die Hören* 1, no. 5, 1795, 97–121 at 115. For a similar, later view of character see G. von Weiler, "Ueber den Begriff der Schönheit, als Grundlage einer Aesthetik der Tonkunst," *Allgemeine musikalische Zeitung* 13, no. 7, February 13, 1811, col. 117–24. See also the translation and commentary of Körner in Robert Riggs, "'On the Representation of Character in Music': Christian Gottfried Körner's Aesthetics of Instrumental Music," *The Musical Quarterly* 81, no. 4 (1997): 599–631.

54. This is the topic of Matthew Pritchard's "'The Moral Background of the Work of Art': 'Character' in German Musical Aesthetics, 1780-1850," *Eighteenth-Century Music* 9, no. 1 (2012): 63–80.

durations would directly affect listeners in any specific way. His shift of emphasis from the composer to the listener is indicative of the incipient rise of a hermeneutic attitude in aesthetics, newly invested in the work of the interpreter.[55]

Meter and character encountered similar issues as they split away from the network of concepts that had once joined them. Theorists like Momigny were exuberant that meter had been freed from notation. Character, too, found itself suddenly missing from the technique of musical inscription. If character was to be a matter of individual deduction, it could not be located anywhere on the page. Just as there were anxieties about the relationship between meter and notation, so too were there worries over how to capture, codify, and transmit character in its new conceptual form.

These different vectors of musical practice help to explain facets of Beethoven's compositional and notational practice. Concerned that the system of *tempo giusto* no longer functioned reliably, Beethoven was an early enthusiast of Maelzel's metronome. Letters from the last fifteen years of his life reflect the belief that tempo required a reliable, external chronometer in order to be accurately transmitted. It was during this same period that he developed a new and distinctive attitude toward paratextual expression markings.[56] Frustrated with the traditional tempo terms, Beethoven pointed out that indications like Allegro, Andante, and Adagio were ineffective guides for both tempo and character. "What can be more absurd than Allegro, which really signifies *merry*, and how very far removed we often are from the idea of that tempo," he wrote to von Mosel in 1817.[57] A fast piece meant to convey fury and rage, for instance, should not bear a marking of Allegro. For Beethoven this term and those like it had become deplorably dissociated from that which moved the listeners, struck their senses, and affected them. This is, of course, an original sense of tempo in the words *mouvement, Bewegung*, and those like them—terms that also served the concept in the older, physical theories of time beating. As Kirnberger remarked, "the name **Gemüthsbewegung**, which we Germans give to passions or affections, already points to their analogy to *Bewegung* [tempo]."[58] At the time of Beethoven's writing the connection was slowly coming undone.

Whereas Beethoven found an answer to the problem of tempo prescription in Maelzel's metronome, he attempted a solution to the problem of character in a new attitude and treatment of paratextual expression markings. "The words describing the character of a composition are a different matter," his letter to von Mosel goes on to say. "We cannot give these up. Indeed the tempo is more like the

55. Rancière, *The Politics of Aesthetics*, 22–30; Wellbery, *Lessing's Laocoon*, esp. 43–49.
56. Pritchard, "'The Moral Background of the Work of Art,'" 75; Riggs, "'On the Representation of Character in Music,'" 611. See also Rudolph Kolisch, "Tempo and Character in Beethoven's Music," trans. Arthur Mendel, *The Musical Quarterly* 29, nos. 1–2 (1943): 169–187, 291–312, reissued in *The Musical Quarterly* 77, nos. 1–2 (1993): 90–131, 268–342.
57. Ludwig van Beethoven to Ignaz Franz, Edler von Mosel, Vienna, 1817, in *Beethoven's Letters*, ed. and trans. Emily Anderson (New York: St Martin's, 1961), 2:727.
58. "Der Name **Gemüthsbewegung**, den wir Deutschen den Leidenschaften oder Affekten geben, zeigt schon die Aehnlichkeit derselben mit der Bewegung an." Kirnberger, *Die Kunst des reinen Satzes in der Musik*, 2:106.

body *but these certainly refer to the spirit of the composition.*[59] The works from the last fifteen years of his life show a dramatic increase in the detail and care taken with these paratexts. Whereas the Piano Sonata in F-sharp major, op. 78 (1809), employs the designations Adagio cantabile, Allegro ma non troppo, and Allegro vivace, the E minor Sonata, op. 90 (1814), begins with "Mit Lebhaftigkeit und durchaus mit Empfindung und Ausdruck" and includes a second movement marked "Nicht zu geschwind und sehr singbar vorzutragen." Likewise the Piano Sonata in A major, op. 101, begins with "Etwas lebhaft und mit der innigsten Empfindung," and the well-known String Quartet op. 130 includes the designations "mit innigster Empfindung," and "neue Kraft fühlend." The extent and detail of the markings speak to the great amount of care Beethoven gave over to notation.

As lengthy and unusual as these paratexts were, though, they were also strangely vague. *Lebhaftigkeit*, or liveliness, goes some way toward detailing the character of the first movement of op. 90, but *Empfindung* and *Ausdruck*—sentiment and expression—are fantastically unspecific. This mixture of precision and vagueness is common in Beethoven's lengthy expression markings and it is an articulation of an important aesthetic orientation. The markings prescribe the character to a certain degree, but they also indicate that the performance is meant to be expressive of something that cannot be specified—something that its interpreters will ultimately divine. The true character of the composition was only to be found in this crucial interpretive act.

Beethoven's notational practices are a revealing site from which to observe the disintegration of the *tempo giusto* system. These practices include all of the metronome markings and anxious discourse thereon Beethoven produced toward the end of his life; they also include his lengthy expression paratexts. These, in connection with his composition of integrated metric shifts, demonstrate the independent pathways that tempo, character, meter, and note values had to take. Now, any meter could have any tempo or employ any note values—with the help of a metronome marking—and any combination of meter, note values, and tempo could create a wide array of characters which, though one could attempt to prescribe them, the listener would ultimately discern. It was only up to the performers to be as expressive as possible.

Meters could no longer be asked to create characters on their own. But in an interesting twist, an older aspect of meter theory retained a place in this new system of expression and reception. The conductor's beat—once a physical theorization of temporal passage—now had the opportunity to do more than simply keep time. With the expansion of discourse on the measure in eighteenth-century treatises on music, information on the practice of time beating also grew. Theorists began to describe distinct patterns for meters of three and four beats.[60] The two-part nature

59. Emphasis in Anderson's edition. Beethoven to Ignaz Franz, Edler von Mosel, Vienna, 1817, in *Beethoven's Letters*, ed. and trans. Anderson, 2:727.
60. The development of this discourse is observable when one compares the remarks in, for instance, Étienne Loulié, *Éléments ou principes de musique* (Paris: Christophe Ballard, 1696), 32–38; with those of Marpurg in the *Anleitung zum Clavierspielen*, (Berlin: Haude and Spener, 1755), 19–22; or Joseph Lacassagne, in the *Traité général des élémens du chant* (Paris, 1766), 39.

of the beat was no longer the primary organizing factor, as the discourse on the action of time beating became independent from the discourse on meter. These new and elaborate specifications for direction emerged alongside the developing notion of the conductor. In the early nineteenth century, this role was increasingly distinct from the concertmaster or composer at the keyboard, one or both of which would have led ensembles while also performing. Early figures in the history of conducing, such as Spohr and Carl Maria von Weber, saw the conductor as an individual whose sole responsibility was to lead an ensemble in coordinated expression.[61] With meter now a universal form of measurement and tempo its assignable rate, the conducted beat became a site of performative interpretation in which expression was intermixed with (rather than created directly by) the notated meter. Though they would always retain meanings associated with each other, the dissolution of the beat, the measure, and character from the *tempo giusto* system meant that each component underwent its own transformations and turbulent reconceptualizations.

As the relationships between these terms were rearranged, meter emerged as a technique in which listeners supplied a formal organization to the sensations of tones as they unfolded. Meter had become an aesthetic activity that was no longer constitutive of character but instead afforded the opportunity to contemplate or imagine it as performers attempted to express it. The process by which meter did this has direct corollaries in the period's aesthetic writings. As discussed in chapter 7, Friedrich Schiller described aesthetic experience as the result of a union between the response to sensation and the drive to create order. In meter, as in Schiller's aesthetics, we react to the undifferentiated tones that unfold in the ongoing and equable flow of time with the desire to instill a law in their unfolding. We direct our attention in an organized fashion to this equable flow, awarding peaks of our attentional energy to certain moments in regularity, ready to respond to any change. The union of this response to sensation and drive to supply it with a formal law can be called meter. It can also be called play, following Schiller, and its product a living form.[62] In the early nineteenth century, the metronome provided a universal law for tempering the sentiment or feeling for tempo. Meter, as attention, created the synthesis of sense and form required for aesthetic play in the ongoing flow of time.

---

61. On the rise of the modern conductor, see especially Clive Brown, *Classical and Romantic Performing Practice: 1750-1900* (Oxford: Oxford University Press, 1999), 390–95; David Schwarz, *Listening Awry: Music and Alterity in German Culture* (Minneapolis: University of Minnesota Press, 2006), 1–26; and José Antonio Bowen, "The Rise of Conducting," in *The Cambridge Companion to Conducting*, ed. Bowen (Cambridge: Cambridge University Press, 2003), 93–113; see also *Oxford Music Online* s.v. "Conducting," by John Spitzer et al., accessed August 20, 2013, <www.oxfordmusiconline.org>; Elliott Washington Galkin, "The Theory and Practice of Orchestral Conducting Since 1752," (PhD diss., Cornell University, 1960); and Georg Schünemann, *Geschichte des Dirigierens* (Leipzig: Breitkopf and Härtel, 1913).

62. This despite the fact that Schiller may have thought music to be lacking in form, as we learn in the twenty-second letter. Friedrich von Schiller, "Über die ästhetische Erziehung des Menschen in einer Reihe von Briefen," in *Gesammelte Werke*, ed. Reinhold Netolitzky (Gütersloh: Sigbert Mohn Verlag, 1961), 5:319–429 at 396; Schiller, "Letters on the Aesthetic Education of Man," trans. Elizabeth M. Wilkinson and L. A. Willoughby in Schiller, *Essays*, ed. Walter Hinderer and Daniel O. Dahlstrom (New York: Continuum, 1993), 150.

Meter, then, is an aesthetic activity. It is a set of actions that constitutes an interface between art and life. Insofar as attention is a way of relating to the world around us, meter would appear to be one of the most aesthetic ways of so doing. Understanding meter this way takes us quite a distance from the casual presumptiveness and assumed familiarity with which it is typically assessed and taught in the twenty-first century. It is perhaps because of its immediate usefulness and utter ubiquity that meter is often able to escape critical inspection. But as the history of music theory demonstrates time and time again, meter is anything but straightforward or simple even while it is so inescapably foundational. It is because of this double appearance that meter has so much to teach us.

Fétis and the Future

In 1831, Fétis published a study in his own *Revue musicale* that attempted a brief history and critique of meter theory since the seventeenth century.[63] At that time, Fétis asserted, a new system of metric notation had arisen in which the whole note (the *ronde* or, by its ancient name, *brève*) assumed the place of primacy in the conceptualization of division. From then on, in Fétis's account, the normative measure contained one whole note divided into either two or four beats. All other measures were derivatives. According to Fétis this problematic origin of modern notation was responsible for the creation of the clumsy system of compounded and simple measures and, in addition to this, had never been able to overcome the challenge of exact tempo precision. Note values were not able to prescribe duration in any sort of precise fashion. The Italian tempo terms were of little help. This lack of specificity was part of the flawed heritage of the modern mensural system, and only recently had musicians found a solution in Maelzel's metronome.

Though apocryphal, Fétis's narrative directs us to an important moment in the history of meter: the incorporation of the metronome into the system of music's temporal inscriptions. With this union of the metronome and the signs of meter, Fétis declared, "the system of time measurement in music has been completed."[64] Maelzel's metronome—linked to the chronometric unit of the minute—was able to provide an external means for the determination of musical tempo, which allowed the signs of meter and the note values to work in other ways.

Fétis's 1831 article might be called one of the first histories of meter theory, making allowances for its rather scant documentation. This historical essay inaugurated his series of writings on the nature and future of meter and rhythm.[65]

---

63. François-Joseph Fétis, "Du temps et de sa mesure dans la musique," *Revue musicale* 11, Vme Année no. 9, April 2, 1831, 65–68.
64. "Le système de la mesure du temps en musique a été complet." Fétis, "Du temps et de sa mesure dans la musique," 68.
65. These include Fétis, "Cours de philosophie musicale de l'histoire de la musique," *Revue musicale* 6, nos. 17, 18, 20, 21, 22, 23, and 24, May 26–July 14, 1832, 131–33, 139–41, 155–58, 161–64, 169–71, 177–79, and 184–87; idem., "De la mesure en musique," *Revue musicale* 8, no. 5, February

Later he would indicate a plan for an entire monograph on the topic to be titled *Traité du rhythme et de la mélodie*, though the final document never appeared in print.[66] In the articles he published, Fétis paints grand visions for the development of the composition and understanding of music's temporal elements. In his judgment these were the least advanced elements of musical practice and theory. "Great things remain to be discovered in this aspect of the art," he urged.[67] His scheme for the future of rhythm and meter paralleled his four-part scheme for the development of harmony and harmonic theory, consisting of four *ordres*. For rhythm and meter, these were the *ordres unirhythmique, transirhythmique, pluri-rhythmique*, and *omnirhythmique*. Unlike harmony, rhythm and meter had been locked in the first *ordre* since the sixteenth century because no one had yet discovered how to modulate with rhythms. Of the subsequent *ordres*, Fétis speculated that the *transirhythmique* would be marked by the ability to modulate between one meter and the next, presenting the same melodic material in both meters; music in the *ordre plurirhythmique* would comingle many meters freely in a single composition.[68] Although he did not remark on the integrated metric shifts discussed above or examples similar to them in the music of his day, Fétis envisioned a future for rhythm and meter that was to be focused on these types of juxtapositions and rapid changes.

In many ways Fétis's 1831 essay can be said to capture the concerns of one age of music theory while inaugurating another. Since the time of his writing, composers and theorists have experimented with myriad ways of integrating metric changes into their compositions and theoretical systems. And indeed, just as the piece forecasts the concerns of much recent music and theory, it also reflects on a critical period in the history of meter: a period in which theorists articulated early assessments of hypermeter, composers experimented with integrated metric shifts, and the discourse on meter moved from the page to the ear. It was during this formative period in the history of meter that the issues still concerning us today came into their present configuration. Hypermeter has remained a curiosity of scholars, and it is not by chance that Edward T. Cone gave the concept its present name in the midst of a discussion about Beethoven and his contemporaries.[69] By the same token the current debate concerning end- and beginning- accentuated phrases was in many ways inaugurated with the polarity

2, 1834, 33–35; and idem., "Du developpement futur de la musique: Dans le domaine de rhythme," *Revue et Gazette musicale de Paris* 19, nos. 35, 36, 37, 40, 43, 44, 48, 50, and 52, August 29–December 26, 1852, 281–84, 289–92, 297–300, 325–27, 353–56, 361–63, 401–4, 457–60, and 473–76.

66. For a detailed treatment of Fétis's larger project see Mary Arlin, "Metric Mutation and Modulation: The Nineteenth-Century Speculations of F.-J. Fétis," *Journal of Music Theory* 44, no. 2 (2000): 261–322.

67. "De grandes choses restent à découvrir sousce rapport dans l'art." Fétis, "Comparaison de l'état actuel de la musique avec celui des époques precedents," *Revue musicale* 14 (1834): 9–12, at 10.

68. Having perhaps arrived at a logical limit in the *ordre plurirhythmique*'s comingling of meters, Fétis did not describe an *ordre omnirhythmique* for rhythm. Fétis, "Du developpement futur de la musique: Dans le domaine de rhythme"; see Arlin, "Metric Mutation and Modulation," 269–86.

69. Cone, *Musical Form and Musical Performance*, 79.

that Weber and Momigny represent. These contemporary scholarly endeavors testify to our enduring concern with how we hear and interpret meter as listeners. This focal point of twenty-first century research on meter includes the study of our most basic cognitive mechanisms and our ability to hear some of the most complex temporal incommensurabilities. It has its foundations in the notion—set forth clearly in Kirnberger's theory—that meter is a mode of attending. Since the time of his writing we have been listening: attempting to understand how meter works as a mode of attending to music in the ongoing flow of time; attempting to understand meter as an aesthetic experience.

With Fétis's historical essay, the narrative that I have traced from the birth of print music theory to the age of the metronome finds its conclusion. Pronouncing the system of time measurement in music complete, Fétis stands at the opening to a long tradition of difficult questions concerning the nature of meter and our relationship to it. These concerns are familiar—hypermeter, grouping and accent, metric shifts and metric conflicts—but the set of intellectual conditions that created the possibility of their emergence is often overlooked and easy to misinterpret. The differences in the ways that musicians have come to know and experience meter are vast. These differences can inspire us to new ways of theorizing; they provide us with the ability to envision new methods for the investigation of music's temporal unfolding. If history provides any lesson here, we are not likely to be satisfied with our conceptualization of meter in the foreseeable future. But as we continue to ask questions about it we can at least attempt to better understand the intellectual legacies of our manners of inquiry. The elusive quality and experience of meter—a perpetual mystery—will continue to ask us to understand it even if we perpetually fail.[70] Meter, it turns out, will always have the last word.

---

70. Following Adorno, "We don't understand music—it understands us." As cited in Rolf Tiedmann, editor's preface to Theodor W. Adorno, *Beethoven: The Philosophy of Music*, ed. Tiedmann and trans. Edmund Jephcott (Stanford: Stanford University Press, 1998), xi.

APPENDIX 1

Representative Writings on the Beat from Gaffurius to Nassarre

Bibliographic data	Year	Geography	Institution/Tradition	Name for the beat	Explicit description as motion?	Explicit Aristotle citation?
Gaffurius, Franchinus. *Practica musice*	1496	Milan	Gaffurius was an important figure in Renaissance Italian music theory, having absorbed the teachings of many predecessors including Guido and De Muris. His practical text is rife with learned citations.	Mensura/mensuram	Yes	No
Wollick, Nicolaus. *Opus aureum*	1501. Later editions through 1509	Cologne	"Cologne School" of Music Theory. His diagram influences Ornithoparchus in particular.	Tactus	Yes	No
Wollick, Nicolaus. *Enchiridion musices.*	1509	Paris; Cologne	"Cologne School" of Music Theory. Cites Tinctoris in his discussion of *modus, tempus,* and *prolatio.*	Tempus and mensura	Yes	No

(Continued)

Bibliographic data	Year	Geography	Institution/Tradition	Name for the beat	Explicit description as motion?	Explicit Aristotle citation?
Quercu, Simon De. *Opusculum musices*	1509	Vienna	De Quercu's text resembles the early German "Cologne School" treatises, which were themselves precursors to the *Lateinschule* tradition. De Quercu was associated with the Imperial court in Vienna.	Tactus	Yes	No
Cochlaeus, Johannes. *Tetrachordum musices*	1511. Later editions 1512–26	Nuremberg	"Cologne School" of Music Theory: Glarean and Heyden were his students. Relied on the work of Wollick and Schanppecher though they are not cited.	Tactus	Yes	No
Koswick, Michael. *Compendiaria musicae artis aeditio*	1517	Leipzig	"Cologne school," though Koswick himself was not a Cologne theorist.	Tactus	Yes	No
Ornithoparchus, Anrdeas. *Musicae activae micrologus…liberis quatuor digestus*	1517 with many later editions	Leipzig	Textbook tradition and wide dissemination. This treatise was later translated by Dowland.	Tactus (tactu)	Yes	No
Agricola, Martin. *Musica figuralis deudsch*	1532	Wittenberg	A contemporary of the German *Lateinschule* theorists, Agricola's treatises are much more substantive than those that are strictly within this tradition.	Schlag odder Tact	Yes	No
Lanfranco, Giovanni Maria. *Scintille di musica*	1533	Brescia	Lanfranco's is the first extensive treatise in the Italian vernacular.	Battuta	Yes	No

Author / Title	Date	Place	Notes			
Listenius, Nicolaus. *Musica…ab authore denuo recognita, multisque novis regulis et exemplis adacta*	1533 with many later editions	Wittenberg; Leipzig; Nuremberg	German *Lateinschule* tradition.	Tactus	No	No
Vanneo, Stephano. *Recanetum de musica aurea*	1533	Rome	Influenced by Pietro Aaron. The first edition of this work was Italian (1551), the second Latin.	Mensura	Yes	No
Milán, Luis. *El maestro*	1536	Valencia	Milán's volume is widely known because it contains the first printed vihuela music. It contains a short introduction that lays out basic musical rudiments.	Compas	Yes	No
Heyden, Sebald. *De arte canendi*	1540	Nuremberg	"Cologne School" of Music Theory: his teacher was Cochlaeus.	Tactus (tactu)	Yes	No
Aaron, Pietro. *Lucidario*	1545	Venice	The *Lucidario* is one of Aaron's more learned texts. He takes issue with other theorists including Gaffurius.	Misura, battuta	No	No
Glarean, Heinrich. *Dodecachordon.*	1547, with ca. 17 editions under other titles	Basel	A student of Cochleaus, Glarean cites Gaffurius frequently and reproduces his examples.	Tactu and Tactus	No. Instead, "measuring"	No
Picitono, Angelo da. *Fior angelico di musica*	1547	Venice	Picitono borrowed entire chapters of this treatise from Ornithoparchus.	M sura	Yes	No

(Continued)

Bibliographic data	Year	Geography	Institution/Tradition	Name for the beat	Explicit description as motion?	Explicit Aristotle citation?
Faber, Heinrich. *Compendiolum musicae pro incipientibus…*	1548, with 46 editions through 1617	Brunswick; Nuremburg; Leipzig	German *Lateinschule* tradition. Translated into German in 1605.	Tactibus	No	No
Bourgeois, Loys. *Le droict chemin de musique*	1550	Geneva	A Swiss *Lateinschule* treatise.	Tact	Yes	No
Martin, Claude. *Elementorum musices practicae pars prior*	1550	Paris	An early French treatise in the *practica* tradition.	Tactu	Yes	No
Coclico, Adrianus Petit. *Compendium musices*	1552	Nuremberg	Coclico, who was raised a Catholic and later became a protestant, disagreed with Lutheran doctrine.	Tactus	No	No
Lusitano, Vincenzo. *Introdutione facilissima*	1553	Rome	Lusitano was very concerned with the reception of Greek theory. His practical writings echo those of his Italian contemporaries.	Battuta	Yes	No
Vicentino, Nicola. *L'antica musica ridotta alla moderna prattica*	1555	Rome	A contemporary of Zarlino, very interested in a revitalization of ancient Greek musical traditions.	batter la misura	Yes	No
Bermudo, Juan. *Comiença el libro llamado declaraciõ de instrumẽtos musicales*	1555	Osuna	Bermudo successfully synthesized elements of the *practica* and *theorica* traditions.	Compas	Yes	No

Author. Title	Date	Place	Notes	Term		
Finck, Hermann. *Practica musica…*	1556 (2 editions)	Wittenberg	German *Lateinschule* tradition. Borrows from Faber and Listenius.	Tactus	Yes	No
Zarlino, Gioseffo. *Le istitutioni harmoniche*	1558	Venice	Famous for its strong synthesis of humanist thought and Scholastic teachings.	Battuta or tempo sonoro, which Augustine calls plauso	Yes	Yes
Salinas, Francisco. *De musica libri septem*	1577	Salamanca	Salinas's lengthy humanist text treats rhythm in an elaborate system of poetic feet.	Tempus, mentions plausus, mensura, and compás	Yes	No
Hoffmann, Eucharius. *Musica practicae Praecepta.*	1588 (original 1572)	Hamburg	German *Lateinschule* tradition. Hoffmann drew on Heyder and Faber.	Tactus	Yes	No
Tigrini, Orazio. *Il Compendio della Musica*	1588	Venice	Tigrini draws heavily on Zarlino (to whom the work is dedicated) and Vicentino.	Battuta	Yes	No
Schneegaß, Cyriacus. *Isagoges musicae*	1591	Erfurt	German *Lateinschule* tradition.	Tactus	Yes	No
Zacconi, Lodovico. *Prattica di musica*	1592 part 1 (Polo); 1596; 1622	Venice: Polo; Carampello; Vincenti	Zacconi's beautifully printed and lengthy treatises owe much to Zarlino's theories.	Tatto	Yes	No
Diruta, Girolamo. *Il transilvano*	1593	Venice	Diruta claims to have studied with Zarlino, Costanzo Porta, and Claudio Merulo.	bettere tasto (tatto)	Yes	No
Bona, Valerio. *Regole del Contraponto et Compositione*	1595	Casale	Bona owes much to Zarlino.	Battuta	Yes	No

(Continued)

Bibliographic data	Year	Geography	Institution/Tradition	Name for the beat	Explicit description as motion?	Explicit Aristotle citation?
Bathe, William. *A Briefe Introduction to the Skill of Song*	1596	London:	Early practical treatise in the English language. Bathe studied at Oxford.	Time	Yes	No
Puteanus, Erycius. *Modulata Pallas, sive septem discrimina vocum*	1599	Milan	Puteanus was a Dutch humanist.	Pallade	Yes	No
Calvisius, Sethus. *Exercitationes musicae duae*	1600	Leipzig	Calvisius, heavily influenced by Zarlino, attempted a historical account of music theory in this document.	Tactus	Yes	No
Banchieri, Adriano. *Cartella overo regole*	1601 with later editions	Venice	Banchieri was an Italian Benedictine monk.	Battuta	Yes	No
Burmeister, Joachim. *Musica…*	1601	Rostock	Studied and taught at Rostock University. He borrowed much from rhetorical theory.	Mensura and Tactus	Yes	No
Maillart, Pierre. *Les tons…*	1610	Tournai	Maillart, a Franco-Flemish musician, influenced later intellectuals such as Doni and Mersenne.	Touchment	Yes	No
Pisa, Agostino. *Breve dichiaratione della battuta musicale* and *Battuta della musica*	1611	Rome	Pisa was a Scholastic: a "doctor of canon and civil law."	Battuta	Yes	Many
Lippius, Johannes. *Synopsis Musicæ*	1612	Strasbourg	This work was mimicked by later authors such as Crüger, Baryphonus, and Alsted.	Tactum, Tactu	Yes	No

Author. Title	Date	Place	Description	Term		
Cerone, Pietro. *El melopeo y maestro*	1613	Naples	Cerone's treatise borrows heavily from Zarlino and Pontio.	Compas ò tiempo	Yes	No
Ravenscroft, Thomas. *A Briefe Discourse…*	1614	London	Cites many theorists including Ornithoparchus, Heyden, Glarean, and Morley.	Tact, Touch, or Time	Yes	No
Fludd, Robert. *Utriusque cosmi…*	1617–24	Oppenheim; Frankfurt am Main	Fludd's tome of neo-Platonic and Rosicrucian thought is an important testament to the persistence of older teachings in the seventeenth century.	Tactus Musicus	Yes	No
Praetorius, Michael. *Syntagma Musicum* III	1618 (vol. III: 1619)	Wolfenbüttel	Although he was a Lutheran church musician, Praetorius did not produce a German *Lateinschule* text. His three large books comprehensively document the state of performance in the early seventeenth century.	Tact, battuta, Schlag	Yes	No
Friderici, Daniel. *Musica figuralis*	1618 with later editions	Rostock	Although written in catechism form, Friderici's text responds to the recent stylistic changes of its day, advocating for performance practices sensitive to an interpretation of the text.	Tactus oder Schlag	Yes	No
Crivellati, Cesare. *Discorsi musicali*	1624	Viterbo	A doctor, Crivellati may have studied with Frescobaldi. His book borrows from Aaron, Zarlino, and others.	Battuta	Yes	No
Crüger, Johannes. *Synopsis musica*	1630	Berlin	Much indebted to Lippius.	Tactus	No	No

(Continued)

Bibliographic data	Year	Geography	Institution/Tradition	Name for the beat	Explicit description as motion?	Explicit Aristotle citation?
Alsted, Johann Heinrich. *Encyclopaedia septem tomis distincta*	1630	Herborn	Part of his encyclopedia. Heavily indebted to Lippius.	Tactus	No	No
Descartes, Rene. *Compendium musicae*	1650 (written 1618)	Utrecht	French philosopher and geometer. His *compendium* was written as a gift for Isaac Beekman.	Percussione, battuta	Yes	No
Kircher, Athanasius. *Musorgia universalis*	1650	Rome	A German Jesuit associated with the Collegio Romano, Kircher knew Zarlino's writings.	Many, including: Tactus, "mensura temporis"	Yes	No
Playford, John. *A Breefe Introduction to the Skill of Musick for Song and Violl*	1654	London	Playford was an important London publisher and teacher of music.	Times	Yes	No
De La Voye-Mignot. *Traité de musique*	1656 with later editions	Paris	This practical treatise was authored by a mathematician, De La Voye-Mignot (whose first name is not known). He was a member of the French scientific academy.	Mesure	Yes	No

Author and Title	Date	Place	Notes	Term		
Du [De] Cousu, Antoine. *La musique universelle, contenant toute la pratique et toute la théorie*	ca. 1658	Paris	Zarlino was an important model for Du Cousu.	Mesure and battuë	Yes	No
Simpson, Christopher. *A Compendium of Practical Musick…*	1667 and many later editions	London	English Jesuit. His *Compendium* was printed into the eighteenth century.	"Keeping Time"; time or measure	Yes	No
Penna, Lorenzo. *Li primi albori musicali*	1672	Bologna	Penna earned a doctorate in theology at Ferrara University. He was a member of the Accademia dei Risoluti and the Accademia dei Filaschisi in Bologna. This explains the Scholasticism of his treatise.	Battuta or tatto	Yes	Yes
Loulié, Étienne. *Éléments ou principes de musique…*	1696	Paris	Loulié was an important part of the regulatory moment at the end of the seventeenth century in France. One of his important goals was to make musical knowledge accessible to his readers.	Battement, Temps	Yes	No
Masson, Charles. *Nouveau traité des règles pour la composition de la musique*	1697 with later editions	Paris	The *Nouveau traité* was an important pedagogical text. Masson was the director of music at the Maison Professe of the Jesuits in Paris.	Mesure	Yes	No
Retzelius, Olaus. "Disputatio musica de tactu"	1698	Uppsala	The "Disputatio" was Retzelius's doctoral dissertation at the University of Uppsala, advised by Vallerius.	Tactus and Tactu	Yes	No

(Continued)

Bibliographic data	Year	Geography	Institution/Tradition	Name for the beat	Explicit description as motion?	Explicit Aristotle citation?
De Saint Lambert. *Les principes du clavecin*	1702	Paris	Saint Lambert's views resemble those of his countrymen Charles Masson and Étienne Loulié. His treatise was important for Rameau.	Mesure and batter la mesure	Yes	No
Tevo, Zaccaria. *Il musico testore*	1706	Venice	Tevo quotes the Scholastic phrase "Tempus est mensura motus" and refers the reader to Othmar Luscinius. He also refers to Pisa, Vanneo, Banchieri, and many other Italian authors.	Battuta	Yes	Yes
Nassarre, Pablo. *Escuela música según la práctica moderna*	1723–24	Saragossa (Spain)	A late example of Renaissance compositional theory. Nassarre cites Salinas as one of his authorities.	Compàs	Yes	Yes

Inventories of Meters from Bononcini to Momigny

Bibliographic data	Year	Meters listed	Classification scheme	Characters described	Musical examples
Bononcini, Giovanni Maria. *Musico prattico*	1673	19	Even and uneven; *maggiore* and *minore*‡	No	12
Penna, Lorenzo. *Li primi albori musicali*	1679 (2nd ed.)	10[1]	Even and uneven; *maggiore* and *minore*‡	No	33
Loulié, Étienne. *Éléments ou principes de musique*	1696	21	Two, three, four, six, nine, and twelve beats.	No	42; two for each meter: one with notes, one with rests.
Mattheson, Johann. *Das neu-eröffnete Orchestre*	1713	15	Even and uneven; simple (*simplice*), compounded (*compositam*); tripled (*mixtam*). Mattheson erroneously included the meter 12/24 (probably intended to be 24/16) in both treatises.	Yes	—

(Continued)

Bibliographic data	Year	Meters listed	Classification scheme	Characters described	Musical examples
Rameau, Jean-Philippe. *Traité de l'harmonie*	1722	37	Two, three, or four beats.*	No (Rameau does this elsewhere)	38
Maier, J. F. B. C. *Museum Musicum*	1732	12	Even and uneven	Yes	—
Mattheson, Johann. *Kleine General-Baß-Schule*	1735	15	Even and uneven; simple (*simplice*), compounded (*compositam*); tripled (*mixtam*). Mattheson erroneously included the meter 12/24 (probably intended to be 24/16 in both treatises.[2]	Yes	—
Montéclair, *Principes de musique*	1736	15	Two, three, or four beats; simple (*simple*); tripled (*composée*)*	No	34; additional examples serve as exercises.
Vion, Charles Antoine. *La musique pratique et theorique*	1742	17	Two, three, or four beats	Yes	70; Vion supplies multiple stylistic examples for each meter. These examples are drawn from actual compositions.
Marpurg, F. W. *Der Kritische Musicus and der Spree* (March 25–April 1, 1749)	1749–50	41[†]	Even and uneven; simple (*einfach*); tripled (*zusammengesetzt*). NB tripled here goes by the term *zusammengesetzt*.	No	12 (at the back in a plate)

Quantz, Johann Joachim. *Versuch einer Anweisung, die Flöte traversiere zu spielen*	1752	10	Even and uneven	Only for *alla breve/alla cappella*	Not for meter signatures
Riepel, Joseph. *Anfangsgründe zur musicalischen Setzkunst (I. De rhythmopoeïa)*	1752	8 (useful); 16 (total)†	Although his examples would suggest his endorsement of compounded measures, some of his statements would seem to contradict this position (as, for example, in vol. 1, 25).	No	More than 100 interspersed through the discussion.
Marpurg, F. W. *Anleitung zum Clavierspielen*	1755	13 (useful); 56 (total)†	Even and uneven; simple (*einfach*); tripled (*zusammengesetzt*). NB tripled here goes by the term *zusammengesetzt*.	Minimally	18
Tans'ur, William. *A New Musical Grammar*	1756	12	Two and three beats; simple ("Vocal Moods"); tripled ("Instrumental Moods")	Only for some	12
Marpurg, F. W. *Kritische Briefe über die Tonkunst* (September 15, September 22, October 6, 1759; July 4–12, 1761)	1759; 1761	16 (useful); 34 (total)†	Even and uneven; simple (*einfach*); compounded (*zusammengesetzt*); tripled (*vermischt*)	For some meters, and especially in relation to musical dance types (July 4–12, 1761)	Refers the reader to musical examples without reproducing them
Marpurg, F. W. *Anleitung zur Musik überhaupt, und zur Singkunst besonders*	1763	12	Simple (*einfach*); compounded (*zusammengesetzt*); tripled (*dreygliedrige*)	Yes	—

(Continued)

Bibliographic data	Year	Meters listed	Classification scheme	Characters described	Musical examples
Rousseau, Jean-Jacques. "Mesure," in the *Encyclopédie*, ed. Diderot and D'Alembert (vol. 10)	1765	16	For Rousseau, the designation *simple* indicated that the meter signature was composed of only one numeral or sign (2, 3, ₵, or C) and *double* indicated signatures with two numerals (e.g., 2/4).	Not explicitly	16 (one for each meter; in the plates volume)
Lacassagne, Joseph. *Traité général des élémens du chant*	1766	14	Two, three, and four beats; simple (*simple*), tripled (*composée*)*	No	158 (many short variations for each meter)
Rousseau, Jean-Jacques. *Dictionnaire de musique*	1768	16	For Rousseau, the designation *simple* indicated that the meter signature was composed of only one numeral or sign (2, 3, ₵, or C) and *double* indicated signatures with two numerals (e.g., 2/4).	Not explicitly	16 (one for each meter)
Mozart, Leopold. *Gründliche Violinschule*	1770 (2nd ed.)	10 (useful); 17 (total)†	Even and uneven.	No	—
Bemetzrieder, Anton. *Leçons de clavecin et principes d'harmonie*	1771	14	Two, three, and four beats	No	—
Schulz, J. A. P. "Takt," in *Allgemeine Theorie der schönen Kunst*, ed. J. G. Sulzer	1771–74	23 (useful); 27 (total)†	Even and uneven; simple (*einfach*); compounded (*zusammengesetzt*); tripled (*vermischt*)	Yes	3

Author / Title	Year	(useful/total)		Meters	
Scheibe, Johann Adolph. *Ueber die Musikalische Composition*	1773	11 (useful); 23 (total)†	Yes	Even and uneven; simple (*einfach*); compounded and tripled (*zusammengesetzt*); NB under the heading of *zusammengesetzt* Scheibe describes both the tripled conception of meters and also the compounded.	7
Eximeno, Antonio. *Dell'origine e delle regole della musica*	1774	10	No	Two and three beats	9 (at the back in a plate)
Manfredi, Vincenzo. *Regole armoniche*	1775	8 (useful); 12 (total)	No	Two, three, and four beats.	8
Kirnberger, Johann Philipp. *Die Kunst des reinen Satzes in der Musik*	1776–79	24 (useful); 34 (total)†	Yes	Even and uneven; simple (*einfach*); compounded (*zusammengesetzt*); tripled (*vermischt*)	58 (including 15 in one large composite example).
Koch, *Versuch einer Anleitung zur Composition*	1782–93	13	Yes	Even and uneven; simple (*einfach*); compounded (*zusammengesetzt*) tripled (*vermischt*)	50 (though these are used in a more demonstrative manner than in the treatises of his contemporaries)
Sabbatini, Luigi Antoni. *Elementi teorici della musica*	1789	11	No	*maggiore* and *minore*‡	14 canons with didactic texts.
Türk, Daniel Gottlob. *Klavierschule*	1789	31	No	Even and uneven; simple (*einfach*); compounded (*zusammengesetzt*); tripled (*triplirten, dreygliedrigen*)	22

(Continued)

Bibliographic data	Year	Meters listed	Classification scheme	Characters described	Musical examples
Galeazzi, Francesco. *Elementi teorico-pratici di musica*	1791–96	11	*maggiore* and *minore*; two, three, and four beats[‡]	No	12 (at the back in a plate)
Kollman, Augustus Frederic Christopher. *An Essay on Musical Harmony*	1796	35 (useful); 44 (total)[†]	Even and uneven; simple (*einfach*); compounded (*zusammengesetzt*); tripled (*vermischt*). Kollman also includes the option that the compounded measures may, themselves, be tripled.	Only for some	19 (for meter; in a plate at the back)
Gervasoni, Carlo. *La scuola della musica*	1800	16	Even and uneven; *maggiore* and *minore*[‡]	Yes	10 (at the back in a plate)
Conservatoire. *Principes élémentaires...*[3]	1800	20	Two, three, and four beats; simple (*simple*), tripled (*composée*)	No	30
Thiémé, Frédéric. *Nouvelle théorie sur les différens mouvemens des airs*	1801	23	For Thiémé (as for Rousseau), the designation *simple* indicated that the meter signature was composed of only one numeral or sign (2, 3, ₵, or C) and *double* indicated signatures with two numerals (e.g., 2/4). Thiémé also includes terms for tripled meters. Tripled meters of two beats: *triples mixtes ou binaire*; tripled meters of three beats: *triples composées ou doubles triples*; and tripled meters of four beats: *triples dosduples ou à quatre temps.*	Only tempi	23 (one for each at the back in a plate)
Koch, *Musikalisches Lexikon*	1802	13	Even and uneven; simple (*einfach*), compounded (*zusammengesetzt*), tripled (*vermischt*)	No	25

Koch, *Kurzgefaßtes Handwörterbuch der Musik*	1807	13	Even and uneven; simple (*einfach*), compounded (*zusammengesetzt*), tripled (*vermischt*)	No	—
Finke, G. W. "Ueber Takt, Taktarten, und ihr Charakteristisches"[4]	1808–9	18	Even and uneven; simple (*einfach*) and compounded (*zusammengesetzt*)	Yes	—
Momigny, Jérôme-Joseph de, in *Encylopédie méthodique…: Musique*, ed. Nicolas-Étienne Framery, Pierre-Louis Ginguené, and Momigny	1818	29	Simple (*simple*), compounded (*double*) and tripled (*ternaires*)[5]	No	25 (within the discussion of meter signatures)
Momigny, Jérôme-Joseph de. *La seule vraie théorie de la musique*	1821	16	Two, three, and four beats	No	52

---

* These texts also include a simplification scheme.

† Includes meters marked as unusable or out of use.

‡ A general note on Italian treatises: these treatises distinguish between *maggiore* and *minore*, which usually indicate degrees of tempo or the length of the beat's duration (as, for example, in Galeazzi's *Elementi teorico-pratici di musica* (Rome: Stamperia Pilucchi Cracas, 1791–6), 34–35). Italians do not seem to be concerned with compounded measures or tripled meters as distinctions. However, these documents describe meters such as 6/4, 6/8, 9/8, and 12/8 that very much resemble the tripled meters of other theorists. A good example is found in F. Luigi Antoni Sabbatini, in his *Elementi teorici della musica* (Rome: Pilucchi Cracas e Giuseppe Rotilj, 1789), 13–17.

1. These include 5/2 and 7/2 which are described as kinds of triples[!]. See Penna, *Li primi albori musicali*, facsimile edition (1684; Bologna: Forni, 1969), 36–37.

2. It should be noted here that Mattheson's celebrated *Der vollkommene Capellmeister* refers readers back to *Das neu-eröffnete Orchestre* and *Kleine General-Baß-Schule* on issues of meter.

3. *Principes élémentaires de musique arrêtés par les Membres du Conservatoire, pour servir à l'étude*, ed. Agus, Catel, Chérubini, Gossec, Langlé, Lesueur, Méhul, and Rigel (Paris: A l'imprimerie du Conservatoire de Musique, Paubourg Poissonniere, 1800), vol. 1.

4. G. W. Finke, "Ueber Takt, Taktarten, und ihr Charakteristisches," Leipzig *AmZ* 11, nos. 13–15, December 28, 1808–January 11, 1809, col. 193–98, 209–18, and 225–31.

5. Momigny's discussion is appended to a reproduction of Rousseau's article for his dictionary; in addition to classifying the meter signatures, Momigny puts forth an anacrustic model of meter that anticipates Riemann's theory.

BIBLIOGRAPHY

Aarslett, Hans. "The Berlin Academy under Frederick the Great." *History of the Human Sciences* 2, no. 2 (1989): 193–206.

Abrams, M. H. *The Mirror and the Lamp*. Oxford: Oxford Unviersity Press, 1953.

Ackermann, Peter. "Die Werke Palestrinas im Repertoire de Cappella Sistina." In *Collectanea II. Studien zur Geschichte der päpstlichen Kapelle. Tagungsbericht Heidelbert 1989*, edited by Bernhard Janz, 405–30. Vatican City: Biblioteca Apostolicae Vaticana, 1994.

Ackrill, J. L., trans. and ed. *Aristotle, Categories and de Interpretatione*. Oxford: Clarendon, 1963.

Adams, Francis, trans. *The Seven Books of Paulus Aegineta*. 3 vols. London: The Sydenham Society, 1846.

Adler, Ken. "A Revolution to Measure: The Political Economy of the Metric System in France." In *The Values of Precision*, edited by M. Norton Wise, 39–71. Princeton: Princeton University Press, 1995.

Adorno, Theodor W. *Beethoven: The Philosophy of Music*. Edited by Rolf Tiedmann. Translated by Edmund Jephcott. Stanford: Stanford University Press, 1998.

Agamben, Giorgio. "What Is an Apparatus." In *What Is an Apparatus and Other Essays*, 1–24. Translated by David Kishik and Stefan Pedatella. Stanford: Stanford University Press, 2009.

Agricola, Martin. *Musica figuralis deudsch*. Wittenberg: G. Rhaw, 1532. Facsimile edition, Hildesheim: Georg Olms, 1969.

Albrechtsberger, Johann Georg. *Gründliche Anweisung zur Composition*. Leipzig: Johann Gottlob Immanuel Brietkopf, 1790.

Aldrich, Putnam. *Rhythm in Seventeenth-Century Italian Monody*. London: J. M. Dent, 1966.

Alexander, Henry Gavin, ed. *The Leibniz-Clarke Correspondence*. Manchester: Manchester University Press, 1956.

Allanbrook, Wye J. *Rhythmic Gesture in Mozart*. Chicago: University of Chicago Press, 1983.

Anawati, G. C., and Albert Z. Iskandar. "Ibn Sīnā, Abū cAlī Al-Husayn Ibn cAbdallāh, also known as Avicenna." In *Complete Dictionary of Scientific Biography*. Detroit: Charles Scribner's Sons, 2008. Online edition, *Gale Virtual Reference Library*. Accessed January 28, 2011. <http://www.gale.cengage.com>.

Apel, Willi. *The Notation of Polyphonic Music: 900-1600*. 5th ed. (revised). Cambridge, MA: The Medieval Academy of America, 1961.

Arbeau, Thoinot. *Orchésographie*. Langres: Jehan des Preyz, 1589.

Arlin, Mary. "Metric Mutation and Modulation: The Nineteenth-Century Speculations of F.-J. Fétis." *Journal of Music Theory* 44, no. 2 (2000): 261–322.

Arthur, Richard T. W. "Newton's Fluxions and Equably Flowing Time." *Studies in the History and Philosophy of Science* 26, no. 2 (1995): 323–51.

Attali, Jacques. *Histoires du temps*. Paris: Fayard, 1982.

Auda, Antoine. *Théorie et pratique du tactus: Transcription et exécution de la musique antérieure aux environs de 1650*. Brussels: Woluwé St. Lambert, 1965.

Avicenna. *Liber canonis*. Venetiis: Apvd Ivntas, 1582.

Bach, Johann Sebastian. *Vingt-quatre preludes et fugues dans tous les tons et demi-tons du mode majeur et mineur pour le clavecin ou piano-forte*. Paris: Richault, 1828.

Baker, Nancy K., and Thomas Christensen, eds. and trans. *Aesthetics and the Art of Musical Composition in the German Enlightenment*. Cambridge: Cambridge University Press, 1995.

Banchieri, Adriano. *Cartella musicale*. Venice: Giacomo Vincenti, 1610.

——. *La Banchierina*. Venice: Alessandro Vincenti, 1623.

Bank, J. A. *Tactus, Tempo and Notation in Mensural Music from the Thirteenth to the Seventeenth Century*. Amsterdam: Annie Bank, Anna Vondelstraat 13, 1972.

Bathe, William. *A Briefe Introduction to the Skill of Song*. London: Thomas Este, ca. 1587. Facsimile edition, edited by Bernarr Rainbow. Kilkenny, Ireland: Boethius Press, 1982.

Batteux, Charles. *Les beaux-arts réduits à un même principe*. Paris: Durand, 1747.

Battista (Padre) Martini, Giovanni. *Esemplare o sia saggio fondamentale pratico di contrapunto sopra il canto fermo*. Bologna: Lelio dalla Volpe, 1774–75.

Baumgarten, Alexander Gottlieb. *Meditationes philosophicae de nonnullis ad poema pertinentibus*. Halle: Grunert, 1735. Modern edition, edited by Benedetto Croce. Naples: Vecchi, 1900.

Beach, David. "The Harmonic Theories of Johann Philipp Kirnberger: Their Origins and Influences." PhD diss., Yale University, 1974.

Beck, Lewis White. *Early German Philosophy*. Cambridge: Harvard University Press, 1969.

Beethoven, Ludwig van. *Letters*. Edited and translated by Emily Anderson. 3 vols. New York: St Martin's, 1961.

Beethoven, Ludwig van, and Antonio Salieri. "Erklärung." Vienna *AmZ* 2, no. 7, February 14, 1818, col. 58–59.

Bemetzrieder, Anton. *Leçons de clavecin et principes d'harmonie*. Paris: Chez Bluet, Libraire, Pont Saint-Michel, 1771. Facsimile edition, New York: Broude Brothers, 1966.

Bent, Ian, Margaret Bent, Geoffrey Chew, David Hiley, David W. Hughes, Thomas B. Payne, Robert C. Provine, Richard Rastall, and Janka Szendrei, with Anne Kilmer. "Notation." In *Oxford Music Online*, edited by Laura Macy. Accessed August 21, 2009. <http://www.oxfordmusiconline.com>.

——. "*Steps to Parnassus*: Contrapuntal Theory in 1725: Precursors and Successors." In *The Cambridge History of Western Music Theory*, edited by Thomas Christensen, 554–602. Cambridge: Cambridge University Press, 2002.

Berlioz, Hector. "Euphonia." *Berlioz's Orchestration Treatise: A Translation and Commentary*. Translated by Hugh Macdonald. Cambridge: Cambridge University Press, 2002.

Berryman, Sylvia. "Ancient Atomism." In *The Stanford Encyclopedia of Philosophy*, edited by Edward N. Zalta. Stanford University, 1997–. Article published Fall 2008. <http://plato.stanford.edu/archives/fall2008/entries/atomism-ancient/>.

Bessel, Friedrich Wilhelm. *Untersuchungen über die Länge des einfachen Secundenpendels.* Berlin: Kgl. Akademie der Wissenschaften, 1828.

Bianchi, Luca. "Continuity and Change in the Aristotelian Tradition." In *The Cambridge Companion to Renaissance Philosophy*, edited by James Hankins, 49–71. Cambridge: Cambridge University Press, 2007.

Blachly, Alexander. "*Mensura* versus *Tactus.*" In *Quellen und Studien zur Musiktheorie des Mittelalters III*, edited by Michael Bernhard, 425–67. München: Bayerischen Akademie der Wissenshaften, 2001.

——. "Mensuration and Tempo in 15th-Century Music." PhD diss., Columbia University, 1995.

Blechschmidt, Eva Renate (Eva Renate Wutta). *Die Amalien-Bibliothek.* Berlin: Merseburger, 1965.

——. *Quellen der Bach-Tradition in der Berliner Amalien-Bibliothek.* Tutzing: H. Schneider, 1989.

Blum, Paul Richard. "Der Standardkursus der katholischen Schulphilosophie im 17. Jahrhundert." In *Aristotelismus und Renaissance: In memoriam Charles B. Schmitt* edited by Eckhard Keßler, Charles H. Lohr and Walter Sparn, 141–48. Wiesbaden: Otto Harrassowitz, 1988.

Bockmaier, Claus. *Die instrumentale Gestalt des Taktes.* Tutzing: Hans Schneider, 2001.

Bonge, Dale. "Gaffurius on Pulse and Tempo: A Reinterpretation." *Musica Disciplina* 36 (1982): 167–74.

Bononcini, Giovanni Maria. *Musico prattico.* Bologna: Giacomo Monti, 1673. Facsimile edition, Hildesheim: Georg Olms, 1969.

Bonus, Alexander Evan. "The Metronomic Performance Practice: A History of Rhythm, Metronomes, and the Mechanization of Musicality." PhD diss., Case Western Reserve University, 2010.

Boone, Graeme M. "Marking Mensural Time." *Music Theory Spectrum* 22, no. 1 (2000): 1–43.

Bowen, José Antonio. "The Rise of Conducting." In *The Cambridge Companion to Conducting*, edited by Bowen, 93–113. Cambridge: Cambridge University Press, 2003.

Boyer, Carl B. *The History of the Calculus and Its Conceptual Development.* New York: Dover, 1949.

Breidenstein, Helmut. *Mozarts Tempo-System.* Tutzing: Hans Schneider, 2011.

Brewster, David, ed. and trans., with additional notes by John Griscom. *Letters of Euler on Different Subjects in Natural Philosophy Addressed to A German Princess.* New York: Harper Brothers, 1846.

Brossard, Sébastien de. *Dictionnaire de musique.* Paris: Ballard, 1703.

Brown, A. Peter. "Eighteenth-Century Traditions and Mozart's 'Jupiter' Symphony K.551." *The Journal of Musicology* 20, no. 2 (2003): 157–95.

Brown, Clive. "Historical Performance, Metronome Marks and Tempo in Beethoven's Symphonies." *Early Music* 19 (1991): 247–58.

——. *Classical and Romantic Performing Practice: 1750-1900.* Oxford: Oxford University Press, 1999.

Burgess, J. Peter. "European Borders: History of Space/Space of History." *CTheory*, article a013 (1994). Accessed November 30, 2011. <http://www.ctheory.net/articles.aspx?id=55>.

Bürja, Abel. *Beschreibung eines musikalischen Zeitmessers.* Berlin: Petit und Schöne, 1790.

Burke, Peter. *The French Historical Revolution: The Annales School, 1929-89.* Cambridge: Polity Press, 1990.

Burney, Charles, ed. *La musica che si canta annualmente nelle Funzioni della Settimana Santa nella Cappella Pontificale.* London: R. Bremner, 1771.

Busse Berger, Anna Maria. *Mensuration and Proportion Signs.* Oxford: Clarendon Press, 1993.

Butt, John. *Music Education and the Art of Performance in the German Baroque.* Cambridge: Cambridge University Press, 1994.

Canales, Jimena. *A Tenth of a Second: A History.* Chicago: University of Chicago Press, 2009.

Čapek, Milič. "The Conflict between the Absolutist and the Relational Theory of Time Before Newton." *Journal of the History of Ideas* 48, no. 4 (1987): 595–608.

Caplin, William. "Theories of Musical Rhythm in the Eighteenth and Nineteenth Centuries." In *The Cambridge History of Western Music Theory*, edited by Thomas Christensen, 657–94. Cambridge: Cambridge University Press, 2002.

Carvalho, Mario S. de. "Time According to the Coimbra Commentaries." In *The Medieval Concept of Time*, edited by Pasquale Porro, 353–82. Leiden: Brill, 2001.

Castilhon, Jean-Louis. "Alla breve." In *Encylopédie méthodique…: Musique.* Edited by Nicolas-Étienne Framery, Pierre-Louis Ginguené, and Jérôme-Joseph de Momigny, volume 1. Paris: Panckoucke, 1791.

——. "Alla Capella." In *Encylopédie méthodique…: Musique.* Edited by Nicolas-Étienne Framery, Pierre-Louis Ginguené, and Jérôme-Joseph de Momigny, volume 1. Paris: Panckoucke, 1791.

Castle, Terry. *The Female Thermometer.* New York: Oxford University Press, 1995.

Chartier, Roger. *The Order of Books: Readers, Authors, and Libraries in Europe between the Fourteenth and Eighteenth Centuries.* Translated by Lydia G. Cochrane. Stanford: Stanford University Press, 1992.

Chen, Jen-Yen. "Catholic Sacred Music in Austria." In *The Cambridge History of Eighteenth-Century Music*, edited by Simon P. Keefe, 59–112. Cambridge: Cambridge University Press, 2009.

——. "Palestrina and the Influence of 'Old' Style in Eighteenth-Century Vienna." *Journal of Musicological Research* 22, nos. 1–2 (2003): 1–44.

Chua, Daniel. "Vincenzo Galilei, Modernity, and the Division of Nature." In *Music Theory and Natural Order*, edited by Suzannah Clark and Alexander Rehding, 17–29. Cambridge: Cambridge University Press, 1993.

Clough, John, and Jack Douthett. "Maximally Even Sets." *Journal of Music Theory* 35, nos. 1–2 (1991): 93–173.

Cochlaeus, Johannes. *Tetrachordum musices.* Nuremberg: Johann Weyssenburger, 1511.

Cohn, Richard. "Complex Hemiolas, Ski-Hill Graphs, and Metric Spaces." *Music Analysis* 20, no. 3 (2001): 295–326.

——. "The Dramatization of Hypermetric Conflicts in the Scherzo of Beethoven's Ninth Symphony." *Nineteenth-Century Music* 15, no. 3 (1992): 188–206.

Collins, Michael. "The Performance of Coloration, Sesquialtera, and Hemiola (1450-1750)." PhD diss., Stanford University, 1963.

——. "The Performance of Sesquialtera and Hemiolia in the 16th Century." *Journal of the American Musicological Society* 17, no. 1 (1964): 5–28.

Commentarii Collegii Conimbricensis e Societate Jesu in octo libros Physicorum Aristotelis Stagiritae. Lyon: Ioannis Baptistae Buysson, 1594. Facsimile edition, Hildesheim: Georg Olms, 1984.

Condillac, Etienne Bonnot de. *La langue des calculs* in *Œuvres Philosophiques de Condillac.* Edited by Georges le Roy. 3 vols. Paris: Presses Universitaires de France, 1948.

Cone, Edward T. *Musical Form and Musical Performance.* New York: Norton, 1968.

Coope, Ursula. *Time for Aristotle*. Oxford: Clarendon Press, 2005

Corwin, Lucille. "*Le istitutioni harmoniche* of Gioseffo Zarlino, Part 1: A Translation with Introduction." PhD diss., The City University of New York, 2008.

Crooke, Helkiah. *Microcosmographia: A Description of the Body of Man* . . . London: William Iaggard, 1615.

Currie, James. "Disagreeable Pleasures: Negotiating Fugal Counterpoint in Classical Instrumental Music." PhD diss., Columbia University, 2001.

Cusick, Suzanne. "Nachtanz." In *Oxford Music Online*, edited by Laura Macy. Accessed August 25, 2009. <http://www.oxfordmusiconline.com>.

Dahlhaus, Carl. *Ludwig van Beethoven: Approaches to His Music*. Translated by Mary Whittall. Oxford: Clarendon Press, 1991.

——. *Die Musiktheorie im 18. und 19. Jahrhundert*. 2 vols. Darmstadt: Wissenschaftliche Buchgesellschaft, 1984–89.

——. *Die Musiktheorie im 18. und 19. Jahrhundert. Zweiter Teil: Deutschland*. Geschichte der Musiktheorie 6. Edited by Ruth E. Müller. Darmstadt: Wissenschaftliche Buchgesellschaft, 1989.

——. "Die Tactus- und Proportionenlehre des 15. bis 17 Jahrhunderts." In *Horen, Messen und Rechnen in der frühen Neuzeit*, edited by Frieder Zaminer, 333–61. Geschichte der Musiktheorie 6. Darmstadt: Wissenschafliche Buchgesellschaft, 1987.

——. "Zur Geschichte des Taktschlagen im frühen 17. Jahrhundert." In *Studies in Renaissance and Baroque Music in Honor of Arthur Mendel*, edited by Robert L. Marshall, 117–23. Kassel: Bärenreiter, 1974.

——. "Zur Rhythmic und Metrik um 1600." In *Studien zur Theorie und Geschichte der musikalischen Rhythmic und Metrik*, edited by Ernst Apfel and Carl Dahlhaus, 1:273–90. Munich: Emil Katzbichler, 1974.

Daston, Lorraine, and Peter Galison. *Objectivity*. New York: Zone Books, 2007.

Davaux, Jean-Baptiste. "Lettre de M. Davaux, aux Auteurs du Journal." *Journal de Paris* 129, May 8, 1784, 559–61.

Day, Thomas. "A Renaissance Revival in the Eighteenth Century." *Musical Quarterly* 57 (1971): 575–92.

de Man, Paul. "Kant and Schiller." In *Aesthetic Ideology*, edited and introduction by Andrzej Warminski, 129–62. Minneapolis: University of Minnesota Press, 1996.

Debuch, Tobias. *Anna Amalia von Preußen*. Berlin: Logos, 2001.

DeFord, Ruth I. "The Evolution of Rhythmic Style in Italian Secular Music of the Late Sixteenth Century." *Studi musicali* 10, no. 1 (1981): 43–74.

——. "Tempo Relationships between Duple and Triple Time in the Sixteenth Century." *Early Music History* 14 (1995): 1–51.

——. "Zacconi's Theories of *Tactus* and Mensuration." *Journal of Musicology* 14, no. 2 (1996): 151–82.

Derrida, Jacques. *The Archeology of the Frivolous*. Translated by John P. Leavy, Jr. Lincoln, NE: University of Nebraska Press, 1987.

Des Chene, Dennis. *Physiologia: Natural Philosophy in Late Aristotelian and Cartesian Thought*. Ithaca: Cornell University Press, 1996.

Descartes, René. *Œuvres de Descartes*. Edited by Charles Adam and Paul Tannery. 11 vols. Revised edition, Paris: Vrin/CNRS, 1964–76.

——. *Principles of Philosophy*. Translated by Valentine Rodger Miller and Reese P. Miller. Dordrecht: Reidel, 1983.

Diderot, Denis, and Jean le Rond d'Alembert, eds. *Encylopédie ou dictionnaire raisonné* . . . 17 vols. Paris: Briasson et Le Breton, 1751–65.

Diderot, Denis. "Projet d'un nouvel Orgue." [1748.] In *Mémoires sur différens sujets de mathématiques* in *Œuvres philosophiques et dramatiques de M. Diderot*, vol. 16. Amsterdam, 1772.

Duns Scoti, Johannis. "In octo libros physicorum Aristotelis." In *Opera Omnia*, 3:1–470. Paris: Apud Ludovicum Vivès, 1891.

Dürr, Walther. "Auftakt und Taktschlag in der Musik um 1600." In *Festschrift Walter Gerstenberg zum 60*, edited by Georg von Dadelsen and Andreas Holschneider, 26–36. Wolfenbüttel: Möseler, 1964.

Earman, John. *World Enough and Space-Time*. Cambridge: MIT Press, 1989.

Eco, Umberto. *The Infinity of Lists from Homer to Joyce*. Translated by Alastair McEwen. London: MacLehose, 2009.

Euler, Leonhard. "Réflexions sur l'espace et le tems." In *Histoire de l'Académie Royale des Sciences et des Belles-Lettres de Berlin 1748*, 324–33. Berlin: Haude et Spener, 1750.

Eustachius a Sancto Paulo. *Summa philosophiae quadripartite*. Leiden: Franciscum Moyardum, 1647.

Eximeno y Pujaver, Antonio. *Delle origini e delle regole della musica colla storia del suo progresso, decadenza, e rinnovazione*. Rome: Michel'Angelo Barbiellini, 1774.

Fallows, David. "Metronome (i)." In *Oxford Music Online*, edited by Laura Macy. Accessed December 4, 2011. <http://www.oxfordmusiconline.com>.

——. "Tempo and Expression Marks." In *Oxford Music Online*, edited by Laura Macy. Accessed November 27, 2011. <http://www.oxfordmusiconline.com>.

——. "Tempo Giusto." In *Oxford Music Online*, edited by Laura Macy. Accessed November 27, 2011. <http://www.oxfordmusiconline.com>.

Febvre, Lucien. *Le Problème de l'incroyance au XVIe siècle: la religion de Rabelais*. Paris: Albin Michel, 1942. Translated by Beatrice Gottlieb as *The Problem of Unbelief in the Sixteenth Century, The Religion of Rabelais*. Cambridge, MA: Harvard University Press, 1982.

——. "Réflexions sur l'histoire des techniques." *Annales d'histoire économique et sociale* 7, no. 36 (November 30, 1935): 531–35.

Fellerer, Karl Gustav. *Der Palestrinastil und seine Bedeutung in der vokalen Kirchenmusik des achtzehnten Jahrhunderts: Ein Beirag zur Geschichte der Kirchenmusik in Italien und Deutschland*. Augsburg: Dr. Benno Filser, 1929. Reprint edition, Walluf bein Wiesbaden: Sändig, 1972.

Fétis, François-Joseph. "Comparaison de l'état actuel de la musique avec celui des époques precedents." *Revue musicale* 14 (1834): 9–12.

——. "Cours de philosophie musicale de l'histoire de la musique." *Revue musicale* 6, nos. 17, 18, 20, 21, 22, 23, and 24, May 26–July 14, 1832, 131–33, 139–41, 155–58, 161–64, 169–71, 177–79, and 184–87.

——. "Du developpement futur de la musique: Dans le domaine de rhythme." *Revue et Gazette musicale de Paris* 19, nos. 35, 36, 37, 40, 43, 44, 48, 50, and 52, August 29–December 26, 1852, 281–84, 289–92, 297–300, 325–27, 353–56, 361–63, 401–4, 457–60, and 473–76.

——. "De la mesure en musique." *Revue musicale* 8, no. 5, February 2, 1834, 33–35.

——. "Sur le métronome de Maelzel." *Revue Musicale* 1, vol. 2, no. 25, August 1827.

——. "Du temps et de sa mesure dans la musique." *Revue musicale* 11, Vᵐᵉ Année no. 9, April 2, 1831.

Finazzi, Giovanni. "Nuovo stromento per battere la musica, chiamato plessimetro, *del medico Finazzi*." In *Propagatore ossia raccolta periodica delle cose appartenenti ai progressi*, 3:387–95. Torino: Alliana e Paravia, 1824–28.

Fludd, Robert. "Utriusque cosmi maioris scilicet et minoris metaphysica." *Physica atque Technica Historia*. 2 vols. Oppenheim and Frankfurt: Johann Theodor de Bry, 1617–21.

Forkel, Johann Nikolaus. *Allgemeine Geschichte der Musik*. 2 vols. Leipzig: Schwickertschen Verlage, 1788. Facsimile edition, Laaber: Laaber-Verlag, 2005.

Foucault, Michel. *The Archaeology of Knowledge*. Translated by A. M. Sheridan Smith. New York: Pantheon Books, 1972.

——. *The Order of Things*. New York: Pantheon Books, 1970. Reprint edition, New York: Vintage, 1973.

Framery, Nicolas-Étienne. "Chronomètre." In *Encylopédie méthodique…: Musique*. Edited by Nicolas-Étienne Framery, Pierre-Louis Ginguené, and Jérôme-Joseph de Momigny, volume 1. Paris: Panckoucke, 1791.

Freud, Sigmund. "The Uncanny." In *Studies in Parapsychology*, 19–60. Edited by Philip Reiff. Translated by Alix Strachey. New York: Collier, 1963.

Friderici, Daniel. *Musica figuralis*. 1618. 5th edition, Rostock, 1638. Facsimile edition in *Deutsche Gesangstraktate des 17. Jahrhunderts*, edited by Florian Grampp. Kassel: Bärenreiter, 2006.

Frobenius, Wolf. "Tactus." In *Handwörterbuch der musikalischen Terminologie*, edited by Hans Heinrich Eggebrecht, 6:1–11. Wiesbaden: Franz Steiner, 1972–2005 [1971].

Fux, Johann Joseph. *Gradus ad Parnassum*. Vienna: Johann Peter van Ghelen, 1725.

Galeazzi, Francesco. *Elementi teorico-pratici di musica*. 2 vols. Rome: Pilucchi Cracas, 1791.

Galen. *De l'usage des parties du corps humain*. Translated and edited by Jacques Dalechamps. Lyon: Guillaume Rouillé, 1566.

Galkin, Elliott Washington. "The Theory and Practice of Orchestral Conducting since 1752." PhD diss., Cornell University, 1960.

Georgiades, Thrsybulos G. "Aus der Musiksprache des Mozart Theaters." In *Mozart-Jahrbuch 1950*. Reprinted in *Kleine Schriften*, edited by Theodor Göllner, 9–32. Tutzing: Hans Schneider, 1977.

——. *Nennen und Erklingen*. Göttingen: Vandenhoeck and Ruprecht, 1985.

——. "Zur Musiksprache der Wiener Klassiker." In *Mozart-Jahrbuch 1951*. Reprinted in *Kleine Schriften*, edited by Theodor Göllner, 33–43. Tutzing: Hans Schneider, 1977.

Gervasoni, Carlo. *La scuola della musica*. 2 vols. Piacenza: Niccolò Orcesi, 1800. Facsimile edition, Bologna: Forni, 1969.

Geslin, Philippe de. *Cours analytiques de musique*. Paris: Chez l'auteur, rue Grenelle-Saint-Honoré, no. 37, 1825.

Geyer, Martin H. "One Language for the World: The Metric System, International Coinage, the Gold Standard, and the Rise of Internationalism, 1850-1900." In *The Mechanics of Internationalism: Culture, Society, and Politics from the 1840s to the First World War*, edited by Martin H Geyer and Johannes Paulmann, 55–92. London: German Historical Institute; Oxford: Oxford University Press, 2001.

Giacon, Carlo. *La seconda scholastica*. Milan: Fratelli Bocca, 1950.

Giddens, Anthony. *The Consequences of Modernity*. Stanford: Stanford University Press, 1990.

Giles of Rome [Aegidii]. *Aegid. Columnii in Porphyrii Isagogen, Aristotelis Categorias, & lib. Peri Hermenias… absolutissima commentaria*. Bergomum, 1591.

Gjerdingen, Robert. *Music in the Galant Style*. Oxford: Oxford University Press, 2007.

Gollin, Edward, and Alexander Rehding, eds. *The Oxford Handbook of Neo-Riemannian Music Theories*. New York: Oxford University Press, 2011.

Grabiner, Judith V. "Was Newton's Calculus a Dead End? The Continental Influence of Maclaurin's Treatise of Fluxions." *American Mathematical Monthly* 104, no. 5 (1997): 393–484.

Graham, Daniel, trans. *Aristotle, Physics, Book VIII*. New York: Oxford University Press, 1999.

Granada, Miguel Angel. "The Concept of Time in Giordano Bruno: Cosmic Times and Eternity." In *The Medieval Concept of Time*, edited by Pasquale Porro, 477–505. Boston: Brill, 2001.

Grant, Edward. *Much Ado about Nothing*. Cambridge: Cambridge University Press, 1981.

——. "Ways to Interpret the Terms 'Aristotelian' and 'Aristotelianism' in Medieval and Renaissance Natural Philosophy." *History of Science* 25, no. 4 (1987): 335–58.

Grant, Roger Mathew. "Epistemologies of Time and Metre in the Long Eighteenth Century." *Eighteenth-Century Music* 6, no. 1 (2009): 59–75.

——. "Four Hundred Years of Meter: Theories, Ideologies, and Technologies of Musical Periodicity since 1611." PhD diss., University of Pennsylvania, 2010.

Grave, Floyd K. "Abbé Vogler's Revision of Pergolesi's *Stabat Mater*." *Journal of the American Musicological Society* 30, no. 1 (1977): 43–71.

Grave, Floyd K. "Metrical Displacement and the Compound Measure in Eighteenth-Century Theory and Practice." *Theoria* 1 (1985): 25–60.

Grendler, Paul F. "The Universities of the Renaissance and Reformation." *Renaissance Quarterly* (2004): 1–42.

Grendler, Paul F. "Italian Schools and University Dreams during Mercurian's Generalte." In *The Mercurian Project: Forming Jesuit Culture 1573-1580*, edited by Thomas M. McCoog, 483–522. Rome: Institutum Historicum Societatis Iesu; St. Louis: The Institute of Jesuit Sources, 2004.

——. *The Roman Inquisition and the Venetian Press, 1540-1605*. Princeton: Princeton University Press, 1977.

Grosholz, Emily. "Space and Time." In *The Oxford Handbook of Philosophy in Early Modern Europe*, edited by Desmond M. Clarke and Catherine Wilson, 51–70. Oxford: Oxford University Press, 2011.

Guicciardini, Niccolò. "Dot-Age: Newton's Mathematical Legacy in the Eighteenth Century." *Early Science and Medicine* 9, no. 3 (2004): 218–56.

Guthmann, F. "Ein neuer Taktmesser, welcher aber erst erfunden werden soll." Leipzig *AmZ* 9, no. 8, November 19, 1806, col. 117–19.

Hacking, Ian. "Historical Meta-Epistemology." In *Wahrheit und Geschichte*, edited by Wolfgang Carl and Lorraine Daston, 53–77. Göttingen: Valdenhoeck und Ruprecht, 1999.

——. *Historical Ontology*. Cambridge, MA: Harvard University Press, 2002.

Hall, A. Rupert. *Philosophers at War*. Cambridge: Cambridge University Press, 1980.

Harding, Rosamond E. M. *The Metronome and it's Precursors* [sic]. Oxfordshire: Gresham Books, 1983.

Harman, Graham. *Tool-Being*. Chicago: Open Court, 2002.

Harnack, Adolf von. *Geschichte der Königlich preussischen Akademie der Wissenschaften zu Berlin*. Berlin: Reichsdruckerei, 1900.

Hass, Max. "Die Musiklehre im 13. Jahrhundert von Johannes de Garlandia bis Franco." In *Die mittelalterliche Lehre von der Mehrstimmigkeit*, edited by Frieder Zaminer, 89–159. Darmstadt: Wissenschaftliche Buchgesellschaft, 1984.

——. "Studien zur mittelalterlichen Musiklehre: I. Eine Übersicht über die Musiklehre im Kontext der Philosophie der 13. und frühen 14. Jahrhunderts." In *Aktuelle Fragen der musikbezogenen Mittelalterforschung: Texte zu einem Basler Kolloquium des Jahres 1975*, edited by Hans Oesch and Wulf Arlt, 323–456. Winterthur: Amadeus, 1982.

Hasty, Christopher. *Meter as Rhythm*. Oxford: Oxford University Press, 1997.

Hatter, Jane. "*Col tempo*: Musical Time, Aging and Sexuality in 16th-Century Venetian Paintings." *Early Music* 39, no. 1 (2011): 3–14.

Hawkins, Sir John. *A General History of Music.* London: T. Payne and son, 1776. Revised edition, London: Novello, Ewer & co., 1875.

Heidegger, Martin. *Being and Time.* Translated by Joan Stambaugh. Albany: SUNY Press, 1996.

——. *What Is Called Thinking.* Translated by J. Glenn Gray. New York: Harper and Row, 1968.

Heilbron, John Lewis. *Weighing Imponderables and Other Quantitative Science Around 1800.* Berkeley: University of California Press, 1993.

Hertzberg, Ewald Friedrich von. *Historische Nachricht von dem ersten Regierungs-Jahre Friedrich Wilhelm II. Königs von Preussen...* Berlin, 1787.

Hiller, Johann Adam. *Anweisung zum musikalisch-richtigen Gesange.* Leipzig: Johann Friedrich Junius, 1774.

——. *Musikalische Nachrichten und Anmerkungen.* 4 vols. Leipzig: In Verlag der Zeitugs-Expedition, 1770.

——. *Treatise on Vocal Performance and Ornamentation.* Edited and translated by Suzanne J. Beicken. Cambridge: Cambridge University Press, 2001.

Hoffmann, E. T. A. "Review of Spohr's First Symphony." *Leipzig AmZ* 13, nos. 48 and 49, November 27–December 4, 1811, col. 797–806 and 813–19.

Holder, Alan. *Rethinking Meter: A New Approach to the Verse Line.* Lewisburg: Bucknell University Press, 1995.

Houle, George. *Meter in Music: 1600-1800.* Bloomington: Indiana University Press, 1987.

Hussey, Edward, ed. and trans. *Aristotle, Physics, Books III and IV.* Oxford: Clarendon Press, 1983.

Janiak, Andrew. *Newton as Philosopher.* Cambridge: Cambridge University Press, 2008.

Janko, Richard, trans. *Aristotle, Poetics.* Indianapolis: Hackett, 1987.

Janvier, Antide. *Étrennes chronométriques, pour l'an 1811, ou précis de ce qui concerne le tems, ses divisions, ses mesures, leur usages, etc.* Paris: Chez Antide Janvier, ou Palais des Arts; J. J. Paschoud; et à Genève, chez le meme Libraire, 1810.

Jones, Mari, Heather Moynihan Johnston, and Jennifer Puente. "Effects of Auditory Pattern Structure of Anticipatory and Reactive Attending." *Cognitive Psychology* 51, no. 1 (2006): 59–96.

Judd, Cristle Collins. *Reading Renaissance Music Theory.* Cambridge: Cambridge University Press, 2000.

Kandler, Franz Sales. "Rückblicke auf die Chronometer und Herrn Mälzels Neuste Chronometerfabrik in London." Vienna *AmZ* 1, nos. 5–8, January 30–February 20, 1817, col. 33–36, 41–43, 49–52, and 57–58.

Kant, Immanuel. *Critique of Judgment.* Translated by Werner S. Pluhar. Indianapolis: Hackett, 1987.

Kircher, Athanasius. *Musurgia universalis.* Rome: Francesco Corbelletti, 1650.

Kirnberger, Johann Philipp. *The Art of Strict Musical Composition.* Translated by David Beach and Jurgen Thym. New Haven: Yale University Press, 1982.

——. *Die Kunst des reinen Satzes in der Musik.* 3 vols. Berlin: Christian Friedrich Voss, 1771-79. Facsimile edition, Hildesheim: Georg Olms, 1968.

Koch, Heinrich Christoph. *Introductory Essay on Composition.* Translated by Nancy K. Baker. New Haven: Yale University Press, 1983.

——. *Musikalisches Lexikon.* Frankfurt am Main: Hermann, 1802. Facsimile edition, Hildesheim: Georg Olms, 1964.

——. *Versuch einer Anleitung zur Composition.* 3 vols. Leipzig: Adam Friedrich Böhme, 1782-93. Facsimile edition, Hildesheim: Georg Olms, 1969.

Kolisch, Rudolph. "Tempo und Charakter in Beethovens Musik." Translated by Arthur Mendel as "Tempo and Character in Beethoven's Music." *The Musical Quarterly* 29, nos. 2–3 (1943): 169–87, 291–312. Reissued as "Tempo and Character in Beethoven's Music." *The Musical Quarterly* 77, nos. 1–2 (1993): 90–131, 268–342.

Kollman, Augustus Frederic Chrostopher. *An Essay on Musical Harmony.* London: J. Dale, 1796.

Körner, Christian Gottfried. "Ueber Charakterdarstellung in der Musik." *Die Hören* 1, no. 5 (1795): 97–121.

Koyré, Alexandre. *From the Closed World to the Infinite Universe.* Baltimore: The Johns Hopkins Press, 1957.

Krebs, Harald. *Fantasy Pieces.* Oxford: Oxford University Press, 1999.

Kula, Witold. *Measures and Men.* Translated by Richard Szreter. Princeton, NJ: Princeton University Press, 1986.

Küster, Martin. "Thinking in Song: Prosody, Text-Setting and Music Theory in Eighteenth-Century Germany." PhD diss., Cornell University, 2012.

LaCapra, Dominick. 2000. *History and Reading: Tocqueville, Foucault, French Studies.* Toronto: University of Toronto Press, 2000.

Lacassagne, Joseph. *Traité général des élémens du chant.* Paris, 1766. Facsimile edition, New York: Broude Brothers, 1967.

Laird, Paul R. "Catholic Church Music in Italy, and the Spanish and Portuguese Empires." In *The Cambridge History of Eighteenth-Century Music,* edited by Simon P. Keefe, 29–58. Cambridge: Cambridge University Press, 2009.

Landes, David. *Revolution in Time.* Cambridge, MA: Belknap, 1983.

Lanfranco, Giovanni Maria. *Scintille di musica.* Brescia: Lodovico Britannico, 1533.

Lawn, Brian. *The Rise and Decline of the Scholastic 'Quaestio disputata': With Special Emphasis on Its Use in the Teaching of Medicine and Science.* Leiden: E.J. Brill, 1993.

Le Breton, Joachim. "Notice des travaux de la Classe des beaux-arts de l'Institut impérial de France, pour l'année 1813." *Magasin encyclopédique ou journal des sciences, des lettres et des arts,* November 1813.

Leong, Daphne. "Metric States, Symmetries, and Shapes: Humperdinck and Wagner." *Journal of Music Theory* 51, no. 2 (2007): 211–43.

Lerdahl, Fred, and Ray Jackendoff. *A Generative Theory of Tonal Music.* Cambridge, MA: MIT Press, 1983.

Leroi-Gourhan, André. *Gesture and Speech.* Translated by Anna Bostock Berger. Cambridge, MA: MIT Press, 1993.

Lessing, Gotthold Ephraim. *Laocoön: oder über die Grenzen der Mahlerey und Poesie.* Berlin: Christian Friedrich Voß, 1766. Second printing, Berlin: Christian Friedrich Voß, 1788.

Lessing, Gotthold Ephraim, and Moses Mendelssohn. *Pope ein Metaphysiker!* Danzig: J.C. Schuster, 1755.

Lester, Joel. *The Rhythms of Tonal Music.* Carbondale, IL: Southern Illinois University Press, 1986.

Levinson, Marjorie. "What is New Formalism?" *PMLA* 122, no. 2 (2007): 558–69.

Lichtenthal, Pietro. *Dizionario e bibliografia della musica.* 4 vols. Milan: Antonio Fontana, 1826.

Lippius, Johannes. *Synopsis musicæ.* Strassburg: Pauli Ledertz, 1612. Facsimile edition, Hildesheim: Georg Olms, 2004.

——. *Synopsis of New Music.* Translated by Benito Rivera. Colorado Springs: Colorado College Music Press, 1977.

Logier, Johann Bernhard. *A System of the Science of Music and Practical Composition.* London: J. Green, 1827.

Lohr, Charles H. "The Sixteenth-Century Transformation of the Aristotelian Natural Philosophy." In *Aristotelismus und Renaissance: In memoriam Charles B. Schmitt*, edited by Eckhard Keßler, Charles H. Lohr, and Walter Sparn, 89–99. Wiesbaden: Otto Harrassowitz, 1988.

London, Justin. *Hearing in Time*. Oxford: Oxford University Press, 2004.

———. "Phrase Structure in 18th- and 19th-Century Theory: An Overview." *Music Research Forum* 5 (1990): 13–50, at 21–23.

Long, Pamela O. "The *Annales* and the History of Technology." *Technology and Culture* 46, no. 1 (January 2005): 177–86.

Loulié, Étienne. *Éléments ou principes de musique*. Paris: Christophe Ballard, 1696.

Luoma, Robert. *Music, Mode and Words in Orlando di Lasso's Last Works*. New York: Edwin Mellen, 1989.

Lütteken, Laurenz. "Moses Mendelssohn und der Musikästhetische Diskurs der Aufklärung." In *Moses Mendelssohn im Spannungsfeld der Aufklärung*, edited by Michael Albrecht and Eva J. Engel, 159–93. Stuttgart-Bad Cannstatt: Frommann-Holzboog, 2000.

Macey, Samuel L. *Clocks and the Cosmos: Time in Western Life and Thought*. Hamden, CT: Archon, 1980.

Malin, Yonatan. *Songs in Motion: Rhythm and Meter in the German Lied*. Oxford: Oxford University Press, 2010.

Manguel, Alberto. *The Library at Night*. New Haven: Yale University Press, 2008.

Mann, Alfred, ed. and trans. *The Study of Counterpoint from Johann Joseph Fux's Gradus ad Parnassum*. New York: W. W. Norton, 1943. Revised edition, New York: W. W. Norton, 1971.

Marion, Jean-Luc. *On Descartes' Metaphysical Prism: The Constitution and Limits of Onto-theo-logy in Cartesian Thought*. Translated by Jeffrey L. Kosky. Chicago: University of Chicago Press, 1999.

Marpurg, Friedrich Wilhelm. *Anleitung zum Clavierspielen*. Berlin: Haude and Spener, 1765.

———. *Anleitung zur Musik überhaupt, und zur Singkunst besonders…* Berlin: Arnold Wever, 1763.

———. *Des critischen Musicus an der Spree*. Berlin: Haude und Spener, 1750. Facsimile edition, New York: Georg Olms, 1970.

———. *Kritische Briefe über die Tonkunst*. Berlin: Birnstiel, 1760–63. Facsimile edition, 2 vols., Hildesheim: Georg Olms, 1974.

Marvin, Clara. *Giovanni Pierluigi da Palestrina: A Guide to Research*. New York: Routledge, 2002.

Marx, Karl. *Capital*. Translated by Ben Fowkes. New York: Vintage, 1977.

Masson, Charles. *Nouveau Traité des regles pour la composition de la musique*. Paris: Ballard, 1699. Facsimile edition, New York: Da Capo, 1967.

Mattheson, Johann. *Kleine General-Baß-Schule*. Hamburg: Johann Christoph Kißner, 1735. Facsimile edition, Laaber: Laaber-Verlag, 1980.

———. *Das neu-eröffnete Orchestre*. Hamburg: The Author and Benjamin Schillers Witwe, 1713. Facsimile edition, Laaber: Laaber, 2002.

———. *Der vollkommene Capellmeister*. Hamburg: Christian Herold, 1739.

Maurer Zenck, Claudia. *Vom Takt*. Vienna: Böhlau, 2001.

Mauss, Marcel. "Techniques of the Body." Translated by Ben Brewster. *Economy and Society* 2, no. 1 (1973): 70–88.

May, Margaret Tallmadge, trans. and ed. *Galen on the Usefulness of the Parts of the Body*. 2 vols. Ithaca: Cornell University Press, 1968.

McAuley, Tomas. "Rhythmic Accent and the Absolute: Sulzer, Schelling and the *Akzenttheorie*." *Eighteenth-Century Music* 10, no. 2 (2013): 277–86.

McLamore, Alyson. "A Tactus Primer." In *Musica Franca: Essays in Honor of Frank A. D'Accone*, edited by Irene Alm, Alyson McLamore, and Colleen Reardon, 299–321. Stuyvesant, NY: Pendragon, 1996.

Meier, Bernhard. *The Modes of Classical Vocal Polyphony: Described According to the Sources*, with revisions by the author. Translated by Ellen S. Beebe. New York: Broude Brothers, 1988.

Mersenne, Marin. *Harmonie universelle*. Paris: Sébastien Cramoisy, 1636–37. Facsimile edition, Paris: Centre national de la recherché scientifique, 1963.

Miller, John Riggs. *Speeches in the House of Commons upon the Equalization of the Weights and Measures of Great Britain*. London: J. Debrett, 1790.

Mirka, Danuta. "Metre, Phrase Structure and Manipulations of Musical Beginnings." In *Communication in Eighteenth-Century Music*, edited by Danuta Mirka and Kofi Agawu, 83–111. Cambridge: Cambridge University Press, 2008.

——. *Metric Manipulations in Haydn and Mozart*. Oxford: Oxford University Press, 2009.

Momigny, Jérôme-Joseph de. *Cours complet d'harmonie et de composition*. Paris: The author and Bailleul, 1806.

——. "Mesure (Théorie de J. J. de Momigny.)." In *Encylopédie méthodique…: Musique*. Edited by Nicolas-Étienne Framery, Pierre-Louis Ginguené, and Jérôme-Joseph de Momigny, volume 2. Paris: Panckoucke, 1818.

——. *La seule vraie théorie de la musique*. Paris: the author, 1821.

Montéclair, Michel Pignolet de. *Principes de musique*. Paris, 1736. Facsimile edition, Geneva: Minkoff, 1972.

Moreno, Jairo. *Musical Representations, Subjects, and Objects*. Bloomington: Indiana University Press, 2004.

Morley, Thomas. *A Plaine and Easie Introduction to Practicall Musicke…* London: Peter Short, 1597.

Mosel, Ingaz Franz von. "Herrn Johann Mälzels Metronome." Vienna *AmZ* 1, no. 48, November 27, 1817, col. 405–10.

Mumford, Lewis. *Technics and Civilization*. New York: Harcourt, Brace and Company, 1934.

Murphy, Scott. "Metric Cubes in Some Music of Brahms." *Journal of Music Theory* 53, no. 1 (2009): 1–56.

Neumann, Frederick. *Performance Practices of the Seventeenth and Eighteenth Centuries*. New York: Schirmer, 1993.

Newton, Isaac. *The Method of Fluxions and Infinite Series; with Its Application to the Geometry of Curve-Lines*. Translated by John Colson. London: Printed by Henry Woodfall and sold by John Nourse, 1736.

——. *Philosophiae naturalis principia mathematica*. Third edition of 1726 with variant readings, edited by Alexandre Koyré and I. Bernard Cohen with the assistance of Anne Whitman. Cambridge: Harvard University Press, 1972.

——. *Sir Isaac Newton's Mathematical Principles of Natural Philosophy and His System of the World*. Translated by Andrew Motte. Revised translation by Florian Cajori. Berkeley: University of California Press, 1934.

——. "Tractatus de quadratura curvarum." In *Opticks*. London: Printed for Sam Smith and B. Walford, 1704.

Ng, Samuel. "Phrase Rhythm as Form in Classical Instrumental Music." *Music Theory Spectrum* 34, no. 1 (2012): 51–77.

Niemöller, Klaus Wolfgang. "Ornithoparchus, Andreas." In *Oxford Music Online*, edited by Laura Macy. Accessed October 29, 2010. <http://www.oxfordmusiconline.com>.

Nikolić, Aleksandar. "Space and Time in the Apparatus of Infinitesimal Calculus." *Novi Sad Journal of Mathematics* 23, no. 1 (1993): 199–218.

Olesko, Kathryn M. "The Meaning of Precision: The Exact Sensibility in Early Nineteenth-Century Germany." In *The Values of Precision*, edited by M. Norton Wise, 103–221. Princeton: Princeton University Press, 1995.

——. "Precision, Tolerance, and Consensus: Local Cultures in German and British Resistance Standards." In *Archimedes* 1, edited by Jed Z. Buchwald, 117–56. London: Kluwer Academic, 1996.

Ong, Walter. *Ramus, Method, and the Decay of Dialogue.* Cambridge, MA: Harvard University Press, 1983.

Ord-Hume, Arthur W. J. G. "Winkel, Diederich Nikolaus." In *Oxford Music Online*, edited by Laura Macy. Accessed November 16, 2008. <http://www.oxfordmusiconline.com>.

Ornithoparchus, Andreas. *Andreas Ornithoparcus His Micrologus, or Introduction, Containing the Art of Singing...* Translated by John Dowland. London: Thomas Adams, 1609. Facsimile edition, New York: Dover 1973.

——. *Musicae activae micrologus... libris quatuor digestus...* Leipzig: Valentin Schumann, 1517.

Pajot d'Ons-en-Bray, Louis-Léon. "Description et usage d'un Métromètre ou Machine pour batter les Mesures et les Temps de toutes sortes d'Airs." In *Histoire de l'Académie Royale des Sciences Année 1732*, 182–95. Paris: De L'Imprimerie Royale, 1735.

Paolucci, Giuseppe. *Arte pratica di contrappunto.* Venice: Antonio de Castro, 1765–72.

Parks, Richard S. *Eighteenth-Century Counterpoint and Tonal Structure.* Englewood Cliffs, NJ: Prentice-Hall, 1984.

Penna, Lorenzo. *Li primi albori musicali.* Bologna: Monti, 1672.

Pisa, Agostino. *Battuta della musica.* Rome: Bartolomeo Zanetti, 1611. Facsimile edition in Pisa, *Breve dichiarazione della battuta musicale* [*sic*], edited by Walther Dürr, Bologna: Forni, 1969.

——. *Breve dichiaratione della battuta musicale.* Rome: Bartolomeo Zanetti, 1611. Facsimile edition, edited and with an introduction by Piero Gargiulo, with extracts from *Battuta della musica*, Lucca: Libreria Musicale Italiana Editrice, 1996.

Piston, Walter. *Harmony.* New York: Norton, 1944.

Porter, Theodore M. *Trust in Numbers: The Pursuit of Objectivity in Science and Public Life.* Princeton: Princeton University Press, 1995.

Praetorius, Michael. *Syntagma musicum.* Wolfenbüttel: Elias Holwein, 1618. Second printing, Wolfenbüttel: Elias Holwein, 1619.

Principes élémentaires de musique arrêtés par les Membres du Conservatoire, pour servir à l'étude. Edited by Agus, Catel, Chérubini, Gossec, Langlé, Lesueur, Méhul, and Rigel. Paris: A l'imprimerie du Conservatoire de Musique, Paubourg Poissonniere, 1800.

Printz, Wolfgang Caspar. *Satyrischer Componist.* Dresden and Leipzig: Johann Christoph Mieth and Johann Christoph Zimmermann, 1696.

Pritchard, Matthew. "'The Moral Background of the Work of Art': 'Character' in German Musical Aesthetics, 1780-1850." *Eighteenth-Century Music* 9, no. 1 (2012): 63–80.

Pyle, Andrew. *Atomism and Its Critics: Problem Areas Associated with the Development of the Atomic Theory of Matter from Democritus to Newton.* Bristol, UK: Thoemmes, 1995.

Quantz, Johann Joachim. *Versuch einer Anweisung, die Flöte traversiere zu spielen.* Berlin: Johann Friedrich Voß, 1752. Third edition, Breslau: Johann Friedrich Korn dem ältern, 1789. Facsimile edition, Kassel: Bärenreiter, 1953.

——. *Versuch einer Anweisung die Flöte traversiere zu spielen.* Berlin: Johann Friedrich Voß, 1752. Facsimile edition, Wiesbaden: Breitkopf und Härtel, 1988.

"Questions Proposées Par L'Académie Pour Les Prix." In *Nouveau Mémoires de L'Académie Royale Des Sciences et Belles-Lettres 1770*, 21–36. Berlin: Chez Chrétien Fréderic Voss, 1772.

Rameau, Jean-Philippe. *Traité de l'harmonie*. 4 vols. Paris: Jean-Baptiste-Christophe Ballard, 1722. Facsimile edition, New York: Broude Brothers, 1965.

Rancière, Jacques. *The Politics of Aesthetics: The Distribution of the Sensible*. Translated by Gabriel Rockhill. London: Continuum, 2004.

——. *The Politics of Literature*. Translated by Julie Rose. Cambridge: Polity, 2011.

Ratner, Leonard G. *Classic Music: Expression, Form, and Style*. New York: Schirmer, 1980.

Renaudin. "Variétés: Chronomètre & Plexichronomètre." *Mercure de France* no. 24, June 12, 1784, 85–89.

"Review of New Musical Publications." *The New Monthly Magazine* 4, January 1, 1817.

Riemann, Hugo. *Musikalische Dynamik und Agogik*. Hamburg: Rahter, 1884.

Riepel, Joseph. *Anfangsgründe zur musicalischen Setzkunst. Erster Teil: De Rhythmopoeia, oder von der Tactordnung*. Regensburg and Vienna: Bader, 1752.

Riggs, Robert. "'On the Representation of Character in Music': Christian Gottfried Körner's Aesthetics of Instrumental Music." *The Musical Quarterly* 81, no. 4 (1997): 599–631.

Riley, Matthew. "Civilizing the Savage: Johann Georg Sulzer and the 'Aesthetic Force' of Music." *Journal of the Royal Musical Association* 127, no. 1 (2002): 1–22.

——. *Musical Listening in the German Enlightenment*. Aldershot: Ashgate, 2004.

Rothstein, William. "Metrical Theory and Verdi's Midcentury Operas." *Dutch Journal of Music Theory* 16, no. 2 (2011): 93–111.

——. "National Metrical Types." In *Communication in Eighteenth-Century Music*, edited by Danuta Mirka and Kofi Agawu, 112–59. Cambridge: Cambridge University Press, 2008.

——. *Phrase Rhythm in Tonal Music*. New York: Schirmer Books, 1989.

Rousseau, Jean-Jacques. "Chronomètre." In *Encylopédie méthodique…: Musique*. Edited by Nicolas-Étienne Framery, Pierre-Louis Ginguené, and Jérôme-Joseph de Momigny, volume 1. Paris: Panckoucke, 1791.

——. *A Complete Dictionary of Music*. Translated by William Warring. London: J. Murray, 1779.

——. *Dictionnaire de Musique*. Paris: Chez le Veuve Duchesne, 1768. Facsimile edition, Hildesheim: Georg Olms, 1969.

——. *Project Concerning New Symbols for Music*. Edited and translated by Bernarr Rainbow. Kilkenny, Ireland: Boethius, 1982.

Rowe, Katherine "'God's handy worke': Divine Complicity and the Anatomist's Touch." In *The Body in Parts: Fantasies of Corporeality in Early Modern Europe*, ed. David Hillman and Carla Mazzio, 287–309. New York: Routledge, 1997.

Royal, Matthew S. "Tradition and Innovation in Sixteenth-Century Rhythmic Theory: Francisco Salinas's *De Musica Libri Septem*." *Music Theory Spectrum* 34, no. 2 (2012): 26–47.

Russell, Bertrand. "The Problem of Infinity Considered Historically." In *Zeno's Paradoxes*, edited by Wesley C. Salmon, 45–58. New York: Bobbs-Merrill, 1970.

Rutherford, Donald. "Metaphysics: The Late Period." In *The Cambridge Companion to Leibniz*, edited by Nicholas Jolley, 124–75. Cambridge: Cambridge University Press, 1995.

Rynasiewicz, Robert. "By Their Properties, Causes and Effects: Newton's Scholium on Time, Space, Place and Motion. II: The Context." *Studies in History and Philosophy of Science* 26, no. 2 (1995): 295–322.

Sachs, Kurt. *Rhythm and Tempo*. New York: Norton, 1953.

Salinas, Francisco. *De musica libri septem*. Salamanca: Mathias Gastius, 1577.

Salzer, Felix, and Carl Schachter. *Counterpoint in Composition*. New York: McGraw-Hill, 1969. New edition, New York: Columbia University Press, 1989.

Sauter, Michael J. "Clockwatchers and Stargazers: Time Discipline in Early Modern Berlin." *American Historical Review* 112, no. 3 (2007): 685–709.

Sauveur, Joseph. "Système General des Intervalles des Sons, et son Applications à tous les Systèmes et à tous les Instruments de Musique. IV: Division et usage de L'Echomètre general." In *Histoire de L'Académie Royale des Sciences Année 1701*, 4:297–364. Paris: Gabriel Martin, Jean-Baptiste Coignard, & Hippolyte-Louis Guerin, 1704.

Schachter, Carl. "Rhythm and Linear Analysis: A Preliminary Study." *The Music Forum* IV, edited by Felix Salzer, Carl Schachter, and Hedi Siegel, 281–334. New York: Columbia University Press, 1974.

——. *Unfoldings*. Edited by Joseph N. Straus. Oxford: Oxford University Press, 1999.

Scheibe, Johann Adolph. *Critischer Musikus*. Leipzig: Bernhard Christoph Breitkopf, 1746. Facsimile edition, Hildesheim: Georg Olms, 1970.

——. *Ueber die Musikalische Composition: Erste Theil Die Theorie der Melodie und Harmonie*. Leipzig: Schwickertschen, 1773. Facsimile edition, Kassel: Bärenreiter, 2006.

Schenker, Heinrich. *Beethoven, Neunte Sinfonie*. 1912. Reprint edition, Vienna: Universal Editon, 1969.

Schiller, Friedrich von. "Letters on the Aesthetic Education of Man." Translated by Elizabeth M. Wilkinson and L. A. Willoughby in Schiller, *Essays*. Edited by Walter Hinderer and Daniel O. Dahlstrom. New York: Continuum, 1993.

——. "Über die ästhetische Erziehung des Menschen in einer Reihe von Briefen." In *Gesammelte Werke*, edited by Reinhold Netolitzky, 319–429. Gütersloh: Sigbert Mohn Verlag, 1961.

Schmitt, Charles B. *Aristotle and the Renaissance*. Cambridge, MA: Harvard University Press, 1983.

Schubert, Peter. "Authentic Analysis." *The Journal of Musicology* 12, no. 1 (1994): 3–18.

Schulenberg, David. "Commentary on Channan Willner, 'More on Handel and the Hemiola.'" *Music Theory Online* 2, no. 5 (1996). Accessed August 28, 2009. <http://mto.societymusictheory.org/issues/mto.96.2.5/mto.96.2.5.schulenberg.html>.

Schulz, J. A. P. "Über die in Sulzers Theorie der schönen Künste unter dem Artikel Verrückung angeführten zwey Beispiele…" Leipzig *AmZ* 2, no. 16, January 15, 1800, col. 273–80.

Schünemann, Georg. *Geschichte des Dirigierens*. Leipzig: Breitkopf and Härtel, 1913.

Schwarz, David. *Listening Awry: Music and Alterity in German Culture*. Minneapolis: University of Minnesota Press, 2006.

Schwindt-Gross, Nicole. "Einfache, zusammengesetzte und doppelt notierte Takte: Ein Aspekt der Takttheorie im 18. Jahrhundert." *Musiktheorie* 4, no. 3 (1989): 203–22.

Seidel, Wilhelm. "Division und Progression: Zum Begriff der musikalischen Zeit im 18. Jahrhundert." *Il saggiatore musicale* 2, no. 1 (1995): 47–65.

——. *Über Rhythmustheorien der Neuzeit*. Bern: Francke, 1975.

Serwer, Howard. "Kirnberger, Johann Philipp." In *Oxford Music Online*, edited by Laura Macy. Accessed March 15, 2010. <http://www.oxfordmusiconline.com>.

Shank, J. B. *The Newton Wars and the Beginning of the French Enlightenment*. Chicago: Chicago University Press, 2008.

Simpson, Christopher. *The Principles of Practical Musick*. London: Will. Godbid for Henry Brome, 1665.

Siraisi, Nancy. "The Music of Pulse in the Writings of Italian Academic Physicians (Fourteenth and Fifteenth Centuries)." *Speculum* 50, no. 4 (1975): 689–710.

Sisman, Elaine. "Genre, Gesture, and Meaning in Mozart's 'Prague' Symphony." In *Mozart Studies 2*, edited by Cliff Eisen, 27–84. Oxford: Clarendon Press, 1997.

——. *Mozart: The "Jupiter" Symphony.* Cambridge: Cambridge University Press, 1993.

Smith, J. A., trans. *The Works of Aristotle.* Edited by W. D. Ross. Oxford: Clarendon, 1931.

Soto, Domingo de. *Reuerendi patris Dominici Soto Segobiensis theologi Ordinis Praedicatorum Super octo libros Physicorum Aristotelis quaestiones.* Salamanca: Andrea de Portonaris, 1555.

Spitzer, John, and Neal Zaslaw. "Conducting." In *Oxford Music Online*, edited by Laura Macy. Accessed 20 August 2013. <http://www.oxfordmusiconline.com>.

Spivak, Gayatri Chakravorty. *An Aesthetic Education in the Era of Globalization.* Cambridge, MA: Harvard University Press, 2012.

Stein, Howard. "Newton's Metaphysics." In *The Cambridge Companion to Newton*, edited by I. Bernard Cohen and George E. Smith, 256–307. Cambridge: Cambridge University Press, 2002.

Steinschulte, Gabriel M. "Palestrina und Deutschland." In *Atti del II Convegno Internazionale di Studi Palestriniani*, edited by Lino Bianchi and Giancarlo Rostirolla, 615–23. Palestrina: Fondazione Giovanni Pierluigi da Palestrina/Centro di Studi Palestriniani, 1991.

Stiegler, Bernard. *Technics and Time, 1: The Fault of Epimetheus.* Translated by Richard Beardsworth and George Collins. Stanford: Stanford University Press, 1998.

Stöckel, G. E. "Noch ein Wort über den musikalischen Zeitmesser." Leipzig *AmZ* 6, no. 4, October 26, 1803, col. 49–55.

——. "Über die Wichtigkeit der richtigen Zeitbewegung eines Tonstücks." Leipzig *AMZ* 2, nos. 38 and 39, June 18–25, 1800, 657–66 and 673–78.

Struik, Dirk Jan. *A Concise History of Mathematics.* Second, revised edition. New York: Dover, 1948.

Suárez, Franciscus. *Metaphysicarum disputationum.* 2 vols. Paris: Apud Michaelem Sonnium, 1605.

Sulzer, Johann Georg. *Allgemeine Theorie der schönen Künste.* 2 vols. Leipzig: M. G. Weidmanns Erben und Reich, 1771–74.

——. *Allgemeine Theorie der schönen Künste.* 2 vols. Leipzig: M. G. Weidmanns Erben und Reich, 1771–74. Second printing, Leipzig: Weidmannschen Buchhandlung, 1792.

Talleyrand-Périgord, Charles Maurice de. *Proposition faite à l'Assemblée nationale sur les poids et mesures.* Paris: De l'imprimerie nationale, 1790.

Tanay, Dorit. *Noting Music, Marking Culture: The Intellectual Context of Rhythmic Notation, 1250-1400.* American Institute of Musicology: Hänssler-Verlag, 1999.

Tans'ur, William. *A New Musical Grammar: or the Harmonical Spector.* London: Jacob Robinson for the author, 1746.

Temperley, David. "End-Accented Phrases: An Analytical Exploration." *Journal of Music Theory* 47, no. 1 (2003): 125–54.

Temperley, David. "Hypermetrical Transitions." *Music Theory Spectrum* 30, no. 2 (2008): 305–25.

Thiémé, Frédéric. *Nouvelle théorie sur les différens mouvemens des airs.* Paris: Laurens jeune, 1801.

Thomas Aquinas, Saint. *Doctoris Angelici divi Thomæ Aquinatis Opera Omnia.* Edited by Eduard Fretté. Paris: Ludovicum Vivès, 1875.

——. *Commentary on Aristotle's Physics.* Translated by Richard J. Blackwell, Richard J. Spath, and W. Edmund Thirlkel. Introduction by Vernon J. Bourke. New Haven,

Yale University Press, 1963. Revised edition with forward by Ralph McInerny. Notre Dame: Dumb Ox, 1999.

Thompson, E. P. "Time, Work-Discipline, and Industrial Capitalism." *Past and Present* 38, no. 1 (1967): 56–97.

Tomlinson, Gary. *Metaphysical Song*. Princeton: Princeton University Press, 1999.

——. *Monteverdi and the End of the Renaissance*. Berkeley: University of California Press, 1987.

——. *Music in Renaissance Magic*. Chicago: University of Chicago Press, 1993.

Türk, Daniel Gottlob. *Klavierschule, oder Anweisung zum Klavierspielen*. Leipzig: Schwickert; Halle: Hemmerde & Schwetschke, 1789. Facsimile edition, Kassel: Bärenreiter, 1962.

Unsigned advertisement for the "Biblioteca di musica moderna." *Gazzetta di Mantova*, no. 11, March 11, 1820.

Unsigned announcement of Maelzel's metronome. Leipzig *AmZ* 15, no. 48, December 1, 1813, col. 784–88.

Unsigned article. "Andrea Christian Sparrevogns Taktur." Leipzig *AmZ* 19, no. 14, April 2, 1817, col. 233–44.

Unsigned article. "Bestimmung der Tempos aller Symphonien von Beethoven, nach Mälzel's Metronom." Leipzig *AMZ* 19, no. 51, December 17, 1817, col. 873–74.

Unsigned article. "Chronomètre du Conservatoire." *Archives des découvertes et des inventions nouvelles, Faites dans les Sciences, les Arts et les Manufactures, tant en France que dans les Pays étrangers, pendant l'année 1813*. Paris: Treuttel et Würtz, 1814.

Unsigned article. "Foglio d'Annunzj." *Gazzetta di Milano*, no. 326, November 22, 1819.

Unsigned article. "Invenzioni—Il metronome." *Teatri arti e letteratura* 7, no. 291, November 12, 1829.

Unsigned article. "Maelzel's Metronome." *Quarterly Musical Magazine and Review*, no. 11 (1821).

Unsigned article. "Notice sur les travaux du Conservatoire impérial de musique et de déclamation, et sur les objets d'invention ou de perfectionnement qui ont été renvoyés à son examen, pour l'année 1812." *Le Moniteur universel* no. 552, December 17, 1812.

Unsigned article. "Notice sur les travaux du Conservatoire impérial de musique et de déclamation, et sur les objets d'invention ou de perfectionnement qui ont été renvoyés à son examen, pour l'année 1812." *Esprit de journaux Français et étrangers par une société de gens de lettres*, February 1813.

Unsigned article. "Rhythmomètre, inventé & exécuté par le sieur Dubos, horloger-méchanicien, qui a eu l'honneur de la présenter au Roi & à la Reine, le 13 Janvier 1787." *Journal général de France* 80, July 5, 1787, 319.

Unsigned miscellaneous contribution. Leipzig *AmZ* 15, no. 18, May 5, 1813, 305–7.

Unsigned miscellaneous contribution. Leipzig *AmZ* 19, no. 37, September 10, 1817, col. 633–36.

Untitled article of correspondence. "Au rédacteur du *Mercure de France*." In *Mercure de France* 66, no. 25, April 1816, 416.

Untitled letter to the editor. *London Times* no. 9888, July 16, 1816, col. 14.

Untitled letter to the editor. *The Morning Chronicle*, no. 14728, July 16, 1816, col. 11.

Valentini, Pier Franceso. *Trattato della battuta musicale*. Rome: MS Barb. Lat. 4417. Biblioteca Apostolica Vaticana, [ca. 1643].

Vecchi, Giuseppe, ed. *Marcheti de Padua Pomerium*. Rome: American Institute of Musicology, 1961.

Vicentino, Nicola. *L'antica musica ridotta alla moderna prattica*. Rome: Antonio Barre, 1555. Facsimile edition, Kassel: Bärenreiter, 1965.

Vion, Charles Antoine. *La musique pratique et theorique.* Paris: Jean-Baptiste-Christophe Ballard, 1742.

Vitodurensi, Albano Torino, trans. *Pauli Aeginetae medici insignis Opus divinium...Albano Torino Vitodurensi interprete.* Basel: Andr. Crantandrum et Io. Bebelium, 1532.

Vogel, Martin. "Die Musikschriften Leonhard Eulers." In *Leonhardi Euleri Opera Omnia,* ser. 3, vol. 11. Turici: Societatis Scientiarum Naturalium Helveticae, 1960.

Vovelle, Michel. *Ideologies and Mentalities.* Translated by Eamon O'Flaherty. Cambridge: Polity Press, 1990.

Waldura, Markus. "Marpurg, Koch, und die Neubegründung des Taktbegriffs." *Musikforschung* 53, no. 3 (2000): 237–53.

Waterfield, Robin, trans. *Aristotle, Physics.* Introduction and notes by David Bostock. Oxford: Oxford University Press, 1996.

Weber, Gottfried. "Chronometer." In *Allgemeine Encyclopädie der Wissenschaften und Künste,* edited by Johann Samuel Ersch and Johann Gottfried Gruber, 17:204–9. Leipzig: J. F. Gleditsch, 1813–89.

Weber, Gottfried. "Mälzel's Metonome Überall Umsonst zu Haben." Vienna *AmZ* 1, no. 37, September 11, 1817, col. 313–14.

Weber, Gottfried. *Ueber chronometrische Tempobezeichnung.* Mainz: B. Schott, 1817.

——. "Über ein Chronometrische Tempobezeichnung, Welche den Mälzel'schen Metronome, so wie Jede Andere Chronometer–Machine Entbehrlich Macht." Vienna *AmZ* 1, no. 25, June 19, 1817, col. 204–9.

——. "Ueber die Jetzt Bevorstehende Wirkliche Einführung des Taktmessers." Leipzig *AmZ* 16, nos. 27–28, July 6–13, 1814, col. 445–49 and 461–65.

——. "Noch Einmal ein Wort über den Musikalischen Chronometer oder Taktmesser." Leipzig *AmZ* 15, no. 27, July 7, 1813, col. 441–47.

——. *Versuch einer geordneten Theorie der Tonsetzkunst.* 3 vols. Mainz: B. Schotts Söhne, 1817–21. Second edition, Mainz: B. Schotts Söhne, 1824.

Weiler, G. von. "Ueber den Begriff der Schönheit, als Grundlage einer Aesthetik der Tonkunst." *Allgemeine musikalische Zeitung* 13, no. 7, February 13, 1811, col. 117–24.

Wellbery, David. *Lessing's Laocoon: Semiotics and Aesthetics in the Age of Reason.* Cambridge: Cambridge University Press, 1984.

Whiteside, Derek T., ed. and trans., with the assistance in publication of M. A. Hoskin. *The Mathematical Papers of Isaac Newton.* 8 vols. Cambridge: Cambridge University Press, 1967–81.

Wiermann, Barbara. "Bach und Palestrina: Neue Quellen aus Johann Sebastian Bachs Notenbibliothek." *Bach-Jahrbuch* 88 (2002): 9–28.

Wilkes, John, ed. "History of Music, Theoretical and Practical." In *Encyclopaedia Londinensis, or Universal Dictionary of Arts, Sciences, and Literature.* London: Printed for the Proprietor, 1819.

Will, Richard. *The Characteristic Symphony in the Age of Haydn and Beethoven.* Cambridge: Cambridge University Press, 2002.

Williams, Raymond. "Structures of Feeling." In *Marxism and Literature,* 128–35. Oxford: Oxford University Press, 1977.

Willner, Channan. "Handel, the Sarabande, and Levels of Genre, a Reply to David Schulenberg." *Music Theory Online* 2, no. 7 (1996). Accessed August 28, 2009. <http://mto.societymusictheory.org/issues/mto.96.2.7/mto.96.2.7.willner.html>.

——. "Metrical Displacement and Metrically Dissonant Hemiolas." *Journal of Music Theory* 57, no. 1 (2013): 87–118.

———. "More on Handel and the Hemiola: Overlaping Hemiolas." *Music Theory Online* 2, no. 3 (1996). Accessed August 28, 2009. <http://mto.societymusictheory.org/issues/mto.96.2.3/mto.96.2.3.willner.html>.

———. "Sequential Expansion and Handelian Phrase Rhythm." In *Schenker Studies 2*, edited by Carl Schachter and Hedi Siegel, 192–221. Cambridge: Cambridge University Press, 1999.

Willner, Channan. "The Two-Length Bar Revisited: Handel and the Hemiola." *Göttinger Händel-Beiträge* 4 (1991): 208–31.

Wintersgill, H. H. "Handel's Two-Length Bar." *Music and Letters* 17, no. 1 (1936): 1–12.

Wise, M. Norton. "Precision: Agent of Unity and Product of Agreement: Part I—Traveling." In *The Values of Precision*, edited by M. Norton Wise, 92–100. Princeton: Princeton University Press, 1995.

Wolf, Uwe. *Notation und Aufführungspraxis: Studien zum Wandel von Notenschrift und Notenbild in italienischen Musikdrucken der Jahre 1571-1630*. Berlin: Merseburger, 1992.

Wolff, Christoph. *Bach: Essays on His Life and Music*. Cambridge, MA: Harvard University Press, 1991.

Wolfson, Susan. "Reading for Form." *Modern Language Quarterly* 61, no. 1 (2001): 1–16.

Wollick, Nicolaus. *Opus aureum*. Cologne: Henricum Quentell, 1501. Revised edition, Cologne, 1508.

Wollick, Nicolaus. *Enchiridion musices*. Paris, 1509. Facsimile edition, Genève: Minkoff Reprint, 1972.

Wright, Peter. "Ligature (i)." In *Oxford Music Online*, edited by Laura Macy. Accessed September 6, 2011. <http://www.oxfordmusiconline.com>.

Yeo, Richard. *Encyclopaedic Visions: Scientific Dictionaries and Enlightenment Culture*. Cambridge: Cambridge University Press, 2001.

Zacconi, Lodovico. *Prattica di musica, seconda parte*. Venice: Alessandro Vincenti. Facsimile edition, Bologna: Forni, 1967.

Zarlino, Gioseffo. *The Art of Counterpoint*. Translated by Guy A. Marco and Claude V. Palisca. New Haven: Yale University Press, 1968. Reprint edition, New York: Norton, 1976.

———. *Le istitutioni harmoniche*. Venice: Francesco de i Franceschi Senese, 1558.

Zmeskall von Domanovecz, Nikolaus. "Tactmesser, zum Praktischen Gebrauch Geeignet." Vienna *AmZ* 1, nos. 35 and 36, August 28–September 4, 1817, col. 293–300 and 305–8.

Zupko, Roland. *French Weights and Measures Before the Revolution: A Dictionary of Provincial and Local Units*. Bloomington: Indiana University Press, 1978.

INDEX